Human Rights and the Unborn Child

Human Rights and the Unborn Child

by

Rita Joseph

MARTINUS NIJHOFF PUBLISHERS

LEIDEN • BOSTON
2009

Printed on acid-free paper.

Library of Congress Cataloging-in-Publication Data

Joseph, Rita.
Human rights and the unborn child / by Rita Joseph.
p. cm.
Includes bibliographical references and index.
ISBN 978-90-04-17560-0 (hardback : alk. paper)
1. Unborn children (Law) 2. Right to life. 3. Abortion--Law and legislation. 4. Human rights. I. Title.
K642.J67 2009
342.08'5--dc22

2009021220

ISBN: 978 90 04 17560 0

PRINTED IN THE NETHERLANDS.

Table of Contents

Introduction

In July 2007, I wrote an article for *The Age*, a mainstream Australian newspaper. The article was entitled "The Right to Life—the most important right of all" and in it I argued against a legislative bill being proposed in the Victorian State Parliament that abortion be decriminalized. My arguments were based entirely on Australia's human rights treaty obligations to provide legal protection for the child before birth.

A reply was published in *The Age* (July 28, 2007)—a letter from John Tobin, senior lecturer in the faculty of law at the University of Melbourne. It was entitled: "International law silent on abortion":

> Rita Joseph (Opinion, 27/7) is entitled to raise concerns in relation to Victorian MP Candy Broad's attempt to decriminalise abortion. But she has no basis upon which to enlist international human rights law in support of her view. International law is silent on abortion and provides no rights to the unborn child.
>
> When states drafted the Convention on the Rights of the Child, the question of when life began was one of the most contentious matters. Catholic states wanted life to begin at conception, while numerous Western states, including Australia, preferred birth. The result is a compromise—each country is entitled to determine when childhood and life begins.
>
> There is no foundation to argue that the right to life under international law prohibits abortion. On the contrary, the Human Rights Committee, the body responsible for monitoring implementation of the International Covenant on Civil and Political Rights, has held that the failure to provide an abortion for a 17-year old girl in circumstances where it would have been lawful under domestic law in Peru was a form of inhuman and degrading treatment because of the mental suffering and trauma experienced by the mother in being forced to give birth.

I was at once intrigued and appalled. I knew that international law is not "silent on abortion". I knew that legal protection for unborn children is one of the founding principles of modern international human rights law, that as one of the Nuremberg judgments, this principle was mandated to be codified in the International Bill of Rights. And I certainly knew that the citation of a judgment made some forty-eight years later was scarcely proof of "no foundation" for arguing the historical fact of such protection!

Indeed, I knew without a doubt that international law *does* recognize rights for the unborn child. I knew this from more than three decades of researching, writing, and lecturing on the language of human rights as contained in the major international human rights instruments. I knew this to be true also from first-hand experience on the circuit of United Nations mega-conferences and from attendance at numerous meetings of UN Commissions and Committees, sometimes as a representative of non-government organizations (NGOs) and sometimes as a member of the Australian delegation in Working Group sessions where the language of human rights was being negotiated.

So why would a senior lecturer from the law faculty of a reputable university deny these truths? Why publish such a palpable untruth? Is it genuine ignorance? Or is it just that pro-abortion ideology has become so entrenched in our universities that all references in international law to legal protection for unborn children have been deliberately suppressed or perhaps just been allowed to fade quietly into obscurity?

Whatever the answer, I began to write a reply in which I gathered together just a small part of what international law has to say about the human rights of the unborn and the serious implications that flow from this for the practice of abortion. At this point, it occurred to me that it would be good to find a book on this subject that I could forward to this senior lecturer in law who believed that international law is silent on abortion. Despite a solid search I could find no such publication.

Thus I came to write this book—to gather in a single volume a selection of the mass of material available from the major human rights instruments, from first drafts, legislative histories, and contemporary commentaries, from more recent scholarship as well as from the *General Comments and Concluding Observations and Recommendations* of the various treaty monitoring bodies.

My selection from the available material is comprehensive enough, I hope, to establish once and for all that the human rights of the unborn child were recognized right from the beginning in the foundation documents of modern international human rights law.

These rights have always been there but regrettably they have been obscured for some decades now by the rise of a new pro-abortion ideology in the form of radical feminism. On the UN conference circuit from Cairo, Beijing, Istanbul, Geneva, The Hague and New York, and at countless meetings of the UN treaty monitoring committees and the UN Commissions, I have seen at first hand a masterly campaign of ideological reinterpretation of the human rights of all members of the human family, a campaign with a singularly ignoble purpose—to exclude the unborn child from the scope of human rights protection.

In this book I have tried to hold some of the most damaging reinterpretations up to the searchlight of historical context, including a reminder of the original purpose and meaning and the philosophical foundation of modern international human rights law.

Chapter 1 UDHR Recognition of the Child before Birth: Analysis of the Texts

A context of inclusiveness

Context shines a powerful light on what the authors of the 1948 Universal Declaration of Human Rights (UDHR) recognized as definitive and universal when they framed that crucial first modern statement of human rights. This is particularly important when we come to examine later human rights documents that derive from and codify the rights expounded in the UDHR, especially as relating to the rights of the child before birth.

In the decade following the UDHR, the General Assembly of the United Nations examined the protection of the rights of the child promised in the UDHR and drew up a list of ten agreed principles which they then proclaimed in the 1959 *Declaration of the Rights of the Child (DRC)*. These principles formed the preliminary outline of fundamental human rights to be codified eventually in the 1989 Convention on the Rights of the Child (CRC).

In the preamble to the 1959 DRC, there is a well-known and often cited paragraph of significance to the unborn child:

> Whereas the child, by reason of his physical and mental immaturity, needs special safeguards and care, including appropriate legal protection, before as well as after birth,

Even examining this paragraph devoid of any context, it is clear that the phrase "before as well as after birth" connotes a consideration that was universally assented. Not only is there no hint of any qualification or mitigation of the entitlements accruing to a child that is unborn, but in fact the inclusion of this phrase actually reflects the determination of the international community in 1959 not to rely on a silent assumption of the rights of the unborn child but to actually give explicit emphasis to those rights.

Although popular practice tends to cite only this paragraph in examining the rights of the child before birth, to do so is to miss the full significance that comes from reading the paragraph in the context of the preamble to which it belongs, as well as in the historical context of contemporary human rights documents. Research on the historical context reveals that the concept of 'the child' as understood at the time of the International Bill of Rights[1] included the child before as well as after birth—from 1924, unbroken conceptual continuity can be established on this issue of inclusion.

Evidence of UN consensus—the child before birth included in human rights protection

The full text of the preamble to the DRC is as follows:

> Whereas the peoples of the United Nations have, in the Charter, reaffirmed their faith in fundamental human rights and in the dignity and worth of the human person, and have determined to promote social progress and better standards of life in larger freedom,
> Whereas the United Nations has, in the Universal Declaration of Human Rights, proclaimed that everyone is entitled to all the rights and freedoms set forth therein, without distinction of any kind, such as race, colour, sex, language, religion, political or other opinion, national or social origin, property, birth or other status,
> Whereas the child, by reason of his physical and mental immaturity, needs special safeguards and care, including appropriate legal protection, before as well as after birth,
> Whereas the need for such special safeguards has been stated in the Geneva Declaration of the Rights of the Child of 1924, and recognized in the Universal Declaration of Human Rights and in the statutes of specialized agencies and international organizations concerned with the welfare of children,
> Whereas mankind owes to the child the best it has to give,

In the second paragraph the DRC reaffirms that everyone is entitled to all rights and freedoms set forth in the UDHR, "without distinction of any kind". Following that reaffirmation, the third paragraph then particularizes the scope of the present Declaration to the special case of "the child … before as well as after birth", thus eliminating any possible ambiguity as to whether the provisions of the Declaration apply to the unborn child. Further, the juxtaposition of the second and third paragraphs clearly implies that the universal human rights enunciated so vigorously and unambiguously in UDHR are understood as applying to "the child … before as well as after birth".

The DRC goes on to state in Principle 1:

> Every child, without any exception whatsoever, shall be entitled to these rights, without distinction or discrimination…

The fourth paragraph provides incontrovertible historical proof that the UDHR "recognized" that the child before birth, no less than the child after birth, is an appropriate subject of human rights law and is entitled to appropriate legal protection. Insertion of the word "such" here and repetition of the words "special safeguards" makes the essential continuity of these two clauses unmistakably clear. It is also unmistak-

1 The International Bill of Rights comprises the UDHR, the 1966 *International Covenant on Civil and Political Rights (ICCPR)*, and the 1966 *International Covenant on Economic, Social and Cultural Rights (ICESCR)*.

ably clear that the UDHR and the statutes of specialized agencies and international organizations concerned with the welfare of children were understood to have committed to provide special safeguards, including appropriate legal protection, for the child before birth.

Here is the nub: though the 1959 DRC may not be legally binding in itself, nevertheless its legal force lies in the formal and irrefutable evidence it provides that as at 20th November 1959 the whole international community understood and agreed that the UDHR (legally binding today as customary law) had for that first decade of its jurisdiction already recognized the legal status of the child before birth and his entitlement to human rights protection. Universal recognition of the child before birth as a juridical personality entitled to legal protection had been established and accepted in the very foundation instrument of modern international human rights law.

Could it have been otherwise? Unlikely, for this was confirmed only eleven years after the UDHR, at the 14th Session of the UN General Assembly at which many of the original authors of that foundation document were present to refute it had it been wrong. For example, veteran UN delegates such as Dr. Charles Habib Malik and Victor Andres Belaunde ensured an unbroken continuity on all such important concepts. Dr. Malik of Lebanon, President of the UN General Assembly (1958-59), had been most prominent in negotiating the text of the 1948 UDHR, while Victor Andres Belaunde of Peru, President of the UN General Assembly (1959-60), had been involved from the very first UN conference in San Francisco in 1945. Professor John P. Humphrey, appointed in 1946 as the first Director of the Human Rights Division in the United Nations Secretariat, where he was the principal drafter of the UDHR, stayed 20 years in the job, a constant presence supervising consistency with UDHR principles in overseeing the implementation of some 67 international conventions.

So it is as an adjunct interpretative document to the UDHR that the 1959 DRC is of immense importance. As a primary source it provides us with an intellectually binding proof that the UDHR is to be understood to apply to all children without discrimination, before as well as after birth, as affirmed by the UN General Assembly on November 20th, 1959.

This consensus is further strengthened in consideration of the fact that it is in the nature of preambular paragraphs to human rights instruments that they recall and record what has already been agreed—in general, a preamble is not the place to introduce controversial new material. Indeed, this reference to the rights of the child before as well as after birth is 'old material', having been "recognized in the Universal Declaration of Human Rights" (as the preamble states) eleven years before.

Refuting "only in the preamble" and "only a Declaration" claims

With regard to legal protection for children before birth, abortion advocates have tried to defuse the powerful truth to be read in the preamble to the DRC by claiming it is "only in the preamble" or that the DRC is "only a Declaration". As far as the preamble-based objection is concerned, the first and most obvious rebuttal that needs to be made is that what is stated in a preamble is by way of foundation and motivation for the substantive content of the relevant document. The DRC and such documents derive their compulsive force precisely from what is stated in the preamble, as a building rests on its foundations or as a mathematical theory rests on its underlying set of axioms. It is precisely what is agreed in the preamble that enables the ensuing content to be asserted and agreed. To attempt to dispense with some part of the preamble is to weaken the foundation, undermine the legitimacy, and dilute the fundamental message of the Declaration.

In relation to the objection based on the status of a declaration, pro-abortion advocates have discounted the DRC as only a declaration, carrying some moral weight but not legally binding (though it's not clear what if any moral weight they are prepared to concede it). This can't be said, however, of the UDHR, which even pro-abortion advocates such as the New York-based Center for Reproductive Rights describe as the foundation document of modern international human rights law.[2] Nor can it be said of the International Covenant on Civil and Political Rights (ICCPR) or the International Covenant on Economic, Social and Cultural Rights (ICESCR), which are the codification in law of the UDHR. These Covenants are legally binding and both contain formal recognition on their very first pages that they are to be "in accordance with the Universal Declaration of Human Rights". That is to say, the Covenants are intended to exhibit a coherence with the UDHR and may not be interpreted in any way that is logically inconsistent with the UDHR. Together these three instruments (UDHR, ICCPR, and ICESCR) comprise the International Bill of Rights and no State Parties may resile from the fundamental rights codified therein.[3]

The term "declaration" has been officially defined by the U.N. Secretariat as "a formal and solemn instrument, suitable for rare occasions when principles of great and lasting significance are being enunciated", and although not legally binding, a declaration "may by custom become recognized as laying down rules binding upon States."[4] The 1959 DRC reaffirms a recognition of the rights of the child before birth which was already agreed in the 1948 UDHR now itself having become, over time, both legally binding and an accepted part of customary law.

Yet it has been argued, disingenuously, that although the 1989 Convention on the Rights of the Child (CRC) is a legally binding document that entails obligations for State Parties (USA being the only country that has not ratified it), those obligations do not extend to the child before birth because the rights of unborn children in the CRC are only mentioned in the preamble:

2 See, for example, Center for Reproductive Rights, "Bringing Rights to Bear: An Analysis of the Work of U.N. treaty Monitoring Bodies on Reproductive and Sexual Rights", 2002, Table of Abbreviations and Glossary, p. 9.

3 UN Committee on Human Rights in General Comment No 26 declared that "international law does not permit a State which has ratified or acceded or succeeded to these Covenants to denounce them or withdraw from them". In the context of a U.N. Convention, the term State Party refers to a U.N. member country that is a signatory (party) to the Convention.

4 U.N. Doc. E/CN.4/L.610, 1962.

> Bearing in mind that, as indicated in the Declaration of the Rights of the Child, the child, by reason of his physical and mental immaturity, needs special safeguards and care, including appropriate legal protection, before as well as after birth.

Dismissing this mention, it is then argued:

> No operative provisions of the CRC, however, refer to the rights of unborn children. Preambular paragraphs do not entail legally binding obligations on State Parties. Therefore, there are no binding legal obligations for a State Party to the CRC to protect unborn children.[5]

However, this argument is in direct contradiction to Article 31, General rule of interpretation of the Vienna Convention on the Law of Treaties (1969):

> 1. A treaty shall be interpreted in good faith in accordance with the ordinary meaning to be given to the terms of the treaty in their context and in the light of its object and purpose.
> 2. The context for the purpose of the interpretation of a treaty shall comprise, in addition to the text ... its preamble...

The operative provisions within the CRC (i.e., in the text) shall be interpreted in good faith in accordance with the ordinary meaning to be given to the terms of the treaty in their context (i.e., in the context of its preamble in addition to the text). Clearly, operative provisions must be read consistently with the perambular paragraphs, which set out the themes and rationale of the Convention. Furthermore, they must be read consistently with the International Bill of Rights. This is confirmed in the full text of the most relevant consecutive preambular paragraphs of the CRC, which are as follows:

> Bearing in mind the need to extend particular care to the child has been stated in the Geneva Declaration of the Rights of the Child of 1924 and in the Declaration of the Rights of the Child adopted by the General Assembly on 20 November 1959 and recognized in the Universal Declaration of Human Rights, in the International Covenant on Civil and Political Rights (in particular in articles 23 and 24), in the International Covenant on Economic, Social and Cultural Rights (in particular in article 10), and in the statutes and relevant instruments of specialized agencies and international organisations concerned with the welfare of children.
> Bearing in mind that, as indicated in the Declaration of the Rights of the Child, "the child, by reason of his physical and mental immaturity, needs special safeguards and care, including appropriate legal protection, before as well as after birth..."

In two earlier preambular paragraphs:

5 Advisory opinion solicited by Australian Senator Gary Humphries, 8th December 2004.

> Recognizing that the United Nations has, in the Universal Declaration of Human Rights and in the International Covenants on Human Rights, proclaimed and agreed that everyone is entitled to all the rights and freedoms set forth therein, without distinction of any kind, such as...birth or other status,
> Recalling that, in the Universal Declaration of Human Rights, the United Nations has proclaimed that childhood is entitled to special care and assistance...

the CRC adopted two precepts established in the UDHR. In regard to the first, note the recognition that entitlement to rights and freedoms set forth in the UDHR applies equally, without distinction of any kind, i.e., before and after birth. In regard to the second, note that such "special care and assistance" includes "appropriate legal protection, before as well as after birth", which was an integral part of "the special safeguards and care" that the DRC asserted had been recognized by the UDHR.

The inescapable conclusion here is that the child before as well as after birth is to be protected by the CRC, if that Convention is interpreted in good faith [without discrimination against the child before birth] in accordance with the ordinary meaning to be given to the terms of the treaty in their context [both text and preamble] and in the light of its object and purpose [recognition of the inherent dignity and of the equal and inalienable rights of all members of the human family, and that human rights should be protected by the rule of law].

Chapter 2 UDHR Recognition of the Child before Birth: The Historical Context

Inclusive meaning—the child before as well as after birth

In support of the recognition of the unborn child in the Universal Declaration, it may be argued that the general term 'the child' was understood to include the child before as well as after birth, that such an understanding was in accordance with common usage at the time. Both the historical and the contemporary meaning of general terms like "the child" and "childhood" as used in the Universal Declaration did include the child before birth: this was the "ordinary"[1] meaning in the sense of it being a well-established understanding, a tradition, that the child before birth, at birth, and after birth, was owed a duty of care because of the inherent vulnerability concomitant with his level of immaturity.

Historically, there had been a long common law tradition of protecting the child before birth from abortion. Historically also, the medical profession formally took the Hippocratic Oath, and continued through the 1940s to take this oath at graduation and profession. The Hippocratic Oath recognized that mother and unborn child as patients were owed a duty of care that precluded deliberate harm to either patient:

> ...and to the law of medicine the regimen I adopt shall be for the benefit of my patients according to my judgment, and not for their hurt or for any wrong I will deny deadly drug to any though it be asked of me. Nor will I counsel such, and especially I will not aid a woman to procure abortion...

This same condemnation of abortion was reaffirmed in June 1947 when the Council of the British Medical Association submitted a statement to the World Medical Association:

> Although there have been many changes in Medicine, the spirit of the Hippocratic Oath cannot change and can be reaffirmed by the profession. It enjoins: ...The motive of service

1 "A treaty shall be interpreted in good faith in accordance with the ordinary meaning to be given to the terms of the treaty in their context and in the light of its object and purpose." Article 31(1) General rule of interpretation of the *Vienna Convention on the Law of Treaties (1969).*

> for the good of patients. The duty of curing, the greatest crime being co-operation in the destruction of life by murder, suicide and abortion.[2]

Textbooks on human embryology at the time recognized that the human embryo is a distinct new human being to be treated by doctors with respect: the end of the process of fertilization "marks the initiation of the life of a new individual".[3]

In the 1940s, 1950s, and 1960s, popular books, magazines and other literature on special care for "motherhood and childhood" regularly included special advice for the care of the child before birth, often referred to as "your baby". Advice columns regularly made recommendations on how best to meet the needs of "your child" through the nine months of gestation. A preliminary survey of popular literature such as *Ladies Home Journal* and *Woman's Day* across these decades furnishes no hint of any common belief that the child *in utero* was not considered to be a member of the human family, and indeed provides much evidence to the contrary. In 1946, Dr. Benjamin Spock published *The Common Sense Book of Baby and Child Care.* Over the next few decades the book was translated into 39 languages; 24 million copies were sold between 1946 and 1972. A typical excerpt from Spock's advice to parents, from the 1968 revised edition of *Baby and Child Care*:

> A great majority of those who admit that their first reaction to pregnancy was predominantly one of dismay (and there are plenty of good people who feel this way) are reassured to find that their acceptance of the pregnancy and their fondness for the baby reaches a comfortable level before he is born.

Eleanor Roosevelt, who wrote regular columns and did many broadcasts on family, women and children, and became Chairwoman of the drafting committee of the Universal Declaration, also endorsed this view: "The women bear the children, and love them before they even come into the world ..."[4]

We now proceed to show that the inclusive meaning of the term 'child' was definitively established by the historical context of contemporary human rights documents.

Geneva Declaration of the Rights of the Child (1924)

The century before the Universal Declaration saw immense advances in pre-natal as well as post-natal care for the child. By 1948 there was a well-delineated tradition of understanding that the child before as well as after birth had special needs. The first

2 Statement by the Council of the British Medical Association to the World Medical Association, June 1947, re-issued by The Medical Education Trust. and reproduced at: http://www.donoharm.org.uk/leaflets/war.htm.

3 Patten, Bradley, "Human Embryology", Philadelphia: The Blakiston Company, 1947, p. 76.

4 Quoted in Glendon, Mary Ann, *A World Made New: A History of the U.N. Charter of Human Rights*, Chapter 6, New York: Random House, 2001.

formal recognition of these special needs in an international human rights instrument is found in the 1924 Geneva Declaration of the Rights of the Child.

The UN General Assembly in 1959 understood the term 'child' as used in the 1924 Declaration to have included the child before as well as after birth:

> ...the need for such special safeguards [including legal protection for the child before as well as after birth] has been stated in the Geneva Declaration of the Rights of the Child of 1924 ...

This human rights tradition of "the need for such special safeguards" for every child before as well as after birth thus goes back to 1924. In the Geneva Declaration, adopted by the League of Nations,

> ...men and women of all nations... declare and accept it as their duty that, beyond and above all considerations of race, nationality or creed:
>
> (1) The child must be given the means requisite for its normal development, both materially and spiritually.

There is no legitimacy to be found here for the modern creed of radical feminism, which has tried to obliterate the right to "normal development" of the child before birth, which believes that the child before birth has no right to special safeguards, no right to legal protection against abortion, that the child before birth is not yet a human being, not yet a person and not entitled to any human rights.

Ironically, it was to redress the dangers of similar creeds that sought to dehumanize others such as Jewish children, children with disabilities, children with mental illness, etc., that the Geneva Declaration was altered after World War II (1948) to include two additional points, the first of which became the new #1 right:

> (1) The child must be protected beyond and above all considerations of race, nationality and creed.

The child before as well as after birth must be protected beyond and above all considerations of modern creeds such as radical feminism that espouse and promote the harmful belief that a child may be aborted at any time during the nine months of normal development from conception until birth. The Geneva Declaration states that the child must be protected, but radical feminism insists that the child before birth has no right to protection, or at best only a limited right contingent on the mother's 'choice'.

The Geneva Declaration's third commitment states:

> (3) The child must be given the means requisite for its normal development...

There is no rational way to reconcile this commitment with the modern practice of abortion, which deliberately and lethally arrests normal development and makes a mockery of the duty of care that was declared and accepted in 1924 by "men and women of all nations".

Nuremberg Trials (1947/8) "...protection of the law was denied to the unborn children..."

In the pain-filled honesty of the immediate aftermath of Nazi atrocities, the international community, through the United Nations, the Nuremberg War Crimes Tribunals and the World Medical Association Organization, issued a clear condemnation of abortion as a crime against humanity[5] and exhibited a common revulsion against the practice.

Historian Dr. John Hunt, in a recent series of research papers on the Nuremberg Trials involving abortion, has established that condemnation of abortion was not simply limited to the practice of forced abortions but extended to voluntary abortions as well.[6] James McHaney, the prosecutor of the *RuSHA/Greifelt* Case, in his summation called abortion an "inhumane act" and an "act of extermination" and stated that even if a woman's request for abortion was "voluntary', abortion was still "a crime against humanity". The men doing the abortions were found guilty at this trial of "encouraging and compelling abortions"; and were sentenced to 25 years in prison. It is part of the Nuremberg record of the trial testimony that the unborn are considered as human beings subject to the protection of the law: "...protection of the law was denied to the unborn children..."[7]

In addition, the Nazi record of decriminalizing abortion in Poland and the Eastern Territories was singled out at the Nuremberg Trials for severe censure. Instructions by Nazi authorities issuing directives to decriminalize abortion were furnished as evidence for the count of crimes against humanity:

---

5 In the *Pohl* case for example, count one charged the commission of crimes against humanity which included abortion as Count 1(b). *Trial of War Criminals before the Nuremburg Military Tribunals,* Volume V, pp.88-9. Available at http://www.mazal.org/archive/nmt/05/NMT05-T0088.htm.

6 Hunt, John:

- "Out of Respect For Life: Nazi Abortion Policy in the Eastern Occupied Territories", *Journal of Genocide Research,* Vol. 1 (3), 1997, pp. 379-385.
- "Abortion and the Nuremberg Prosecutors: A Deeper Analysis", *Life and Learning* Vol.VII, Proceedings of the Seventh University Faculty for Life Conference, June, 1997.
- "Abortion and Nazism: Is There Really a Connection?" *Linacre Quarterly,* November, 1996.
- "Perfecting Humankind: A Comparison of Progressive and Nazi Views on Eugenics, Sterilization and Abortion", *Life and Learning,* Vol.VIII, Proceedings of the Eighth University Faculty for Life Conference, June, 1998.
- "The Abortion and Eugenics Policies of Nazi Germany", Association for Interdisciplinary Research in Values and Social Change, Volume 16 (1), 2001.

7 *Nuremberg Trials Record*: "The *RuSHA* Case", March 1948, Volume IV, p. 1077. Available at http://www.mazal.org/archive/nmt/04a/NMT04-T1076.htm.

> Abortion must not be punishable in the remaining territory... Institutes and persons who make a business of performing abortions should not be prosecuted by the police.[8]

The crime of "encouraging abortions" was widely condemned by the international community. The British Medical Association's June 1947 submission *War Crimes and Medicine* reaffirmed, under the "Ethics" heading, "the duty of curing, the greatest crime being co-operation in the destruction of life by murder, suicide and abortion". The World Medical Association's Geneva Declaration of September 1948 proclaims:

> I will maintain the utmost respect for human life from the time of conception, even under threat; I will not use my medical knowledge contrary to the laws of humanity.

And the *International Code of Medical Ethics* in 1949 concurs: "A doctor must always bear in mind the importance of preserving human life from the time of conception until death".

Regarding the term "compelling abortions", it is important to note that it is the abortion itself that is an atrocity against human life from the time of conception. Compulsion is an additional factor of rights violation but it is clear from the Nuremberg records that it does not constitute the whole violation.[9]

The real significance of the Nuremberg judgment lies in the fact that it is part of the very foundation of international human rights law. The human rights obligation to provide legal protection for the unborn child was established universally via the Nuremberg principles and judgments and their codification in the International Bill of Rights.

In the Affirmation of the Principles of International Law recognized by the Charter of the Nuremberg Tribunal, Resolution 95 (1) of the United Nations General Assembly, 11 December 1946, the UN committee on the codification of international law was directed to establish a general codification of "the principles recognized in the Charter of the Nuremberg Tribunal and in the judgment of the Tribunal". These became the foundation of all the human rights instruments to come.

Indeed, during the final General Assembly debate on the Universal Declaration in December 1948, "opposition to the barbarous doctrines of Nazism and Fascism"[10] was recognized as the primary inspiration for the Declaration. René Cassin, one of

8 *Trial of Ulrich Greifelt and Others Indictment* [Tr. pp. 1-18, 7/1/1947.] p. 10. http://www.mazal.org/archive/nmt/05/NMT05-T0111.htm.

9 Historian John Hunt, after extensive research of Nazi abortion programs and the Nuremberg prosecution's evidence, concludes that the Nazis saw abortion as "an act of killing" and that Nuremberg condemned both the violations of liberty and the violations of life as far as abortion was concerned: "Like the kidnapping of children and the seizing of newborns also prosecuted at this trial, abortions were seen as wrong at any time, not just when done for racial-genocidal reasons." Hunt, John: "Abortion and the Nuremberg Prosecutors: A Deeper Analysis", *op. cit.*, p. 205.

10 Charles Malik, quoted in Morsink, Johannes, *Universal Declaration of Human Right: Origins, Drafting and Intent,* Philadelphia: University of Pennsylvania Press, 1999, p. 36.

the principal drafters, affirmed that the Universal Declaration was indeed drafted on the principle of universal inclusion, on "the fundamental principle of the unity of the human race", and this was necessary because Hitler had started "by asserting the inequality of men".[11] Johannes Morsink, in his seminal study of the origins of the Universal Declaration, concludes that the "moral outrage thus created" gave the drafters "a common platform from which to operate and do the drafting".[12]

First Draft of the International Covenant (1947)—"from the moment of conception"

At the very first session of the Drafting Committee of the Commission on Human Rights, the concept of human rights protection for "any person, from the moment of conception" was recognized. The term "from the moment of conception" was used in this original text for Article 1 of the Draft International Covenant on Human Rights:

> It shall be unlawful to deprive any person, from the moment of conception, of his life or bodily integrity, save in the execution of the sentence of a court following on his conviction of a crime for which this penalty is provided by law.[13]

This text became the basis of Article 6 of the Draft International Covenant on Civil and Political Rights (ICCPR) when subsequently, it was decided that two covenants would need to be drafted—the ICCPR and the International Covenant on Economic, Social and Cultural Rights (ICESCR).

Post-World War II Geneva Conventions

The Geneva Conventions at the heart of international humanitarian law are explicit in the kind of special protection and assistance that must be provided to expectant mothers in all situations.[14] The emphasis is always on authorities providing comprehensive care for the expectant mother and her child. Completely absent from the Geneva Conventions is the modern concept being pushed by the current UN Secretariat, that expectant mothers in war and refugee situations should be provided with abortion services.[15] Always the Geneva Conventions emphasize that expectant

11 Ibid., p. 38.

12 Ibid., p. 36.

13 UN Doc.E.CN.4/21.

14 *Geneva Convention relative to the Protection of Civilian Persons in Time of War, e.g.* Articles 14, 23, 50 & 89; also *Protocol Additional to the Geneva Conventions of 12 August 1949, and relating to the Protection of Victims of International armed Conflicts* (Protocol I), Articles 70, 76 & 77.

15 See, for example, the UN's *Reproductive Health in Refugee Situations: An Inter-Agency Field Manual*, Geneva, UNHCR, 1999. "Emergency Management of Post-Abortion Complications" is redefined so as to provide a right to "uterine evacuation" (abortion). The manual has broadened the symptoms which require vacuum extraction and dilata-

mothers in distress are to be given first call on access to nutrition, health care and basic needs for safe passage of both mother and child through pregnancy. This is a very important commitment, consistently presented—recognition that the expectant mother is to be given priority assistance by virtue of the fact that she is carrying within her another human life that is particularly vulnerable by reason of his/her physical and mental immaturity, and entitled to special care.

Fourth Geneva Convention (1949)

The human rights language of the *Fourth Geneva Convention* (August 12, 1949), for example, illustrates the point that only a matter of months after the Universal Declaration (December 1948), concern for the child before birth was very well understood and accepted as a fundamental humanitarian duty. In Articles 14, 33(5), and 50, special protection measures are enumerated specifically for "children under fifteen, expectant mothers and mothers of children under seven". This term provides important confirmation that the expectant mother is to receive special assistance because she has in her care a child before birth who is entitled, along with children under fifteen, to special provisions. The expectant mother, although her child is unborn, yet is to be provided with the same benefits and protections as mothers of children under seven. Special legal protections and other provisions are to be extended to children under fifteen and to mothers of children before as well as after birth.

Children, and their need for special safeguards, are the common factor in all three terms "children under fifteen, expectant mothers and mothers of children under seven". In light of this acknowledgment, it is most plausible that the Universal Declaration of 1948, less than a year earlier, was understood to provide similar protections, i.e., protections that included the child before as well as after birth. Indeed, during the signing ceremony of the Geneva Convention in 1949, the President of the Geneva Convention Conference, Max Petitpierre, specifically affirmed the fundamental connection between the UDHR and the Fourth Geneva Convention:

> Our texts are based on certain fundamental rights proclaimed in it [the Universal Declaration]...respect for the human person, protection against torture and against cruel, inhuman or degrading punishments or treatment...The Universal Declaration... and the Geneva Convention are both derived from one and the same ideal.[16]

---

tion and curettage (D&C abortion) to the point where any woman or girl may present with just a claim of cramping and/or lower abdominal pain and no menses for over one month to be considered "as potential patients with a threatened or incomplete abortion." Experienced obstetricians are agreed, however, that a genuine threatened or incomplete abortion will always need careful examination to reveal at least some evidence of vaginal bleeding or loss, and of the cervix opening. Without this evidence, "uterine evacuation" and "emergency management of post-abortion complications" may be used as mere euphemisms employed to legitimize abortion on demand in those countries where abortion is against the law.

16 *Final Record of the Diplomatic Conference of Geneva of 1949*, Vol. II, p. 536.

Geneva Protocol II (1977)

The Fourth Geneva Convention's commitment to protecting the child before birth, implicitly maintained throughout the next 28 years, was then reaffirmed and extended in the 1977 *Protocol Additional to the Geneva Conventions of 12 August 1949, and Relating to the Protection of Victims of Non-International Armed Conflicts* (Protocol II). Article 6(4) of this Protocol provides an important indicator of the strength of the Geneva Conventions' well-established fundamental concern for the right to life of the unborn child:

> Article 6(4) The death penalty shall not be pronounced on persons who were under the age of eighteen years at the time of the offence and shall not be carried out on pregnant women or mothers of young children.

Again, the common focal point is children. The object and purpose is to provide special safeguards and care including legal protection for all children before and after birth, and protection for mothers who are a critically essential conduit for the provision of special safeguards and care to the child before birth and to "very young children".

This concern to protect children before and after birth from the cruel effects of the death penalty was a reaffirmation and reiteration of these protections in the 1966 International Covenant on Civil and Political Rights, Article 6.

We see here important evidence of continuity of the concept of human rights protection for the child before as well as after birth.

Convention on the Prevention and Punishment of the Crime of Genocide (1948)

This *Genocide Convention* was approved by the UN General Assembly on December 9th, 1948, the day before the Universal Declaration of Human Rights.

The Contracting Parties considered genocide to be a crime under international law contrary to the spirit and aims of the United Nations and condemned by the civilized world, an odious scourge, that at all periods of history has inflicted great losses on humanity. Regarding crimes against children specifically, the acts that comprise genocide include "imposing measures intended to prevent births within the group" and "forcibly transferring children of the group to another group".

Here is a clearly implied concern for the child both before as well as after birth:

> In the present Convention, genocide means any of the following acts committed with intent to destroy, in whole or in part, a national, ethnical, racial or religious group, such as: (a) Killing members of the group; (b) Causing serious bodily or mental harm to members of the group; (c) Deliberately inflicting on the group conditions of life calculated to bring about its physical destruction in whole or in part; (d) Imposing measures intended to prevent births within the group; (e) Forcibly transferring children of the group to another group.

The first draft of this Genocide Convention (prepared in May 1947) referred more explicitly to "biological" genocide, which included restricting births by "compulsory abortion". In Section II (2), abortion was seen as a tool for "biological genocide".

For the purpose of understanding the concepts at that time, it is interesting to note that the first draft began:

> The High Contracting Parties proclaim that Genocide, which is the intentional destruction of a group of human beings, defies universal conscience, inflicts irreparable loss on humanity by depriving it of the cultural and other contributions of the group so destroyed, and is in contradiction with the spirit and aims of the United Nations.

But it is interesting also to consider how aptly this ethic may be applied to our own times. The aggregate of voluntary and compulsory abortions performed globally each year on some 42 million children who may be designated as "unwanted" is encompassed quite intelligibly by the phrase "the intentional destruction of a group of human beings". May it not be said that such intentional destruction "defies universal conscience, inflicts irreparable loss on humanity by depriving it of the cultural and other contributions of the group so destroyed, and is in contradiction with the spirit and aims of the United Nations"?

Draft American Declaration of the International Rights and Duties of Man (1948)—"...the right to life from the moment of conception"

The Inter-American Juridical Committee's *Draft American Declaration of the International Rights and Duties of Man* (commissioned in March 1945) and submitted to the Ninth International Conference of American States (April 1948) was prepared by the eminent jurists Dr. Francisco Campos, Dr. José Joaquin Caicedo Castilla, Dr. E. Arroyo Lameda, and Dr. Charles G. Fenwick. It explicitly recognized the right to life of the unborn:

> Every person has the right to life. This right extends to the right to life from the moment of conception; to the right to life of incurables, imbeciles, and the insane.[17]

The fact that an almost identical sentence was proposed during the *UDHR* negotiations on text relating to the right to life provides testimony to the prevalence of this concept at the time (1948).

As set out below, the reason for deletion of right-to-life references to specific groups within the umbrella term "all members of the human family" in the very first line of the UDHR was the need for conciseness and not, as has been claimed, the

17 Article 1—Right to Life in Novena Conferencia International Americana—Actas y Documentos, Vol. V, p. 449.

intention to delete the human rights of the unborn, the incurables, the mentally disabled, and the insane.[18]

World Medical Association Declaration of Geneva (1948)—"the utmost respect for human life from the time of conception"

The *Declaration of Geneva* (1948), also known as the *Physician's Oath*, to be taken at the time of being admitted as a member of the medical profession, asserts:

> I solemnly pledge myself to consecrate my life to the service of humanity: I will maintain the utmost respect for human life from the time of conception, even under threat; I will not use my medical knowledge contrary to the laws of humanity; I make these promises solemnly, freely and upon my honour.

This Declaration was a principled response by the World Medical Association of national medical bodies to the atrocities committed by doctors in Nazi Germany, atrocities that included using medical knowledge contrary to the laws of humanity to abort many human lives. Abortion in 1948 was not compatible with the solemn pledge to observe the "utmost respect for human life from the time of conception, even under threat, I will not use my medical knowledge contrary to the laws of humanity".

This document was adopted by the World Medical Association only three months before the UN General Assembly adopted the Universal Declaration. The concept of a duty to protect the child before birth was well established and included a solemn duty to maintain respect for human life from the time of conception and to protect human life from the time of conception according to the laws of humanity.

This promise was reaffirmed *verbatim* in the *Declaration of Geneva* (1968), thus proving that from three months before the Universal Declaration (1948) till two years after the ICCPR and the ICESCR, this understanding of human rights to include the child before birth ("from the time of conception") was indeed universally accepted.

American Declaration of the International Rights and Duties of Man (1948)

The *American Declaration of the International Rights and Duties of Man* (1948) (also called the *Bogotá Declaration*) and the Universal Declaration are very closely aligned in both time and concepts. As Paola Wright-Carozza has pointed out:

18 It is a perverse anachronism to interpret past texts without any regard for the generally held assumptions of the epoch in which they were written, and in particular to construe inclusions or exclusions that were never intended, merely because the corresponding exclusions or inclusions were not explicitly mentioned. One might as well cite any past reference to marriage that did not explicitly mention the union of a man and a woman and claim that therefore such a restriction on the sexual composition of the married parties was never intended.

> In 1948 the Latin American nations were engaged in drafting two bills of rights, the Bogotá one for their own region and the other for the United Nations. Almost all of the Latin American countries sent delegates to both events and no doubt many of these did double duty.[19]

The significance of the 1948 American Declaration for our argument here lies chiefly in the regrettable fact that its protection for the unborn child has been misrepresented in the infamous *Baby Boy* case.[20] It is important for us to re-examine this case, as it has been used in a number of recent international legal cases to seriously damage the rights of the unborn.

Certain courts today maintain a pretence that international human rights instruments are "silent" on the right to life of the unborn child. Recently, for example, the European Court of Human Rights (ECHR) in the *Vo v France* judgment made the following statement:

> Unlike Article 4 of the American Convention on Human Rights, which provides that the right to life must be protected "in general, from the moment of conception", Article 2 of the [European] Convention is silent as to the temporal limitations of the right to life and, in particular, does not define "everyone" ("toute personne") whose "life" is protected by the Convention.[21]

The judgment fails to discern that the 'silence' of the European Convention is eloquent in what it does *not* say—as in the Universal Declaration upon which the European Convention was based, "everyone" was deliberately left undefined in order to emphasize that absolutely everyone was included—no human being was to be excluded or 'defined out' of their human entitlement to human rights.

Exploration of the historical context, including the *travaux préparatoires* for the Universal Declaration, sheds some light on this 'silence'. An amendment proposed by Chile to the UDHR article on the right to life went thus:

> Unborn children and incurables, mental defectives and the insane shall have the right to life.[22]

Unborn children at the time were recognized to have the right to life and it may be argued that the amendment was removed chiefly in the cause of keeping to the broadest simplest expression of the principle in order to produce a more concise text.

19 Wright-Carozza, Paolo, "From Conquest to Constitutions: Retrieving a Latin American Tradition of the Idea of Human Rights", *Human Rights Quarterly*, Volume 25(2), May 2003, pp. 281-313.

20 Inter–American Commission on Human Rights, Resolution No 23/81 Case 2141 (United States), 1980.

21 European Court of Human Rights, *Vo v France*, Judgment of 8 July 2004.

22 E/CN.4/21, p. 59.

Conceptually, this was the same text considered only a few months before in the Inter-American Juridical Committee's draft of Article I of the American Declaration:

> Toda persona tiene derecho a la vida, inclusive los que están por nacer así como también los incurables, dementes y débiles mentales. (Every person has the right to life, including those who are not yet born as well as the incurable, mentally defectives, and the insane.)[23]

Much of the UDHR document had in fact been based on the preparatory work for the Bogotá Declaration.[24]

Dr. Marco Gerardo Monroy Cabra, of the Inter-American Commission on Human Rights, argues that one cannot conclude from the elimination of the sentence "This right extends to the right to life from the moment of conception" that life should not be protected from conception, inasmuch as the phrase "to the right to life of incurables, mentally defectives, and the insane" was also eliminated.[25] No one, he argues, could reasonably say that the life of incurables, mentally defectives, or the insane should not be protected.

Dr. Luis Demetrio Tinoco Castro, also of the Inter-American Commission on Human Rights, goes further:

> ...the reason for that elimination was none other than that expressed by the Rapporteur, Mr. Lopez de Mesa, in these terms: "likewise, it was decided to draft them (the rights and duties) in their mere essence, without exemplary or restrictive listings, which carry with them the risk of useless diffusion and of the dangerous confusion of their limits." And the reason cannot be other, because there would not be another for explaining the elimination of the phrase that recognizes the right to life for 'incurables, mentally defectives, and the insane'.[26]

It seems reasonable also to infer a similar explanation for why the UDHR amendment (proposed by the same Chilean delegation and in the same year as the Bogotá Declaration) was not passed:

23 Novena Conferencia Internacional Americana, Actas y Documentos, Vol. V, (1948), at 449.

24 Hernán Santa Cruz, « Cooperar o Perecer El Dilema de la Comunidad Mundial » Buenos Aires: Grupo Editor Latinoamericano, 1984, pp. 184–93. Johannes Morsink, in *The Universal Declaration of Human Rights: Origins, Drafting, and Intent*, Philadelphia: University of Pennsylvania Press, 1999, also confirms that in drafting the right to life Article 3 of the UDHR, Canadian Secretary of the Drafting Committee, John P. Humphrey, drew heavily on the Bogotá Declaration.

25 Dr Marco Gerardo Monroy Cabra, Dissenting opinion, Inter–American Commission on Human Rights, Resolution No 23/81 Case 2141(United States), 1980.

26 Dr Luis Demetrion Tinoco Castro, Dissenting opinion, Inter–American Commission on Human Rights, Resolution No 23/81 Case 2141(United States), 1980.

> ...that the supplementary phrase was eliminated because it was considered unnecessary, and that the concept—not discussed or put in doubt by anyone—that every person has the right to life, including those yet unborn, as well as the incurables, imbeciles and the insane, was implicitly maintained.[27]

Dr. Castro makes the further point:

> That principle [right to life of the unborn child] was not one exclusively of the Internationalists of the Inter-American world, but the predominant one on the matter in the broader circles of the United Nations as is shown by considerandum 111 of the Declaration of the Rights of the Child on November 20, 1959, by the XIV Session of the General Assembly...[28]

In further support of this reasoning, Dr. Castro points to the *International Code of Medical Morality*, and the Declaration of Geneva as principles of professional ethics that together with the scientific principles cited from a number of eminent medical texts establish the widespread recognition of the unborn child that pertained at the time.

Given this widespread recognition of the unborn child in 1948, it seems reasonable to conclude that it was the need for conciseness that accounted for dropping the specific inclusion of unborn children, incurables, the mentally disabled and the insane in the right to life article. Australian delegation documents from 1948 negotiating sessions on the UDHR text confirm this preoccupation with conciseness: "In general any expansion of Declaration articles is illustrative rather than exhaustive"[29] and a recommendation was made that "...the present text should be replaced by a more concise statement of general principles".[30]

Professor Tore Lindholm of the Norwegian Institute of Human Rights, applauds this minimalism of the UDHR as one of its strengths:

> ...the more maximalist a declaration is the more exclusive it is. This is because the more ideas or practices are specified in detail, the more ideas and practices are omitted, contradicted or distorted. The search for universal values or rights must begin with the challenges that are experienced as universal.[31]

Absolutely *everyone* began existence as a human embryo—there are few other challenges that are experienced quite so universally.

27 Ibid.

28 Ibid.

29 Hodgson to Department of External affairs: Dispatch 1, Paris, 5 January 1948, "Report on session held 2-17 December 1947".

30 Cablegram 183, Canberra, 13 April 1948, 4.30 pm: "Australian response to the draft Declaration in the form proposed by the Second Session of the Commission".

31 Lindholm, Tor, "Universal Ethics: From the Nordic perspective", Regional Experts Meeting, Lund, Sweden, 3-5 June, 1999.

The truth which emerges here is that the 1981 majority judgment by the Inter-American Commission on Human Rights on the *Baby Boy* case was wrong when it denied that "article 1 of the declaration has incorporated the notion that the right of life exists from the moment of conception". The Resolution provides no evidence for the claim that: "...the conference faced this question but chose not to adopt language which would clearly have stated that principle".

A decision was taken that there was no need to mention by name the unborn, the mentally disabled, the insane and the incurable. These four vulnerable groups were recognized as human beings with equal rights in keeping with the purpose and intention of the whole Declaration of the Rights and Duties of Man where "Man" was understood to encompass everyone, all human beings, including women, children, the unborn, the mentally disabled and the incurable.

It is interesting to note that there was some discussion in 1948 of a resolution to include the phrase "and women" in certain clauses of the American Declaration. One wonders what would be the outcry if the Inter-American Commission on Human Rights in 1981 had extended their argument to women: "...the conference faced this question but chose not to adopt language which would clearly have stated that principle". By this reasoning, all women also, along with the unborn, the mentally disabled and the insane, might be excluded today from the protection of their rights under the Declaration.

International Code of Medical Ethics (1949)—"the importance of preserving human life from the time of conception"

The *International Code of Medical Ethics* (1949) adopted by the World Medical Association stipulated:

> A doctor must always bear in mind the importance of preserving human life from the time of conception until death.

This principle was reaffirmed without change at the 1968 World Medical Association General Assembly.

Here is concrete evidence that from the time of the Universal Declaration till at least two years after the Conventions of 1966, the international medical community understood very clearly that there is a duty to preserve human life from the time of conception. Doctors recognized a duty of care towards the child before birth, and that duty pertained from the time of conception. Dr. Paul Cibrie, chairman of the committee appointed to prepare the International Code of Medical Ethics, affirmed that "abortionists" were implicitly condemned in the Declaration of Geneva.[32]

---

32 Cited in Hilgers, Thomas W. and Horan, Denis J., *Abortion and Social Justice*, New York, Sheed and Ward, 1972, p. 317.

Draft Declaration on the Rights of the Child (1950)—"even from before birth"

The concept of human rights entitlement for children "even from before birth" was a definitely accepted part of international human rights discourse around this time. The very first Draft Declaration on the Rights of the Child (1950) recognized the child before birth:

> He shall be entitled even from before birth to grow and develop in health....[33]

The understanding here is clearly that human rights entitlement begins before birth—the unborn are entitled to human rights protection.

European Convention for the Protection of Human Rights and Fundamental Freedoms (1950)

In the *European Convention for the Protection of Human Rights and Fundamental Freedoms* (1950), the High Contracting Parties undertook to "secure to everyone within their jurisdiction" the right to life.

The High Contracting Parties included Belgium, Denmark, France, Ireland, Italy, Luxembourg, the Netherlands, Norway, Sweden, and the United Kingdom. These founding member governments of the Council of Europe framed and signed the European Convention in 1950. All these governments were represented at and in agreement with the Universal Declaration. They were also represented at and in agreement with the General Assembly (Session XIV) in 1959 which reaffirmed the right to legal protection for the child before birth.

Is it likely that the Council of Europe, signing in Rome on 4th November 1950 a document that was billed in the international media as "the first international legal instrument to guarantee the protection of human rights", could have dissented so radically from the Universal Declaration on such a fundamental issue as legal protection for the child before birth? It is not likely, especially considering that the preamble to the European Convention proclaims:

> Being resolved, as the governments of European countries which are like-minded and have a common heritage of political traditions, ideals, freedom and the rule of law, to take the first steps for the collective enforcement of certain of the rights stated in the Universal Declaration

This "common heritage of... the rule of law" included, we must remember, not only a tradition of common law protection for the unborn child but also widespread legal protection for the child at risk of abortion.[34]

33 *Draft Declaration on the Rights of the Child* (1950) Principle 3.

34 A/3764 para. 113. "It was pointed out that the legislation of many countries accorded protection to the unborn child." A/C.3/SR 817 para. 25; A/C. 3/SR 818 para. 28.

Indeed, for the High Contracting Parties to exclude the child before birth from their jurisdiction cannot make sense in the light of the fact that these same Council of Europe member governments subsequently agreed in 1959 that the need for legal protection for the child before as well as after birth was recognized "in the Universal Declaration and in the statutes of specialized agencies and international organizations concerned with the welfare of children." If the Council of Europe had indeed excluded the child before birth from his human rights jurisdiction in the 1950 Convention, why did their member governments recognize the need for legal protection for the child before birth in 1959?

Where is the evidence that the right to legal protection for the child before birth recognized in the Universal Declaration was never accepted by the European Court of Human Rights? How could this be when this Court was established in Strasbourg under the European Convention, specifically to ensure observance of the codified UDHR obligations undertaken by contracting states? The Court was brought into existence by the Council of Europe on 18th September, 1959. This was just two months before these same Council of Europe member governments agreed at the UN General Assembly that the UDHR "recognized" the right to legal protection for the child "before as well as after birth".

It stands to reason that recognition of the child before birth as needing legal human rights protection must have been accorded in the absence of any formal reservation or statement of interpretation to the contrary by the Council of Europe or by any of the individual governments who were signatories both to the Universal Declaration (as member nations of the UN) and to the European Convention (as members of the Council of Europe).

In the European Convention's "Right to Life" Article 2, absolutely no provision was made for intentionally depriving the child before birth of the right to life. The conditions[35] laid down for lawful deprivation of life are clearly not applicable—for the child before birth, there has been no crime, and no sentence of a court following his conviction. The child before birth is utterly incapable of offering any person unlawful violence or of participating in a riot or insurrection.

Failure to make any lawful provision here for intentional deprivation of the life of the unborn child is consistent with the general understanding at the time that the child before birth is entitled to the right to life, entitled to have the right to life secured, and entitled to legal protection as recognized in the Universal Declaration, upon which the European Convention is based.

On inclusion of the unborn child in human rights protection, it is only prudent to assume that the European Convention was in complete agreement with the Universal Declaration—in fact, the detailed history of the negotiations actually records that there was no discussion whatsoever about excluding the child before birth from the

35 The exemptions listed in the *European Convention* are borrowed from the very first list of exemptions submitted to the Human Rights Commission by the UN's International Covenant Drafting Committee. Of the 12 items listed, none were related to abortion. E/CN.4/AC.1/SR.29.

right to life or from human rights protection.[36] Around this time also, during the 5th *Session* (1949), *6th Session* (1950), and *8th Session* (1952) of the UN *Commission on Human Rights,* it should be noted that "consideration for the interests of the unborn child" was one of the specific concerns which was recorded as having "inspired" the discussions on prohibition in the draft ICCPR of the death sentence on pregnant women.[37]

> The provisions of paragraph 4(5) of the draft article aimed at the protection of the life of the unborn child whose mother was sentenced to death; that protection should be extended to all unborn children.[38]

Finally, John P. Humphrey, the Canadian Professor of International Law who was appointed by the UN to oversee the drafting of all the foundational human rights instruments, has reminded us of the real source for the drafting of the European Convention:

> ...the European Convention for the Protection of Human Rights and Fundamental Freedoms was modelled on the draft of the Covenant on Civil and Political Rights as it existed in 1950.[39]

So what did the Covenant on Civil and Political Rights "as it existed in 1950" have to say on the right to life?

The UN Commission on Human Rights at the 6th Session (1950) had agreed on the following text for the Draft ICCPR:

> Every human being from the moment of conception has the inherent right to life.[40]

36 Committee on Legal and Administrative Questions Report, Section 1, para.6, 5 September 1949, in *Collected edition of the 'Travaux Préparatoires' of the European Convention on Human Rights,* Vol. III, The Hague: Martinus Nijhoff Publishers, 1975-85, p. 194.

37 United Nations, *Official Records of the General Assembly* (GAOR) , *Tenth Session, Annexes,* (1955), A/2929, Chapter VI, para. 10.

38 Bossuyt, Marc J., *Guide to the "Travaux Préparatoires" of the International Convenant on Civil and Political Rights,* Dordrecht, Boston, Lancaster: Martinus Nijhoff Publishers, 1987, p. 121. A/3764 para. 113; A/C.3/SR.810 para. 2; A/C.3/SR.811 para. 9; A/C 3/SR.812 para. 7; A/C.3/SR.813 para. 36; A/C 3/SR 815 para. 28.

39 John P. Humphrey's Preface to Bossuyt, Marc J.: *Guide to the "Travaux Préparatoires" of the International Convenant on Civil and Political Rights,* Dordrecht, Martinus Nijhoff Publishers, 1987, p. xv.

40 E/CN.4/L.365, p. 24.

Draft Declaration on the Rights of the Child (1957)

The established concept of human rights for the unborn child as well as human rights for the child's mother was reaffirmed in the 1957 *Draft Declaration on the Rights of the Child.*

Following negotiations on Principle 5, the following wording was agreed:

> The child shall enjoy the benefits of social security. He shall be entitled to grow and develop in health; to this end special care and protection shall be provided both to him and to his mother, including adequate prenatal and post-natal care.

This wording makes it clear that the drafting team were in agreement that there are two distinct human beings here, the child and his mother, both entitled to human rights, including adequate "prenatal care".

UN Declaration of the Rights of the Child (1959)—"...legal protection before as well as after birth"

The Preamble to the UN Declaration of the Rights of the Child (1959) acknowledges that "the child, by reason of his physical and mental immaturity, needs special safeguards and care, including appropriate legal protection, before as well as after birth". It acknowledges further that "the need for such special safeguards has been... recognized in the Universal Declaration of Human Rights".

Juxtaposition of these two acknowledgements with the non-discrimination principle articulated in the same Preamble signifies that any distinction between the rights of the child before birth and the rights of the child after birth is to be prohibited as a form of discrimination. The child before birth is not to be treated as an exception to human rights protection. Principle 1 of he 1959 *Declaration* stipulates: "Every child, without any exception whatsoever, shall be entitled to these rights, without distinction or discrimination..."

In other words, the Universal Declaration of Human Rights, having "recognized" that the child before birth, no less than the child after birth, is an appropriate subject of human rights law and human rights entitlement, was understood to have committed governments to provide special safeguards, including appropriate legal protection for the child before birth.

The legal force of the 1959 Declaration lies in the formal evidence it provides that as at 20th November 1959 the whole international community understood and agreed that the Universal Declaration had for that first decade of its jurisdiction *already recognized* the legal status of the child before birth including entitlement to human rights protection. Universal recognition of the child before birth as a person before the law entitled to legal protection had been established and accepted.

Draft American Convention on Human Rights (1959)—"protected by law from the moment of conception"

> This right shall be protected by law from the moment of conception. No one shall be arbitrarily deprived of his life

In 1959, the Inter-American Council of Jurists wrote the first draft of the *American Convention on Human Rights*. The Inter-American Year-book (1968) of the Organization of American States affirms that this draft developed and codified the principles of the American Declaration (1948) and "was influenced also by other sources, including the work in course at the United Nations".[41]

Certainly, the right-to-life article written by the Inter-American Council of Jurists in 1959 was very much in agreement with the "before as well as after birth" human rights language of "the work in course at the United Nations", viz. the 1959 Declaration of the Rights of the Child as a development of the original rights of the child as recognized in the Universal Declaration.

In the 1980 *Baby Boy* case,[42] however, the Inter-American Commission on Human Rights majority resolution has misrepresented this continuity. The commission claimed that the Draft's "definition of the right to life (article 2)...reintroduced the concept that 'This right shall be protected by law from the moment of conception'".

The Commission in 1980–1 was wrong to impose such a reinterpretation on the historical facts. The concept was not "reintroduced" at all—it was already there. It had been there consistently from the Draft Declaration of the International Human Rights and Duties of Man (April 1948). It remained implicit in the Declaration itself which was signed 2 May, 1948. Seven months later, in December 1948, the concept of human rights protection before birth was recognized in the Universal Declaration and was reaffirmed by the UN General Assembly in 1959, the very same year as this Draft American Convention was written.

It is significant that the UN General Assembly in Session XIV in 1959 saw no need to "reintroduce" the concept of the right to life of the unborn. Clearly, the UN General Assembly understood that this right was already there, even from the Geneva Declaration of the Rights of the Child of 1924, and had indeed been recognized by the Universal Declaration, as well as in the statutes of specialized agencies and international organizations concerned with the welfare of children. How can this concept of the rights of the unborn be reintroduced when it was already there, accepted, and recognized by the international community? The specific wording "This right shall be protected by law from the moment of conception" may have been reintroduced but it is a great mistake to assume that the concept itself had any need to be reintroduced.

The 1980–81 Commission's judgment was faulty in that it did not take sufficient account of its own admission that the Draft Convention had been influenced "by the

41 Organization of American States (OAI), *Inter-American Year-book, 1968*, Washington: 1973, pp. 67 & 237.

42 Inter-American Commission on Human Rights in resolution N° 23/81 Case 2141 (United States).

work in course at the United Nations". That work, most importantly, concluded that same year in the UN Declaration on the Rights of the Child.

As Dr. Luis Demetrio Tinoco Castro of the Inter-American Commission on Human Rights points out in his dissenting opinion in the *Baby Boy* case:

> The draft prepared by the Inter-American Juridical Committee, as well as the United Nations Declaration of the Rights of the Child (Resolution 1386/XIV), ... expressly recognized that the human being exists, and has rights, and needs protection, including legal protection, in the period preceding his birth.

International Covenant on Civil and Political Rights (1966)—"to save the life of an unborn child"

The *International Covenant on Civil and Political Rights* (ICCPR), Article 6 (5) asserts:

> Sentence of death shall not be imposed for crimes committed by persons below eighteen years of age and shall not be carried out on pregnant women.

Juxtaposition in the one sentence of concern to protect the right to life (remember this is the human right being articulated in Article 6) of "persons below eighteen years of age" with the protection of "pregnant women" signifies that the child before birth is entitled to the rights of "persons below eighteen years of age". It signifies that the pregnant woman does indeed carry within her womb another human being, a new member of the human family who is entitled, by reason of the child's physical and mental immaturity (an immaturity that distinguishes every person below eighteen years of age) to special protection from the death sentence. Articles prohibiting execution of pregnant women acknowledge that the child, from the State's first knowledge of that child's existence, is to be protected.

So this article is a single right, not two separate rights, in a single sentence. This article focuses powerfully on the child and in it every child is recognized to have a right to life. Every child, i.e., every child before birth, every child after birth, every person below the age of 18 years, has a right to State protection from capital punishment: "sentence of death...shall not be carried out on pregnant women". The child before birth is recognized as being innocent of any crime and so the right to life of that child is to be preserved and protected by the State in circumstances where the right to life of the child's mother was to have been forfeited.

During the 5th Session (1949), 6th Session (1950), and 8th Session (1952) of the UN Commission on Human Rights, the *travaux préparatoires* for the ICCPR refer specifically to the intention to save the life of the unborn child in recognition of the human rights principle that protection should be extended to all unborn children.

The provisions of paragraph 4(5) of the draft article aimed at the protection of the life of the unborn child whose mother was sentenced to death; that protection should be extended to all unborn children.[43]

Again in the 12th Session (1957) of the Third Committee, the right to life of "an innocent unborn child" is recognized:

> The principal reason for providing in paragraph 4 [now Article 6(5)] of the original text that the death sentence should not be carried out on pregnant women was to save the life of an innocent unborn child'.[44]

It is important to understand here that this intention was not just a fleeting one-off expression of concern for the right to life of the unborn child. It was in fact the culmination of a long constant and consistent concern and commitment to protecting the unborn child, a concern arising out of the Nuremberg judgments, finding expression in the Geneva Conventions and impacting on the very earliest drafting sessions of the ICCPR, specifically in the Draft Committee's 1st Session (1947):

> It shall be unlawful to deprive any person, from the moment of conception, of his life or bodily integrity, save in the exercise of the sentence of a court following on his conviction of a crime for which this penalty is provided by law.[45]

The only recorded attempt to introduce abortion as an exception to the right to life Article 4 (now Article 6) of the ICCPR Draft occurred in the Working Group's 2nd Session (1947):

> It shall be unlawful to procure abortion except in a case in which it is permitted by law and is done in good faith in order to preserve the life of the woman, or on medical advice to prevent the birth of a child of unsound mind to parents suffering from mental disease, or in a case when the pregnancy is the result of rape.[46]

It was put to a vote in the Commission on Human Rights and was resoundingly defeated. A principle was adopted in which the only exception to the unlawfulness of deprivation of life was to be as follows:

> It shall be unlawful to deprive any person of his life save in the execution of the sentence of a court following on his conviction of a crime for which the penalty is provided by law.[47]

---

43 Bossuyt, *op. cit.*, p. 121. A/C.3/SR.810 para. 2; A/C.3/SR.811 para. 9; A/C 3/SR.812 para. 7; A/C.3/SR.813 para. 36; A/C 3/SR 815 para. 28.

44 A/C.3/SR.819 para. 17 & para. 33.

45 E/CN.4/21 This was one of the two original texts for Article 1 (now Article 6) of the ICCPR.

46 E/CN.4/SR.35, p. 16.

47 Ibid.

the only grounds for opposing insertion of the words "from the moment of conception" were two practical obstacles:

> That it was impossible for the State to determine the moment of conception and hence, to undertake to protect life from that moment;[49] and
> That the proposed clause would involve the question of the rights and duties of the medical profession in different countries where legislation on the subject was based on different principles.[50]

This first practical obstacle appears to be the most reasonable and the most likely explanation of the addition of the phrase "in general" to the concept of protection of the right to life "from the moment of conception". Certainly, the subsequent article, prohibiting execution of pregnant women, acknowledges that the child, from the State's first knowledge of that child's existence (if not *precisely* from the moment of conception), is to be protected.

Furthermore, the fact that Inter-American Conference reviewing the draft text rejected the Brazilian and Dominican motion to delete the whole term "in general, from the moment of conception"[51] indicates clearly that the Conference was committed to protecting the right to life in general from the moment of conception. There were absolutely no indications that the Conference was removing protection of the right to life of the unborn from conception to birth.

The ICCPR negotiators' second practical obstacle to protecting the right to life from the moment of conception is also mirrored in the objection of the Inter-American Conference regarding the different laws in different countries. Yet this reason seems less than convincing in the light of the fact that the World Medical Association seemed to have had no difficulty in getting international agreement from doctors in all parts of the world across many different jurisdictions on the need to protect life from the moment of conception. The Geneva Declaration (1948) was agreed by the World Medical Association (an association of national medical bodies) only three months before the UN General Assembly adopted the Universal Declaration. The concept of a duty to protect the child before birth was well established and included a solemn duty to maintain respect for human life "from the time of conception" and to protect human life "from the time of conception according to the laws of humanity".

This promise was reaffirmed *verbatim* by the World Medical Association in the Declaration of Geneva (1968), thus verifying that from three months before the Universal Declaration until two years after the ICCPR, this understanding of human rights to include the child before birth ("from the time of conception") was indeed universally established and agreed.

49 A/C 3/SR.817 para. 37.

50 A/C. 3/SR 815 para. 37; and A/C.3/SR.818 para. 13.

51 Inter-American Commission on Human Rights in resolution N° 23/81 Case 2141 (United States) paras. 27 & 28.

Chapter 3 Fundamentals of the Universal Declaration's Human Rights Protection

Legally binding principles

The *Universal Declaration of Human Rights* (UDHR) recognizes the rights of the child before as well as after birth and, since it was adopted by a resolution of the General Assembly,[1] the principles contained therein are considered now to be legally binding on States both as customary international law and as fundamental principles of humanity as originally formulated. In 1980, in regard to the Tehran hostages case, for example, the International Court of Justice clearly affirmed that "the fundamental principles enunciated in the...Declaration" are legally binding in international law.[2]

The Universal Declaration is a specification of the human rights recognized in the *Charter of the United Nations*. The Universal Declaration originally and ultimately derives its authority from the legal standing of this international Charter.

In 1950, Cambridge University's Professor Hersch Lauterpacht, perhaps the most eminent international law consultant to the Nuremberg judges and to the birth of the United Nations and its foundation instruments, commented on the Charter's human rights provisions. He stressed that the members of the United Nations are under a legal obligation to act in accordance with the purposes of the Charter. It is their legal duty to respect and observe fundamental human rights and freedoms. These provisions, he asserted, are no mere embellishment of an historic document; they were not the result of an afterthought or an accident of drafting. They were adopted, with deliberation and after prolonged discussions before and during the San Francisco Conference (1945), as part of the philosophy of the new international system and as a most compelling lesson of the experience of the inadequacies and dangers of the old.[3]

This abiding obligation for UN member states to encourage and respect human rights is affirmed in Article 1(3) of the UN Charter, which identifies among the purposes of the UN the specific purpose "to achieve international cooperation...in pro-

---

1 United Nations General Assembly Resolution 217 A (III) 10 December 1948.

2 *United States of America v. Iran*, Judgment, ICJ Reports 1980, p. 42, para. 91.

3 Lauterpacht, Hersch: *International Law and Human Rights*, London, Stevens and Sons, 1950, pp. 147-8.

moting and encouraging respect for human rights and fundamental freedoms for all." These rights are elaborated in the Universal Declaration of Human Rights.

UDHR recognition of child before birth still pertained in 1959

As an adjunct document to the Universal Declaration, the 1959 Declaration on the Rights of the Child is of immense importance. Its *gravitas* lies in its character as an intellectually binding primary source It furnishes historical proof that on the critical question of whether or not the Universal Declaration is to be understood to apply to all children without discrimination before as well as after birth, the UN General Assembly, on November 20th, 1959, gave a resounding "Yes!"[4]

In the years since that consensus in the 1959 Declaration there has been no unanimous or even near-unanimous reneging on that position. On this question, that vital "Yes!" still stands.

To date, this historical affirmation retains its integrity. The 1959 Declaration retains its full force as reaffirming and providing proof that, eleven years earlier in the Universal Declaration, an international consensus was reached recognizing the need for human rights protection for the child before birth. It also testifies to the fact that this recognition still pertained in 1959. Indeed, it is the only real and substantial UN consensus on the rights of the child before birth that we possess either contemporary with or since the International Bill of Rights, those first three great human rights instruments establishing modern international human rights law.

This is the only formal consensus definition that we have ever had of how, with regard to the child before birth, the United Nations is to understand and implement not only the Universal Declaration of Human Rights (1948) but also the International Covenant on Civil and Political Rights (1966) and the International Covenant on Economic, Social and Cultural Rights (1966) that followed only seven years after the clear reaffirmation in the 1959 Declaration.

This formal consensus definition stands unassailably in the middle of the first two decades of discussion, negotiation, and formulation of the initial great human rights instruments of the modern world. Inclusion of the child before as well as after birth for human rights protection was the single consensual understanding at the time (1959) and the closest understanding that we have contemporaneous with the International Bill of Rights that emerged between 1948 and 1966.

This consensus definition has never been formally revoked since, despite tremendous efforts (both fair and foul) from pro-abortion lobbies on the recent circuit of UN mega-conferences. An exceptionally devious ploy by some pro-abortion delegates to remove recognition of the child before birth from the definition of the child in the Convention on the Rights of the Child (1990) was unsuccessful.[5]

Thus, recognition by the Universal Declaration that the child before as well as after birth has a human rights entitlement to special safeguards and care, including legal

4 Only one delegation voted against it.

5 See Chapter 8 below on the legislative history of the Convention on the Rights of the Child.

protection, holds grave implications today for how member nations of the international community are to treat these smallest members of the human family.

Irrevocable nature of Universal Declaration tied to inalienability of human rights

Human rights are of their essence inalienable and timeless. The opening paragraph of the Universal Declaration proclaims:

> Whereas recognition of the inherent dignity and of the equal and inalienable rights of all members of the human family is the foundation of freedom, justice and peace in the world...

The right to legal protection "before as well as after birth" is one of the equal and inalienable rights of all members of the human family. No one may destroy that right, nor deprive any human being of that right, nor transfer that right, nor renounce it—that's what inalienable means. And when the Preamble goes on to say:

> ...it is essential...that human rights should be protected by the rule of law

it is clear that no one may remove the human rights of the unborn child from the protection provided by the rule of law. The term "no one" means no treaty monitoring committee, no commission, no legislature, no judiciary—none of these has the authority to de-recognize the human rights of any individual human being or any selected group of human beings.

The human rights recognized in the Universal Declaration may not be revoked. To undermine or attempt to revoke any of these human rights set down in this foundation document of modern international human rights law is to undermine the whole international human rights legal system. If it is permissible to withdraw legal protection for the human rights of any one group of "members of the human family" (such as children before birth), then it may be permissible some time in the future to withdraw legal protection for any other group (such as children immediately after birth, children with a disability, Jewish children, middle-aged women with dementia, old men with incontinence...).

Withdrawal of legal protection of the human rights of unborn children is not permissible, as it is tantamount to the deliberate destruction of human rights that have been recognized to belong to them inalienably. Destruction of human rights recognized by the Universal Declaration is not permissible—under any circumstances. This is made clear in Article 30:

> Nothing in this Declaration may be interpreted as implying for any State, group or person any right to engage in any activity or to perform any act aimed at the destruction of any of the rights and freedoms set forth herein.

With appropriate substitution of the terms used here, this means that *no government legislature or judiciary, no radical feminist abortion advocacy group, no doctor, no judge, no mother of an unwanted child, not even the UN Human Rights Committee itself has any right to advocate decriminalization of abortion violence against mothers and their unborn children or to intentionally deprive an unborn child of life, or in any other way to seek to destroy any of the rights and freedoms granted to the unborn.*

Charles Malik, President of the Economic and Social Council and Rapporteur of the Commission on Human Rights in 1948, called the last article of the Universal Declaration "the article of inner consistency":

> ...it states that nothing should flow from this Declaration that can contradict or nullify its effect. Thus no person aiming at the destruction of the fundamental rights can take cover under any of the freedoms granted by this Declaration...[6]

Under Article 30, there is no right for pro-abortion advocates to engage in activity aimed at the destruction of the rights of the child before birth. They should not be campaigning to remove from the children at risk of abortion the special safeguards and care including appropriate legal protection that have been put in place for them. There is no right for any State, group or person to initiate or participate in any action aimed at the destruction of laws that protect the child at risk of abortion.

Yet today the inalienability of human rights is being deliberately undermined. Among many academics it has become convenient to refashion the history of the Universal Declaration to represent it as having been based on "a metaphysical blank tablet"[7]—this make-over is being promoted in order to facilitate the incorporation of present-day "Western lifestyle values" and some peculiarly non-traditional "Asian values", as well as to accommodate current radical feminist dogma.

Such a modern reinterpretation of the historical Declaration is not supported by Johannes Morsink's careful examination of the factual records of debate at the time of drafting. Morsink's meticulous research on the drafting history of the Universal Declaration traces and reveals that the metaphysical foundation of the human rights therein was acknowledged to be natural rights—the drafters, according to Morsink, had recognized a "connection between human rights and human nature".[8] There was an understanding that our appreciation of these natural rights could be deepened and strengthened over time but they could never be revoked.

6 Malik, Charles, "International Bill of Human Rights", *United Nations Bulletin*, July, 1948.

7 This term is taken from Morsink, Johannes: "Review of: The Universal Declaration of Human Rights: A Commentary", *Human Rights Quarterly*, Volume 17, Number 2, May 1995, pp. 398-402.

8 Morsink, Johannes, *The Universal Declaration: Origins, Drafting and Intent*, Philadelphia: University of Pennsylvania Press, 1999, pp. 281-2, also p. 190.

Universal human rights—natural, inalienable, "a permanent guide"

At the inaugural meeting of the Commission on Human Rights (29April 1946), Henri Laugier, UN Assistant Secretary-General, instructed the Commission to develop "a permanent guide for men of good will", articulating essential human rights based on "a minimum of common principles".[9] Thus was the Universal Declaration founded on principles shared among men of good will and intended as a permanent statement of the rights enunciated therein.

At the outset of the UN project, a UNESCO group of philosophers representing all major philosophies and creeds were consulted about the practical possibility of drafting a statement of universal principles. They were justifiably optimistic. After a global questionnaire and survey of eminent representatives of all the major philosophies and creeds, they concluded that there are indeed a few basic practical concepts of human rights which are so widely shared that they "may be viewed as implicit in man's nature as a member of society".[10] Jacques Maritain, an eminent French philosopher deeply involved in the discussions and drafting, described this fortuitous human commonality as:

> ...basic principles of action implicitly recognized by the consciousness of free peoples, this happens to constitute grosso modo a sort of common residue, a sort of unwritten common law, at the point of convergence of extremely different theoretical ideologies and spiritual traditions.[11]

At the same time, Maritain was alert to the difficulties posed by the fact that natural law, though recognized by all peoples and all cultures, is yet interpreted sometimes very differently and defended by very different arguments. The law and the knowledge of the law, Maritain says, are "two different things", since natural law exists *a priori* but our knowledge of natural law is interpreted through experience.[12]

Recognition of natural-law rights—clarified through Holocaust experience

And for a short time, post-World war II and pre-Cold War, in a moment of grace and honesty and good will, the nations of our troubled world did unite to recognize natural-law rights through the scarifying but extraordinarily unifying experience of stark Nazi violations of those basic universal human rights. Indeed, Morsink observes that

---

9 *E/HR/6* p. 2.

10 UNESCO, (ed.), *Human Rights: Comments and Interpretations*. London & New York: Wingate, 1949, p. 267.

11 Maritain, Jacques: "The Possibilities for Co-operation in a Divided World": inaugural address to the Second International Conference of the United Nations Educational. Scientific and Cultural Organization, Mexico, November 6, 1947. See Jacques Maritain Center, "The Range of Reason". Available at: http://maritain.nd.edu/jmc/etext/range.htm.

12 Maritain, Jacques: *Natural Law: Reflections on Theory & Practice*, (Ed.) William Sweet, South Bend: St. Augustine's Press, 2001, pp.33-4.

this experience was sufficient: "They did not need a philosophical argument in addition to the experience of the Holocaust."[13]

The Indian delegate Lakshimi Meron confirmed that the Universal Declaration "was born of the need to reaffirm these rights after their violation during the war".[14] Eleanor Roosevelt concurred at the closing session:

> The realization that the flagrant violation of human rights by Nazi and Fascist countries sowed the seeds of the last world war has supplied the impetus for the work which brings us to the moment of achievement here today.[15]

From the recurring pattern of debate in the detailed history of the drafting process, Morsink draws this conclusion about the *modus operandi* of the drafters and the delegates:

> While they often differed in specific wording to be used, once it was shown that a violation of a certain clause or article had in some way helped create the horrors of the war, the adoption of that clause or article was virtually assured.[16]

In such a powerful context, it is unthinkable that these people in framing their response to the destructive violence of the war would have proposed (or even concealed) in the Universal Declaration some prescient endorsement of the scale of abortion violence we have today.

Absolutely no one to be excluded from human rights protection

Certainly there is no evidence whatsoever that the drafters ever contemplated the removal of legal protection from unborn children. Remember that the Nazi abortion programs had been severely condemned in the very recent Nuremberg judgments: "...protection of the law was denied to the unborn children..." [17] If the drafters were clear and united about anything, they were clear and united on this: that henceforth, absolutely no one was to be excluded from human rights protection, and no jurisdiction was ever again to be exempt from the universality of that protection.

To infer in retrospect, as do some human rights experts like Professor Tore Lindholm, that the drafters who framed Article 1 back in the late 1940s were keen to

13 Morsink, Johannes, "World War Two and the Universal Declaration", *Human Rights Quarterly*, Vol. 15, 1993, pp. 357-405.

14 Morsink, "The Universal Declaration". *op. cit.*, p. 36.

15 Eleanor Roosevelt's speech, December 9, 1948. "Adoption of the Declaration of Human Rights" available at: http://www.udhr.org/history/ergeas48.htm.

16 Ibid., p. 37.

17 *Nuremberg Trials Record*: "The *RuSHA* Case", March 1948, Volume IV, p. 1077. http://www.mazal.org/archive/nmt/04a/NMT04-T1076.htm.

make human rights "sensitive to shifting societal and historical circumstances"[18] is not borne out by the factual account of the major debates of the time. Indeed, it is hard to reconcile any such alleged 'sensitivity' with the feisty spirit of determination that operated throughout the negotiations, a spirit signified by the cry *Never Again!* Today's make-over of that spirit to render it more "sensitive" to changes (such as the present annual abortion toll of some 42 million children) is quite possibly motivated by a desire to provide wiggle room for new populist violations of human rights condoned by current ideological and cultural aberrations.

Lindholm is right however, in his understanding that what he calls "a genuine natural rights doctrine" of human rights "excludes interpretations of historically changing societal conditions from being an essential part of the rationale of human rights".[19] But he is wrong to condemn such a principled foundation as "insensitive to the structural and cultural circumstances of human rights". In fixing their human rights principles in the stone foundation of natural rights, the drafters of the Universal Declaration were far from insensitive—in fact they were exquisitely *sensitive* to the possibility that future "structural and cultural circumstances" could throw up infinitely ingenious variations of Nazi-style excuses and justifications based on ideology or culture and demonstrating the "necessity" of violating the most basic human rights of some vulnerable group of human beings.

Universal Declaration and the fragility of medical ethics

Both Dr. Leo Alexander and Dr. Andrew Ivy, the American physicians who testified for the prosecution in the Nuremberg Trials, commented on the gradual seduction of the German medical profession by Nazi ideology and on the incremental nature of the profession's fall from grace. Deeming some lives "not worthy to be lived", Nazi ideologues authorized systematic medical killing on a large scale.

Dr. Alexander, writing in the *New England Journal of Medicine* in 1947, observed that the fall of the medical profession started with a "subtle shift in emphasis in the basic attitude of the physicians…the acceptance of the attitude…that there is such a thing as life not worthy to be lived" and then moved gradually from "the severely and chronically sick" to encompass "the socially unproductive, the ideologically unwanted, the racially unwanted, and finally all non-Germans".[20] Dr. Alexander warned that prevention of doctors succumbing again to this "disease" requires "observation and recognition of early signs and symptoms":

> In looking for these early signs one may well retrace the early steps of propaganda on the part of the Nazis in Germany as well as in the countries that they overran and in which

18 Lindholm, Tore: "Article 1" in (eds.) Godnundur Alfredson and Asbjorn Eide, *The Universal Declaration of Human Rights: A Common Standard of Achievement*, The Hague, Martinus Nijhoff Publishers, 1999, p. 71.

19 Ibid., pp. 71-3.

20 Alexander, Leo, "Medical Science Under Dictatorship", *New England Journal of Medicine*, 14 July 1949, pp. 39-47.

> they attempted to gain supporters by means of indoctrination, seduction and propaganda.[21]

Indeed, Nazi propaganda was highly effective in perverting public opinion and public conscience in a remarkably short time: "In the medical profession this expressed itself in a rapid decline in standards of professional ethics."[22]

Dr. Ivy, writing in 1949, also emphasizes this point:

> What happened to the medical profession of Germany is stern testimony to the fact that… acquiescence in or even silence before the violation of sacred professional ethics, the service by medical men of any goal but truth for the good of humanity, can lead to dishonour and crime in which the entire medical profession of a country must in the last analysis be considered an accomplice.[23]

And in 1961, while the human rights prescribed by the Universal Declaration were in the process of being codified in the Conventions (the ICCPR and the IESCR), this warning was reiterated in the highly publicized Eichmann Trial. Dr. Robert Servatius (Defense Counsel for Eichmann) astutely draws on a truth that was understood and accepted at that time:

> From the interweaving of the various connections must be drawn the lesson that what happened to the Accused can in the future happen to anyone, no one is immune. Concepts are remodeled, the capable ones are needed, they are lured and won over and they are the very ones who become guilty. What happened to the German people can come to pass in every people. The entire civilized world is confronted by this problem. Recognizing this truth should heal and teach us how to prevent new disasters.[24]

Indeed, "to prevent new disasters" was the *raison d'être* of the Universal Declaration, and still had a powerful thrust in the International Covenants being drawn up at that time. Written into the Universal Declaration is a profound appreciation of the fragility of medical ethics. The drafters' awareness of that fragility had been finely honed by still very recent and searing revelations of Nazi atrocities carried out by 'civilized' and well-educated physicians. The drafters recognized that painful truth which was summed up much later by Dr. Edmund Pellegrino of the Center for Clinical Bioethics at Georgetown University:

21 Ibid.

22 Ibid., p. 39.

23 Ivy, A. C., Statement in Mitscherlich A, Mielke F., *Doctors of infamy: the story of the Nazi Medical Crimes*, New York: Schuman, 1949, pp. xii-xiii.

24 *Shofar FTP ArchShofar FTP Archive File*, available at: www.nizkor.org/ftp.cgi/people/e/eichmann.adolf/.../ftp.py?people/e/eichmann.adolf/transcripts/Sessions/Session-120-03.

> The German physicians indicted at Nuremberg had been taught by some of the world's best historians of medicine and ethics. They could not plead ignorance of ethics and, in fact, made constant allusions to medical ethics and the Hippocratic tradition in their testimony. They even convinced themselves that their heinous acts were consistent with those principles.[25]

Moral Relativism—no place in the Universal Declaration

In the light of this experience, it is not surprising that when it came to establishing a strong conceptual framework of human rights principles, the theories of relativism and positive law, untethered from universal principles, had no place in the drafting of the Universal Declaration. Certainly there was pragmatism in the negotiations, to gain agreement on the text; as well as a certain amount of hard-headed cynicism concerning immediate or even ultimate realization of the ideals. But these should not be presumed to have contaminated the drafters' concept of permanent foundational principles.

While they quibbled over the words, they agreed on the basic principles—indeed, the subtext of the whole long and earnest negotiation history was that an expression of a single definitive set of universal principles was possible and was even now in the making.

Even the most vigorous debates maintained a robust optimism that they could make here a definitive *Declaration* of the 'universal' principles that would be the bedrock of international human rights law. Confident that it could be done, they went ahead and did it. Not for them the sceptical denial of the possibility of non-relative human values. Nor were they to be seduced by a popular form of legal positivism that emerged in the 20th century, which allows for the moral law to be endlessly reconstructed to accommodate the idiosyncrasies of States and special interest groups in different times and places.

Natural-law principles declared by the drafters to be universal

The dignity and worth of the human person is the founding premise of the Universal Declaration. The UN Charter Article 55 requires States to promote and encourage respect for human rights and fundamental freedoms; but nowhere does the Charter define precisely what these rights are. From the outset, according to Charles Malik, the Universal Declaration was seen as:

> a filling out of this gap in the Charter; it is the definitive explication of the pregnant phrase of the preamble, 'the dignity and worth of the human person.'[26]

25 Pellegrino, Edmund D., "The Nazi Doctors and Nuremberg; Some Moral Lessons Revisited", Annals *of Internal Medicine*, 1997, pp. 127-307.

26 Charles Malik: "International Bill of Human Rights", *United Nations Bulletin*, July, 1948.

And indeed, all the human rights of the Universal Declaration are premised on the second preambular paragraph of the UN Charter of Human Rights, which reads: "…to reaffirm faith in fundamental human rights, in the dignity and worth of the human person." [27]

And this in turn is traced back to Field Marshal Smuts' original text in that first proposal at the San Francisco Conference 1945: "To re-establish faith in fundamental human rights, in the sanctity and ultimate value of human personality."

Dr. Johannes van Aggelen, a close associate of John Humphrey, Director of the UN Division of Human Rights, first appointed to oversee the drafting of the Universal Declaration, has made the point that although the text of the Smuts' proposal was changed, "the spirit of his words remained intact".[28] Eleanor Roosevelt affirmed this, too, at the adoption of the Universal Declaration on December 9, 1948 when she quoted Gladstone Murray:

> The central fact is that man is fundamentally a moral being… Man's status makes each individual an end in himself. No man is by nature simply the servant of the state or of another man.[29]

The concepts of dignity, sanctity, status, worth, and ultimate value—*each individual an end in himself*—underpin the Declaration's understanding and acceptance of the first principle of natural law, viz., the moral imperative to do good and avoid evil, and emanating from this, the precept that affirms preservation of each human life and proscribes arbitrary deprivation of any human life.

Natural law principles such as these found concrete expression in the Declaration and were declared by the drafters to be universal. Martti Koskenniemi has gathered convincing evidence that references to World War II were deleted from the original Cassin draft of the Preamble as well as from all other passages that sought to situate the Declaration in the specific post-war period.[30] Many speakers in the UN General Assembly Third Committee consultations affirmed that "this was necessary in order to highlight the ahistorical, universally applicable aspects of the declaration".[31]

Fereydoun Hoveyda, looking back to his experience as a young Iranian law graduate assistant to René Cassin in drafting the Universal Declaration and also as an adviser to the Iranian delegate in the Third Committee debates, confirms this great emphasis on the universality of the Declaration. He recalls that the Universal Decla-

27 "Preamble to the Charter of the United Nations submitted by the South African Delegation", *UNCIO*, Vol. III, p. 476, document 2, G/14 d(1), May 3, 1945.

28 Van Aggelen, Johannes: "The Preamble of the United Nations Declaration of Human Rights", *Denver Journal of International Law and Policy*, Vol.28 (2), 2000, pp. 133-4.

29 Eleanor Roosevelt's speech, December 9, 1948. "Adoption of the Declaration of Human Rights" available at: http://www.udhr.org/history/ergeas48.htm

30 Koskenniemi, Martii, "The Preamble of the Declaration of Human Rights" in Godnundur Alfredson and Asbjorn Eide, (eds.), *The Universal Declaration of Human Rights: A Common Standard of Achievement*, The Hague, Nijhoff, 1999, pp. 32-3.

31 Ibid., p. 33.

ration was "conceived as a bulwark against what happened in the thirties and forties in several European countries and that prompted World War II."[32] He is troubled now, however, that the very concept of the universality of the Universal Declaration of Human Rights is being harmed:

> A few years back, within the framework of UNESCO, Muslim states elaborated an Islamic Declaration of Human Rights. Different ethnic communities in advanced societies like the United States claim the privilege of safeguarding their "traditions" even when some of them contradict parts of the Universal Declaration. Such a fragmentation would certainly nullify the Universal Declaration. Indeed what was new and important in the Declaration in 1948 was justly the concept of universality. Abandoning it in the name of "cultural differences" would constitute a setback. There are no Islamic, Buddhist, Hindu, Zoroastrian, Christian, Judaic, etc. rights. There are human rights, pertaining to human beings wherever they live and whatever their creeds.[33]

And here in addition we would extrapolate that abandoning the concept of universality in the name of a radical feminist ideology would also constitute a setback. For there are no "feminist" rights—there are only human rights, pertaining to human beings wherever they live, pertaining even to the smallest human beings who, for a short nine months, enjoy the natural right to live and grow *in utero*.

Universal rights—a bulwark against ideological manipulation

Pope Benedict XVI, who as a youth saw at first hand the disastrous adaptation of law to Nazi ideology, states a profound truth that is relevant here:

> Natural law is, definitively, the only valid bulwark against the arbitrary power or the deception of ideological manipulation. The knowledge of this law inscribed on the heart of man increases the progress of the moral conscience.

The writing of the Universal Declaration represents, we would argue, just such a bulwark. It represents also a tremendous leap in the progress of the moral conscience. The Preamble does not dissemble as to the spur that made possible such a leap:

> Whereas disregard and contempt for human rights have resulted in barbarous acts which have outraged the conscience of mankind...

In the Preamble language, there is none of the modern academic quibbling over what constitutes a barbarous act or the sneering cynicism as to whether any act can be intrinsically evil. Nor is there any of today's dilettante dabbling in theories of law *sans*

32 Hoveyda, Fereydoun, "The Universal Declaration and 50 Years of Human Rights", *Transnational Law and Contemporary Problems*, Vol. 8, 1998, p. 435.

33 Ibid.

morality or in theories that deny the existence of any conscience not elastic enough to accommodate the most popular vices of the day.

"Never Again!" commitment at the heart of the Universal Declaration

Yet the rock-firm intractable *Never Again!* commitment at the heart of the Universal Declaration still resonates today. Modern commentators recognize this:

> Nothing legitimizes human rights work more than the slogan 'Never Again!' And behind that imperative is the memory of the Holocaust. It is a mark of just how deeply that memory has saturated our everyday consciousness that the phrase 'Never Again' does not require any further specification for us to know to what it refers.[34]

It is that *Never Again!* commitment that continues to shore up the inalienability of human rights. The term "inalienable rights of all members of the human family" applied to the child before birth means that these human rights cannot be taken from the child by anyone, not by a neo-Nazi State, not by doctors, and not even by the child's mother.

Thus, the right to life, because it is inalienable, rules out procured abortion. The natural law principles relevant here are that a human entity should be allowed to persist in being and that one must not directly attack any basic good in any person, not even for the sake of avoiding bad consequences. This last principle, that the basic aspects of human well-being are never to be directly suppressed, is cited by Professor John Finnis as the principle of natural law that provides the rational basis for *absolute* human rights, for those human rights that prevail *semper at ad semper* (always and on every occasion), and even against the most specific human enactment and commands.[35]

Protection of our unborn children is a natural ethical principle inscribed in our humanity. It has been observed that respect for human life from conception is a part of "the ethical message" inscribed in our very being and remains always one of the "unbreakable and contingent norms that do not depend on the will of the legislator and not even on the consensus that the State can and must give".[36] These are in fact norms that "precede" any State law, and as such, "they are not subject to modification by anyone".[37] The drafters of the Universal Declaration would have agreed with this for according to Morsink, they indeed recognized human rights as "logically anteced-

34 Levy, Daniel and Sznaide, Natan, "The institutionalization of cosmopolitan morality: The Holocaust and human rights", *Journal of Human Rights*, Vol. 3 (2), June 2004, p. 144.

35 Finnis, John: *Natural Law and Natural Rights*, Oxford; Clarendon Press, 1980; and *Aquinas: Moral, Legal and Political Theory*, Oxford University Press, 1998, pp.164-171.

36 Pope Benedict XVI: "Address at the International Congress on Natural Law", Pontifical Lateran University of Rome, 12th February, 2007.

37 Ibid.

ent to the rights spelled out in various systems of positive law" and that human rights "are seen as inherent and inalienable... and thus are held independent of the state".[38]

This continued to be acknowledged at the 5th Session (1949) and the 6th Session (1950) of the Commission on Human Rights, as the commissioners drafted the codification of the Declaration rights into the Conventions:

> ...it was argued that the rights of man appertained to him as a human being and could not be alienated and that they constituted a law anterior and superior to the positive law of civil society.[39]

Inherent dignity and children at risk of abortion

Inherent dignity became the core natural law value at the heart of the International Bill of Rights:

> ...recognition of the inherent dignity and inalienable rights of all members of the human family is the foundation of freedom, justice and peace in the world.

This appears in the Preamble of all three instruments and was characterized by the Commission of Human Rights as "a statement of general principle which was independent of the existence of the United Nations and had an intrinsic value of its own."[40] As such, it is a foundational premise upon which all rights that follow are based. It is "the foundation of...justice", i.e., it is the foundation of international human rights law.

On this foundation, there is no right to abortion. There is no human right for one human being to abort the life of another human being before or after birth. Dependency of a weaker human being on a stronger human being confers neither ownership nor disposal rights, i.e., there is no right to terminate the life of the one who is dependent.

Human rights derive from the inherent dignity of the human person—it is the nature of human rights that they are inherent, that they belong to every human being "by nature". Charles Malik, Rapporteur of the Commission on Human Rights at the time of drafting the Universal Declaration, explained the rationale thus:

> ...if my fundamental rights and freedoms belong to me by nature, then they are not a chance assemblage of items: they must constitute an ordered whole. Responsible inquiry must then exhibit their inner articulation.[41]

---

38 Morsink: "The Universal Declaration", *op. cit.*, pp. 333-4.

39 United Nations, *Official Records of the General Assembly* (GAOR) , *Tenth Session, Annexes*, (1955) A/2929 Chapter III para. 6.

40 GAOR, A/2929 Chapter III para. 4.

41 Malik, Charles, "International Bill of Human Rights", *United Nations Bulletin*, July, 1948.

Responsible inquiry into the "ordered whole" of inherent human rights could not have produced an irrational and discordant judgment that the human rights that belong by nature to every human being do not belong to the human child growing and developing in his/her mother's womb. What could be argued to warrant withholding the human rights that belong to the child "by nature"? Only that the human child is not human—and both science and logic refute this as nonsense.

Dehumanizing language cannot legitimize human rights violations

Giving the human child at the early stages of development other names such as "embryo" or "fetus" and referring to the child as "it" does not alter the child's human nature or the child's entitlement "by nature" to the "inherent dignity and inalienable rights of all members of the human family".

Yet dehumanizing language intended to make mothers feel more comfortable about rejecting their children at risk of abortion is freely available today on pro-abortion Web sites. For example, note the vilifying language used to describe the human embryo in this passage from Carl Sagan:

> It destroys tissue in its path. It sucks blood from capillaries. It bathes itself in maternal blood, from which it extracts oxygen and nutrients. It establishes itself as a kind of parasite on the walls of the uterus...By the third week...It looks a little like a segmented worm. By the end of the fourth week...It's recognizable now as a vertebrate, its tube-shaped heart is beginning to beat, something like the gill arches of a fish or an amphibian become conspicuous, and there is a pronounced tail. It looks rather like a newt or a tadpole. By the sixth week...The eyes are still on the side of the head, as in most animals, and the reptilian face has connected slits where the mouth and nose eventually will be. By the end of the seventh week...The face is mammalian but somewhat piglike. By the end of the eighth week, the face resembles that of a primate but is still not quite human.[42]

The child at risk of abortion is likened to a blood-sucking parasite, a worm, a fish, an amphibian, a newt, a tadpole, an animal with a reptilian face, a mammal with a piglike face and finally the child is described as having a face that *resembles that of a primate but is still not quite human.*[43]

In justifying extermination programs which included termination of unborn children, Nazi propagandists used similar language to dehumanize those who were deemed to threaten others' health:

42 Quoted in "When does the fetus become human?", Abortion Access and Information. Available at: http://www.abortion.org.au/.

43 The perverse irony in this is that there are individuals and organizations today who would grant the apes "person" status on a par with humans!

> In National Socialism, the German people...is again on the path to health, and therefore offers the Jewish parasite no further nourishment...[44]

Under National Socialism, millions of human beings, including unborn children, were denied their inherent human dignity. Dehumanizing language paved the way for medicalized killing. The phrase "extermination of life not worth living" has been traced back to a 1933 *Deutsches Arzteblatt* article "The Physician and Genetic Improvement" by Professor F. Lommel.[45]

It is important to remember this here, for the Universal Declaration was framed in response to Nazi atrocities that were based on attempts at systematic dehumanization of vulnerable human beings. Small Jewish children were called "Jew-dogs", children who were disabled were disparaged as "life unworthy of life", and the unborn children of Polish and Eastern workers were labeled "racially inferior offspring". Always the dehumanizing language came first, then came the exterminations, the aborting of human lives ideologically reclassified as less than human, and totally expendable.

Universal Declaration built on "the inherence view of human rights"

And so the Universal Declaration was adopted and proclaimed, and began with "recognition of the inherent dignity and inalienable rights of all members of the human family". Morsink gathers carefully from diverse delegations a prolific number of references giving support to "the inherence view of human rights" and affirming that the drafters did indeed establish a fundamental connection between human rights and human nature.[46] The drafters concurred that human beings have an inherent dignity that belongs to them by nature, and from the beginning, and they made it clear that membership of the human family was never again to be subjected to the imposition of Nazi-like conditions of exclusivity.

At no time in the drafting history was any consent given to the idea that any group of human beings at any particular stage of life or condition of dependency should be excluded from human rights protection. The term "inherent dignity", applied in the spirit and purpose of the Universal Declaration, means that every human being, from the first moment of existence as a discrete, genetically unique human entity right up to the point of natural death, has an immutable dignity, a dignity that does not change with external circumstances such as levels of maturity, mental or physical health, prognoses of quality of life, functionality, or 'wantedness'.

There is no conceivable condition or deprivation or mental or physical deficiency that can ever render a human being "non-human". Pejorative terms such as "clump of cells", "spare embryo", "non-viable fetus", "a major fetal abnormality" or "a non-person

---

44 "Parole 21: "Den Juden kennen heißt den Sinn des Krieges verstehen!", *Sprechabenddienst*, Sept./Oct. 1944. Available at www.calvin.edu/academic/cas/gpa/sprech44a.htm.

45 Hanauske-Abel, Hartmut, M., "Not a slippery slope or sudden subversion: German medicine and National Socialism in 1933", *British Medical Journal*, Vol. 313, Nuremberg Doctors' Trial special edition, 7th December, 1996, pp. 1453-1463.

46 Morsink, "The Universal Declaration", *op.cit.*, pp. 281-2, also p. 190.

in a permanent vegetative state" cannot justify violation of the human rights of the human person so described, nor can such terms destroy *the inherent dignity of the human person.* As long as a human being exists, from growth and development in the womb to enfeeblement and debilitation in old age, he or she retains all the rights of being human, all the rights that derive from his or her inherent dignity as a human being.

Chapter 4 The Inaugural Human Right—To Be Born Free and Equal

Rights of the child exist before birth

The *Universal Declaration of Human Rights* Article 1 begins: "All human beings are born free and equal in dignity and rights.....".

Some pro-abortion advocates have opined that this first article is not a right at all—merely a statement. This is disingenuous. It is no mistake that this is the inaugural right—for this first right, in the Declaration of Human Rights, the right to be born free and equal, is the basis of all rights to come. As a logically necessary first premise, Article 1 establishes at the outset this first right upon which all other rights are predicated. It stands to reason, then, that if some human beings are denied the right to be born, then all human beings are not "born free and equal in dignity and rights".

The term "all human beings" includes the child before birth—the Universal Declaration was understood by the UN General Assembly in 1959 to have specifically included appropriate legal protection for the child before birth as well as for the child after birth.[1] The child before birth has human rights to be protected by the rule of law and this protection includes the right to born free and equal in dignity and rights. The child's rights pre-exist birth—they inhere in the child's humanity and therefore cannot be conferred or granted at birth.

So all children, including the child before birth, have the inaugural right "to be born" and more than that, they have a right to be "born free and equal in dignity and rights". Recognition of that right requires that any existing discrimination against the child before birth must be eliminated.

The child before birth is equal in dignity and rights to the child after birth These rights, like all human rights are inalienable. Being born cannot be used as an exclusionary criterion to "disappear" the rights of the child before birth. No one child has a greater right to be born than any other. Disability, non-preferred sex, illegitimacy, father a rapist, mother doesn't want the child—none of these distinctions can be used to deny the child before birth the right to be born free and equal in dignity and rights.

1 See Chapters 1 & 2 above.

Being human confers human rights—not the act of "being born"

It is not the act of "being born" that grants or confers human rights, it is being human. Common language has always recognized the human identity of what medical textbooks have long called the embryo and the foetus. In biblical and old English traditions, a woman is said to be 'with child'. In more modern language, a woman is said to be 'expecting a child'. The 20th century *Geneva Conventions* consistently use the term "expectant mother". Digressing here for a moment, suppose I were to say I was expecting a guest, a child, to arrive by train; suppose I then arranged to have the train sabotaged so the child's life is terminated. Suppose I claimed that, while I was perfectly prepared to treat the child with dignity and care once the child arrived, I recognized no such constraint to honour my obligations as a host while the child was in transit, so to speak. You might quite rightly condemn my behavior as discriminating between the child in transit and the child on arrival. You might point out to me that this is the very same child, *in transit* and *upon arrival*. And you would be right.

Each child existentially unique—the same child before as well as after birth

That unique child who comes into being at conception and who makes that pre-natal journey *in utero* to birth is one and the same individual throughout the nine-month continuum of development (in transit), one and the same individual "at birth", and one and the same individual "after birth". That unique human being who exists before birth is the same unique human being who exists after birth. It is reason and science, not just the Catholic Church, that affirms that the human embryo is a subject identical with the human being which will be born at the term of this vital initial stage of human growth and development. Both reason and science tell us that every child has the same genetic identity before birth as after birth.

Each human embryo is an embryonic human being: he or she[2] is not part-human and part-something else. Each embryonic human being is completely human, essentially human, possessing inherently a unique set of human characteristics that, in a single natural pre-ordained continuum, will mature and unfold through the natural stages of human growth and development: embryonic, fetal, newborn, infant and toddler, girlhood or boyhood, adolescence, young adulthood, middle age, old age.

Children before birth—"human beings without frills"

The child before birth at whatever stage of life, embryonic or fetal, is a distinctly *human* being, a new and unrepeatable human being, an identifiable "member of the human family", whose rights are equal and inalienable. For all members of the human

2 The sex of the embryo can be identified at the very earliest stage of existence. See, for example, the research on 3-day-old human embryos in Hardy K., Martin K.L., Leese H.J., Winston R.M., Handyside A.H., "Human preimplantation development in vitro is not adversely affected by biopsy at the 8-cell stage", Human Reproduction, Vol. 5, No. 6, 1990, pp. 708-714.

family (and the child before birth is a member of the human family, biologically, genetically, and genealogically), human dignity is inherent and human rights are equal and inalienable. According to the opening proclamation of the UDHR, the ICCPR and the ICESCR:

> Whereas recognition of the inherent dignity and of the equal and inalienable rights of all members of the human family is the foundation of freedom, justice and peace in the world...

To be eligible for membership of the human family, one has only to be human. Johannes Morsink, in his meticulous study of the drafting history of the Universal Declaration, observes that when all prohibited discriminations are eliminated:

> ...what we have left is just a human being without frills. And the Declaration says that the human rights it proclaims belong to these kinds of stripped down people, that is to everyone, without exception.[3]

From conception to birth, children are 'human beings without frills', without the extras that come with maturity, stripped down certainly but yet possessing all the essentials of a new human life. Lacking much in physical size, weight, age, and independence, without a voice, without the power to fend off attacks on their tiny human bodies, our children *in utero* are, nevertheless, human beings. To qualify for human rights protection, to be eligible to be born free and equal in dignity and rights, remember that one has only to be human.

UDHR Article 1: Reason, conscience and the spirit of brotherhood

Article 1 of the Universal Declaration continues: "...They are endowed with reason and conscience and should act towards one another in a spirit of brotherhood."

For human beings endowed with reason and conscience, it is impossible to characterize the violent and discriminatory act of abortion that takes the life of an unborn child as acting towards that child in a spirit of brotherhood.

For one of the chief drafters of this article, René Cassin, an eminent French jurist and Zionist who himself had suffered the loss of many family members in Nazi concentration camps, the equality of all human beings and their brotherhood in one family were vital truths. These truths, he believed, needed to be urgently re-established as the guiding principles of human rights protection under the new international rule of law.[4] Cassin convinced the Drafting Committee that they must start with "the fundamental principle of the unity of the human race" precisely because Hitler had started

3 Morsink, Johannes, "Women's rights in the Universal Declaration", *Human Rights Quarterly*, Vol. 13, 1991, p. 230.

4 Morsink, Johannes, *The Universal Declaration: Origins, Drafting and Intent*, Philadelphia: University of Pennsylvania Press, 1999, p. 38.

his pogroms "by asserting the inequality of men".[5] Cassin also put forward a second principle, that every human being has "a right to be treated like every other human being"; and a third principle, "the concept of solidarity or brotherhood among men".[6] All three concepts were incorporated in Article 1 of the Universal Declaration.

In the drafting history, the Belgian delegate perceived the true significance of Article 1 as a principle governing the entire field of human rights:

> Article 1 was important as a first article of a solemn document, since it affirmed a principle in which some measure summed up the articles that followed.

As Charles Malik reminded the Drafting Committee, acting towards one another "in a spirit of brotherhood" is a clear moral directive rooted firmly in natural law obligations that stem from "reason and conscience", the characteristics of man that distinguish him from the animals.[7]

Reason and the rules of conscience

It was actually Peng-Chun Chang, Chinese philosopher and diplomat and Vice-Chairman of the Drafting Committee, who proposed that the word "conscience" [8] be added to Malik's original draft:

> All men are brothers. Being endowed with reason and conscience as members of one family, they are free and possess equal dignity and rights.

From the start, these concepts of brotherhood and membership of one family were universally accepted, as was implicitly the understanding that reason and conscience could determine the practical principles of morality and ethics consistent with treating each other in the spirit of brotherhood and as members of one family: "Each is responsible for the life, liberty and dignity of all".[9].

---

5 Ibid., p. 39.

6 UN Document E/CN.4/AC.1/SR.2. p. 2.

7 Charles Malik, a Lebanese philosopher and diplomat, was President of the UN Economic and Social Council and Rapporteur of the Commission on Human Rights at the the time of drafting the Universal Declaration.

8 Tore Lindholm, "Article 1", in *UDHR: A Common Standard of Achievement, op.cit,*. p. 43. Professor Lindholm argues that 'conscience' was a heavily Westernized rendition of 'ren', a fundamental normative notion in Confucian ethics. But Lindholm's quote from Confucian ethicist Joseph Chan seems to indicate that the concept is very close to the Socratic principle that "it is never right to do wrong" and also to the Golden Rule principle, both of which are at the heart of the Western concept of conscience: "For Confucius, *ren* is the basis of all human virtues…it requires us to show concern and respect to other people… *Ren* also requires reciprocity: we should not impose on others what we do not desire." *The Analects*, VX:24.

9 From an earlier French version of Article 1 in UN doc. E/CN.4/82, Add, 8. p. 2.

The Declaration was openly, vigorously, and unashamedly a formidable and forthright response to the massive human rights atrocities of World War II. This great concern was expressed in the second clause of the Preamble:

> Whereas disregard and contempt for human rights have resulted in barbarous acts which have outraged the conscience of mankind...

The drafters of the Declaration clearly understood their role as representatives of "the conscience of mankind". They all had vivid, still red raw memories of how ideologues exercised their positions of power in villages and cities, prison camps, and even in hospitals, where they flouted with impunity the basic rules of conscience—the Golden Rule that one may not do to another what one would not have done to oneself, and the universal principle that one may not do evil even that good may come of it.

It is inconceivable that the drafters of the Declaration had it in mind at this time to authorize the removal of unborn children at risk of abortion from the human rights protection they were designing for all members of the human family.

The injunction to "act towards one another in a spirit of brotherhood" is no mere platitude. Rather, from the beginning it has identified clear and grave duties recognized by reason and conscience to be owed and exercised by those in power towards others in positions of weakness or helplessness. Positions of power were never again to be exercised to proclaim the inequality of some human beings, and then to divest them of dignity and human rights, and of life itself.

Though there was some small quibbling from certain women delegates over the term 'brotherhood', Eleanor Roosevelt was able to resolve this by pointing to the inclusiveness of the term 'mankind' used in the UN Charter. Perhaps today the concept 'in the spirit of brotherhood' may be better understood (in language less irksome to the radical feminist sisterhood) as 'human solidarity', as willing the good of all other members of the human family for the sake of our shared humanity.

For ultimately the human race is not some exclusive little club where the power of incumbency—those who are in the prime of life—confers the right to abort the lives of others who are just starting out, by declaring them "unwanted", disabled, having the wrong sex or the wrong father, etc. The power of incumbency does not authorize the exclusion and destruction of children at risk of abortion. On the contrary—the universal rules of conscience oblige those whose lives at the earliest stages had once been protected and nurtured to provide now that same protection and care towards other human beings in those same early vulnerable stages.

Acting in the spirit of brotherhood—"Everyone has duties to the community..."

Ensuring that children before birth are given appropriate legal protection is not the sole responsibility of government authorities but involves everyone and every community:

> Everyone has duties to the community in which alone the free and full development of his personality is possible.
> Universal Declaration Article 29(1)

Ghandi's contribution to the drafting of the Universal Declaration was an insistence that human rights be grounded in universal duties: "The Ganges of rights flows from the Himalaya of duties." Right from the outset of negotiations on of the text of the Universal Declaration, there was a common understanding of the general principle that individual rights entailed duties.[10]

In the Cassin draft of Article 3, it was proposed that each man "owes to society fundamental duties which are: obedience to law, exercise of a useful activity, acceptance of the burdens and sacrifices demanded for the common good." [11]

Stephen Hall, in an article in the *European Journal of International Law*, warns that it is when we are "unmindful of the richness of the common good under the natural law" that the temptation to turn moral wrongs into human rights arises; he offers the establishment of a human or fundamental right to abortion under the positive law as an example of an attempt to transform a moral wrong into a human right:

> Laws authorizing abortions, and buttressing access to abortions, are radically unjust (and radically immoral) in that they permit choosing directly against a self-evident form of human flourishing; i.e. life.[12]

The human rights of mothers and their corresponding duties to other human beings include their duty to protect life, to sustain rather than to destroy their children before birth.

The Universal Declaration (as well as the Preambles to both ICCPR and the ICESCR) establish the human rights duties of individuals towards other individuals.

Mothers have duties to the community that include a duty of care for the child before birth who belongs already to the youngest generation, the newest generation, the regeneration of that community.

That the child before birth already belongs to the community and is entitled to be born into that community is recognized in Article I of the *Geneva Convention on the*

---

10 Morsink concludes from the drafting history of Article 29 (1) that it was introduced in order to avoid "the extreme individualism often associated with a natural rights philosophy of human rights". See Morsink, Johannes, "The Philosophy of the Universal Declaration", *Human Rights Quarterly*, Vol. 6(3), 1984, pp. 319-320.

11 See the June 1947 Draft revised by Cassin (Cassin Draft) in Glendon, Mary Ann: *A World Made New A History of the U.N. Charter of Human Rights*, New York: Random House, 2001, Appendix 2.

12 Hall, Stephen: "The Persistent Spectre: Natural Law, International Order and the Limits of Legal Positivism", *European Journal of International Law*, Vol. 12 (2), Oxford: 2001, p. 269.

Prevention and Punishment of the Crime of Genocide. Herein lies recognition that imposing measures intended to prevent births within the group will harm that group or community. What is 'granted' to the mother—'abortion rights' conferring permission to abort her child—is most certainly 'imposed' on her child. To harm the child before birth is to harm also the community to which that child belongs.

The term "everyone" in Article 29 of the Universal Declaration means just that: everyone has duties to the newest generation of a community. The mother is not alone in her duties toward the child before birth. Everyone must share that duty, and help her to provide for the basic needs of the child. Everyone includes fathers, families, grandparents, uncles, aunts, doctors, nurses, neighbors, friends, employers and work colleagues—as well as the government departments of health, housing, child welfare, employment, etc.

As Mary Ann Glendon, Harvard law professor and author of a formidable amount of research on the framers of the Universal Declaration, correctly discerns:

> ...the most pressing task for friends of human rights today is to re-unite what the framers of the Universal Declaration put together, to reunite the two halves of the divided soul of the human rights project – the love of freedom and the sense of one human family for which we all bear a common responsibility.[13]

Particularly with regard to honouring and protecting the child before birth, our "love of freedom" needs to be reconciled with our duties towards the child in keeping with "the sense of one human family for which we all bear a common responsibility".

Indeed, in the negotiations of the text of this section of Article 1, the French delegation's understanding of 'acting in the spirit of brotherhood' sheds valuable light: "Each is responsible for the life, liberty and dignity of all"[14]

Current ideological revamping of Article 1—invalid

Yet Article 1 of the Universal Declaration of Human Rights, which reads:

> All human beings are born free and equal in dignity and rights...

is currently being interpreted as excluding unborn children from human solidarity and human rights entitlement. Whether this reinterpretation is being misshaped by academic dishonesty, ideological zeal, or careless incompetence, we shall leave to the reader to judge—for the time being, anyway.

A false claim has appeared recently in a number of academic journals and on Web sites that the text and negotiating history of Article 1 of the Universal Declaration

13 "A World Made New", Radio National Encounter Interview with Mary Ann Glendon, 11th August, 2002.

14 From an earlier French version of Article 1 in UN doc. E/CN.4/82, Add, 8. p. 2.

explicitly premises human rights on birth.[15] This false claim appears on the web site of the New York-based Center for Reproductive Rights (CRR)[16] and is being disseminated as truth in *amici curiae* briefs for national and international court cases related to abortion:[17]

> Article 1 opens the Universal Declaration of Human Rights with the fundamental statement of inalienability: "All human beings are born free and equal in dignity and rights" (Art.1). Significantly, the history of the negotiations (travaux préparatoires) indicates that the word "born" was used intentionally to exclude the fetus or any antenatal application of human rights. An amendment was proposed and rejected that would have deleted the word "born", in part, it was argued, to protect the right to life from the moment of conception. One of the drafters, a representative from France, explained that the statement "All human beings are born free and equal..." meant that the right to freedom and equality was "inherent from the moment of birth". Article 1 was adopted with this language by 45 votes, with nine abstentions. Thus, a fetus is not a holder of rights under the Universal Declaration of Human Rights. The deliberately gender-neutral term "everyone has the right to life...", utilised thereafter in the Declaration to define the holders of human rights, refers to born persons only.[18]

Yet a careful and thorough reading of the negotiating history of Article 1 confirms that there is no evidence whatsoever that "the word 'born' was used intentionally to exclude the fetus or any antenatal application of human rights".

The authors of this false claim (Copelon, Zampas, Brusie and Devore) would have done better had they heeded the advice of Johannes Morsink, the world's pre-eminent authority on the drafting of the Universal Declaration. Morsink enumerates eight drafting stages and warns:

> Thus to comment on the original intent of the drafters of the Universal Declaration is not an easy thing to do. A thorough investigation into this intent would require a scrutiny of each of the stages for each of the articles of the Declaration. One is tempted to skip over the earlier stages and rely exclusively on the General Assembly stages, especially on what was said at stage seven in "the great debates" of the Third Committee.[19]

---

15 Copelon, R., Zampas, C., Brusie, E., Devore, J., "Human rights begin at birth: international law and the claim of fetal rights", Reproductive Health Matters, Vol.13 (26), November, 2005, pp. 120-9.

16 http://www.reproductiverights.org/pdf/ww_poland_constitution.pdf.

17 CRR's amici curiae record includes Tysiac v. Poland / Amici (European Court of Human Rights); Achyut Prasad Kharel v. His Majesty's Government of Nepal / Amici (Supreme Court of Nepal); Abortion Law Challenge in Colombia / Amici (Constitutional Court of Colombia); and D. v. Ireland / Amici (European Court of Human Rights).

18 Copelon, R., Zampas, C., Brusie, E., Devore, J., *op. cit.*, p. 120.

19 Morsink, Johannes, "Book Review on the Universal Declaration of Human Rights—a Commentary", *Human Rights Quarterly*, Vol.17 (2), 1995, p. 400.

The word 'born' was introduced and discussed only at the penultimate stage of negotiations of this text. The discussions at that stage in this particular great debate centered on some very complex philosophical and metaphysical meanings none of which could have been said to focus on an intention "to exclude the fetus or any antenatal application of human rights".

Restoring the word 'born' to its true context

Diverse understandings of the term 'born' enunciated during negotiations on the text included the following:[20]

- A moral birth took place when people were *born into the human family*
- People had rights *when born, but that they could later lose them* (Charles Malik, Third Committee Chairman); also *All the human beings are born free and equal because the reality of the freedom and the equality of the men exists for them because of their birth, whatever the subsequent events* ... René Cassin (French jurist involved in the original drafting)
- Equality existed only *at birth* (Venezuela)
- Equality rights in law were determined *not by the fact of birth, but by the social structure of the state* (Soviet Union)
- The right to freedom and equality was inherent *from the moment of birth* (France)
- All men are *born free* (New Zealand)

Careful reading of the drafting history shows that this flux of meanings was being proffered tentatively in the ongoing exploration of a deeper issue about the very meaning of human rights.

In the context of this larger debate, Capelon *et al.* are being ingenious but not ingenuous when they make their facile assertion:

> An amendment was proposed and rejected that would have deleted the word "born", in part, it was argued, to protect the right to life from the moment of conception. The representative from France explained that the statement "All human beings are born free and equal..." meant that the right to freedom and equality was "inherent from the moment of birth".

The words "in part it was argued, to protect the right to life from the moment of conception" carry the implication that it was specifically this particular part that was the reason or even a significant part-reason for the deletion.

Not so. There was no proposal to drop 'born' to protect the right to life from the moment of conception. There was no perceived necessity—the right to life for un-

20 Morsink, Johannes: *Universal Declaration of Human Rights: Origins, Drafting and Intent*, Philadelphia, University of Pennsylvania Press, 1999, pp. 284-296.

born children was accepted by the international community at that time as a given.[21] The proposal to drop the term 'born' came from Lebanon's representative, Mr. Azkoul, who made explicit his reason for the proposal: it was because the sentence: 'All human beings are born free and equal', in his opinion, constituted a threat in so far as it could suggest that a man could be deprived of his rights for an unspecified reason.[22]

The Chinese delegate rejected the term 'born' because of its connotations regarding Rousseau's theory that all men are born naturally good. The Iraqi delegate wanted 'born' replaced with 'should be' so as to render more clearly a right rather than a mere fact. Among various other expressions of support for Lebanon's proposal, there was only one brief affirmation from Venezuela, offering the *additional* grounds that it would avoid the implication that equality existed only at birth and not continuously from conception through to complete development of each human being. No expression of dissent was offered in reply to this and the debate swirled on to the real issue at stake—the inherency of human rights.

The real issue at stake—are rights inherent or are they granted by governments?

The singularly significant reason for rejection of the proposal to delete the word 'born' was that it was at the very heart of a fierce philosophical debate on another issue altogether that had been conducted over many sessions. The real debate was about whether rights are granted by governments or are 'endowed' and 'inherent' by 'nature'. Morsink summarizes the outcome:

> The words "inherent," ...and "born" in the first recital and in Article 1 make the same point as did the phrase "by [their] nature" that was traded away. Together the drafting fragments comprising these words add up to what I shall call the inherence view of human rights. This is the view that human rights inhere in people as such; people have these moral rights because of their membership in the human family, not because of any external force or agency.[23]

21 *Convention on the Prevention and Punishment of the Crime of Genocide* (1948) prohibited "...Killing members of the group; Causing serious bodily or mental harm to members of the group; Imposing measures intended to prevent births within the group..." The World Medical Association's *Declaration of Geneva* (1948) solemnly pledged to "maintain the utmost respect for human life from the time of conception"; The *Draft American Declaration of the International Rights and Duties of Man*,(1945-8) affirmed "...the right to life from the moment of conception" The *International Code of Medical Ethics* (1949) pronounced as a doctor's duty "the importance of preserving human life from the time of conception...".

22 Verdoodt, Albert, *Naissance et Signification de la Déclaration Universelle des Droits de l'Homme*, Société d'Etudes Morales, Sociales et Juridiques, Louvain-Paris: Editions Nauwelaerts, 1964, pp. 80-1.

23 Morsink: *Universal Declaration of Human Rights: Origins, Drafting and Intent, op. cit.*, p. 290.

In this context, France's explanation was not a response urging the rejection of "the right to life from the moment of conception" as Capelon *et al.* have implied. In fact, France's explanation on which Capelon *et al.* have placed so much reliance was in reply to Sergei Pavlov, the Soviet Union delegate, who was espousing the philosophy that equality of rights before the law is "determined not by the fact of birth, but by the social structure of the state." He went on to insist that it was thus "obvious that in the days of feudalism men had not been born free and equal".

It was in reply to this specific philosophical point that the French representative, Grumbach, explained to the Russian that "[a]ll representatives agreed that inequality did, in fact, exist, but the statement 'All human beings are born free and equal' meant that the right to freedom and equality was inherent from the moment of birth."

In the context of the particular "great debate" that was going on at this time, the emphasis here was never on the strict literal meaning of the phrase 'from the moment of birth' but rather on the 'inherency' of the rights of all human beings as opposed to the rights of human beings as constructs of the State. The Soviets were claiming that human rights are "determined not by the fact of birth, but by the social structure of the state." France's very pertinent point here to the Soviet representative was that the inherency of our human rights is not by virtue of a benign State, nor by virtue of 'being born', but by virtue of 'being born human'. France's reply comes down very strongly on the side of "the inherency view" in this great debate summarized succinctly by Morsink:

> "… people have these moral rights because of their membership in the human family, not because of any external force or agency".[24]

Excluding the idea of hereditary slavery

Capelon *et al.* have only to return to the drafting history and place the intervention by France's delegate Mr. Grumbach in its true context, in order to understand the authentic meaning that was revealed in the immediate responses supplied by Egypt's representative Mr. Bagdad and by Syria's representative Mr. Kayaky. Both supported Grumbach by affirming inclusion of the word 'born' for the specific reason that it would exclude the idea of hereditary slavery.

So, to sum up, both delegates responding to Grumbach's intervention offer support for inclusion of the word 'born' in the common understanding that it is being proposed in order to establish human rights as *inherent*, thus excluding the idea of hereditary slavery. It's clear that Capelon *et al.* are without credibility in their claim that it was introduced in order to exclude the unborn child from human rights.

Significantly, Mr. Bogomolov (also a Soviet Union delegate) then wanted the whole of Article 1 deleted, judging it "devoid of meaning" because of its "abstract philosophical or religious notion." The South African delegate, representing an apartheid regime, also supported deletion on the grounds of his personal belief that it did not define any right or freedom at all.

24 Ibid.

Article 1 "should state the philosophical basis of human rights"

It was at this point that the New Zealand delegate argued that "the declaration should, however, state the philosophical basis of human rights and fundamental freedoms" and proposed a new wording for Article 1:

> All men are born free, equal in dignity and rights as human beings endowed with reason and conscience, and bound in duty to one another as brothers...

Here we see what was understood to be the true core values being discussed. New Zealand brings the whole discussion back to the original principles of the French Revolution—separated by commas—freedom, equality, brotherhood:

1. *All men are born free,*
2. [all men are] *equal in dignity and rights as human beings endowed with reason and conscience, and*
3. [all men are] *bound in duty to one another as brothers...*

There is no recognition here that "the word 'born' was used intentionally to exclude the fetus or any antenatal application of human rights" as the Capelon *et al.* article surmises. The focus was always on freedom, equal dignity and rights, and brotherhood.

The centrality of these three principles stood continuously , from René Cassin's very first draft (16thJune 1947) of Article 1 ("All men, being members of one family are free, possess equal dignity and rights, and shall regard each others as brothers.") to the very last draft of the Universal Declaration ("All human beings are born free and equal in dignity and rights. They are endowed with reason and conscience and should act towards one another in a spirit of brotherhood".)

This understanding was confirmed in very clear terms by Charles Malik, who was chairman of ECOSOC and of the Third Committee that steered the Universal Declaration to its conclusion:

> Then in Article I human beings are said to be "born free and equal in dignity and rights." Certainly the word "born" means that our freedom, dignity and rights are natural to our being and are not the generous grant of some external power. Finally, Article I goes on to say that human beings 'are endowed with reason and conscience.' Obviously, the word 'endowed' can only mean that our nature is such that we originally possess those rights and freedoms.[25]

So the case put forward by Capelon *et al.* collapses. They offer no other evidence whatsoever for their additional claim: "The deliberately gender-neutral term "every-

25 From a speech on human rights to the U.S. Chamber of Commerce Committee on International, Political, and Social Problems given at the Waldorf Astoria in New York, November 4, 1949. Available at: http://www.udhr.org/history/talkon.htm.

one", utilized thereafter in the Declaration to define the holders of human rights, refers to born persons only." The material they reference here from Morsink applies only to the gender-neutrality of the term 'everyone' and supplies no indication that either this term or the term 'all human beings' in Article 1 "refers to born persons only". Their interpretation appears to owe more to fertile imaginations than to any rigorous analysis of the historical records.

Verdoodt on abortion in the drafting history of the Universal Declaration

In his seminal study on the drafting of the Universal Declaration, Johannes Morsink concludes that nothing was specifically stated during the drafting process on the issue of abortion.[26] Albert Verdoodt, however, sheds further light on this issue in his authoritative 1964 work on the birth and significance of the Universal Declaration.[27] Verdoodt had the advantage of personal consultation with many of the original drafters, especially with René Cassin who wrote the preface to Verdoodt's work.[28] Certainly, Verdoodt casts doubts on the legality of all legislation that permits abortion, even abortion permitted only in "certain cases". This was noted by Lars Adam Rehof in an essay on UDHR Article 3 ("Everyone has the right to life, liberty and security of person.") in a volume marking the fiftieth anniversary of the Universal Declaration, in which he says:

> Verdoodt concludes that the interpretation of article 3 leaves a certain amount of doubt as to the legality of (all) provoked abortions and that it is not settled when exactly the protection starts.[29]

However, Verdoodt's comment regarding no exact commencement of legal protection has an added significance that Rehof overlooks. Verdoodt maintains that the right to life in Article 3 of the Universal Declaration as it relates to abortion and euthanasia, the death penalty, and legal protection by the State from criminal attacks, is to be understood "only in the context of the entire Declaration"[30].

---

26 Morsink: *Universal Declaration of Human Rights: Origins, Drafting and Intent, op. cit.*, pp.291-2.

27 Verdoodt, Albert, *Naissance et Signification de la Déclaration Universelle des Droits de l'Homme*, Société d'Etudes Morales, Sociales et Juridiques, Louvain-Paris: Editions Nauwelaerts, 1964.

28 Verdoodt had extensive consultations with many of the drafting committee and the Third Committee that were present at the negotiations, including Cassin, Malik, Santa Cruz, Garcia Bauer, Austregesilo de Atheida—also Verdoodt listened to tape recordings of the critical sessions, so he was able to distinguish the nuances of the debate.

29 Rehof, Lars Adam : *Article 3* in Alfredsson, Gudmundur & Eide, Asbjorn (eds.): *The Universal Declaration of Human Rights: A Common Standard of Achievement*, The Hague, Martinus Nijhoff, 1999, p. 92.

30 "De même aucune condamnation explicite n'est portée contre l'euthanasie des incurables et des faibles d'esprit, ni contre la condamnation légale pour crime grave à la peine capi-

Regarding the laws that permit abortion "in certain cases", Verdoodt says that from the *travaux préparatoires* one can interpret Article 3 as "Each individual has the right to physical existence".[31] He then goes on to emphasize:

> It was not stated precisely when this existence commences. In the same way any explicit condemnation of euthanasia against the incurable and the mentally disabled was not pronounced.... [32]

What is Verdoodt's real point here? He is saying that there was no need for specifying when the physical existence of the child being considered for abortion begins. Just as, he implies, there was no need for any explicit condemnation of euthanasia against the incurable and the mentally disabled ... for these and for the unborn he concludes that each individual has the right to liberty and security of person, as this right is spelled out in the articles of the Universal Declaration that follow.

Verdoodt understands protection for all of these—the unborn child, the incurable, and the mentally disabled—to be lawful, as affirmed by Article 5, which prohibits cruel, inhuman, or degrading treatment, and to include the right to "physical integrity" in the "right to physical existence". Verdoodt asserts that these rights are "explained" in the articles that follow Article 3, i.e., "in the context of the entire declaration".

Conforming domestic abortion legislation to human rights principles

In truth, this great debate was not about whether rights begin 'from the moment of birth'—indeed, protecting the right to life of the unborn child was implicitly agreed, the only voice of dissent coming from Madame Begtrup, representative for the Commission for the Status of Women, because, she said, legislation in many countries included "the possibility of provoked abortions in certain cases".[33] This reasoning was ignored by the UN's Third Committee (where all UN members were revising the draft text), as it had ignored every other appeal (regardless of the issue) that was based on protecting existing domestic laws, and in any case it did not reflect any substantive objection to the principle of protection for the unborn. The object and purpose of the Universal Declaration and the subsequent Conventions were always to universalize the rule of law on protections for human rights. Indeed, the main thrust of the 20th century human rights movement was precisely to eliminate the wide variety of domestic legislation that made convenient concessions for various degrees of human rights abuses such as slavery, racial discrimination, child labor, child marriage, and child soldiers.

---

tale ou contre le manque de protection de l'Etat contre les tentatives criminelles. Chaque individu a droit à la liberté et à la sureté de sa personne, comme cela est précisé dans les articles suivants." ibid., p. 99.

31 "Chaque individu a droit à l'existence physique." ibid., p. 100.

32 "Il n'est pas précisé quand cette existence commence eu égard à des législations permettant l'avortement dans certains cas." ibid., pp. 99-100.

33 UN doc. E/CN. 4/AC.2/SR3.

The Australian delegation understood this point to be very important, relating as it does to each State's future obligation to voluntarily eschew some of the State's sovereignty in order to ensure that domestic laws comply with the Conventions:

> A close study of the Declaration in any country will, of course, make it clear that domestic legislation does not correspond precisely with the Declaration itself. It is inevitable, therefore, that private individuals or groups of people will quote the Declaration from time to time, claim that domestic legislation lags behind the Declaration, and bring pressure to bear upon governments to modify domestic legislation in order to make to conform with the Declaration. All countries will be in this position, and most countries in a far worse position than Australia in this regard. The point I wish to make is that any direct attempt by an individual country to limit the scope of the Declaration of Human Rights so that it conformed precisely to domestic legislation in that country would have been brushed aside in Committee Three.[34]

Consistently throughout the entire negotiations, the Human Rights Commission and the UN delegates in Committee Three had insisted that domestic laws must progressively and eventually be conformed to the human rights principles being enumerated, rather than conforming human rights to existing domestic laws. From the very beginning, it was established that these Conventions were to codify in international human rights law the principles of the Universal Declaration as a "common standard of achievement for all peoples and all nations".[35]

Misreading post-World War II Declaration with a 21st century bias

It is important to understand that abortion in 1948 was quite simply not a controversial issue as it is now in today's society. In 1948 the international community, including the World Medical Association, was experiencing a well-documented[36] and universal revulsion against abortion. Recall that abortion had been condemned at the Nuremberg Trials as a failure by the Nazi state to provide legal protection for unborn children: "...protection of the law was denied to the unborn children...".[37] René Cas-

34 Ibid.

35 Preamble, Universal Declaration.

36 See note 19 above.

37 It is part of the Nuremberg record of the trial testimony in the RuSHA or Greifelt Case that the unborn are considered as human beings subject to the protection of the law. Though the Nazis had decriminalized abortion in Poland and the Eastern territories, the Nuremberg Tribunal still judged that "...protection of the law was denied the unborn children" and two SS Officers Richard Hildebrandt and Otto Hofmann were convicted for "compelling and encouraging abortion" receiving sentences of 25 years. Richard Hildebrandt was Higher SS and Police Leader at Danzig-West Prussia from October 1939 to February 1943, and simultaneously leader of the Administration District Danzig-West Prussia of theAllgemeine SS and deputy of the RKFDV. From 20 April 1943 to the end of the war, he was chief of RuSHA. Also Otto Hofmann, as chief of RuSHA from 1940

sin, one of the principal drafters, insisted that the principles of liberty, equality, and fraternity in Article 1 of the Universal Declaration, which "had been ruthlessly flouted" and which "had come to extinction", were to be proclaimed in order to "refute the abominable doctrine of fascism."[38] It was a well-known fact of what was very recent Nazi history at that time that abortion was one of the Nazi tools for exterminating the ideologically and socially unwanted. Indeed, this was an essential part of what Cassin condemned as "the abominable doctrine of fascism".

Regrettably, ideologically committed academics like Capelon make the mistake of reading the historical post-World War II Declaration with their 21st century bias. It is completely inimical to the context of the time to impute the drafters of the Declaration with an intention to exclude the child before birth from human rights. The Declaration was a creation of its times—and the focus of those times was firmly, even passionately, on 'non-exclusion'. Morsink places great emphasis on this aspect of the drafting of the Declaration. From his study of the copious documents and records of the drafting sessions, he discerns "...an intended literal meaning of the words 'everyone' and 'no one'" and goes on to confidently assert:

> They intentionally chose words like 'everyone' and 'no one' and meant them to be taken literally. [39]

In fact, Morsink has a warning about the importance to women of a literal inclusive interpretation of the human subjects covered by the Declaration. His article *Women's Rights in the Declaration* [40] concludes thus:

> The Universal Declaration contains few references to women's rights...as far as explicit references go, this is not much, which is why it is crucial that we read 'everyone' and 'no one' literally. The drafters intended it this way.

There is irony here in the fact that women academics today who advocate abortion as a woman's human right would argue for an *inclusive* rendition of 'everyone' and 'no one' for their own 'women's rights' but for an *exclusive* interpretation when it comes to the human rights of the child before birth.

to 1943. See *Nuremberg Trials Record*: "The *RuSHA* Case", Opinion and Judgment, "War Crimes and Crimes Against Humanity", Vol. V, pp. 152 to 154 and pp. 160-2. Available at: http://www.mazal.org/archive/nmt/05/NMT05-T0152.htm.

38 Morsink: *Universal Declaration of Human Rights: Origins, Drafting and Intent, op. cit.* p. 39.

39 Morsink, Johannes: "Women's Rights in the Universal Declaration", *Human Rights Quarterly*, Vol. 13, p. 256.

40 Ibid., p. 255.

Chapter 5 What Is "Appropriate" Legal Protection Before As Well As After Birth?

Non-discriminatory legal protection

First and foremost, appropriate legal protection for every child before as well as after birth must be non-discriminatory:

> Everyone is entitled to all the rights and freedoms set forth in this Declaration, without distinction of any kind, such as race, colour, sex, language, religion, political or other opinion, national or social origin, property, birth or other status. *Universal Declaration of Human Rights, Article 2.*

The term 'everyone' must include the child before birth, since the Universal Declaration "recognized" that "the child, by reason of his physical and mental immaturity, needs special safeguards and care, including appropriate legal protection, before as well as after birth..."[1]

Since it was universally recognized that the child before birth is entitled to appropriate legal protection, it follows that the child before birth (as well as after birth) is entitled to "all the rights and freedoms set forth in this Declaration, without distinction of any kind..."

Morsink asserts that when this article was being drafted, the authors of the Declaration decided, after much discussion, to go beyond the short list of non-discrimination items in the *Charter of the United Nations* to prohibit "any kind" of discrimination based on "race, colour, sex, language, religion, political or other opinion, national or social origin, property, birth or other status".[2] Though the meaning of the phrase "of any kind" is clear enough, the drafters were evidently determined to spell it out for the international community by then enumerating specific criteria on which discrimination had been practiced on a vast scale and in a most heinous form (the presence of "race" at the head of the list clearly reflecting the awareness of the recent Nazi abominations). And finally, just in case some might still want to construe residual grounds for discrimination, the phrase "or other status" was included so as to preempt any such notion in the future.

1 See Chapter 1 above.

2 Morsink, *The Universal Declaration, op. cit.*, p. 3.

Peter Heyward, the Australian member of the drafting team, affirmed that their intention in the deliberate use of the terms "every person" or "everyone" throughout the Declaration was to extend the prohibition of discrimination in the application of every human right in the Declaration: "...logically, discrimination was prohibited by the use in each article of the phrase 'every person' or 'everyone'".[3]

The clear intention was that all rights accorded to the child after birth must also be accorded to the child before birth.

Applying the human rights principle—"without distinction of any kind"

The term "before as well as after birth" is irrevocably embedded in the foundation framework for protecting the human rights of every child, and Article 2 of the Universal Declaration prohibits discrimination "of any kind" in the entitlement to those rights, including discrimination on the grounds of "birth or other status". Thus is proscribed discrimination on the basis of such birth-related attributes as sex, disability, illegitimacy, father's crimes of rape or incest, or any status that might be construed to devalue the child as unwanted, inferior, or otherwise undeserving of human dignity and inalienable human rights. In regard to discrimination against a child because of the father's crimes of rape or incest, the observation made by the delegate from India in the UDHR negotiating sessions is pertinent: "The sins of the fathers must not be visited on the children."[4]

Appropriate legal protection—part of "special safeguards" entitlement

The right to legal protection is recognized for the child before birth, as well as (i.e., no less than) the child after birth, "by reason of his physical and mental immaturity" (i.e., both the child before birth and the child after birth are characterized by a physical and mental immaturity), and this immaturity entitles both of them without discrimination to "special" safeguards and care. These special safeguards include "appropriate" legal protection (i.e., "special" legal protection) both consistent with the principles of equality and non-discrimination as well as compensating for the child's extra vulnerability "by reason of his physical and mental immaturity".

Legal protection is to provide a "special safeguard", formulated appropriately, designed especially for the needs of children before as well as after birth. Appropriate legal protection of their rights must by reason of their physical and mental immaturity necessarily be of a higher order than that accorded adults. All children, because of their vulnerability, should receive always more protection, never less protection than adults.[5]

---

3 Morsink: "Women's rights in the Universal Declaration", *Human Rights Quarterly*, Vol. 13, p. 230.

4 Morsink, *The Universal Declaration: Origins, Drafting and Intent*, *op. cit.*, p. 256.

5 This principle has been reaffirmed more recently in the *Guiding Principles of the Report of the Independent Expert for the United Nations Study on Violence against Children* (1996) "Regarding children, their uniqueness—their potential and vulnerability, their de-

Appropriate legal protection must seek to compensate the child's vulnerability to adult manipulation and exploitation of the child's physical and mental immaturity. The child, before as well as after birth, is unable to defend his or her own right to life with the competency, skills, and resources available to most adults.

Inappropriate legal status—the child before birth an inferior being?

There is a crying need for a major human rights education campaign to raise sensitivity to the plight of children selected for abortion. Analysis of the status of child victims of abortion reveals some appalling attitudes and outcomes arising from discrimination against the child before birth. Such discrimination amounts to treating the child before birth as inferior to the child after birth.

An impartial status analysis should seek to identify and examine inequalities that arise from the unequal power relationships between the unborn child at risk of abortion and the child's mother (along with her 'abortion provider'). The dire consequences of this inequity on her child's development, health, well-being, and life prospects need to be acknowledged. Critical analysis should also reveal and publicize inequitable differences in access to provision of the child's developmental and healthcare needs, noting that in general the child at risk of abortion has no access to fulfillment of basic needs except what his or her mother will allow and what the family and community will provide.

The Inter-American Court of Human Rights has given us a clear definition of the concept of equality in international human rights law, a definition that deserves to be widely publicized:

> The notion of equality springs directly from the oneness of the human family and is linked to the essential dignity of the individual. That principle cannot be reconciled with the notion that a given group has the right to privileged treatment because of its perceived superiority. It is equally irreconcilable with the notion to characterize a group as inferior and treat it with hostility or otherwise subject it to discrimination in the enjoyment of rights which are accorded to others not so classified. It is impermissible to subject human beings to differences in treatment that are inconsistent with their unique and congenerous character.[6]

Children at risk of abortion are indeed subject to a treatment "inconsistent with their unique and congenerous character". Regarding this 'treatment', children at risk of abortion are in an invidious position of weakness, of silent helplessness against adult relatives and medical personnel in positions of power and authority over their survival and development.

---

pendence on adults—makes it imperative that they have more, not less, protection from violence."

6 I-A Court HR, Proposed Amendments to the Naturalization Provisions of the Constitution of Costa Rica, Advisory Opinion OC-4/84 of January 19, 1984, Series A, No. 4, p. 104, para. 55.

Appropriate legal protection—the right to recognition as a person before the law

Legal protection that is 'appropriate' for the child before as well as after birth must be in accord with Article 6 of the Universal Declaration:

> Everyone has the right to recognition everywhere as a person before the law.

The term "everyone" means "all members of the human family" and, as recognized by the Universal Declaration,[7] includes the child before birth. The Universal Declaration construes the child's existential presence in the mother's womb "before birth" as both recognition of the child's membership in the human family and recognition of the child as a person before the law. Every child "without any exception whatsoever"[8] is entitled to "appropriate legal protection before as well as after birth".

The child before birth, therefore, has a right to legal personality on an equal basis with the child after birth. This right is absolute and must be guaranteed in all circumstances and at all times.

Cassin and Roosevelt on juridical personality

Article 6 on "the right to recognition everywhere as a person before the law" was first advanced by René Cassin in the early days of discussion in the Human Rights Commission entrusted with the task of drawing up the Universal Declaration. Cassin presented a forthright justification for this article:

> Such a declaration might seem unnecessary if the most recent history did not offer an example of forms of slavery under which juridical personality had been withdrawn from certain individuals. . . . they should be guaranteed certain elementary rights indispensable to their well-being and to their dignity.[9]

Eleanor Roosevelt, who chaired the Drafting Committee, recalls that the debate over Article 6 illustrated not only the difficulties of different legal systems but also the belief held by many representatives in the Commission, to the effect that certain things must never happen again because they had been one of the causes that brought on World War II:

> His [Cassin's] suggestion was that we have an article that would read in French, "Personne ne doit être privé de sa personalité juridique," and I, without any legal knowledge, translated it into English as "No one shall be deprived of their juridical personality."

7 See Chapter 1 and Chapter 2 above.

8 The *Declaration on the Rights of the Child* states in Principle 1 "Every child, without any exception whatsoever, shall be entitled to these rights, without distinction or discrimination..."

9 Third Session Fifty-Eighth Meeting, S/R.58/, p. 3.

> Well, I didn't know what I had started. Behind my back, where lawyers sit from the departments in Washington, there was a storm. They all said, "There is no such expression as 'juridical personality' in English or American law." And all the United Kingdom gentlemen who were lawyers put their heads together and said "No" very firmly at me. So I knew that I hadn't gotten the right word. Behind my back they kept arguing, saying what it means is "without due process of law," but how do you say it? Well, it took a long while to argue that out and finally one day one of my Department of Justice youngish lawyers handed me a piece of paper and said, "You can accept the translation 'juridical personality,' it was once used in American law."
>
> And when do you think it was used? It was used in the Dred Scott case when Justice Taney said "a slave has no juridical personality." So I accepted it.
>
> There was no trouble at all with any of the Latin American countries, all of which accepted the French idea quite happily because they had the same system of law. The trouble lay with the Anglo-Saxon people, and finally our United Kingdom delegate said that it didn't mean anything in English law, but he couldn't think of any better expression, so for the time being, he would accept it. Professor Cassin himself finally thought of something better in the way of wording and the idea is in the document, though the words are changed.[10]

We have quoted here at length because Eleanor Roosevelt has highlighted the really important issue here, the fundamental injustice of denying juridical personality to any member of a group of human beings. She relates such instances of denial of juridical personality to both the World War II victims of Nazi ideology and the slaves of an earlier ideologically racist American era. The current conspiracy to deny *personalité juridique* to the child before birth on the strength of an extreme feminist ideology that empowers mothers to abort their children may be seen to be in this same shame-filled tradition.

Denying legal personality to the child before birth—a "punishment by civil death"

Decriminalization of abortion may well represent an unconscionable reversion to the barbaric practice in ancient Roman law of reducing certain human beings to mere objects of law and of denying them their human status as persons before the law. In truth, de-recognition of the child before birth as a person before the law is a most despicable form of punishment. What crime has the child at risk of abortion committed that he or she should deserve such a terrible punishment—indeed any punishment at all?

Michael Bogdon and Birgitte Kofod Olsen conclude a discussion on Article 6 with the claim that punishment by "civil death", i.e., by depriving the offender of his or her legal personality, seems no longer to be in use in any country.[11] But they are wrong.

10 Eleanor Roosevelt, "Making Human Rights Come Alive", Speech to the Second National Conference on UNESCO (1949). Available at: http://www.udhr.org/history/114.htm.

11 Bogdon, Michael and Olsen, Birgitte Kofod, "Article 6" in Godnundur Alfredson and Asbjorn Eide, (eds.), *The Universal Declaration of Human Rights: A Common Standard of Achievement*, The Hague, Martinus Nijhoff Publishers, 1999, p. 151.

Under decriminalization or legalization of abortion that now obtains in many countries, millions of children at risk of abortion are objectified. Unborn children are reduced to mere objects of the law, deprived of recognition as persons before the law, treated as offenders, already punished by 'civil death', and branded as candidates for 'lawful abortion'. Children suffer risk of abortion, an arbitrary form of capital punishment inflicted for such innocuous 'offences' as being in their mothers' wombs at the wrong time, having disabilities, being of the wrong sex, having fathers who have committed crimes of rape or incest, or even just being 'unwanted'.

Bogdon and Olsen suggest that the "everyone" to whom Article 6 applies does not include unborn children because they are regarded by law as mere objects in need of protection "just as animals are the objects of laws forbidding cruelty to animals":

> Thus, provisions of domestic criminal or administrative law whose aim is to protect the life of unborn children by prohibiting or limiting provoked abortions cannot be seen as implying a recognition of the legal personality of the fetus.[12]

Yet no historical evidence is provided that the drafters of Article 6 had any such intention to deny unborn children the "right to recognition everywhere as a person before the law". Nor is there any evidence that the drafters would have approved de-recognition of the *personalité juridique* of the unborn child at risk of abortion. On the contrary.

The child before birth entitled to the same legal protection as after birth

When the General Assembly elaborated on the child's need for appropriate legal protection "before as well as after birth" in the subsequent *Declaration on the Rights of the Child* (1959), it is notable that both the child before birth and the child after birth were to be beneficiaries of such protection.

In the light of that early spirit of determination to extend human rights to *all members of the human family*, it reflects yet another instance of academic dishonesty or careless scholarship to resort to the extravagantly revisionist theory being popularized today. There is no historical evidence that the drafters of the Universal Declaration or those of the Declaration on the Rights of the Child intended the child before birth to be entitled only to such "legal protection" as is appropriate to "objects of the law", and so to be denied the recognition as a person before the law that is clearly accorded to the child after birth. Had a distinction of such significance been contemplated, it would have been thoroughly debated and articulated.

Such an unequal and discriminatory distinction does not accord with the facts that the "right to recognition everywhere as a person before the law" in Article 6 is followed immediately by a clear statement of the equality and non-discrimination principles regarding protection of the law for "all", and that both sets of rights began as a single composite article in the drafting process. Indeed, Article 7 of the Universal Declaration states clearly:

12 Ibid., pp. 148-9.

> All are equal before the law and are entitled without any discrimination to equal protection of the law.

Article 7 precludes any notion that the child before birth be assigned a lesser status before the law, or inferior protection of the law, than the child after birth.

The right to recognition as a person before the law lays the basis for the right of the child before birth to enjoy human rights and freedoms on an equal basis and for the same reason as the child after birth. Moreover, this right to recognition is reaffirmed in Article 16 of the International Covenant on Civil and Political Rights (ICCPR), Article 4(2) of which stipulates that this is a right that cannot in any circumstances be derogated from, not even in times of public emergency.[13] This means that the right of the child before birth to recognition as a person before the law and on an equal basis with the child after birth must be respected in times of peace and in times of war, in all exigencies and all situations, such as in refugee camps or in IVF laboratories.

The right of everyone to be recognized everywhere as a person before the law is particularly pertinent for children before birth, for whom life is often curtailed by reason of immaturity (age), or sex, or disability, or circumstances in which the child was conceived. This right to recognition implies that children before birth may not be treated as objects to be discarded. Legal personality also means that children before birth must have full and unimpeded representation of their best interests in the legal institutions of their country for the purpose of vindicating their rights and obtaining protection against premeditated violation of their rights.

In this respect, the current global push to decriminalize abortion is in grave breach of this fundamental human rights obligation.

Appropriate legal protection—equal before the law and equal protection of the law

So we can argue that legal protection in order to be 'appropriate' must be in accord with Article 7 of the Universal Declaration:

---

13 *ICCPR* Article 16: Everyone shall have the right to recognition everywhere as a person before the law.

ICCPR Article 4:

1. In time of public emergency which threatens the life of the nation and the existence of which is officially proclaimed, the States Parties to the present Covenant may take measures derogating from their obligations under the present Covenant to the extent strictly required by the exigencies of the situation, provided that such measures are not inconsistent with their other obligations under international law and do not involve discrimination solely on the ground of race, colour, sex, language, religion or social origin.
2. No derogation from articles 6, 7, 8 (paragraphs I and 2), 11, 15, 16 and 18 may be made under this provision.

> All are equal before the law and are entitled without any discrimination to equal protection of the law. All are entitled to equal protection against any discrimination in violation of this Declaration and against any incitement to such discrimination.

This entitlement to equal protection before the law and by the law, without any discrimination, is a fundamental principle conditioning the entire field of international human rights law.

The subjects of this entitlement are designated as "All...without any discrimination", and so must include the child "before as well as after birth".

The child before birth must be "equal before the law" to the child after birth, and both "are entitled without any discrimination to equal protection of the law".

In addition, both the child before birth and the child after birth are "entitled to equal protection... against any incitement to such discrimination". The violation of this principle is the great human rights scandal of our time. There is a highly organized "incitement to such discrimination" against the child before birth by numerous national judiciaries, legislatures, academics, and media, as well as by many international human rights advocates, even at the UN level. Also party to this subterfuge are individuals like former High Commissioners for Human Rights Mary Robinson and Louise Arbour and groups like the United Nations Population Fund (UNFPA) and the Human Rights and CEDAW Committees.[14] Instead of calling for equal protection for all children before as well as after birth as recognized by the Universal Declaration, they are inciting discrimination by promoting abortion of selected children before birth as a woman's 'right'.

Appropriate legal protection—protection of the law against 'arbitrary interference'

Any genuinely 'appropriate' legal protection for the child before as well as after birth must include protection of the law against arbitrary interference:

> No one shall be subjected to arbitrary interference with his privacy, family, home or correspondence, nor to attacks upon his honour and reputation. Everyone has the right to protection of the law against such interference or attacks. *Universal Declaration of Human Rights, Article 12.*

The child at risk of selective abortion has the right to protection of the law against arbitrary interference or attacks, especially as such interference constitutes a threat not only to the child's actual place of habitation but also to the child's most intimate familial relationships. Ultimately, of course, abortion deprives the child not just of

14 The Human Rights Committee monitors compliance with the ICCPR and the CEDAW Committee monitors compliance with the *Convention on the Elimination of All Forms of Discrimination Against Women* (CEDAW).

home and family but of survival and development.[15] Express concern for the normal development of the unborn child is recorded in the ICCPR *travaux préparatoires*.[16]

Abortion represents a deliberate attack on the child's life, yet abortion advocates deny that such lethal interference with the child's survival and development is arbitrary.

The records of negotiation on this article reveal that a careful discussion took place about the term 'arbitrary'. The New Zealand delegate, Mrs. Newlands, proposed replacing the word "unreasonable" with the word "arbitrary", arguing that "arbitrary" signified everything that was not in accordance with well established legal principles.[17] The United Kingdom delegate, Mrs. Corbet, supported her with the following definition: "Any action taken at the will and pleasure of some person who could not be called upon to show just cause for it." [18] Albert Verdoodt concludes that the word "arbitrary" should be interpreted as "without justification in valid motives and contrary to established legal principles."[19] It is precisely in this sense that the vast majority of selective abortions being carried out today may be seen to be "arbitrary" attacks on children before birth for they are contrary to the established legal principle that children before birth are entitled to appropriate legal protection.

This right to protection of the law from arbitrary interference is reaffirmed and codified in Article 17 of the ICCPR and in Article 16 of the Convention on the Rights of the Child (identical wording):

1. No child shall be subjected to arbitrary or unlawful interference with his privacy, family, home...
2. The child has the right to the protection of the law against such interference or attacks.

It is interesting to note that the UN Human Rights Committee in its *General Comment* on Article 17 has affirmed that:

15 The child's right to development was affirmed way back in 1924, in the *Geneva Declaration of the Rights of the Child*, in Principle 1; it was reaffirmed in the *Declaration on the Rights of the Child* (1959) Principle 4: "The child...shall be entitled to grow and develop in health; to this end, special care and protection shall be provided both to him and to his mother, including adequate pre-natal and post-natal care."; also in the *Convention on the Rights of the Child* Article 6(2): "State Parties shall ensure to the maximum extent possible the survival and development of the child.".

16 In the debate on the death sentence for convicted mothers and their unborn children, it was reasoned: "The normal development of the unborn child might be effected if the mother were to live in constant fear that, after the birth of the child, the death sentence would be carried out". Third Committee 12th Session (1957) A/3764, para. 18.

17 Verdoodt, Albert, *Naissance et Signification de la Déclaration Universelle des Droits de l'Homme*, Société d'Etudes Morales, Sociales et Juridiques, Louvain-Paris, Editions Nauwelaerts, 1964, p. 141.

18 Ibid., p. 142.

19 Ibid., p. 143 : "...arbitraires (c'est-a-dire sans justification pour des motifs valables et contraires a des principes juridiques bien établis)...".

> Interference authorized by States can only take place on the basis of law, which itself must comply with the provisions, aims and objectives of the Covenant".[20]

Regarding the expression "arbitrary interference", the Committee goes on to say:

> The introduction of the concept of arbitrariness is intended to guarantee that even interference provided for by law should be in accordance with the provisions, aims and objectives of the Covenant...[21]

Legal abortion may be seen then to be "interference provided for by law" that nonetheless is not "in accordance with the provisions, aims and objectives of the Covenant". This application of the term 'arbitrary' to what may be 'legal' but is nevertheless 'unjust' was reaffirmed very clearly in the *travaux préparatoires* for the ICCPR.[22]

Indeed, abortion may be viewed as an unjust attack on privacy (there are few places more private than the womb!) and certainly abortion unjustly deprives the child before birth of his family and his home. It would be hard to find a more vicious attack or a more arbitrary interference than the use of abortion against the child in his or her mother's womb.

Decriminalization of abortion—incompatible with appropriate legal protection

> Everyone is entitled to a social and international order in which the rights and freedoms set forth in this Declaration can be fully realized. *Universal Declaration of Human Rights, Article 28*

So what kind of international order are children at risk of abortion entitled to so that their right to "special safeguards and care, including appropriate legal protection, before...birth" can be "fully-realized" as promised in Article 28?

It is necessary to establish and to maintain an international order that operates under the rule of law. Logically, there can be no legitimate decriminalization of the violent act of abortion, for decriminalization will result in arbitrary removal of legal protection of the child at risk of abortion and will condone arbitrary deprivation of countless human lives.

In every country the emphasis must be on "building democratic institutions, the rule of law and effective legal systems that function to protect the human rights of all without discrimination".[23] As a main player in any truly democratic system, the State

20 UN Human Rights Committee, General Comment No 16 on *ICCPR* Article 17, para. 3.

21 Ibid.

22 E/CN.4/SR.310 p. 9; 5th (1949), 6th (1950) and 8th (1952) Sessions of the Commission on Human Rights.

23 Mary Robinson, former United Nations High Commissioner for Human Rights, addressing the Plenary Session of the Earth Summit in Johannesburg, 29 August 2002.

has a grave duty—to maintain a rule of law that will function to protect the human rights of all *without discrimination*.

Decriminalizing abortion means that abortion would not be considered a crime, and that the State therefore could no longer exercise the duty or power to arrest, investigate, prosecute, convict, or punish those who perform abortions.[24] The drafters of the Universal Declaration could have had no truck with decriminalization of abortion. The Nazi record of decriminalizing abortion in Poland and the Eastern Territories was still fresh in the public perception. Decriminalization of abortion was judged and condemned at Nuremberg as encouraging abortions. Instructions by Nazi authorities issuing directives to decriminalize abortion were furnished as evidence for the count of crimes against humanity:

> Abortion must not be punishable in the remaining territory… Institutes and persons who make a business of performing abortions should not be prosecuted by the police.[25]

A systematic program of decriminalized abortion was set in place. Eastern women workers were induced or forced to undergo abortions. In addition, to the charge of "compelling" abortions there was also the charge of "encouraging" abortions among Polish women by removing abortion from prosecution in Polish courts:

> Abortions on Polish women in the General Government were also encouraged by the withdrawal of abortion case from the jurisdiction of the Polish courts. The defendants Greifelt, Creutz, Meyer-Hetling, Schwarzenberger, Hofmann, Hildebrandt, Schwalm, Huebner, Lorenz, and Brueckner are charged with special responsibility for and participation in these crimes."[26]

Though the Nazis had decriminalized abortion, the Nuremberg Tribunal still judged that "…protection of the law was denied the unborn children"; and two SS Officers, Richard Hildebrandt and Otto Hofmann, were convicted for "compelling and encouraging abortion", receiving sentences of 25 years.[27]

Historian John Hunt, after extensive research of Nazi abortion programs and the Nuremberg prosecution's evidence, concludes that the Nazis saw abortion as "an act

24 Mollmann, M., "Decisions Denied", *Human Rights Watch*, Vol 17, No 1 (B), June 2005.

25 *Nuremberg Trials Record: Trial of Ulrich Greifelt and Others Indictment* [Tr. pp. 1-18, 7/1/1947.] Vol.V. at pp.95 6.http://www.mazal.org/archive/nmt/05/NMT05-T0095.htm.

26 Ibid., para. 13.

27 Richard Hildebrandt was Higher SS and Police Leader at Danzig-West Prussia from October 1939 to February 1943, and simultaneously he was leader of the Administration District Danzig-West Prussia of theAllgemeine SS and deputy of the RKFDV. From 20 April 1943 to the end of the war, he was chief of RuSHA. Also Otto Hofmann, as chief of *RuSHA* from 1940 to 1943. See *Nuremberg Trials Record*: "The *RuSHA* Case", Opinion and Judgment, "War Crimes and Crimes Against Humanity", Vol.V, pp. 152 to 154) and pp. 160-2. http://www.mazal.org/archive/nmt/05/NMT05-T0152.htm.

of killing" and that Nuremberg condemned both the violations of liberty and the violations of life as far as abortion was concerned:

> Like the kidnapping of children and the seizing of newborns also prosecuted at this trial, abortions were seen as wrong at any time, not just when done for racial-genocidal reasons.[28]

For the Nazi leadership, decriminalization of abortion was a significant tool in the genocidal program to prevent births in particular groups that were deemed ideologically or socially unwanted. For those at the United Nations who, subsequent to these Nazi atrocities, were drafting human rights safeguards, including "appropriate legal protection" for the child before birth, there could have been no thought of decriminalizing abortion.

Legalization of abortion—incompatible with appropriate legal protection

Similarly, legalizing abortion was not envisaged as "appropriate legal protection" for the child before birth by the drafters of those early human rights instruments. The current clamor for legalization of abortion as a simple regulated health procedure under State control and interest is heedless of the State's fundamental human rights duty to provide "appropriate legal protection" for the child at risk of abortion. What is classified as a health procedure for the child's mother is actually an intentionally lethal procedure for her child.

If State parties go ahead to legalize the abortion of selected human beings, then they fail grievously to protect the human rights of a class of human beings that has been separated out from the human family in a most discriminatory way. Legalizing abortion would authorize discrimination against children at risk of abortion. Mothers and abortionists would be authorized to discriminate between those children who are deemed 'wanted', to whom benign medical treatment and care will be accorded, and those children who are deemed 'unwanted' to whom lethal treatments are to be applied. In short, legalization effectively authorizes and licenses abortionists to violate the unborn child's human right to be protected by law without *discrimination*.

Appropriate legal protection—universality, objectivity and nonselectivity

All the nation members of the international community solemnly agreed at the UN *World Conference on Human Rights* in Vienna (1993) to uphold "the importance of ensuring the universality, objectivity and non-selectivity of the consideration of human rights issues".[29] The recently appointed (as of late 2008) UN High Commissioner

28 Hunt, John: *Abortion and The Nuremberg Prosecutors: A Deeper Analysis, Life and Learning VII,* Proceedings of the Seventh University Faculty for Life Conference, June, 1997, p. 205.

29 *Vienna Declaration and Programme of Action,* adopted by the World Conference on Human Rights in Vienna on 25 June 1993, para. 32.

for Human Rights, Navanethem Pillay, reaffirmed this importance in her inaugural address to the Human Rights Council in September 2008:

> Foremost of importance in this effort, I believe, is impartiality in the operation of this system and adherence to the single and consistent standard represented by the Universal Declaration that is applied equally to all without political consideration....I start from the premise that the credibility of human rights work depends on its commitment to truth, with no tolerance for double standards or selective application.[30]

Indeed, tolerance of decriminalization and legalization of abortion represents both double standards and selective application in denying Universal Declaration protection to children before birth:

Universality of human rights application: Legalized abortion excludes certain children before birth from human rights protection because of certain circumstances beyond their control, viz., they happen to have come into existence in the wrong place at the wrong time, in the wrong circumstances, or with the wrong set of attributes, e.g., wrong sex, wrong physiology, wrong father, wrong mother.

Non-selectivity of human rights application: Legalized abortion condones a most reprehensible selectivity—it permits particular human beings to be selected *in utero* on blatantly discriminatory grounds, on the ethically trivial grounds of 'unwantedness', on the quality of being deemed 'imperfect'; on grounds of sex or disability, or on the grounds that their fathers have committed criminal acts. Legalized abortion means that those children selected for termination are to be denied their inherent human rights, the rights due to all human beings by the very nature of their being human.

Objectivity of human rights application: Decriminalization of abortion compromises objectivity by implicit acceptance of false arguments that purport to deprive certain children at risk of abortion of the fundamental respect due to all human beings. Disingenuous insults, such as claiming that the unborn child is not human or not 'wanted' or too small or too dependent or too disabled to warrant equal human rights, are purposely designed to influence the feeble-minded and to destroy true objectivity.

Appropriate legal protection "...meeting the just requirements of morality, public order and the general welfare..."

Laws against abortion are truly valid limitations on women's rights and freedoms, because they are limitations determined by law solely for the purpose of securing due recognition and respect for the rights of children before birth who are at risk of selective abortion.

30 Address by Navanethem Pillay, UN High Commissioner for Human Rights, at the opening of the 9th Session Human Rights Council, 8 September, 2008.

> In exercise of his rights and freedoms, everyone shall be subject only to such limitations as are determined by law solely for the purpose of securing due recognition and respect for the rights and freedoms of others and of meeting the just requirements of morality, public order and the general welfare in a democratic society. *Universal Declaration, Article 29(2)*

Laws limiting abortion are legitimized in this clause. The mother's rights and freedoms are "subject only to such limitations as are determined by law solely for the purpose of securing due recognition and respect for the rights and freedoms of others", i.e., of her child before birth.

This duty that one individual (the mother) has towards another (her child before as well as after birth) and to the community to which she belongs is spelled out subsequently in the Preambles to both ICCPR and the ICESCR:

> Realizing that the individual, having duties to other individuals and to the community to which he belongs, is under a responsibility to strive for the promotion and observance of the rights recognized in the present Covenant...

So while it is the individual who is "under a responsibility to strive for the promotion and observance of the rights recognized in the present Covenant", it is the State Parties to these Covenants that are also undertaking that responsibility. Among those rights "recognized" in the Covenants and the UDHR that comprise the International Bill of Rights is the right of the child to "special safeguards and care, including legal protection before as well as after birth".

The mother (the individual) has a duty to protect the child before as well as after birth, and the State parties and the community have a duty to protect and support both the mother and the child before as well as after birth.

One notable early statement of natural law duties regarding human rights was by Samuel von Pufendorf in 1673:

> Among the absolute duties, i.e., of anybody to anybody, the first place belongs to this one: let no one injure another. For this is the broadest of all duties, embracing all men as such. It is also the easiest, as consisting in mere refraining from action.... Again, it is likewise the most necessary duty, because without it the social life could in no way exist.[31]

Abortion intentionally injures another, the child before birth, and abrogates the duty to refrain from action that harms that child. Given that pregnancy is still the sole means of natural human propagation, protection of mothers and their unborn children through pregnancy is "the most necessary duty" critical to the ordered protection, cohesion and continuity of "the social life".

31 Von Pufendorf, Samuel, On *The Duty of Man and Citizen According to the Natural Law (1673)* [1682 Edition] translated by Frank Gardner Moore, New York: Oxford University Press, 1927, Book 1, Chapter 6, para. 2.

Legalized abortion is "...contrary to the purposes and principles of the United Nations"

Provision of legal protection that is "appropriate" for the child before as well as after birth requires also the prohibition of any exercise of asserted rights (such as women's "reproductive rights") that is contrary to the purposes and principles of the United Nations.

In Article 29(3), the Universal Declaration warns that the rights in the Declaration "may in no case be exercised contrary to the purposes and principles of the United Nations". Those who advocate that women should be permitted to exercise their rights by lawfully aborting the life and human rights of their own children are indeed advocating an exercise of women's rights *contrary to the purposes and principles of the United Nations.* In particular, so-called abortion rights are contrary to the original Charter of the United Nations and its foundational purposes to reaffirm the dignity and worth of the human person (Preamble) and to promote universal respect for, and observance of, human rights and fundamental freedoms for all without distinction (Article 55). Aborting the lives of children before birth who are members of the human family is also contrary to the very first principle of the UN International Bill of Rights:

> Whereas recognition of the inherent dignity and of the equal and inalienable rights of all members of the human family is the foundation of freedom, justice and peace in the world.

So-called abortion rights are in contravention of the Universal Declaration's recognition of the rights of the child before birth as a member of the human family.

Recognition of human rights prohibits "destruction of any of the rights"

Given that the Universal Declaration recognized the child before birth as deserving of human rights protection, in particular of the right to special safeguards and care, including appropriate legal protection, those who engage in advocacy for decriminalization and/or legalization of abortion are aiming at the destruction of rights set forth in the Declaration, rights that encompass the child *by reason of his physical and mental immaturity,* and *before as well as after birth.*

Human rights are by definition inherent and inalienable and thus can never be de-recognized. Therefore it is critical that the child before birth enjoy formal universal recognition as a legitimate subject of human rights, including entitlement to legal protection. Once we establish that the human rights of the unborn child were recognized by the original framers of modern international human rights law, then there is no way that anyone can legitimately de-recognize them—not any government, not any court, not any UN human rights treaty monitoring committee, and not even the UN General Assembly. The concept of 'recognition' of human rights is absolutely integral to the foundation of modern international human rights law. Dr. Frederick Nolde, in the discussions at that time, constantly emphasized the principle that governments could not grant human rights—they "could do no more than recognize the human rights which human beings by virtue of their being and destiny already possessed".[32]

This principle of recognition was understood and accepted by those who, following the horrors of World War II, framed the first modern international human rights instruments. Charles Malik, who at the time of drafting the Universal Declaration was the President of the UN Economic and Social Council as well as Rapporteur with the Commission on Human Rights, explained:

> A careful examination of the Preamble and of Article I will reveal that the doctrine of natural law is woven…into the intent of the Declaration. Thus it is not an accident that the very first substantive word in the text is the word "recognition": "Whereas recognition of the inherent dignity and of the equal and inalienable rights, etc." Now you can "recognize" only what must have been already there, and what is already there cannot, in the present context, be anything but what nature has placed there… dignity and rights are natural to our being and are not the generous grant of some external power.[33]

The Universal Declaration warns in Article 30:

> Nothing in this Declaration may be interpreted as implying for any State, group or person any right to engage in any activity or to perform any act aimed at the destruction of any of the rights and freedoms set forth herein.

Article 30 is an explicit prohibition of revisionist reinterpretation aimed at the destruction of any of the rights recognized in the Declaration. Having recognized the human rights of the child before birth, the Universal Declaration may not be reinterpreted to condone activities such as decriminalization or legalization of abortion aimed at the destruction of the right to life of the child at risk of abortion.

Children at risk of abortion—protected by the rule of law

Article 26 of the International Covenant on Civil and Political Rights reaffirms and further codifies Article 7 of the Universal Declaration:

---

32 Sir Ronald Wilson affirms this as the contemporary understanding of this principle "enshrined in the first Preamble" in: "Why human rights matter for everyone", *Human Rights*, Volume 3 (3), September, 1996. He recalls the work of his friend Dr Frederick Nolde, the director of the Churches Commission in Geneva on International Affairs, influential and indefatigable in the great human rights drafting debates that led to the Universal Declaration of Human Rights.

33 From a speech on human rights to the U.S. Chamber of Commerce Committee on International, Political, and Social Problems held at the Waldorf Astoria in New York, November 4, 1949.

> All persons are equal before the law and are entitled without any discrimination to the equal protection of the law...

Why, then, is the child before birth so often maltreated, experimented upon, discarded in laboratories, or aborted in the mother's womb, with legal impunity for the perpetrators of such actions?

There is an urgent need for major human rights education in order to raise sensitivity to the poignant vulnerability of the child in that critical stage of life between conception and birth. For as long as the child before birth is allowed to be dehumanized and routinely subjected to lethal discrimination and stigmatization, these children at risk of abortion are not being accorded the "appropriate legal protection" promised to them in the founding instruments of modern international human rights law.

These children are woefully exposed to the most arbitrary lethal abuse when selective abortion is decriminalized and/or legalized. Such failure to provide legal protection for these children is not just "inappropriate"—it is in grave contravention of a most fundamental principle of human rights law: "...it is essential...that human rights should be protected by rule of law..."[34]

34 *Universal Declaration of Human Rights*, Preamble.

Chapter 6 The Right to Life and to the Necessities of Life

Each individual has the right to physical existence

Article 3 of the Universal Declaration stipulates that the right to life, liberty and security of person for everyone (including for the child before as well as after birth) is to be protected by the rule of law.[1]

> Everyone has the right to life, liberty and security of person.

In the drafting of Article 3, laws that permit abortion in certain cases were understood to be problematic for the protection of the right to life by the rule of law. From the beginning, Article 3 was understood to entail the most complex and comprehensive of the human rights in the Universal Declaration. In the second session of the Working Group created by the Human Rights Commission, the notions of liberty and of integrity of the person established at the first session were placed under the far more extensive umbrella of the right to life.[2] Albert Verdoodt, after consultation with the original drafters and careful research of the recorded history of the drafting process, declares:

> Article 3 is understood only in the context of the entire Declaration. Considering the *travaux préparatoires*, it may be interpreted as follows: *Each individual has the right to physical existence.*[3]

Although Verdoodt concedes that there was no explicit statement as to when this existence begins, he intimates that it was understood at the time Article 3 was drafted

1 "...it is essential...that human rights should be protected by the rule of law..." *Universal Declaration*, Preamble.

2 Commission on Human Rights, Second Session report, UN doc. E/600, 1947.

3 Verdoodt, Albert, *Naissance et Signification de la Déclaration Universelle des Droits de l'Homme*, Société d'Etudes Morales, Sociales et Juridiques, Louvain-Paris: Editions Nauwelaerts, 1964. "Bref, l'article 3 ne se comprend que dans le contexte de la Déclaration toute entière. On peut, en raison des travaux préparatoires, l'interpréter comme suit: *Chaque individu a droit à l'existence physique*." pp. 95-100.

that laws permitting abortion in certain cases would be incompatible with the right of each individual to physical existence. He draws a parallel between abortion and "euthanasia against the incurable and the mentally weak", of which, he points out, the drafters also failed to pronounce any explicit condemnation but nevertheless had agreed to include such categories of persons in the human rights protections of Article 3. Both abortion and euthanasia, covered in Article 3, were to be fully understood in the light of subsequent articles. Each individual in each of these groups was to be accorded the right to life as understood, he says, *in the context of the whole declaration.*[4]

"Everyone has the right to life..."

Indeed, the *Declaration on the Rights of the Child* (1959) got this right when it affirmed in its Preamble that the Universal Declaration recognized the need for legal protection for the unborn child:

> Whereas the child, by reason of his physical and mental immaturity, needs special safeguards and care, including appropriate legal protection, before as well as after birth,

These "special safeguards" are designed to compensate for the increased vulnerability that is naturally concomitant with the child's immaturity, and must include "appropriate legal protection" consistent with the principles of equality and non-discrimination. For the child *before as well as after birth,* legal protection of his right to life must be "special", i.e., of a higher order than that accorded adults. Against the crime of arbitrary deprivation of life, children, because of their inherent vulnerability, should receive more protection, never less protection than adults:

> Regarding children, their uniqueness—their potential and vulnerability, their dependence on adults—makes it imperative that they have more, not less, protection from violence.[5]

The Universal Declaration proclaims a right to life that is equally valid for adults and children, before birth and after birth, without qualification other than that children may need *special* safeguards and care in order to protect that right.

Codification of this right to life in the *International Covenant on Civil and Political Rights* (ICCPR) ensures that the right to life is protected by international human rights law. This means, *inter alia,* that States must at no time engage in, or condone, arbitrary or extrajudicial killings of children before or after birth; and that States have a strict legal duty to prevent, investigate, prosecute, punish, and redress violations

4 Ibid., "Bref, l'article 3 ne se comprend que dans le contexte de la Déclaration toute entière." p. 99.

5 *Guiding Principles of the Report of the Independent Expert for the United Nations Study on Violence against Children* (1996).

of the right to life.[6] The legal duty to take positive and effective steps to protect the right to life for everyone is equally valid in times and states of public emergency—for example, in war, national disasters, or refugee camps. It follows that States cannot pretend at any time to hold a discretionary power to decriminalize or legalize the arbitrary taking of a child's life through procured abortion.

Procured abortion contravenes principles of necessity and proportionality

Regardless of time or circumstances, the State's legal duty to protect the right to life against any act of intentional deprivation is as valid for the child before birth as for the child after birth. Cognizant of the need to provide "special safeguards and care, including appropriate legal protection, before as well as after birth", domestic judiciaries and international treaty monitoring bodies must exercise the fundamental principle of proportionality in the formulation and application of abortion laws that purport to base justification for the deprivation of life on the grounds of "necessity".[7] In every selective abortion, deprivation of the child's life is the intended outcome. Growing tolerance of routine abortions carried out for psycho-social reasons must be challenged. The proportionality principle requires that any force used against any human being must be strictly proportional to the extent of the danger that the use of that degree of force is intended to avert. In the use of lethal force against any human being, the danger to be averted must be a clear and lethal danger and there must be absolutely no other way, no less deadly way to avert that danger.

States have a duty to scrutinize all decisions concerning children at risk of abortion and to assess objectively the common law defences of necessity and proportionality in relation to such decisions. This has devastating logical implications for the rhetoric of "choice". Subjective choice is never sufficient basis for the taking of a human life. When the life of an innocent human being is at stake, there is no room whatsoever for decisions made on mere choice. The use of a medical or surgical intervention that is intended to save the life of the mother, though it result in the unintended loss of life of the unborn child, may be considered necessary only when, tragically, it is all that remains. When every other less devastating avenue for saving the mother's life without lethal harm to the life of her baby has been genuinely and thoroughly examined, it may be absolutely necessary in some very rare cases to proceed with medication or surgery that will have the unintended outcome of loss of the life of her child. Every effort should be made to maintain the best possible medical care for both the child and the mother, to save both lives. A lethal act performed directly on the child—abortion

6 See ICCPR Article 4 and Article 6. See also Human Rights Committee General Comment No.6.

7 As the grave human toll of selective abortions has become more visible, the euphemistic language of pro-abortion advocacy is being abandoned and more forthright, brutally honest language is breaking through: for example, the recent Plan Report, *Because I am a Girl: The State of the World's Girls 2007*, Plan, UK Branch, cites the fact "that girls are more likely to be killed in the womb". (p. 23). Abortion is acknowledged here as a form of killing.

per se—must not continue to be misrepresented routinely in law as a necessary treatment for preservation of the life of the child's mother.

Procured abortion not within recognized exceptions to the right to life

An eminent *Libertarians for Life* legal attorney, Dr. Edwin Vieira, Jr., has argued that the right to life implies a correlative duty in all other persons not to take the life of the unborn child, except in two cases:

> These cases involve: (i) the privilege of self-defense, which permits a victim of aggression to defend his own life, even if that defense requires taking the aggressor's life; and (ii) the privilege of self-preservation, which permits an innocent individual to take the life of another innocent individual in an 'emergency' situation in which both cannot survive, and the survival of one depends upon the denial to the other of the means of survival.[8]

Dr. Vieira points out that abortion is not an exercise of the privilege of self-defense, since the unborn child is not an aggressor and that abortion is not an exercise of the privilege of self-preservation, since, in the usual case, the mother's life is not endangered by the pregnancy.

Since abortion does not come within the two recognized exceptions to the right to life, and is inconsistent with the right as far as the unborn child is concerned, Dr. Vieira concludes that abortion must itself be a form of aggression repugnant to libertarian principles.[9]

"Everyone has the right to... liberty"

As an essential element of the right to life, the child before birth has also a right to liberty in the sense that the child is not to be seen as the chattel of the mother—the mother/child relationship is not to be an unequal one of ownership, of a master/slave kind. Every expectant mother is doing for her child *in utero* only what her own mother once did for her—giving birth to one's child is not to be misrepresented as an inequitable burden that justifies a decision to abort the life of one's child. The mother has a duty of care towards her child before birth, and where this duty for whatever reason becomes too onerous for the mother, both the State parties and society are

8 Dr. Edwin Vieira, Jr., "If the Unborn Child is a Person Entitled to Rights, Abortion is Aggression", 6th November, 1999. Available at Libertarians for Life: http://www.l4l.org/library/pers-agg.html.

9 However we must part with Dr. Vieira in his assertion that in extraordinary cases "the mother would have the privilege to defend her life through abortion". The term "through abortion" is troubling in that it would seem to imply that a deliberate decision may be taken to mount a direct attack upon the child's life. If the life of the child is inadvertently lost in the course of treatment genuinely necessary to save the life of the mother, this should not be characterized as a procured abortion. It should not be described as an exercise of "the privilege to defend her life through abortion".

required under the terms of the human rights instruments to assist both mother and child.[10]

The child before birth also has a right to liberty in the sense that the child should remain free to grow and develop. The child should enjoy a natural freedom to pass through the first nine months of existence and growth, the first stage of life, in the protective, nourishing environment of the mother's womb, without the threat of lethal chemical or surgical attacks mounted specifically with the intention of harming, indeed terminating, that natural, purposeful, lively development. A mother's womb should not be transformed intentionally into an execution cell from which her child shall not be allowed to depart alive. A mother's body is designed by nature to protect, nourish and prosper life—it must not be converted perversely to a death trap where her unborn child is to be deliberately destroyed.

Yet radical feminist abortion advocates are now promoting a new euphemism for a mother aborting her child, "voluntary motherhood", which they describe as "a refusal to be enslaved to another whether that be the advocate or enforcer of patriarchal obligation or its surrogate, the fetus".[11] They go on to say: "No fully developed person has the right to subordinate another in the way that unwanted pregnancy subordinates a woman."[12] The unborn child, "the fetus", is demonized as a surrogate advocate or enforcer of patriarchal obligation! This is ideological madness, matching even the intemperate extremes of Nazi rhetoric.

In a metaphorical sleight-of-hand, the term "unwanted pregnancy" is personified as the human rights violator. Ultimately the guilt of being unwanted is being transferred to the tiny child who, it is intimated, is guilty of subordinating his or her mother in a way that "[n]o fully developed person has the right to subordinate another". The tiny child, innocent and powerless, is grotesquely misrepresented as the enforcer, the violator of the mother's human rights, to be executed for those unwitting violations over which the child had no knowledge, intention or control.

Unwantedness—attitudinal prejudice—not a reason for abortion

What pro-abortion advocates refuse to acknowledge is this: that in an "unwanted pregnancy" the quality of 'unwantedness' is not inherent in the child. The child is not to be blamed or held accountable for this quality. Rather, the 'unwantedness' is *per se* an attitudinal attribute of the child's mother (and/or of other parties such as the father, other family members, and the community). It is this attitudinal prejudice that needs to be worked on and reformed. The child is not to be placed at risk of abortion because others reject the child as curtailing their own rights and freedoms.

10 International Covenant on Economic, Social and Cultural Rights (ICESCR) Articles 10 and 12; also Convention on the Rights of the Child, Articles 3(2), 6(2), 16, 18(2), 19, 23, 24 & 37.

11 Copelon, R., Zampas, C., Brusie, E., Devore, J., "Human rights begin at birth: international law and the claim of fetal rights", Reproductive Health Matters, November, 2005,Vol. 13(26), pp. 120-9 at p. 125.

12 Ibid.

In short, it is the attitudes of those responsible for the child at risk of abortion that need to be changed, not the laws protecting the child from abortion.

Procured abortion—an exercise of ownership over the child *in utero*

Article 4 of the Universal Declaration states:

> No one shall be held in slavery or servitude; slavery and the slave trade shall be prohibited in all their forms.

The rise of extreme feminism has brought a terrible distortion of the fundamental principle of the equal and inalienable rights of all members of the human family, in that it has crassly inflated "women's reproductive rights" so as to blot out the rights of their children before birth, and indeed to transform genuine rights into a gross travesty of what has always been implied in motherhood.

Some feminist historians have rightly condemned the shameful old injustices where sometimes and in some places children (and their mothers) were sometimes considered the property of their fathers. But over time, they say, a shift has occurred, and "we are beginning to understand children... as rights-bearers, not simply as objects of protection".[13] The tragic irony, however, is that to pro-abortion feminists, children before birth are now considered neither as objects of protection nor as rights-bearers but rather as the property of their mothers, subject to arbitrary treatment and disposal at least as vile as anything that paternalism was ever responsible for. In effect, these pro-abortion feminists have reduced the child before birth to an object, a 'choice', a thing of less-than-human status, suspended in a slave-like state between life and death, pending an arbitrary decision by the "owner" to abort or to keep the child. Yet from the first drafts of Article 4 the comprehensive term "slavery, in all its forms" was accepted.[14] Protection of all human beings from all forms of the powerlessness of slavery was to be unlimited in scope.

A clear understanding of the scope of application and real substance of this protection was already established in the *Slavery Convention* of 1926 and reaffirmed in 1956 in Article 7 of the *Supplementary Convention on the Abolition of Slavery, the Slave Trade, and Institutions and Practices Similar to Slavery:*

> "Slavery" means, as defined in the Slavery Convention of 1926, the status or condition of a person over whom any or all of the powers attaching to the right of ownership are exercised, and "slave" means a person in such condition or status.

Article 8 of the ICCPR codifies Article 4 of the Universal Declaration and explicitly prohibits slavery "in all its forms". It is difficult to construe the condition or status of the child at risk of abortion as anything but a form of slavery, in which the concepts of

13 For example, see Kilbourne, Susan: "Placing the CRC in an American Context", available at: http://www.amnestyusa.org/children/newsletters/2000summer.

14 Commission on Human Rights, Second Session report, UN doc. E/600, 1947.

'ownership' and 'absolute power' over a dependent are used to violate human dignity and rights.

Nina Lassen in her research on the ICCPR drafting record found annotations to the draft text of Article 8 that explain why the drafters split the Universal Declaration concept of slavery into two distinct concepts:

> Slavery was considered a relatively limited and technical notion, which implied the destruction of the juridical personality of the victim, and servitude a more general idea covering all possible forms of one person's domination of another.[15]

Abortion may be seen as a form of slavery on both counts:

- Decriminalization of abortion is essentially an attempt to effect "the destruction of the juridical personality of the victim", the unborn child; and
- the concept of a mother's right to abort the life of her own child is certainly at the extreme end of servitude, the most extreme of "all possible forms of one person's domination of another."

To accord mothers the "right" to abort their children is to allow them the most pernicious of all the powers attaching to the alleged rights of ownership and domination—powers of life and death. The pseudo-right to abortion stands in direct contradiction to the long, hard-won tradition of human rights and freedoms, a tradition forbidding that any one human being should have ownership and disposal rights over any other human being, no matter how small or dependent or troublesome or unwanted.

"Everyone has the right to...security of person"

Both in the nine months of life in the womb and in the first years of infancy, the right of children before as well as after birth to security of person is exceedingly dependent on the goodwill and protection owed them, but not always given them, by their mothers, fathers, families, and communities, including members of the medical profession. Abortion violates the right of the child before birth to security of person in the privacy of the womb, no less than domestic violence against the child after birth violates the right of the child to security of person in the privacy of the home.

Every child at risk of abortion is a child at risk of extreme violence. The *World Report on Violence and Health* (2002) defines violence as

> the intentional use of physical force or power, threatened or actual, against a child, by an individual or group, that either results in or has a high likelihood of resulting in actual or potential harm to the child's health, survival, development or dignity.[16]

15 Lassen, Nina, "Article 4 " in (eds.) Godnundur Alfredson and Asbjorn Eide, *The Universal Declaration of Human Rights: A Common Standard of Achievement*, The Hague: Nijhoff, 1999, p. 109.

16 Krug, E.G., Dahlberg, L.L., Mercy, J. A., Zwi, A. B., and Lozano, R., (eds.), *World Report on Violence and Health*, Geneva: World Health Organization, 2002, p. 5.

Abortion, although described euphemistically as a "reproductive health service" for women, is an act that involves the deliberate infliction of lethal physical violence against a small, defenceless human being trapped *in utero*.

The UN Secretary-General's *Report on Violence against Children* (2006) asserts that every society, no matter its cultural, economic or social background, can and must stop violence against children.[17] This does not mean sanctioning perpetrators only, but requires transformation of the "mindset" of societies and the underlying economic and social conditions associated with violence.[18] No violence against children is justifiable; all violence against children is preventable.[19] Adult justification and societal acceptance of abortion violence against children *in utero* as inevitable and normal must be challenged. Abusive treatment of a child before birth is neither inevitable nor normal.

Socially guaranteed necessities of life for child's survival and development

The right of the child before as well as after birth to security of person includes not just legal protection against intentional violence but also a socially guaranteed provision of the benign conditions necessary for the child's survival and development. The drafting record of Article 3 reveals that about half of the UN General Assembly's Third Committee wanted to add to "the right to life, liberty and security of person" the words: "and to economic, social and other conditions necessary to the full development of the human personality".[20] This proposal was defeated but the concept was accepted and enshrined in Article 22 of the Universal Declaration where it affirms:

> Everyone...is entitled to realization...of the economic, social and cultural rights indispensable for...dignity and the free development of...personality.

The drafters understood that the State has an obligation here to ensure enabling conditions for the full and free development of each human personality, and recognized its corollary that the state must protect every human being from anything that threatens that dignity and free development of personality.

The deliberated use of the term "free development" signifies that the whole natural process of development of any human being, no matter how young or immature, is to be protected from deliberate harm such as from the intentional withdrawal or destruction of the necessary or "indispensable" conditions or rights that are owed to the "dignity" of each developing personality. For the drafters, this right to security of person is linked to concepts of 'social security' and 'social justice', a secure environment conducive to and respectful of the dignity and free development of each human being. There is no place here for the contemporary radical feminist

17 UN Secretary-General's *Report on Violence against Children* (2006) p. 6.

18 Ibid.

19 Ibid., p.3.

20 General Assembly Official Records, A/C.3/SR.95-179, 1948.

revisionism that insists that the right to "security of person" applies exclusively to the mother and not to "everyone". Both the mother and the child at risk of abortion are entitled to security of person.

Since "Everyone has the right to...security of person", the child before birth has the right to grow and develop in the natural security and protection of his or her mother's womb, and that right to security of person must be respected from the first knowledge of that child's existence to the birth of the child, and beyond that, through all stages of life until the moment of natural death.

Guarding children against "measures intended to prevent their birth"

The Universal Declaration has recognized that the right to security of person is equally valid for the child before birth as for the child after birth and this right to security of person means that the right to life is to be protected and secured for each child. Children are to be protected by law from all attempts against their life, including "measures intended to prevent their birth" as guaranteed in the *Convention on the Prevention and Punishment of the Crime of Genocide* (1948).

This Convention was approved by the UN General Assembly on December 9th, 1948, the day before the Universal Declaration of Human Rights. The Contracting Parties described genocide as a crime under international law, contrary to the spirit and aims of the United Nations and condemned by the civilized world, an odious scourge that at all periods of history has inflicted great losses on humanity. "Imposing measures intended to prevent births within the group" was one of the criminal acts against children, a category of crime specifically condemned as genocide.

To understand the extent of the revulsion against Nazi war crimes that included the use of abortion measures to prevent births within selected groups, it might be helpful to recall the Statement by the Council of the British Medical Association to the World Medical Association in June 1947, entitled "War Crimes and Medicine". It begins:

> The evidence given in the trials of medical war criminals has shocked the medical profession of the world. These trials have shown that the doctors who were guilty of these crimes against humanity lacked both the moral and professional conscience that is to be expected of members of this honourable profession. They departed from the traditional medical ethic which maintains the value and sanctity of every individual human being.[21]

The statement ends by enjoining the international medical profession to proclaim this principle *inter alia*:

> The duty of curing, the greatest crime being co-operation in the destruction of life by murder, suicide and abortion.

21 Statement by the Council of the British Medical Association for submission to the World Medical Association, June 1947 (re-issued by The Medical Education Trust and reproduced by donoharm.org.uk/leaflets/war.htm).

and to publish and apply such principles nationally and internationally in medical education and in medical practice.

There has arisen in present times the despicable modern practice, a genocide endorsed by a significant part of the current membership of the international medical profession, to commend to expectant mothers of children with disabilities such as Down Syndrome "measures intended to prevent births within the group". The UDHR right to security of person for children at risk of abortion includes also the right to security of person in the event of disability or genetic disease or dysfunction. UDHR Article 25 (1) extends UDHR Article 3 to apply to those members of the human family in situations of disability or helplessness:

> Everyone has...the right to security in the event of...disability...in circumstances beyond his control.

The right to security entitles the child before birth (who by definition is in circumstances totally *beyond his control*) to special safeguards and care. Pre-natal detection of disability in children does not justify violating their right to security by imposing, or even by offering, measures to prevent their birth.

"...the right to physical integrity from the moment of conception"

Rightly understood, human rights must be directed towards sustaining the well-being of both mother and child. All human rights derive from the dignity of the human person. In every pregnancy, there are at least two human beings entitled to safeguards and care, mother and child, and both sets of human rights, when rightly ordered, must strive towards sustaining both human persons in their being. The right to life for both human beings includes a right to physical integrity. This was understood clearly and accepted without controversy during the drafting process, even from very first session (1947) of the Drafting Committee of the Commission on Human Rights:

> It shall be unlawful to deprive any person, from the moment of conception, of his life or bodily integrity...[22]

In order to understand properly the right to life, liberty and security of person, Verdoodt emphasizes the importance of describing "the essentials of the debate" which gave rise to this article.[23] He draws special attention to Charles Malik's earlier variant of René Cassin's final draft noted in the report of this committee:

---

22 UN Doc. E.CN.4/21.

23 Verdoodt: *op. cit.*, pp. 95-100.

> Everyone has the right to life and to the integrity of his body from the moment of his conception, irrespective of his physical or mental condition, and he has also the right to liberty and security of person.[24]

In this context, abortion may be seen to be a double attack on everyone's right to security of person—it constitutes arbitrary interference with the physical integrity of the expectant mother and a lethal violation of the physical integrity of her child.

The right to life and Article 5

In Verdoodt's comprehensive study of the drafting of Article 3, "Everyone has the right to life, liberty and security of person", he concludes that its full meaning can be understood only "as is explained in the Articles following."[25] From the legislative history of the drafting of Article 3, he traces and discerns a very definite and important connection between the right to life and Article 5 of the Universal Declaration:

> No one shall be subjected to torture or to cruel, inhuman or degrading treatment or punishment.

Although only a few countries had interpreted the right to life to include the right to physical integrity—to be contained in the legal notion of personal security–Verdoodt avers that based on Article 5, which prohibits cruel, inhuman or degrading treatment, it is lawful to include the right to physical integrity. The "entire context of the Declaration" affirms such a right.[26]

The right to life for the child before birth, therefore, includes the right to physical integrity and is contained in the legal notion of personal security. In other words, the child before as well as after birth is entitled to legal protection of his or her personal security, physical integrity, and right to life. The authority for legal protection of these children at risk of abortion, the "lawfulness" of prohibition of abortion, was understood by the drafters to be based on Article 5.

Truly, a child at risk of abortion is a child at risk of an act of *cruel, inhuman or degrading treatment or punishment,* and the fact that such an act is perpetrated in medical or quasi-medical settings by abortion "providers" does not validate the violation of this right, but it certainly degrades the profession and practice of medicine.

The wording of this article came *verbatim* from Article 5 of the 1948 *American Declaration of the International Rights and Duties of Man.* In all four Geneva Conventions of 1949, this same right is enunciated in Article 3, which in peace time as well as situations of armed conflict, prohibits "mutilation, cruel treatment and torture...and degrading treatment". The crime of "mutilation" has particular relevance to some second-term abortions and to many third-term abortions, where the child may be dismembered and the head crushed in order to facilitate "delivery". Anyone who

24 Ibid., p. 97.

25 Ibid., pp. 99-100.

26 Ibid.

has seen the mutilated remains of such abortions could deny neither the humanity of the unborn child nor the inhumanity of those responsible for this egregious act.

Legal protection against "...cruel treatment"

It has been argued that abortion law has failed to keep pace with rapid advances in medical science, particularly in embryology and foetal medicine and surgery.[27] Evidence continues to mount that abortion of the life of a child at the earliest stages of the child's existence is *cruel treatment* of the child and contravenes the age-old first principle of medical treatment *primum non nocere* –"first do no harm".

The violence of abortion is intensely physical and can be cruelly painful. Studies in the United Kingdom and in Germany have indicated that pain is felt by unborn children as early as 16 weeks.[28] But Bernard J. Baars, a scientist at the University of California at Berkeley, has asserted that these results—sentience at 16 weeks—should be considered far too conservative:

> As a scientist working on the brain basis of consciousness...I am not a fundamentalist enemy of all abortions, but I am concerned about the way abortion advocates avoid the question of fetal pain. We now know a great deal about pain perception in utero. The nervous system develops early, and the pain system is a complex part of all nervous tissue. Sonograms performed during abortion procedures seem to show fetuses trying to escape surgical damage. Fetal electroencephalograms suggest that consciousness occurs early as well...Medically, at least, we must anaesthetize fetuses before surgical procedures. Caution is indicated here, since we do no know the lower limit in gestation for the origins of pain perception.[29]

Dr. Vincent J. Collins, in his text *Principles of Anesthesiology*, teaches that neurological structures necessary to feel pain, pain receptive nerve cells, neural pathways, and the thalamus of the brain begin to form eight weeks after conception and become functional during the thirteenth week.[30] A new collection of research papers, *Neo-*

27 See for example, Mary Joseph, *One Pregnancy, Two Lives*, November, 1999; and *Medical and legal treatment of the fetus; a growing disjunction?* July, 1999. Available at: http://www.catholicculture.org/library/view.cfm?recnum=710.

28 Ranalli, Paul, "Abortion and the Unborn Baby: the Painful truth", Statement to the House Judiciary Committee of the State of Ohio, June 27, 1997. Dr. Paul Ranalli was a neurologist at the University of Toronto at the time. See also the comprehensive survey of the literature in the testimony of Dr. Jean Wright, Professor & Chairman of Pediatrics Mercer School of Medicine before the Senate Committee on Health, Children, Families, Aging and Long Term Care, "Understanding Fetal Pain", April 19, 2005. Available at: http://www.legis.wisconsin.gov/assembly/asm97/news/features/200504.../Fetal%20Pain%20-%20Wisconsin%20Briefing.ppt.

29 Letters, *New York Times*, 5 November, 1997.

30 Collins, Vincent J., *Principles of Anesthesiology*, Third Edition, Baltimore:Williams and Wilkins, 1992.

natal Pain: Suffering, Pain and the Risk of Brain Damage in the Fetus and Unborn, edited by Giuseppe Buonocore and Carlo Bellieni, also affirms the reality of fetal pain and fetal stress that can be scientifically observed now with the introduction of three-dimensional and four-dimensional ultrasonography.[31]

Significantly, there has emerged clear evidence, documented by Dr. K.J.S. Anand, a pediatric anesthesia specialist at Emory University, Atlanta, that premature newborn babies, and hence second-trimester unborn babies, experience pain *more* intensely than do babies delivered at full term, because the neurotransmitters that mediate pain are present in the second trimester, but the neurotransmitters that dull or inhibit pain do not emerge largely until later in pregnancy, around 28 weeks. This means that the premature baby or second-trimester unborn child lives through a vulnerable period when, as Dr. Paul Ranalli has described it, "raw pain impulses from the body may roar through unchecked by the modifying inhibitory system that we enjoy as adults".[32] The distinctive nature of fetal pain manifests the potential for very real cruelty in the aborting of the lives of these tiny patients.

Increasingly, in the mainstream press this truth is at last being given due prominence. The *New York Times* (10th February 2008) published a well-researched in-depth report on fetal pain and the grave implications for the practice of abortion: "The First Ache" by Annie Murphy Paul.[33] The pain of abortion for mother and child cannot remain hidden—it is always a cruel business.

Cruelty is more than the absence of loving care—it is treatment that is insensitive to the harm inflicted. The cruelty of abortion lies in its intention and purpose to do harm to the unborn child; it is an act that withdraws love and care and good-will from one of the newest most defenceless members of the human family. Abortion of a tiny thriving human being *in utero* is never an ethically neutral act—rather it is actively callous, even merciless. It is medical maltreatment of the child, and requires a hardening of heart in any normal human being who would inflict such maltreatment. Even the most sophisticated rationalization cannot cloak the fact that it takes ruthlessness to deliberately inflict such cruelty on these smallest children.

---

31 Buonocore, Giuseppe & Bellieni, Carlo (eds.): *Neonatal Pain: Suffering, Pain and the Risk of Brain Damage in the Fetus and Unborn*, Milan: Springer, 2008. See especially Chapter 6, Noia, G., Cisari, E., Ligato, M. S., Visconti, D., Tintoni, M., Mappa, I., Greco, C., Fortunato, G.P., and Caruso, A., "Pain in the Foetus", which explores a new set of foetal pain indicators.

32 Ranalli, *op cit.*

33 Annie Murphy Paul, "The First Ache", *New York Times*, February 8, 2008. See also "Babies feel pain before 24-week abortion limit" by Rosa Prince and Bonnie Malkin, *Daily Telegraph* (UK) 29th January, 2008; and Roger Highfield (Science Editor), "Babies may feel pain of abortion" *Daily Telegraph* (UK),Tuesday August 29, 2000.

Legal protection against "...inhuman treatment"

The term "inhuman treatment" signifies treatment that denies the humanity of the victim—it denies the care that is owed "in the spirit of brotherhood"[34] by one human being to another. Abortion violates the child's right to be treated not just humanely (even animals are to be treated humanely), but as a human being. This right to be treated as a human being belongs inherently and inalienably to every child as a member of the human family. The child at risk of abortion is at risk of being subjected to inhuman treatment and is entitled to legal protection against such treatment.

Legal protection against "...degrading treatment"

The term "degrading treatment" refers to treatment that degrades and disparages the inherent human dignity of the child before birth. Abortion destroys a small dependent human being, reducing him or her to mere matter, a small unit of non-recyclable refuse to be summarily removed and discarded. Degrading terms are routinely applied to the child at risk of abortion—in the material on abortion on the World Health Organization's Web site, the child is referred to as "contents of the uterus to be expelled" and "aspirated tissue to be examined".[35]

Abortion debases the humanity of the child, stripping the child of inherent dignity and of life itself: the child at risk of such treatment is in desperate need of "appropriate legal protection before as well as after birth".

Legal protection against "...cruel, inhuman or degrading... punishment"

In regard to cruel, inhuman or degrading "punishment", tragically there has developed a relatively widespread cultural practice of using abortion as a vicarious capital punishment for the crimes of rape and incest. However, since the child before birth is innocent of any crime, the child conceived in rape or incest is not to be subjected to "legal" execution—to deliberate State-sanctioned extermination of the child's life because of the crimes of the child's father. Such unjust punishment of one of these smallest and most palpably innocent members of the human family is incompatible with the opening premise of the Universal Declaration:

> Whereas recognition of the inherent dignity and of the equal and inalienable rights of all members of the human family is the foundation of freedom, justice and peace in the world...

34 Universal Declaration of Human Rights, Article 1: "All human beings are born free and equal in dignity and rights. They are endowed with reason and conscience and should act towards one another in a spirit of brotherhood."

35 See also World Health Organization (WHO), *Safe abortion : technical and policy guidance for health systems*, Geneva: WHO, 2003, pp. 34-43.

Indeed, abortion violence, though it is perpetrated in medical or quasi-medical settings, still amounts to subjecting the child before birth *to cruel, inhuman or degrading treatment or punishment.* That health-care clinics for mothers and children, reproductive health centres, and accredited hospitals offer abortion violence as a "treatment" or "service" for expectant mothers and their children may be seen as a heinous form of treachery. The use of euphemisms like 'safe abortion' cannot disguise or excuse medicalized killing of children before birth.

Right to life—the right to the necessities of life for mother and her unborn child

In accordance with UDHR Article 25(1), both the mother and the child before birth ("everyone" is inclusive) have a right to a standard of living adequate for their health and well-being, including food, housing, medical care, and necessary social services. as well as the right to security in the event of sickness, disability and in circumstances beyond their control.

This last phrase is particularly relevant to both child and mother—the child has zero control over the circumstances in which he or she is developing, and the pregnancy itself is a natural event which, once in motion, moves beyond any honourable or legitimate "control" by the mother. Pregnancy is an innately ordered, exquisitely integrated natural process which should not be subject to deliberate sabotage aimed at extinguishing the life of the child whose continued growth and survival depends totally on that natural process. Both mother and child, in whatever the difficult circumstances *beyond their control,* are entitled to adequate pre-natal care and assistance. Codification of this right to adequate health care in the *International Covenant on Economic, Social and Cultural Rights* (ICESCR) is very careful to exclude no one from health rights. It places particular emphasis on the need for special health provisions for the child before as well as after birth "for the reduction of the still-birth-rate and of infant mortality and for the healthy development of the child".[36]

It is logically incoherent to insist that good pre-natal health care services include "safe abortion services", when such services violate the human rights to survival and development of the unborn child. Abortion deprives the child before birth of the right to adequate food, housing, and medical care.

A "socially guaranteed" right to life and security of person includes "the provision of subsistence at least to those who cannot provide for themselves" and includes the

36 Article 12(1) of the ICESCR states:

> The States Parties to the present Covenant recognize the right of everyone to the enjoyment of the highest attainable standard of physical and mental health.

Article 12(2a) states:

> The steps to be taken by the States Parties to the present Covenant to achieve the full realization of this right shall include those necessary for: (a) The provision for the reduction of the stillbirth-rate and of infant mortality and for the healthy development of the child.

duty "not to eliminate a person's only available means of subsistence".[37] Morsink's commentary on the drafting record of Article 25 quotes Henry Shue's perception that food, housing and medical care are "basic rights" because "the enjoyment of them is essential to the enjoyment of all other rights".[38] In Shue's explanation of how these rights came into the Declaration and of why they stayed in, he observed:

> Because of their fundamentality, they are everyone's minimum and reasonable demands on the rest of humanity.[39]

Adequate nutrition, the protective environment of the mother's womb, and benign medical care are part of the "need for special safeguards and care before…birth" recognized by the Universal Declaration. They are "basic rights" and because of their fundamental necessity to the nurturing of life, they are the unborn child's minimum and reasonable demands on the rest of humanity. The mother's minimum and reasonable demands must also be met—to which end every support must be given by the rest of humanity. The subsistence rights of both the mother and her unborn child must be socially guaranteed.

Mothers and children at risk of abortion—"entitled to special care and assistance"

> Motherhood and childhood are entitled to special care and assistance. All children, whether born in or out of wedlock, shall enjoy the same social protection. *Universal Declaration, Article 25(2).*

Because this is a clause in a human rights instrument, this is a statement of the human rights of persons in particular states of being. Both the state of being a mother and the state of being a child carry therein equal entitlement to special care and assistance.

The well-being of the mother and her child are so intimately connected that the special care and assistance must endeavor to be holistic, comprehensive of *both* sets of needs. Care and assistance for those in one state should not be pursued to the detriment of those in the other state, the single exception being when treatment needed to save the life of the mother leads unavoidably to the unintended death of her child.

Yet under the guise of "special care and assistance" to mothers, it is claimed by pro-abortion feminists that abortion is a right, part of the "reproductive health services" governments must provide for every woman. But this is to ignore the fact that abortion can never be endorsed as a genuine service to her unborn child. Abortion can

---

37 Shue, Henry, *Basic Rights: Subsistence, Affluence, and U.S. Foreign Policy*, Princeton: Princeton University Press, 1980. p. 24 and 53.

38 Morsink, Johannes: *The Universal Declaration Origins, Drafting and Intent*,, *op. cit.*, p. 19.

39 Ibid.

never be characterized rationally as an act of "special care and assistance" promised the child.

A "special" set of rights for mothers and children was easily agreed in the very earliest drafts of the Declaration:

> Mothers and children have the right to special regard, care and resources.[40]

This special set of rights was reaffirmed by the UN Declaration on the Rights of the Child to include an entitlement to special care and assistance for children before birth:

> ...special safeguards and care, including appropriate legal protection, before as well as after birth...the need for such special safeguards has been...recognized in the Universal Declaration of Human Rights and in the statutes of specialized agencies and international organizations concerned with the welfare of children.[41]

From the very beginning, States parties to the *Constitution of the World Health Organization* (WHO) declared, in conformity with the Charter of the United Nations, the principle:

> Healthy development of the child is of basic importance; the ability to live harmoniously in a changing total environment is essential to such development.[42]

Principle 2 of the WHO Constitution goes on to state:

> In order to achieve its objective, the functions of the Organization shall be...to promote maternal and child health and welfare and to foster the ability to live harmoniously in a changing total environment.[43]

Here is recognition of the obligation to foster the ability of both mother and child (interdependent) to live harmoniously in a changing total environment—good health care fosters the healthy development of the child in the changing total environment of the mother's womb, works for the health and welfare of the mother and her child so that both may live harmoniously, each making adaptations as the natural continuum that is life brings continuous development and change. Abortion is the very antithesis of this objective.

Abortion is an abrogation of the Universal Declaration commitment: "All children... shall enjoy the same social protection". It is an abrogation also of the principle of Article 2, "without distinction of any kind", for the child at risk of abortion

40 UN Doc. E/CN.4/20 p. 80.

41 *UN Declaration on the Rights of the Child* (1959).

42 Preamble to the *Constitution of the World Health Organization*, July 22, 1946.

43 Ibid., Chapter 2, "Functions", Article 2.

is denied the same human rights protection as is recognized for children after birth. Abortion is based on a prohibited distinction, an irrational prejudice that the "before birth" status of a child is inferior and less deserving of human rights protection than the "after birth" status of the same child or of other children.

In regard specifically to children, the Universal Declaration recognizes in Article 25 a second application of the principle that prohibits discrimination:

> All children, whether born in or out of wedlock, shall enjoy the same social protection.

These two terms, "before as well as after birth" and "whether born in or out of wedlock", comprise an essential framework for protecting, without discrimination on grounds of opinion, birth or other status, the human rights of every child.

The right "...to share in scientific advancement and its benefits"

One area, however, in which discrimination against the child before birth is rampant and impinges directly on the right to life relates to many scientific "advancements" that are being used to place unborn children at increased risk of abortion. Article 27(1) of the Universal Declaration states:

> "Everyone has the right...to share in scientific advancement and its benefits."

Under this article, "everyone [including the child before as well as after birth] has the right...to share in scientific advancement and its benefits". This includes for all children the right to the benefits of medical and surgical advancement in pre-natal health care, including fetal surgery and fetal medicine, where needed. Recent breakthrough treatment of open fetal surgery has been developed and refined to the point of being able to treat the child before birth as early as 22 weeks' gestation.[44]

For most human embryos involved in IVF and its scientific "advancements", there are no benefits—only the indignity of being used in risky projects or destroyed. The embryonic child's right to security of person is violated in IVF clinics and in laboratories where the human embryo is deliberately subjected to greater risk than in the mother's womb.[45] Many human embryos are brought into existence *in vitro*, and "on

---

44 Crisis Pregnancy Centers Online News Service, 13 July, 1998, reports the case of Noah Kipfmiller, whose abnormal spinal growth was diagnosed at 20 weeks, and was successfully operated on 3 weeks later by surgeons at the Philadelphia Children's Hospital in the USA. According to Dr. Joseph Bruner, director of fetal diagnosis and therapy at Vanderbilt University Medical Center, early medical treatment for unborn children with physical problems is critical. Many other fetal patients had also undergone the surgery, but at 28 weeks: "Conducting the surgery sooner [as in Noah Kipfmiller's case] can reduce the chance of spinal damage". Also, more recently in late 2007, Australian surgeons at Melbourne's Monash Medical Centre saved the leg of an unborn baby girl by performing *in utero* surgery at just 22 weeks' gestation. (AFP news, 9 June, 2008).

45 Bellieni, Carlo, Buonocore, Giuseppe, "Assisted Procreation: Too Little Consideration for the Babies?", *Ethics & Medicine*, Summer 2006. The authors argue that recent studies

the basis of crude tests" a few are chosen, and of those few, even fewer survive the trauma of implantation.[46] Many are stored, neglected, abused as experimental material, harvested for their stem cells, and then discarded.

Abortion—part of ktenology, the science of killing—not genuine health care

Some scientific advancement does not deliver benefits to the child *in utero*. The dangers of scientific advancement in which some human beings may be victims rather than beneficiaries were well understood by those who were drafting Article 27(1) in the Universal Declaration. Dr. Leo Alexander observes what was well publicized at the time, viz., that a large part of Nazi research "was devoted to the science of destroying and preventing life", for which he proposed the term "ktenology", the science of killing.[47] Raphael Lemkin, also writing at the time of the drafting of the Universal Declaration, recalls:

> The concept of genocide was also used recently by the Chief of Counsel in subsequent Nuremberg proceedings. Brigadier General Telford Taylor, in the case against Nazi doctors who experimented on human beings in concentration camps. In this classical genocide case the defendants practiced experiments in order to develop techniques for outright killings and abortions...[48]

The juxtaposition of "outright killings" and "abortions" verifies the understanding at this time that abortion has a moral equivalence with outright killing. Scientific advancement in methods of abortion was clearly condemned.

In much the same way, the new pre-natal medical testing for disabilities such as Down Syndrome cannot be said to be genuine scientific advancement when any benefits in which the children being tested may share are so often withheld. Indeed, a systematic literature review found that some 92% of these children detected with

---

have revealed much higher risks of cerebral palsy and malformations in babies conceived by in vitro fertilization (IVF) than in babies conceived naturally. They question whether parents can legitimately accept this risk on behalf of offspring. They argue that parents can expose their baby to a risk only to preserve it from a worse possibility, and this is not the case of IVF, which is not a therapeutic tool for children because when the IVF decision is taken, the child has not yet been conceived.

46 See also, Roger Highfield, "IVF success rate is too low, says Lord Winston", Telegraph (UK) 9th June, 2008. Lord Winston, Britain's leading fertility expert, says: "the success rate of in vitro fertilisation, or IVF, has remained static for the past few decades At present, it is around 30 per cent, but that is only possible by 'picking the right patients to treat'...there is no reliable way of the best quality embryos most likely to create a successful pregnancy, and clinic staff tend to decide which embryos to implant on the basis of crude tests...32,600 women underwent treatment resulting in 11,000 births."

47 Alexander: *op. cit.*

48 Lemkin, Raphael, "Genocide as Crime under International Law", *The American Journal of International Law*, Vol. 41(1), January, 1947, pp. 145-151, at pp. 147-8.

the disability are routinely aborted.[49] There is no benefit for these children. Indeed, improved medical testing for these children *in utero* has led to an increased risk of abortion for them. Scientific advancement in pre-natal testing has become part of ktenology, the science of killing, that was implicitly prohibited as a human rights violation in the drafting of Article 27(1).

The Human Rights Commission's initial draft of this article stipulated that all human beings are entitled to share "in the advantages of science" but this was significantly clarified and replaced with the phrase "in the goods which result from scientific discoveries". So when a revised text reached the Third Committee debates with the phrase "to share in scientific advancement" , there was still the clear intention of guaranteeing everyone a share in the "goods" which result from scientific advancement, and so the words "and its benefits" were added as a further protection against the misuse of scientific discoveries.[50]

This protection in Article 27 of the Universal Declaration has been codified in Article 15(1)(b) of the International Covenant on Economic, Social and Cultural Rights:

> The State Parties to the present Covenant recognize the right of everyone... [t]o enjoy the benefits of scientific progress and its applications.

The Committee on Economic, Social and Cultural Rights has spelled out the State's obligations inherent in this right, which include:

> Measures taken to prevent the use of scientific and technical progress for purposes which are contrary to the enjoyment of all human rights, including the rights to life, health, personal freedom, privacy and the like.[51]

The right to life of the Down Syndrome child at risk of abortion because of "improved" pre-natal "fetal abnormality" diagnostic tests and the right to life of the girl child at risk of abortion because of "more advanced" pre-natal sex-selection technology are victims of "the use of scientific and technical progress for purposes that are contrary to the enjoyment of all human rights, including the rights to life, health ..." States are obliged to take measures "to prevent" such uses.

The terms "scientific advancement and its benefits" and "the benefits of scientific progress and its applications" endorse only positive connotations of the right to a benign sharing of new knowledge and treatments. Research that uses and discards an embryonic human being as research material is by its very nature in violation of this

49 Mansfield C., Hopfer S., Marteau T.M., "Termination rates after prenatal diagnosis of Down Syndrome, spina bifida, anencephaly, and Turner and Klinefelter syndromes: a systematic literature review. European Concerted Action: DADA (Decision-making After the Diagnosis of a fetal Abnormality)", *Prenatal Diagnosis*, Vol.19(9), September, 1999, pp.808-12.

50 General Assembly Official Records—TC 3, pp. 619-27.

51 UN Doc. E/C.12/1991/1 Revised guidelines by the Committee on Economic, Social and Cultural Rights, under *Article 17 of the Covenant* 2(c).

right. Such a human subject definitively does not "share in scientific advancement and its benefits". These particular human beings are instead to be selected for laboratory use only, sacrificed in the cause of scientific advancement and benefits in which others share, but they themselves are not permitted even to live to share.

A "social and international order" in which the right to life is "fully realized"

Recalling Verdoodt's conclusion that the right to life as stated in Article 3 of the Universal Declaration can be understood only in the context of the entire Declaration, it is necessary to take special note of the wider environment in which the right to life is to be protected:

> Everyone is entitled to a social and international order in which the rights and freedoms set forth in this Declaration can be fully realized. *Universal Declaration, Article 28.*

To what kind of social order are children at risk of abortion entitled so that their right to special *safeguards and care, including appropriate legal protection, before as well as after birth* can be fully-realized as promised in Article 28?

Children at risk of abortion, and their mothers, have a right to a social order based on the principle of solidarity (or brotherhood), which is best expressed in the term "all members of the human family". Solidarity is a duty of care towards all our fellow members of the human race from the very newest to the oldest. This duty of solidarity with "all members of the human family" is owed precisely because of each member's inherent human dignity. Solidarity is the growth and exercise of a sincere consciousness of a common good that extends to the whole human family, *without any exceptions.*

Children at risk of abortion, and their mothers, are entitled also to a social order where expectant mothers and their children in conflict situations and in peace time are protected, where nations strive for political stability as well as for economic development and prosperity. They are entitled to a social order where equitable distribution of material goods and services (including medical services) ensure for "all members of the human family" the necessities of life, realization of the economic, social and cultural rights "indispensable" for dignity and the free development of personality (Article 22), and social security "adequate for his health and well-being", both "in the event of disability" and "in circumstances beyond his control" (Article 25).

Provision of these necessities of life was understood by the drafters not as "charity" but as obligations of social justice. From a thorough study of the drafting history of the economic, social, and cultural rights set out in the Universal Declaration, Bard-Anders Andreaason describes the tremendous advance that was made by the drafters:

> Key components of the normative justification of social and economic human rights are equality and social justice, whose function is to secure, against societal threats, the inherent dignity and integrity of every human being... The Basic shift has been from "charity"...

> to a notion of universal entitlement based on rights claimed by the human being *per se*.[52]

Indeed, it is as a human being *per se* that the child at risk of abortion lays claim to have the right to life made secure "against societal threats" to inherent dignity and integrity. For every mother and child at risk of abortion, governments, communities, and families must strive together to provide an adequate share in the necessities of life to which there is universal entitlement.

It is important here to recognize that even while better prenatal and post-natal programs are being developed, a lack of economic or social security cannot in the meantime be allowed to excuse a lack of legal protection for expectant mothers and their unborn children.[53]

A constant devious theme used by radical feminism to promote abortion is that pregnancy threatens women and girls' access to education, employment, self-determination and economic independence.[54] Such arguments, however, rely on denying the presence in every pregnancy of a human child with human rights, on disregarding the lethal physical harm done to a child who is aborted, and on trivializing the physical trauma and psychological anguish experienced by the child's mother. One experienced counselor for abortion grief, Teresa Burke, founder of Rachel's Vineyard, a global network for helping women hurt by abortion, describes abortion thus:

> Abortion is a death experience. It is the demise of human potential, relationship, responsibility, maternal attachment, connectedness and innocence.[55]

Sadly, "safe" abortion programs cannot produce a safe environment for expectant mothers and their children—they cannot provide the environment of nurture, support and protection in which the right to life of both the mother and her child can be fully realized.

---

52 Bard-Anders Andreaason, "Article 22" in *The Universal Declaration of Human Rights: A Common Standard of Achievement*, Gudmundur Alfredsson and Asbjorn Eide, (eds.), The Hague: Martinus Nijhoff, 1999, pp. 476-7.

53 John P. Humphrey, Director of the UN Division of Human Rights, recalls that even as early as 1951, the immediate priority of civil and political rights was understood: "The Economic, Social and Cultural Rights were programme rights, most of which depended on the availability of resources, and could therefore only be implemented progressively, but the Commission did not consider progressive implementation appropriate for the Covenant on Civil and Political Rights since the rights enunciated by it required immediate implementation." Letter to the Editor, *Human Rights Quarterly*, Issue 4, p. 539.

54 For example, see The Alan Guttmacher Institute, "Into a New World: Young Women's Sexual and Reproductive Lives", New York: 1997.

55 Quoted in "Breaking the silence on abortion", by Dr. Brigid McKenna, *The Catholic Weekly*, May 18, 2008.

Chapter 7 Decriminalization—A Treaty Interpretation Manifestly Unreasonable

"In accordance with the Declaration of Human Rights"

Recognition of the rights of the child before birth in the *Universal Declaration of Human Rights* (UDHR) implies recognition of these rights in all subsequent human rights instruments.

Because the Universal Declaration recognizes that the child before birth has human rights that are to be protected by the rule of law, then all subsequent UN human rights instruments that state they are "in accordance with the Universal Declaration of Human Rights"[1] (or reference the Universal Declaration to that effect) must, in the words of the Declaration, apply these human rights *without distinction of any kind* to the child *before as well as after birth*. Every major international human rights instrument, including every regional instrument, acknowledges the Universal Declaration of Human Rights as foundational, as a source document of fundamental human rights principles with which the new instrument undertakes to be consistent.

The Universal Declaration of Human Rights and the International Covenants interpreted correctly (i.e., in good faith and in the context of their Preambles[2]) indeed "recognize" the rights of the child before birth to legal protection, i.e., to laws protecting them from harmful treatment such as abortion.

Once a treaty has entered into force and is legally binding, the States Parties must perform the treaty obligations "in good faith" (*pacta sunt servanda*). A human rights treaty must be interpreted on the basis that any interpretation must respect the rights and interests of each individual human being and also must be logically consistent

---

1 This exact phrase is used, for example, in the Preambles to the *International Covenant on Civil and Political Rights* (ICCPR), the *International Covenant on Economic, Social and Cultural Rights* (ICESCR) and the *American Convention on Human Rights.*

2 Article 31(1) General rule of interpretation of the Vienna Convention on the Law of Treaties:

> A treaty shall be interpreted in good faith in accordance with the ordinary meaning to be given to the terms of the treaty in their context and in the light of its object and purpose.
>
> 2. The context for the purpose of the interpretation of a treaty shall comprise, in addition to the text ... its preamble...

with both the context of the treaty and the principles and purpose of the treaty as a whole.

Authentic interpretation of modern international human rights instruments must respect the rights of the child before as well as after birth. The Universal Declaration came into being because, the Preamble says,

> ...disregard and contempt for human rights resulted in barbarous acts which have outraged the conscience of mankind...

Among the Nazi atrocities encompassed in this statement was disregard and contempt for the human rights of unborn children which resulted in barbarous acts of abortion. Legal protection "denied to the unborn children" was condemned at the Nuremberg Trials.[3] Programmed abortion by the Nazi medical establishment was certainly understood at the time of the drafting of the Universal Declaration as one manifestation of the "barbarous acts which have outraged the conscience of mankind".[4]

UN Declaration principles—"of great and lasting significance"

Significantly, this phrase 'the conscience of mankind' points to *jus cogens*, which consists essentially of international principles based on the common conscience of mankind. An enduring and essential concept of the universal law, *jus cogens* has been commonly understood and practised over the centuries by civilized human societies. Throughout history, the principle of providing protection for the child before birth has been an integral part of *jus cogens* and as such, it belongs to that class of international customary law that is self-executing, has peremptory force, and cannot be abrogated by domestic law or treaty. Since ancient times, protection of the rights of the child before birth and recognition of the child's juridical personality have been understood and upheld by Ulpian, Justinian, Gratian and numerous others.[5] The major faiths of the world, Judaism, Christianity and Islam, also have maintained and defended a common respect for the rights of the child before birth.

The *travaux préparatoires* of the 1989 *Convention on the Rights of the Child* (CRC) records that the representative of Italy stated (significantly without contradiction) that no State was manifestly opposed to the principles contained in the *Declaration of the Rights of the Child* and, therefore, according to the *Vienna Convention on the Law of Treaties*, the rule regarding the protection of life before birth could be consid-

3 *Nuremberg Trials Record*: "The RuSHA Case", March 1948, Volume IV, p. 1077. Available at: http://www.mazal.org/archive/nmt/04a/NMT04-T1076.htm.

4 See, for example, Statement by the Council of the British Medical Association to the World Medical Association, June 1947, re-issued by The Medical Education Trust and reproduced at: http://www.donoharm.org.uk/leaflets/war.htm.

5 Pontifical Council for the Family, *The Family and Human Rights*, Vatican City: 1999, para. 33.

ered as *jus cogens* since it formed part of the common conscience of members of the international community.[6]

It should be understood also that the term "declaration" has been officially defined by the U.N. General Assembly as "a formal and solemn instrument, suitable for rare occasions when principles of great and lasting significance are being enunciated", and although not legally binding, a declaration "may by custom become recognized as laying down rules binding upon States."[7] The 1959 Declaration on the Rights of the Child reaffirms a recognition of the rights of the child before birth which was already agreed in the 1948 Universal Declaration.[8] It is now generally accepted that the Universal Declaration itself has become, over time, both legally binding and an accepted part of customary law.[9] Professor Peter Bailey has summed this up succinctly:

> The very large and increasing number of ratifications of the two human rights Covenants, and the fact that the rights stated in the UDHR are commonly recognised as well founded in moral and good practice terms, means that there are now virtually unchallengeable grounds for asserting that the UDHR rights have become part of international customary law. That means that, unlike treaties, which only bind a country once it has accepted the treaty obligations, all countries in the world are bound, whatever their particular view may be. A country cannot repudiate international customary law, as it can a treaty obligation.[10]

So having established in Chapters 1 and 2 above that the term "everyone" includes the child before birth, and given that the Universal Declaration Article 3 says "Everyone has the right to life...", we would argue here that prohibition of abortion, like prohibition of slavery, is a legal norm considered to be so fundamental that it is a peremptory norm of international law.

Protection of the child before as well as after birth is a fundamental principle of *jus cogens*, of our system of international protection of human rights based on universal recognition by the international community. It is recognized irrevocably in "this Universal Declaration of Human Rights as a common standard of achievement for all peoples and all nations..." (UDHR Preamble). And since a "country cannot repudiate international customary law, as it can a treaty obligation", the UDHR commitment to protect the right to life of all members of the human family (including children before as well as after birth) remains obligatory.

6 Report of the Working Group to the Commission on Human Rights (1989), E/CN.4/1989/48, para. 40.

7 U.N. Doc. E/CN.4/L.610 (1962).

8 See Chapter 1 above.

9 See, for example, International Court of Justice Judgment, *United States of America v. Iran*, ICJ Reports 1980, p. 42, para. 91.

10 Bailey, Peter: "The Creation of the Universal Declaration of Human Rights". Available at: http://www.universalrights.net/main/creation.htm.

Reinterpretation of human rights instruments to exclude the child before birth: legally and morally an invalid process

So how can it be right for some UN treaty monitoring bodies to collude in pressuring legislatures and judiciaries around the world to remove all legal protections for the child at risk of abortion with the clear intention of repudiating international customary law protecting such children? How can it be legally or morally right for those in positions of power to scheme to bring into force a "new" customary law that denies fundamental protection to the most defenceless, the most vulnerable members of the human family?

Would such a scheme constitute a legally and morally valid process if this scheme were being used to pressure some critical number of States Parties into repealing anti-slavery laws (which like abortion laws protect non-derogable rights)? Upon the successful execution of such a scheme, would ownership of slaves become a human right? Upon successful completion of a campaign in international, regional and domestic courts and legislatures to decriminalize slavery, would it be legally and morally valid to declare then that the right to own slaves has now been made to enter into international customary human rights law? Is clever manipulation of customary human rights law by the ideological forces of the day to be allowed to undermine the equal and inalienable rights of all members of the human family?

The intellectually honest answer must be "no". When aimed at the destruction of non-derogable human rights, this process is neither legally nor morally valid. If slavery once again becomes commonplace, and if international, regional, and domestic courts of justice refuse to prosecute those who claim to be exercising the so-called right to own slaves, the practice will enjoy immunity from the law. And the human rights of the victims of slavery will be removed from case law and will remain hidden from public consciousness, will remain hidden even from "the conscience of mankind" that gave rise to the great modern human rights instruments.

It is time for all intellectually honest, non-ideologically-driven legal experts to denounce the ruse in progress now. This ruse involves encouraging domestic courts to discover an international "right to abortion" by consulting executive, legislative and judicial precedents, and the recorded expertise of jurists and commentators, all ideologically reinterpreting international agreements.

Careful scrutiny needs to be applied to this dubious legal process. There can be little virtue in repealing the fundamental human rights of one group in order to enhance and advance some subset of human rights for another group (such as a mother's 'right' to abort her own children or an individual's 'right' to own slaves). This designer-programmed tampering with non-derogable human rights in customary law must be scrutinized more closely. If this devious process continues to be utilized and legitimized, then a situation may arise where human rights of the most vulnerable groups may be abused once again with legal impunity. Governments around the world may be pressured one by one to remove legal protection of non-derogable rights from a select category of human beings such as the slave-child, the disabled child, the Jewish child, until by appeal to common practice and customary law, decriminalization of abuses of their human rights is accepted as compatible with international human rights law.

It was precisely to prevent these kinds of large-scale human rights abuses happening ever again that the modern international human rights instruments were drawn up after World War II. Of the Universal Declaration principles, Johannes Morsink, after meticulous examination of the drafting debates, asserts:

> These are not mere Enlightenment reflexes, they are deep truths rediscovered in the midst of the Holocaust and put on paper again shortly thereafter.[11]

Truly it is contrary to the purpose and principles of the United Nations and is thus in violation of UDHR Article 29(iii), this "process" of pressuring countries to repeal laws protecting non-derogable rights with a premeditated agenda of removing, from international law, those rights for a particular group of human beings.[12]

If we legitimize this process, we shall reach the point of absurdity, where there are no non-derogable human rights for any group of human beings. And if a process is set up to enable countries and court systems to remove non-derogable rights from international human rights law, the law becomes simply what the Human Rights Committee and some sub-set of international, regional and domestic courts decide at that particular time according to the particular ideological wind that prevails at that time. In effect, the whole structure of international human rights law that began with a universal agreement in 1948 is undermined so that it becomes ineffectual as a new ideology takes hold and begins to reinterpret the human rights instruments to enhance the rights of those particular groups who espouse the new ideology, whether it be radical feminism, eco-utopianism, neo-Nazism or whatever.

Decriminalization of abortion—"a result... manifestly unreasonable"

The current ideologically-driven reinterpretation of the non-derogable right to life "leads to a result which is manifestly absurd or unreasonable", viz., the selection for exclusion of children at risk of abortion from the human rights protection of "all members of the human family". According to the Vienna Convention on the Law of Treaties Articles 31 and 32(b), when an interpretation "leads to a result which is manifestly absurd or unreasonable", then "recourse may be had to supplementary means of

11 Morsink, Johannes, "World War Two and the Universal Declaration", Human Rights Quarterly, Vol. 15, No. 2, May 1993, pp. 357-405.

12 A masterly stratagem was devised by pro-abortion feminist ideologues to move a woman's "right" to abortion into international human rights "customary" law. This stratagem was drawn up and agreed to in 1996 at the *Round Table of Human Rights Treaty Bodies on Human Rights Approaches to Women's Health, with a Focus on Sexual and Reproductive Health and Rights.* (Published jointly in 1998 by UNDAW, UNFPA & UNHCHR) In agreeing to this, the Human Rights Treaty Monitoring Bodies went not only beyond their mandate but against it.

interpretation, including the preparatory work of the treaty and the circumstances of its conclusion, in order… to determine the meaning".

As I have set out in Chapters 1 and 2 above, the preparatory work for the Universal Declaration and the circumstances of its conclusion determine without doubt that the meaning of "child" is inclusive—it was understood at the time in both the text and the context to mean that the child "before as well as after birth" is recognized to have human rights entitlement to *special safeguards and care, including legal protection before as well as after birth.*

Moreover, according to Article 53 of the Vienna Convention on the Law of Treaties, a treaty is simply "void if, at the time of its conclusion, it conflicts with a peremptory norm of international law". UDHR Article 3, "Everyone has the right to life…" ("everyone" including the child before as well as after birth), is a peremptory norm of general international law. Thus treaties subsequent to the Universal Declaration are void if at the time of their conclusion they conflict with this norm. So when treaty monitoring bodies or legislatures or courts of international law pretentiously reinterpret their international or regional human rights instruments to withdraw legal protection from children at risk of abortion, they are espousing a nonsensical interpretation which, if true, would have rendered the particular treaty void at the time of its conclusion.

Also according to Article 53 of the Vienna Convention on the Law of Treaties, such a norm is described as "a norm from which no derogation is permitted and which can be modified only by a subsequent norm of general international law having the same character".

There can be no doubt that treaty-monitoring bodies, legislatures, and judiciaries around the world are colluding in ideological manipulation of a principle of customary law—legal protection for children at risk of abortion—in order to replace it with a modified subsequent norm of general international law that is not *of the same character*, namely decriminalization of abortion. To remove legal protection from the child before birth is of a *contrary* character—it conflicts with the original peremptory norm of international law, the obligation to provide appropriate legal protection for the child before as well as after birth.

Decriminalization—a most inappropriate legal protection for the child at risk of abortion

The term "appropriate legal protection" in the context of the founding international human rights instruments means application of the UDHR principles of equality and non-discrimination in the administration of justice for children at risk of abortion as well as for all other children. Decriminalization of abortion flouts these principles.

The Universal Declaration "recognized" that the child before birth, no less than the child after birth, is an appropriate subject of human rights law and is entitled to appropriate legal protection. The child before as well as after birth is entitled to legal protection that respects the fundamental principles of the child's right to equality and non-discrimination in the administration of justice.

Following the prohibition of discrimination in the *Charter of the United Nations*,[13] the adoption of the Universal Declaration of Human Rights together with the *Convention on the Prevention and Punishment of the Crime of Genocide* in 1948 established the principles of non-discrimination and equality before the law. For the child at risk of abortion, decriminalization of abortion contravenes these principles.

The Universal Declaration, in recognizing the child before birth and the child's need for legal protection, recognizes that the child before birth has a right to be "born free and equal in dignity and rights" (Article 1) and is entitled to all the rights and freedoms set forth in this Declaration without distinction of any kind, such as race, colour, sex, language, religion, political or other opinion, national or social origin, property, birth or other status" (Article 2). No distinction is to be made regarding universal human rights entitlement—it was recognized to apply "before as well as after birth".

Furthermore, with regard to the right to equality, Article 7 of the Universal Declaration stipulates that:

> All are equal before the law and are entitled without any discrimination to equal protection of the law. All are entitled to equal protection against any discrimination in violation of this Declaration and against any incitement to such discrimination.

In the Commission on Human Rights discussions during the Third Session relating to the draft of what was to become Article 7 of the Universal Declaration, the Soviet delegate, Alexei Pavlov, made the critical point that even when discrimination is based on law it is not acceptable. Morsink reports it thus:

> ...the article talks 'only of arbitrary discrimination' and incitement thereto..." He pointed out that the article "condoned and justified 'the so-called non-arbitrary' discrimination, i.e., discrimination based on law". As examples, he gave "the mass discrimination, most disgraceful and offensive to human dignity, which is embodied in the laws against Negroes in the United States of America or against Indians in the Union of South Africa.[14]

An example in today's world of discrimination "based on law" is embodied in those laws that now make it "lawful" to discriminate against unborn children, to subject them to selective abortion with legal impunity. Both the general discriminatory opinion that the child before birth is inferior in rights to the child after birth and particular forms of discrimination against girl children before birth, against unborn children with disabilities and against children whose fathers are guilty of rape or incest should not be tolerated by law.

It should be emphasized also that Article 7 of the Universal Declaration prohibits "any incitement to such discrimination". This means that incitement to discrimination against anyone, including against the child before birth, cannot be legally toler-

13 *Charter of the United Nations* (1945) Article 1(3) and Article 55(c).

14 Morsink, Johannes, *Universal Declaration of Human Rights: Origins, Drafting and Intent*, Philadelphia: University of Pennsylvania Press, 1999, p. 94.

ated. However, as we have seen, this prohibition has been ignored by some of the international monitoring bodies which continue to promote today "abortion rights" which disguise a deadly discrimination against children at risk of selective abortion. Together with other assemblies such as the Council of Europe which recently caved into ideological prejudice,[15] they conspire to incite States parties to decriminalize abortion—to repeal abortion laws that seek to protect the rights of every child to "special safeguards and care".

Convention on the Rights of the Child—"appropriate legal protection"

The UN Committee on the Rights of the Child, however, appears to be moving towards better protection for the child before as well as after birth, a protection more consistent with the Universal Declaration:

> The preamble to the Convention on the Rights of the Child affirms, in accordance with the principles in the Charter of the United Nations, repeated in the preamble to the Universal Declaration, that "recognition of the inherent dignity and of the equal and inalienable rights of all members of the human family is the foundation of freedom, justice and peace in the world". The preamble to the Convention also recalls that, in the Universal Declaration, the United Nations "has proclaimed that childhood is entitled to special care and assistance.[16]

Regarding this "special care and assistance", the UN Committee on the Rights of the Child has issued very clear guidelines in their General Comment No 5 on how governments, parliaments and judiciaries are to understand their obligations under the Convention on the Rights of the Child.[17] States parties are required to take "all appropriate legislative, administrative and other measures" for implementation of human rights protection for all children. Their task of implementation—of making a reality of the human rights of children—needs to engage all sectors of society. Ensuring that all domestic legislation is fully compatible with the Convention and that the Convention's principles and provisions can be directly applied and appropriately enforced is fundamental.[18] These obligations of direct application and appropriate enforcement of legal protection for the child before as well as after birth in domestic legislation are certainly not being met when abortion is decriminalized.

The Committee says that when a State ratifies the Convention on the Rights of the Child, it takes on obligations under international law to implement it, to take ac-

15 "Access to safe and legal abortion in Europe", Resolution 1607. 2008. Available at: http://assembly.coe.int/Main.asp?link=/Documents/AdoptedText/ta08/ERES1607.htm.

16 UN Committee on the Rights of the Child: General Comment No 8, para. 17.

17 UN Committee on the Rights of the Child: General Comment No 5 (2003) General measures of implementation of the Convention on the Rights of the Child (arts. 4, 42 and 44, para. 6).

18 Ibid., para. 1.

tion to ensure the realization of all rights in the Convention for all children in their jurisdiction.[19]

It is completely illogical to intimate as some pro-abortion advocates have done that the child before birth is not "within their jurisdiction" –if this were so, then the commitment (dating back to recognition in the Universal Declaration) to provide the child with *"special safeguards and care, including legal protection before as well as after birth"* is meaningless.

Ideological re-interpretation aimed at accommodating prevalent abortion practices reduces this commitment to just nonsense words added for no sensible reason—"a result which is manifestly absurd or unreasonable". The Vienna Convention on the Law of Treaties asserts that when interpretation "leads to a result which is manifestly absurd or unreasonable", then we are to have recourse to "supplementary means of interpretation, including the preparatory work of the treaty and the circumstances of its conclusion, in order... to determine the meaning". And so we must turn to the history of the concept of appropriate legal protection for the child before as well as after birth, and critically examine some of the recent reinterpretations in the light of that history.

Attempts to gut "appropriate legal protection" of meaning for the child before birth

In truth, the preambular commitment in the Convention on the Rights of the Child provides an insurmountable problem to pro-abortion advocates who try to re-write the phrase "before as well as after birth" by deleting the "before as well as" and by reducing the need for appropriate legal protection to "only after birth". Capelon *et al.* attempt an interpretation which departs quite imaginatively from the original concept but appears to bear little relation to the actual text:

> This reflects, at most, recognition of a state's duty to promote, through nutrition, health and support directed to the pregnant woman, a child's capacity to survive and thrive after birth.[20]

Another "creative" reinterpretation of the critical preambular provision for appropriate legal protection for the child before as well as after birth is advanced by the quintessentially ideological feminist Rebecca Cook who opines:

---

19 Ibid.

20 Copelon, R., Zampas, C., Brusie, E., Devore, J., "Human rights begin at birth: international law and the claim of fetal rights", Reproductive Health Matters, Nov. 2005, Vol. 13(26), pp. 120-9.

> The Convention gives no guidance to what the Preamble means by 'appropriate'. Such protection might include provision of reasonable prenatal care, nutrition and essential obstetric care to ensure safety in delivery and care for the newborn.[21]

Neither of these curiously perverse interpretations are what reasonable people would understand as "the ordinary meaning" of the preambular commitment in accordance with the rules of interpretation in the Vienna Convention on the Law of Treaties. The "ordinary meaning" criterion is in itself a strong argument in favour of a common sense approach to treaty interpretation, whereby legislators, judges, academics and treaty monitoring bodies in deciding the meaning of a particular commitment, are expected to avoid giving that provision a meaning which plainly thwarts the drafting intention behind the commitment.

Reading *"appropriate legal protection"* for the child as primarily a women's rights statement?

Capelon's ideologically-driven revisionist version of the text relies on ignoring the word "legal" in the phrase "including appropriate legal protection before as well as after birth". It ignores also the context in which this legal protection is promised:

> Whereas the child, by reason of his physical and mental immaturity, needs special safeguards and care, including appropriate legal protection, before as well as after birth...

The text relates specifically to "the child", to the child's vulnerability "by reason of his physical and mental immaturity", to the child's need for "special safeguards and care, including appropriate legal protection, before as well as after birth". The state's duty is not just to promote "a child's capacity to survive and thrive after birth" but to provide as stated clearly "appropriate legal protection, before as well as after birth".

Cook's interpretation is also logically garbled for it would allow for "the provision of reasonable prenatal care" to include the provision of abortion. For reasonable people, aborting a child is the antithesis of providing "essential obstetric care to ensure safety in delivery... for the newborn". Cook's sleight-of-hand here should not deceive reasonable people into accepting her re-definition of 'prenatal' and 'postnatal'—"special safeguards and care, including legal protection before as well as after birth"—to apply only to the newborn (i.e., the child after birth) and not to the child "before as well as after birth" as is actually and clearly stated.

It should be remembered that the wording of this commitment was developed in the context of the Declaration on the Rights of the Child (1959) specifically out of a genuine and primary concern for the child that had already been recognized in the Universal Declaration. It was reaffirmed in the Convention on the Rights of the Child, a Convention focusing first and foremost on the child—it should not be read

21 Cook, Rebecca and Dickens, Bernard M., "Human Rights dynamics of Abortion Law Reform" Human Rights Quarterly, Vol. 25, No. 1, February 2003, p. 24.

today from the contemporary bias of radical feminist ideology as primarily a women's rights statement.

Each State determines for itself what is "appropriate legal protection"?

Nor should it be read as an optional extra the States can decide for themselves to take up or reject as they please. Philip Alston advances this fiction in yet another contemptible push to strip the child of "appropriate legal protection" before birth:

> ...its significance is to endorse the already widespread practice of taking whatever measures the state considers 'appropriate' with a view to protecting the fetus...What is 'appropriate' in that regard is for each state to determine for itself and it is not a matter to which the Draft Convention addresses itself.[22]

Alston, who is not an ignorant man, is being disingenuous here for he knows full well that "the significance" of a human rights instrument is never primarily or by default "to endorse the already widespread practice of taking whatever measures the state considered 'appropriate' with a view to" any serious human rights protection for any group of human beings!

Cultural pragmatism is no sound basis for international human rights protection. When it comes to universal human rights, the international community cannot endorse that each state determines for itself what is appropriate legal protection for vulnerable groups such as child soldiers in parts of Africa, or for sexual slaves in parts of Asia—certainly not when completely inadequate protection is being deemed "appropriate" by some individual States.

Human rights not constricted by existing national legislation

From the very beginning of the drafting of the first human rights instruments, it was understood that selectivity and discrimination were never "appropriate" in providing legal protection, that human rights protection for any group of human beings was not to be left to the individual discretion of individual states but rather that human rights protection was to be universal. Under the rule of law in all States, all members of the human family were to have equal human rights protection.

Morsink writes of "the international strand" of the non-discrimination articles 2 and 7 of the Universal Declaration which prohibit discrimination in terms of "all rights and freedoms set forth in this Declaration":

> In other words, the Universal Declaration is being set up as a definitive, identifiable and external standard of judgment over whatever legal system happens to be in place at what-

22 Alston, Philip, "The Unborn Child and Abortion under the draft Convention on the Rights of the Child", *Human Rights Quarterly*, Vol.12(1), 1990, pp. 156-178, at p. 172.

ever place and time we pick. The intent of Article 2 is to judge any systems that fall short of the standard.[23]

It was made clear during the 1948 negotiations that legal protection of universal human rights was never envisaged as being restricted by whatever domestic laws were already in place:

> In its preamble the Declaration is stated to be 'a common standard of achievement for all peoples and all nations'. As such, any such Declaration naturally goes beyond the present state of domestic legislation in all countries. It was inevitable, therefore, that the Assembly approved, in this Declaration of Human Rights, a number of principles which are not yet enshrined in national legislation in all countries. Occasional attempts were made by various delegations…to bring the Declaration in certain respects into line with existing national legislation. This, however, had to be done with the utmost care in order to avoid publicising and drawing severe criticism upon national legislation which Committee Three would have regarded as not sufficiently liberal or advanced.[24]

The Australian delegation understood this point to be very important, relating as it does to each State's future obligation to eschew voluntarily some of the State's autonomy and sovereignty in order to ensure that domestic laws comply with the Universal Declaration's "common standard of achievement" in international universal human rights:

> A close study of the Declaration in any country will, of course, make it clear that domestic legislation does not correspond precisely with the Declaration itself. It is inevitable, therefore, that private individuals or groups of people will quote the Declaration from time to time, claim that domestic legislation lags behind the Declaration, and bring pressure to bear upon governments to modify domestic legislation in order to make to conform with the Declaration. All countries will be in this position, and most countries in a far worse position than Australia in this regard. The point I wish to make is that any direct attempt by an individual country to limit the scope of the Declaration of Human Rights so that it conformed precisely to domestic legislation in that country would have been brushed aside in Committee Three.[25]

Thus right from the outset, all countries understood that their domestic legislation would have to be conformed to human rights and not human rights to "whatever measures the state considers appropriate", as Alston now posits.

Again, a secret memorandum from the Australian delegate at the Paris 1948 Committee Three negotiations of the Universal Declaration text makes another very strong point: that it was clearly understood that countries could not secure exclusion

23 Morsink, *op. cit.* p.92.

24 Report of Australian Alternate on Human Rights Drafting Committee, Second Session, May 3-21, 1948.

25 Ibid.

of the Declaration principles, once they had been accepted by the Commission on Human Rights and "embodied" in the forthcoming Covenant:

> During the discussions in Paris, it was always possible to fall back, in the last resort, upon the view that the Declaration of Human Rights was not a legally binding instrument, and any government which does not desire to conform immediately to the Declaration is perfectly entitled to refrain from so doing. This attitude, however, cannot be adopted regarding the Covenant of Human Rights. Once the principles are accepted by the Commission on Human Rights and are embodied in the draft Covenant, it will be extremely difficult, if not impossible, to secure the exclusion of those principles.[26]

This clear understanding that States entering a Convention would not have discretion "to secure exclusion" of UDHR principles, once accepted, does not support Alston's theory that each State who is a party to the Convention on the Rights of the Child remains free to determine for itself whether or not the child before birth is to have any legal protection. The Convention on the Rights of the Child embodies in its Preamble the Declaration on the Rights of the Child principle of providing special safeguards and care for children, "including appropriate legal protection before as well as after birth", a principle that had already been "recognized" by the Universal Declaration.

Conventions and Declarations on which they are based must be logically compatible

Each new UN human rights convention must be logically compatible not only with the foundational Universal Declaration principles but also with the principles of each new UN Declaration upon which the new treaty is based. Conventions were never meant to contradict or supercede the Declaration of principles upon which they are based. A Convention is drawn up to codify in international law the principles of the Declaration. The International Covenant on Civil and Political Rights (ICCPR) and the International Covenant on Economic, Social and Cultural Rights (ICESCR) do not supercede the Universal Declaration, nor does the Convention on the Rights of the Child supercede the Declaration on the Rights of the Child.

Tracing the path from *Declaration* to *Convention*

A concise history of the Convention on the Rights of the Child written by Defence for Children International (an active participant in negotiations) places the Convention accurately as the culmination of the children's rights movement last century:

> The entry into force of the UN Convention on the Rights of the Child on 2 September 1990 marked the culmination of nearly 70 years of efforts designed to ensure that the

26 Memorandum, (188 Watt to Burton) London, 22 December 1948, United Nations Assembly, Paris, 1948: Committee Three.

> international community give proper recognition to the special needs and vulnerability of children as human beings.
>
> The first expression of international concern about the situation of children came in 1923, when the Council of the newly-established non-governmental organisation "Save the Children International Union" adopted a five-point declaration of the rights of the child, known as the Declaration of Geneva, which was endorsed the following year by the Fifth Assembly of the League of Nations. In 1948, the General Assembly of the United Nations approved a slightly expanded version of that text, and went on to adopt a new Declaration, containing ten basic principles of child welfare and protection, in 1959.
>
> The 1959 Declaration—which, it can be noted, has not been superceded, but only supplemented, by the 1989 Convention—served as the springboard for the initiative to draft the Convention on the Rights of the Child.[27]

The need for human rights protection for the child before birth recognized in the 1959 Declaration could not have been superceded, either logically or legitimately, by a rejection of that specified need in the Convention that followed.

Pre-natal care and protection—"provided both to him and to his mother"

Pro-abortion re-interpretations of the rights of the child to special safeguards and care contradict one of the "ten basic principles of child welfare and protection, in 1959" – the child's right to prenatal care, a right that belongs "both to him and to his mother":

> ...he shall be entitled to grow and develop in health; to this end, special care and protection shall be provided both to him and to his mother, including adequate pre-natal and post-natal care... Declaration on the Rights of the Child, Principle 4.

It is nonsense to intimate as Cook does that the child's entitlement to grow and develop in health applies only from birth as a newborn. From the State's first knowledge of the child's existence and of the mother's pregnancy, adequate pre-natal care should be provided "both to him and to his mother". From the moment of fertilization, i.e., from the earliest moment of biologic existence, the child begins "to grow and develop in health". There is no reputable physician or obstetrician who would be so foolish as to say that the child begins "to grow and develop in health" only after birth, as a newborn.

Cook's claim that the "Convention gives no guidance to what the Preamble means by 'appropriate'" is not true—the Preamble's term "appropriate legal protection" is formally sourced from the Declaration on the Rights of the Child where very specific

27 Defence for Children International, *The Convention on the Rights of the Child,* Introduction by Nigel Cantwell. Available at: http://child.cornell.edu/childhouse/childrens_rights/dci_crc.html.

guidance as to what "appropriate" means is to be found in Principle 2 of the Declaration:

> The child shall enjoy special protection, and shall be given opportunities and facilities, by law and by other means, to enable him to develop physically, mentally, morally, spiritually and socially in a healthy and normal manner and in conditions of freedom and dignity. In the enactment of laws for this purpose, the best interests of the child shall be the paramount consideration.

In the Convention itself, further reference is made under Article 3(2) to "appropriate" legislative measures which should be read in conjunction with the Preambular commitment to provide "appropriate legal protection, before as well as after birth":

> States Parties undertake to ensure the child such protection and care as is necessary for his or her well-being, taking into account the rights and duties of his or her parents, legal guardians, or other individuals legally responsible for him or her, and, to this end, shall take all appropriate legislative and administrative measures.[28]

The phrase "protection and care" takes on particular significance for the well-being of children at risk of abortion in the light of the commitment in the Preamble to provide "special safeguards and care, including legal protection before as well as after birth". And so "to this end", that is, to ensure the child before as well as after birth "such protection and care as is necessary for his or her well-being", States have undertaken, *inter alia*, to enact legislative protection for children at risk of abortion and to provide administrative measures to help mothers whose unborn babies are at risk.

The CRC Committee entirely concurs with the Committee on Economic, Social and Cultural Rights[29] in asserting that "even where the available resources are demonstrably inadequate, the obligation remains for a State party to strive to ensure the widest possible enjoyment of the relevant rights under the prevailing circumstances ..." Whatever their economic circumstances, States are required to undertake all possible measures towards the realization of the rights of the child, paying special attention to the most disadvantaged groups.[30] This includes children at risk of abortion because their mothers are in difficult economic or social circumstances.

The Committee emphasizes that, in the context of the Convention, States must see their role as fulfilling "clear legal obligations to each and every child"— implementation of the human rights of children must not be seen as a charitable process, bestowing favours on children.[31] If the human rights of children to "special safeguards and

28 On "all appropriate legislative and administrative measures", see UN CRC Committee: General Comment No 5 (2003) General measures of implementation of the Convention on the Rights of the Child (arts. 4, 42 and 44, para. 6) para. 4.

29 UN Committee on Economic, Social and Cultural Rights: General Comment No 3 para. 11.

30 UN CRC Committee: General Comment No 5 (2003), para. 6.

31 Ibid., para. 9.

care, including legal protection before as well as after birth" are to be implemented in accordance with the Convention, then legal protection for the child at risk of abortion is to be seen as part of the State's "clear legal obligations to each and every child".

Applying the general principles of the CRC inclusively

1. Non-discrimination

The development of a children's rights perspective throughout Government, parliament and the judiciary is required for effective implementation of the whole Convention on the Rights of the Child and, in particular, in the light of the following articles in the Convention identified by the Committee as general principles:

> Article 2: the obligation of States to respect and ensure the rights set forth in the Convention to each child within their jurisdiction, before as well as after birth, without discrimination of any kind.

This non-discrimination obligation requires States actively to identify individual children and groups of children [e.g., children at risk of selective abortion], the recognition and realization of whose rights may demand special measures. For example, the Committee highlights, in particular, the need for data collection to be disaggregated to enable discrimination or potential discrimination to be identified [e.g., data collection of specific and verifiable reasons given for performing abortion].

The UN Human Rights Committee points out:

> Addressing discrimination may require changes in legislation, administration and resource allocation, as well as educational measures to change attitudes.[32]

The Committee on the Rights of the Child commends the Human Rights Committee on this for it "has underlined the importance of taking special measures in order to diminish or eliminate conditions that cause discrimination" [e.g., discriminatory attitudes towards female unborn children, or towards the unborn children whose fathers have committed rape or incest, or towards unborn children with disabilities].

Article 2(1) of the Convention on the Rights of the Child provides that States must ensure children can enjoy their rights without discrimination.[33] Article 2(2) of the Convention goes a step further and requires States to ensure that a child is protected

32 UN Human Rights Committee General Comment No 18, 1989.

33 UN Convention on the Rights of the Child, Article 2(1):

> States Parties shall respect and ensure the rights set forth in the present Convention to each child within their jurisdiction without discrimination of any kind, irrespective of the child's or his or her parent's or legal guardian's race, colour, sex, language, religion, political or other opinion, national, ethnic or social origin, property, disability, birth or other status.

against "all forms of discrimination" based on the status or opinions of their parents.[34]

In other words, article 2(2) of the CRC affirms a stand alone right which protects children from suffering any discrimination on the basis of the status or opinions of their parents–including the opinions of their parents or their "abortion providers", that these children should not have the right to good prenatal care or the right to life, survival and development.

2. *The best interests of the child*

Article 3(1) of the Convention on the Rights of the Child upholds the best interests of the child as a primary consideration in all actions concerning children:

> In all actions concerning children, whether undertaken by public or private social welfare institutions, courts of law, administrative authorities or legislative bodies, the best interests of the child shall be a primary consideration.

The article refers to actions undertaken by "public or private social welfare institutions, courts of law, administrative authorities or legislative bodies". The Committee on the Rights of the Child asserts that the principle requires active measures throughout Government, parliament and the judiciary. Every legislative, administrative and judicial body or institution is required to apply the best interests principle by systematically considering how children's rights and interests are or will be affected by their decisions and actions.[35]

Thus, in the light of the Preamble's commitment to legal protection for the child before as well as after birth, the requirements relate to any proposed or existing law or policy or administrative action or court decision that tolerates arbitrary deprivation of life for unborn children or authorizes their selective abortion or encourages removal of legislative protection from children at risk of abortion.

The best interests principle requires the legislature of each State, the executive (including private institutions acting on their behalf) and the judiciary to ensure that the best interests of the child are a primary consideration in all actions concerning children.

Jurisdictions which decriminalize abortion and promote "lawful" abortion as a "health right" for mothers will have a negative impact in that they discriminate against children before birth, denying them a right to survival and development and having the intended dire outcome for these children of arbitrary deprivation of life. If such a negative impact is a reasonably foreseeable outcome of a particular change

34 UN Convention on the Rights of the Child, Article 2(2):

> States Parties shall take all appropriate measures to ensure that the child is protected against all forms of discrimination or punishment on the basis of the status, activities, expressed opinions, or beliefs of the child's parents, legal guardians, or family members.

35 UN CRC Committee: General Comment No 5 (2003), "General measures of implementation of the Convention on the Rights of the Child", para. 12.

in the law, it suggests strongly that the best interests of the child principle was not a primary consideration in the decision to enact such legislative changes.

3. *The child's inherent right to life*

> Article 6: the child's inherent right to life and States parties' obligation to ensure to the maximum extent possible the survival and development of the child.

The UN Committee on the Rights of the Child expects States to interpret 'development' in its broadest sense as a holistic concept, embracing the child's physical, mental, spiritual, moral, psychological and social development. Implementation measures, according to the Committee, should be aimed at achieving the optimal development for all children. Logically, this should be read in the light of the *Preamble's* direction to provide legal protection before as well as after birth, and also in the powerful light shed by modern embryology and fetology on our most intimate knowledge of the child's vitally complex development from the moment of fertilization to the moment of birth. States must "ensure to the maximum extent possible the survival and development" of these children before as well as after birth.

Inclusiveness fundamental to all human rights treaties

In view of the States' grave obligation to provide "appropriate legal protection before as well as after birth" and "to ensure to the maximum extent possible the survival and development of the child", decriminalization of abortion is irrational and counterproductive. Any interpretation of "appropriate legal protection" for the child at risk of abortion that leads to decriminalization of abortion is indeed "a result which is manifestly absurd or unreasonable". It is an "absurd and unreasonable" attempt to derecognize the rights of the child before birth. Decriminalization of abortion can have no validity for it is entirely out of character with the original and abiding determination by the post World War II international community to include all human beings under universal human rights protection.

The Universal Declaration of Human Rights is fundamentally an inclusive document. All subsequent human rights instruments were intended to reaffirm and expand on that inclusiveness, not to reduce it. Reverting to the old injustice of excluding a particular class of vulnerable human beings (unborn children in this case) is perverse. It is contrary to the formidable sweep of history that brought the international community to found the modern international human rights instruments which proclaimed the inclusion of "all members of the human family".

In contravention of this concept of 'inclusiveness' that characterized the human rights movement at its very deepest level, removal of human rights protection for unborn children represents an unconscionable act of exclusion. Such exclusion is irrevocably and totally incompatible with the principles and the purpose of the UN human rights instruments.

Chapter 8 CRC Legislative History and the Child Before Birth

Strong support for recognition of the rights of the unborn child

The recent UN publication *Legislative History on the Convention on the Rights of the Child* issued by the Office of the High Commissioner for Human Rights (Geneva, 11th June 2007) provides strong support for the Convention's recognition of the human rights of the unborn child and States parties' obligations to protect them.[1]

In distinct contrast, the *Legislative History* provides only feeble and disjointed support for the theory advanced in the Introduction that the Convention successfully excluded unborn children from the Convention's definition of the child in Article 1. For as conceded in the Introduction, the Convention's Preamble reaffirms what was agreed in the 1959 *Declaration on the Rights of the Child* that the States parties have a specific obligation to recognize the human rights entitlement of the unborn child:

> ...the child, by reason of his physical and mental immaturity, needs special safeguards and care, including appropriate legal protection, before as well as after birth...

Understanding this in the context of Principle 1 of the Declaration, it is clear that the degree of this immaturity is not to be allowed to diminish in any way the child's inherent humanity: human rights are equally valid for the child before birth as for the child after birth *without any discrimination whatsoever*.[2]

Preamble integral to the Convention

The *Legislative History* provides clear evidence that, although certain delegates attempted to quarantine the Preamble's human rights protection for the child before birth from the obligations set out in the articles of the Convention, the attempt was

1 Office of the High Commissioner for Human Rights (OHCHR), *Legislative History on the Convention on the Rights of the Child*, Geneva: OHCHR, 2007.

2 *UN Declaration on the Rights of the Child* (1959) Principle 1: "Every child without any exception whatsoever is entitled to these rights ..."

ill-conceived and set for failure.[3] Legal Counsel, requested by the representative of the United Kingdom at the time of negotiation and included here in the *Legislative History,* gave fair warning that such an attempt was inconsistent with the rules of interpretation as set out in the *Vienna Convention on the Law of Treaties.*

> The preamble to a treaty serves to set out the general considerations which motivate the adoption of the treaty. Therefore, it is at first sight strange that a text is sought to be included in the travaux préparatoires for the purpose of depriving a particular preambular paragraph of its usual purpose, i.e., to form part of the basis for the interpretation of the treaty.[4]

The theory that preambular paragraphs do not entail legally binding obligations on States parties to a Convention is a direct contradiction of Article 31 General rule of interpretation of the Vienna Convention on the Law of Treaties:

> 1. A treaty shall be interpreted in good faith in accordance with the ordinary meaning to be given to the terms of the treaty in their context and in the light of its object and purpose.
> 2. The context for the purpose of the interpretation of a treaty shall comprise, in addition to the text, its preamble…

In other words, the operative provisions within the Convention on the Rights of the Child (i.e., in the text) shall be interpreted in good faith in accordance with the ordinary meaning to be given to the terms of the treaty in their context (i.e., in the context of its preamble in addition to the text). Clearly, operative provisions must be read *consistently* with the preambulatory paragraphs, which set out the themes and rationale of the Convention.

Furthermore, operative provisions must be read *consistently* with commitments already established in the International Bill of Rights and in the whole accumulative body of human rights protection for the child before as well as after birth beginning with the Geneva Declaration of the Rights of the Child of 1924. This agreement to honour all previous human rights commitments is confirmed in the full text of the most relevant consecutive preambular paragraphs of the Convention on the Rights of the Child which are as follows:

> Bearing in mind that the need to extend particular care to the child has been stated in the Geneva Declaration of the Rights of the Child of 1924 and in the Declaration of the Rights

3 The validity of the attempt to exclude the child before birth from rights protection was first seriously questioned in some original research by Dr. John Fleming and Dr. Michael Hains. See Fleming, John I. and Hains, Michael G., "What Rights, if Any, Do the Unborn Have Under International Law?" *Australian Bar Review*, December 1997.

4 Response of the Legal Counsel (Carl August Fleischhauer) 9 December 1988, Annex to the 1989 report of the Working Group to the Commission on Human Rights. E/CN.4/1989/48.

> of the Child adopted by the General Assembly on 20 November 1959 and recognised in the Universal Declaration of Human Rights, in the International Covenant on Civil and Political Rights (in particular in articles 23 and 24) in the International Covenant on Economic, Social and Cultural Rights (in particular in Article 10) and in the statutes and relevant instruments of specialized agencies and international organisations concerned with the welfare of children...
> Bearing in mind that, as indicated in the Declaration of the Rights of the Child, "the child, by reason of his physical and mental immaturity, needs special safeguards and care, including appropriate legal protection, before as well as after birth...

Inclusion of well-established and documented human rights concerns for the child before birth in the Preamble casts significant doubt on the theory that the international community proceeded in Article 1 to redefine 'the child' so as to exclude the child before birth from human rights protection.

A far more coherent case exists for inclusion rather than exclusion. The child before as well as after birth is to be protected by the Convention on the Rights of the Child, when that Convention is *interpreted in good faith* [without discrimination against the child before birth] *in accordance with the ordinary meaning to be given to the terms of the treaty in their context* [both text and preamble] *and in the light of its object and purpose* [recognition of the inherent dignity and of the equal and inalienable rights of all members of the human family and protection of these human rights by the rule of law].

Long tradition of human rights protection before as well as after birth

Recognition of the child before birth was established and maintained with consistency and continuity throughout the entire body of international human rights and humanitarian foundation instruments.[5] Unbroken continuity of this concept of human rights protection for the child before as well as after birth can be traced, for it is a continuity that stretches from the *Geneva Declaration* (1924) through the *Geneva Declaration* (1948), the *Universal Declaration* (1948), the *Fourth Geneva Convention*(1949) and the *Second Protocol to the Geneva Convention* (1949), the *European Convention* (1950) and the *Declaration of the Rights of the Child*(1959) to the *International Covenant on Civil and Political Rights* (1966) and the *American Convention on Human Rights* (1969).

Even the extremely sketchy historical record as presented in this *Legislative History* does not support the initial claims in its Introduction by Adam Lopatka who had been Chairman/Rapporteur of the Working Group on the Draft Convention:

> As set out in its Article 1, the Convention on the Rights of the Child deals with the protections necessary for the child after his or her birth. Decisions as to the form and scope of legal protection of the child before birth have been left to individual States.

5 See above Chapter 1 UDHR Recognition of Child before Birth: the Historical Context and Chapter 2 UDHR Recognition of the Child before Birth: Analysis of the Texts.

These two claims, colored regrettably by a contemporary bias towards preserving liberal abortion laws now operating in many States, fail to take sufficient account of the existing precedents for providing legal protection for unborn children, precedents that were set irrevocably in the foundation documents of modern international human rights and humanitarian law.

Legislative history supports "before as well as after birth" human rights protection

Lapotka's claims also misrepresent the actual negotiations as recorded in this *Legislative History on the Convention on the Rights of the Child.* In particular:

1. The text of the *Legislative History* does not substantiate Lapatka's claim in the Introduction: "As set out in its Article 1, the Convention on the Rights of the Child deals with the protections necessary for the child after his or her birth." Most significantly, the wording proposed in Article 1 of the 1979 *Draft Convention on the Rights of the Child,* "from the moment of his birth" was, in fact, rejected.[6]
2. The representative of Italy observed (significantly without contradiction) that no State was manifestly opposed to the principles contained in the Declaration of the Rights of the Child and, therefore, according to the Vienna Convention on the Law of Treaties, the rule regarding the protection of life before birth could be considered as *jus cogens* since it formed part of the common conscience of members of the international community.[7]
3. Malta and Senegal were satisfied that it was not necessary for the words "from conception" to be included in Article 1 as it was taken as understood that the rights of the child before birth were adequately covered by inclusion of the phrase "before as well as after birth" in the Preamble. Their proposal to insert the phrase "from conception" was withdrawn "in light of the text of preambular paragraph 6 as adopted..."[8]
4. In an attempt to quarantine Article 1 from this preambular commitment to provide legal human rights protection for the child before birth, a statement was placed by a small number of delegations in the *travaux préparatoires:*

> In adopting this preambular paragraph, the Working Group does not intend to prejudice the interpretation of Article 1 or any other provision of the Convention by States Parties.[9]

6 Discussion and adoption by the Working Group (1980), paras. 30-31 from E/CN.4/L.154.

7 1989 Report of the Working Group to the Commission on Human Rights, E/CN.4/1989/48, para. 40.

8 Ibid., paras. 76 & 77.

9 Ibid., para. 43.

As already explained, this attempt was, in effect, quashed by the subsequent Legal Counsel requested by the representative of the United Kingdom and annexed to the report. As pointed out by Legal Counsel:

> The preamble to a treaty serves to set out the general considerations which motivate the adoption of the treaty. Therefore, it is at first sight strange that a text is sought to be included in the travaux préparatoires for the purpose of depriving a particular preambular paragraph of its usual purpose, i.e., to form part of the basis for the interpretation of the treaty. Also, it is not easy to assess what conclusions States may later draw, when interpreting the treaty, from the inclusion of such a text in the travaux préparatoires. Furthermore, seeking to establish the meaning of a particular provision of a treaty, through an inclusion in the travaux préparatoires may not optimally fulfil the intended purpose, because, as you know, under Article 32 of the Vienna Convention on the Law of Treaties, travaux préparatoires constitute a "supplementary means of interpretation" and hence recourse to travaux préparatoires may only be had if the relevant treaty provisions are in fact found by those interpreting the treaty to be unclear.

In other words, Legal Counsel warned that inclusion of the statement is not sufficient to ensure its "intended purpose". Its purpose was a devious one: to empty of significance the international community's re-commitment in the Preamble to the long-held understanding that "the child, by reason of his physical and mental immaturity, needs special safeguards and care, including appropriate legal protection, before as well as after birth..." The ploy, however, lacked sufficient validity to exclude the child before birth from "the interpretation of Article 1" and subsequently from the operative protective provisions of the Convention.[10]

Protecting liberal abortion laws or protecting the child before birth?

As Cynthia Price Cohen of the Child Rights International Research Institute has pointed out, abortion *per se* was not extensively discussed by the working group:

> In fact, the word "abortion" was never used in the drafting of the substantive articles of the Convention; it appears in only three paragraphs of the 1980 Working Group Report in reference to an ultimately rejected proposal to include the words "before as well as after birth" in preambular paragraph 6. Even when this proposal was reintroduced during the second reading of the convention causing heated debate, the word "abortion" itself was not part of the discussion. The focus was always on "the rights of the unborn child".[11]

---

10 Dr. John Fleming and Dr. Michael Hains first raised doubts about the validity of the ploy in their ground-breaking study: Fleming, John I and Hains, Michael G., "What Rights, If Any, Do the Unborn Have Under International Law?", Australian Bar Review, Vol. 16 (2), December 1997, pp. 181-198.

11 Cohen, Cynthia Price, "Review", The American Journal of International Law, Vol. 89 (4), October, 1995, pp. 852-855. Cohen's footnote (p.853) on this: "See UN Doc. E/CN.4/

Nevertheless, pro-abortion advocates continue to advance the fiction that States can decide for themselves to exclude human rights protection from the child before birth at risk of abortion. Disquieting considerations point to some intellectually dishonest reinterpretation of the historical records on this issue as presented in the *Legislative History*. Regrettably, this reinterpretation is being propelled, no doubt, by sustained pressure from those States who have removed most domestic legal protections for the unborn child at risk of abortion. Given that the international community in the founding documents of modern international human rights law reached a formal and virtually unanimous agreement on the need for safeguards and care including legal protection for the child before birth[12] and in view of the *Legislative History*'s own testament that a valid alternative consensus to the contrary was not reached,[13] the original consensus must remain in effect.

Having reneged on this original consensus and abandoned the fundamental principle that the unborn child at risk of abortion has a right to legal protection, abortion advocates (even within the UN) are now trying to maintain an untenable position.

Human rights advocates everywhere are being pressured by the zealously organized global politics of an extreme feminist ideology to exclude the child before birth from the legal protection promised in the universally agreed foundation human rights instruments. They are warned not to disturb the *status quo* in some UN member States where tens of thousands, even hundreds of thousands of unborn children are aborted 'legally' each year. It is prejudice not logic that induces a gullibility that allows for the pretence that abortion is the one exception where the human rights principles of indivisibility and *best interests of the child* can be discarded.

Legally and administratively, the fundamental human rights principles of indivisibility and *best interests of the child* should operate on all public decisions concerned with children at risk of abortion. The Convention on the Rights of the Child (Articles 3, 9, 18, 20, 21, 37 and 40) requires that the *best interests of the child* principle be applied to each and every proposed or existing law or policy or administrative action or court decision directly or indirectly affecting the well-being of children.[14] The indivisibility

L.1543, 1980, paras. 6, 10 & 18. The word 'abortion' does not appear anywhere else in the travaux préparatoires."

12 In the UN Declaration on the Rights of the Child, the UN General Assembly, November 20th, 1959, reaffirmed explicitly the UDHR's "recognition" of the rights of the child before birth. The concept of formal universal recognition of the child before birth as a legitimate subject of inherent and inalienable human rights including entitlement to legal protection is critical for it is the nature of inherent and inalienable human rights that they can never be de-recognized by courts of law or legislatures.

13 "Other delegations, including Norway, the Netherlands, India, China, the Union of Soviet Socialist Republics, Denmark, Australia, Sweden, the German Democratic Republic and Canada, however, opposed what in their view amounted to reopening the debate on this controversial matter which, as they indicated, had been extensively discussed at earlier sessions of the Working Group with no consensus achieved." Legislative History, p. 295, para. 36.

14 UN Committee on the Rights of the Child General Comment No 5 (2003), General measures of implementation of the Convention on the Rights of the Child, para. 10.

principle requires human rights protection of both the mother and her unborn child; and prohibits the individual state from abandoning laws that protect the unborn child on the grounds that it has a priority obligation to protect the 'the abortion choice' of the child's mother. Ironically, the *best interests of the child* principle is legally binding on individual mothers and abortionists as well as individual states.[15]

Human rights authorities condemn 'choices' that entail lethal damage to the child's health and development.[16] Abortion 'choices' as human rights violations by adults in positions of power over children in positions of dependency are logically incompatible with protection of the child before birth. When the indivisibility principle is applied, the individual State's misperceived duty to provide expectant mothers with abortion 'services' cannot be performed at the neglect of the more fundamental duty to uphold the rights of their children to "special safeguards and care including appropriate legal protection before as well as after birth". The right to life is "the supreme right" and "basic to all human rights".[17]

Ideological reinterpretation of human rights

And so the *Introduction* to this *Legislative History* is trying to do the impossible—to reconcile an expectant mother's putative "right to abortion", a relatively new but central invention of the extreme feminist ideology prevailing at the time the Convention was concluded (1989), with the original international human rights legal framework which recognized her child's right to "appropriate legal protection before as well as after birth".

There can be no intellectually honest evasion of the truth that appropriate legal protection means that legal protection for the child at risk of abortion before birth should be equally effective as the legal protection of that same child at risk of infanticide after birth. In the whole historical context of the development of modern human rights law, unequal rights to legal protection are most inappropriate. Any new ideology that advocates unequal protection for a particularly vulnerable group such as unborn children should be exposed as unacceptable, inhumane and unjust.

Ironically, some UN human rights personnel seem to have forgotten that it was precisely in order to proof us against our human susceptibility to new extreme ide-

15 UN Human Rights Committee General Comment General Comment No 31 (2004), para. 8. "It is also implicit in Article 7 that States Parties have to take positive measures to ensure that private persons or entities do not inflict...cruel, inhuman or degrading treatment... on others within their power".

16 The Inter-American Court of Human Rights concurs with the European Court of Human Rights on this: see *Inter-American Court of Human Rights advisory opinion: oc-17/2002 on children's juridical status and human rights*, paras. 74 & 137.9.

17 UN Human Rights Committee General Comment 6, paras. 1 & 3. See also Inter-American Court of Human Rights in *Jailton Neri Da Fonseca* v. Brazil, (2004): "The human right to life is a fundamental human right, the basis for the exercise of the other human rights. ...enjoyment of the right to life is essential for the exercise of all other human rights. If it is not respected, all rights lack meaning."

ologies that the modern human rights instruments, including the Convention on the Rights of the Child, were specifically proposed for universal ratification. The original purpose for the establishment of a universal human rights law was to ensure that new ideologies will conform to human rights, not human rights to new ideologies.

"The Polish contribution"

It is unfortunate that, in the *Introduction* to the *Legislative History on the Convention on the Rights of the Child*, Lopatka's eloquent summary of the terrible plight of Polish children under the Nazi regime excludes the significant acts of violence perpetrated by the Nazis against unborn Polish children. Conveniently, it seems, for Lopatka's thesis that the Convention on the Rights of the Child has no mandatory application to children before birth, he has failed to mention Nazi atrocities involving selective extermination of unborn children.

Errant Nazi morality that represented the lethal act of abortion to Polish mothers as "a simple and pleasant affair"[18] also considered it should be left up to individual states to provide or to withhold legal protection for the unborn child. The "individual" Nazi State claimed absolute authority over "decisions" to validate arbitrary deprivation of the lives of unborn children selected for abortion.

Almost immediately after the occupation of Poland, a Nazi RKFDV decree was issued:

> All measures which have the tendency to limit the births are to be tolerated or to be supported. Abortion in the remaining area [of Poland] must be declared free from punishment.[19]

Abortion of "racially substandard offspring of Eastern workers and Poles" was cleverly sanitized:

> A pregnancy interruption should go off without incidents and the Eastern worker or Pole is to be treated generously during this period in order that this may get to be known among them as a simple and pleasant affair.[20]

---

18 Letter from the SD office in Koblenz to the branch offices, 18 February 1944, *Nuremberg Military Trials, Vol IV*, p. 687. Available at: http://www.mazal.org/archive/nmt/04a/NMT04-T0687.htm.

19 Document received by Himmler on the 25th November 1939 from the Stabshauptamt des Reichskommissars fuer die Festigung des Deutschen Volkstums (Staff Main Office of the Reich Commissioner for the Strengthening of Germanism) usually referred to as the RKFDV. This excerpt is from Kamenetsky, Ihor, *Secret Nazi Plans for Eastern Europe: A Study of Lebensraum Policies*, New York: Bookman Associates, 1961, p. 171.

20 Letter from the SD office in Koblenz to the branch offices, 18 February 1944, *Nuremberg Military Trials, Vol IV*, p. 687. Available at: http://www.mazal.org/archive/nmt/04a/NMT04-T0687.htm.

Nazi eugenic programs at home and in the Occupied Territories peddled the original seductive notion of "saving the German people from a steady stream of new moral and economic burdens resulting from genetic illnesses..."[21] In Poland, Russia and the Eastern Occupied Territories, Nazi ideologues had set about "encouraging" abortion of the unwanted:

> ...the press, radio, and movies, as well as pamphlets, booklets, and lectures, must be used to instill... the idea that it is harmful to have several children. We must emphasize the expenses that children cause, the good things that people could have had with the money spent on them. We could also hint at the dangerous effect of child-bearing on a woman's health... It will even be necessary to open special institutions for abortion, and to train midwives and nurses for this purpose. The population will practice abortion all the more willingly if these institutions are competently operated. The doctors must be able to help out, there being any question of this being a breach of their professional ethics.[22]

Himmler's March 1943 decree coined the excuse (familiar these days) that "the pregnancy is being interrupted for reasons of social distress".[23]

In the pain-filled honesty of the immediate aftermath of these Nazi atrocities, the international community, through the United Nations, the Nuremberg War Crimes Tribunals and the World Medical Association Organization, issued a clear condemnation of abortion as a crime against humanity and exhibited a common revulsion against the practice.[24]

To claim that the international community, in drawing up the Convention on the Rights of the Child, excluded the child before birth from the human rights protections

21 Gerhard Wagner, "Rasse und Bevölkerungspolitik," Der Parteitag der Ehre vom 8. bis 14. September 1936. Offizieller Bericht über den Verlauf des Reichsparteitages mit sämtlichen Kongreßreden, Munich: Zentralverlag der NSDAP, 1936. Available at: http://www.calvin.edu/academic/cas/gpa/pt36rasse.htm.

22 Dr. Erich Wetzel, Director of the Nazi Central Advisory Office Memorandum: *Stellungnahme und Gedanken zum Generalplan Ost des Reichsführers SS* (Opinion and ideas Regarding the General Plan for the East of the *Reichsführer SS*) 27 April 1942. (Presented as evidence in the RuSHA/Greifelt Case). This excerpt is quoted in Poliakov, Léon, *Harvest of Hate: The Nazi Program for the Destruction of the Jews of Europe*, New York: Holocaust Library [distributed by Schocken Books], 1979, p. 274.

23 *Nuremberg Military Trials Volume V*, p. 109. Available at: http://www.mazal.org/archive/nmt/05/NMT05-T0109.htm.

24 *UN Convention on the Prevention and Punishment of the Crime of Genocide* (1948) prohibited "...Killing members of the group; Causing serious bodily or mental harm to members of the group; Imposing measures intended to prevent births within the group..." World Medical Association *Declaration of Geneva* (1948) solemnly pledged to "maintain the utmost respect for human life from the time of conception"; *Draft American Declaration of the International Rights and Duties of Man* (1945-8) affirmed "...the right to life from the moment of conception" *International Code of Medical Ethics* (1949) pronounced as a doctor's duty "the importance of preserving human life from the time of conception..."

of the Convention is to ignore the historical roots of the great mid-century human rights initiative that brought into being the International Bill of Rights and led on to the Convention. It is to intimate that, on the original commitment to protect the unborn child, the Convention broke with the Bill of Rights in order to resurrect and reinstate Nazi concepts condemned by the international community at Nuremberg: "...protection of the law was denied to the unborn children...Abortion was encouraged..."[25] Such a regression is inconceivable—certainly, it remains unsubstantiated in this Legislative History.

Child's right to pre-natal care—inconsistent with legal abortion

What the *Legislative History* does substantiate, however, is that the unborn child's right to prenatal care is an enduring concept that has been reaffirmed many times over the years, despite the obvious obstacles it presents for abortion advocacy. The record shows that the Draft Convention articulated the basic concept of a human rights duty to provide the unborn child with adequate prenatal care.[26] This principle had appeared in the 1950 Draft Declaration on the Rights of the Child and was universally acknowledged in Principle 4 of the UN Declaration on the Rights of the Child (1959):

> He shall be entitled to grow and develop in health; to this end, special care and protection shall be provided both to him and to his mother, including adequate pre-natal and post-natal care...

The *Legislative History* shows that from the very first formal discussion of the Draft Convention by the Working Group, the Austrian delegation pointed out quite prophetically:

> There is a possible inconsistency between "the child's" right to adequate prenatal care and the possibilities for legal abortion provided in some countries.[27]

Indeed, records in the *Legislative History* confirm that this "possible inconsistency" emerged in the negotiations as a "definite" inconsistency that abortion advocates were unable to resolve.

Logical consistency with human rights obligations owed to the child at risk of abortion continues to be a grave obstacle to legalized abortion— the UN Committee on the Rights of the Child (CRC Committee) recently issued *General Comment on the Rights of Children with Disabilities* which reaffirms that children before birth

25 *Nuremberg Trials Record*: "The RuSHA Case", March 1948, Volume IV, p 1077. Available at: http://www.mazal.org/archive/nmt/04a/NMT04-T1076.htm.

26 *Polish Draft Convention* (1978) Article IV: "He shall be entitled to grow and develop in health; to this end, special care and protection shall be provided both to him and to his mother, including adequate prenatal and post-natal care."

27 From document E/CN.4/1324, *Legislative History*, p. 581.

are 'children' not just 'foetuses'—they are children with rights, and specifically with a right to prenatal care.

> The Committee recommends that States parties introduce and strengthen prenatal care for children...[28]

Moreover, the Committee insists that each and every child's right is not a "favour" to be bestowed or withheld by the State but rather "a clear legal obligation".[29] In addition, the Committee has condemned selective abortion as discrimination against children and as "a serious violation of their rights, affecting their survival".[30] The Committee denounces not only selective abortion of girl children on the grounds of gender discrimination, but also goes on in the same paragraph to condemn "multiple discrimination (e.g. related to ethnic origin, social and cultural status, gender and/or disabilities)".

Contrary to the claim in the *Introduction* to the *Legislative History* that the Convention deals with the protections necessary for the child [only] "after his or her birth", these General Comments (which are the most authoritative statements that can be issued by the UN Committee on the Rights of the Child) reaffirm that the operative provisions of the Convention include the child before birth. The problem, initially flagged by Austria, of "inconsistency between 'the child's' right to adequate prenatal care and the possibilities for legal abortion provided in some countries", remains a dilemma of moral and logical incompatibility in those States where legal protection for unborn children at risk of abortion has been withdrawn or is being withheld.

Ascertaining "...the form and scope of legal protection of the child before birth"

No rational reconciliation is possible between today's mass abortion statistics and the core concepts fundamental to all human rights. The principles of indivisibility, non-discrimination and the inherent and inalienable dignity of all members of the human family are binding on all individual States.

These core principles can neither be abandoned nor made optional by leaving "decisions as to the form and scope of legal protection of the child before birth to individual States", not even in order to accommodate existing individual State's laws that allow for abortion of 'unwanted' children before birth. This discretionary open-

28 UN Committee on the Rights of the Child, General Comment No 9 (2006), para. 46.

29 UN Committee on the Rights of the Child, General Comment No 5 (2003) para. 9 "The Committee emphasizes that, in the context of the Convention, States must see their role as fulfilling clear legal obligations to each and every child. Implementation of the human rights of children must not be seen as a charitable process, bestowing favours on children."

30 UN Committee on the Rights of the Child (CRC), General Comment No 7 (2005), "Right to Non-discrimination".

In a subsequent session, the New Zealand delegate also questions the definition of the child: "Does the definition begin at conception, at birth, or at some point in between?"[38]

These two observations/questions/suggestions, both tentative in nature, are nevertheless quoted and requoted many times through the *Legislative History* until they seem to take on far more weight than they deserve. The authors of the *Legislative History* use and re-use these mild musings to bulk up their exceedingly slender evidence that the child before birth is not included under the Convention's mantle of protection for every child.

The Barbados question relating to the unborn child was rhetorical only. It had already been answered affirmatively in the Preamble to the Declaration on the Rights of the Child (1959) which specifically stated that

> ...the child, by reason of his physical and mental immaturity, needs special safeguards and care, including appropriate legal protection, before as well as after birth...

This wording was reaffirmed by its inclusion *verbatim* in the Preamble to the Convention on the Rights of the Child, as recorded in the *Legislative History.*

Yet the *Legislative History* also confirms that there was considerable effort by some delegates to devise ways to discount or evade the solemn 1959 UN General Assembly commitment to protecting the child before as well as after birth. For example,

> The view was... expressed that the Declaration of 1959, being a document of almost 30 years, is to be superseded by the present new draft and, therefore, there was no need to stick to all of its provisions.[39]

This view, unfortunately, was based on ignorance. The term "declaration" had already been officially defined by the U.N. Secretariat in 1962 as "a formal and solemn instrument, suitable for rare occasions when principles of great and lasting significance are being enunciated", and although not legally binding, a declaration "may by custom become recognized as laying down rules binding upon States." [40]

As argued in Chapter 1 above, the 1959 Declaration on the Rights of the Child reaffirms a recognition of the rights of the child before birth which was already agreed in the 1948 Universal Declaration now itself having become, over time, both legally binding and an accepted part of customary law.

The New Zealand question was more unsettling, but it could have and should have been settled definitively with just a little research into what had already been agreed in this regard at Nuremberg, in the UDHR, the ICCPR and in the Geneva Conventions. The meaning of 'the child', though not always articulated, was well understood in practical terms to apply to every child from the State's first knowledge of the child's existence. In the era in which these original human rights instruments were agreed,

38 E/CN.4/1324/Add.5.

39 *Legislative History*, p. 295, para. 36.

40 U.N. Doc. E/CN.4/L.610, 1962.

a simple pregnancy test affirmed the child's existence *in utero*. (Today's IVF technicians and researchers also can apply a simple test to affirm that a distinct new embryonic human being has been formed, that a small new genetically unique human child has come into existence and is developing *in vitro*.)

When the unborn child's right to legal protection was reaffirmed in the Nuremberg judgments ("...protection of the law was denied to the unborn children..."), there was no doubt that protection of the law should have been given from the State's first knowledge of each child's existence:

> ...every pregnancy had to be reported to the dreaded Gestapo.[41]

Subsequently, the human rights of unborn children were affirmed in the UDHR's recognition of the child before birth who "by reason of his physical and mental immaturity" is entitled to "special safeguards and care including appropriate legal protection before as well as after birth."; and also reaffirmed in Article 6 of the *ICCPR* which protects the right to life of *all members of the human family*[42] and includes the unborn child.

ICCPR consensus on "when life begins"

The ICCPR's *travaux préparatoires* stated this explicitly:

> The principal reason for providing in paragraph 4 [now Article 6(5)] of the original text that the death sentence should not be carried out on pregnant women was to save the life of an innocent unborn child.[43]

The State, in order to protect the child's inherent right to life, must prohibit and prevent the death penalty for the unborn child's mother.

> Sentence of death shall not be imposed for crimes committed by persons below eighteen years of age and shall not be carried out on pregnant women. [ICCPR Article 6(5)]

Juxtaposition in the one sentence of concern to protect the right to life (remember this is the human right being articulated in Article 6) of "persons below eighteen years of age" with the protection of "pregnant women" signifies that the child before birth is entitled to the rights of "persons below eighteen years of age". It signifies

41 *Nuremberg Military Trials, Vol IV*, p 687. Available at: http://www.mazal.org/archive/nmt/04a/NMT04-T0687.htm.

42 "...recognition of the inherent dignity and inalienable rights of all members of the human family is the foundation of freedom, justice and peace in the world" This is a core value of the International Bill of Rights. It appears in the Preamble of all three instruments and as such is a foundational premise upon which all the rights that follow are based. It is "the foundation of...justice" i.e., it must be the foundation of international human rights law.

43 A/C.3/SR.819, para. 17 & para. 33.

that the pregnant woman does indeed carry within her womb another human being, a new human person who is entitled, by reason of the child's physical and mental immaturity (an immaturity that distinguishes every person below eighteen years of age) to special protection from the death sentence. Articles prohibiting execution of pregnant women acknowledge that the child, from the State's first knowledge of that child's existence, is to be protected.

It is logically indefensible to deny a child human rights protection on the grounds that there is some perceived difficulty in making a consensual statement on "when life begins". The international community which drafted the "right to life" Article 6 of the ICCPR faced that problem and solved it. For all practical purposes, they recognized that a life has begun when a woman is pregnant, that pregnancy signifies that the first stage of life, the child's nine months of growth and development in the womb, has begun already and that there is a State responsibility "to save the life of the unborn child":

> The provisions of paragraph 4(5) of the draft article aimed at the protection of the life of the unborn child whose mother was sentenced to death; that protection should be extended to all unborn children.[44]

Not only did they recognize the unborn child as having a life to be saved but also that legal protection is to be extended to all unborn children—that is, in practical terms, from the first moment that an unborn child's existence in a new pregnancy is acknowledged and verified.

No "margin of appreciation" on the form and scope of the child's right to life

Given these ICCPR right to life obligations, Lapotaka's misreading of the *Legislative History*—"Decisions as to the form and scope of legal protection of the child before birth have been left to individual States"—is incompatible with the human rights principles of inalienability and non-derogability. Right from the beginning of the whole modern international human rights project, all UN members understood clearly that the new human rights instruments would require that domestic laws be made consistent with international human rights law and not *vice versa*.

Recognition of the child before birth as a person entitled to legal protection is enshrined in the 1948 Universal Declaration of Human Rights. (The UN General Assembly, November 20th, 1959, reaffirmed explicitly the UDHR's "recognition" of the rights of the child before birth.) Given this as well as the ICCPR obligations, it stands to reason that individual States are not free to decriminalize abortion, to reduce to nothing "the form and scope of legal protection of the child before birth". They are not free to remove all substantial legal protection of the child's inalienable rights. The

44 Bossuyt, Marc J., *Guide to the "Travaux Préparatoires" of the International Convenant on Civil and Political Rights*, Dordrecht, Martinus Nijhoff Publishers, 1987, A/C.3/SR.810 para. 2; A/C.3/SR.811 para. 9; A/C 3/SR.812 para. 7; A/C.3/SR.813 para. 36; A/C 3/SR 815 para. 28.

concept of formal universal recognition of the child before birth as a legitimate subject of inherent and inalienable human rights including entitlement to legal protection is critical for it is the nature of inherent and inalienable human rights that they can never be de-recognized by the courts of law or legislatures of individual states.

Failure by individual states to protect children at risk of abortion violates a specific human right from which domestic laws are not permitted to derogate. The right to life in international human rights covenant law is a non-derogable right.[45] It is the universal nature of non-derogable human rights that individual States do not have a wide discretionary power to legislate against these rights for any particular group selected on discriminatory grounds from "all members of the human family". When it comes to withholding the right to life from children *in utero*, the 'margin of appreciation' being claimed by certain European Union states (in contravention of the International Covenant on Civil and Political Rights to which all are a party) is illusory, a semantic legerdemain. Charles Yourow, writing on the 'margin of appreciation', warns that "the essence of a right" must never be encumbered.[46] Yet this 'margin of appreciation' doctrine has generally served in European Court of Human Rights jurisprudence to compromise the universality of human rights by favoring reversion to moral relativism as a basis for enactment of human rights law in individual States. The 'margin of appreciation' doctrine has been used in recent years precisely to erode the right to life, to provide greater discretionary power for some European states with liberal abortion laws to maintain those laws with impunity.[47]

It is an absurdity to claim thus that the right to life as articulated in Article 2 of the *European Convention on Human Rights* or in Article 6 of the *Convention on the Rights of the Child* is substantially less than and different from the right to life in the ICCPR and the UDHR.[48] While it is true that under international human rights law, each sovereign state's legislature remains the primary defender of the human rights of all members of the human family within their jurisdiction, individual states must conform to universally recognized rights to which they have already committed. As explained by Nobel laureate René Cassin, one of the principal authors of the Bill of

45 *ICCPR* Article 4, paras. 2 & 6.

46 Yourow, Howard Charles, *The Margin of Appreciation Doctrine in the Dynamics of the European Court of Human Rights Jurisprudence*, London: Martinus Nijhoff Publishers, 1996.

47 In *Tysiac v Poland* (March, 2007), for example, the European Court of Human Rights (ECHR) reaffirmed that the margin of appreciation doctrine grants States wide discretion in regulating abortion.

48 "...the right to life enunciated in the first paragraph of Article 6 of the International Covenant on Civil and Political Rights is the supreme right from which no derogation is permitted even in time of public emergency. The same right to life is enshrined in Article 3 of the Universal Declaration of Human Rights adopted by the General Assembly of the United Nations on 10 December 1948. It is basic to all human rights." UN Human Rights Committee, General Comment No 14 (Article 6) para. 1.

Rights, "...the states consent to exercise their sovereignty under the authority of international law."[49]

Individual states which have ratified the *ICCPR* have committed to providing protective laws for the child before as well as after birth. Individual states must, then, at all times take positive steps to effectively protect the right to life, a legal duty of the State that is equally applicable to the child before birth as to the child after birth.[50] The right to life, as protected by international human rights law, means, *inter alia*, that States have a strict legal duty that is non-derogable, a duty at all times to prevent, investigate, prosecute, punish and redress violations of the right to life wherever such violations occur, both in private and in public, and even in public emergencies threatening the life of the nation (Article 4(2) ICCPR).

That the right to life is non-derogable means also that at no time are States permitted to engage in or condone the arbitrary or extrajudicial taking of a human life, including the life of a child before birth. Intentional deprivation of the life of an unborn child contravenes ICCPR Article 6(5)[51] and fails the common law tests of absolute "necessity" and strict "proportionality".[52]

Historical context invalidates Lopatka's claims

Legal protection for unborn children is one of the founding principles of modern international human rights law. As one of the Nuremberg judgments, this principle was mandated to be codified in the International Bill of Rights.[53]

---

49 Cassin, René, Nobel Lecture, December 11, 1968. Available at: http://nobelprize.org/nobel_prizes/peace/laureates/1968/cassin-lecture.html.

50 The child before birth having been recognized by the Universal Declaration of Human Rights as being included in "*all the members of the human family*" cannot be excluded by any subsequent human rights instrument or committee or judiciary without undermining the very foundation of modern international human rights law. Should international society even once permit the 'de-recognition' of the human rights of even one group of human beings, then the human rights of no group of human beings are secure. (This lesson from the Nazi experience of dehumanization of one group after another was still very vivid at the time of writing the *Universal Declaration*.)

51 *The ICCPR's* travaux préparatoires acknowledges that the unborn child's right to life, from the State's first knowledge of that child's existence, is to be protected: "The principal reason for providing in paragraph 4 [now Article 6(5)] of the original text that the death sentence should not be carried out on pregnant women was to save the life of an unborn child."

52 CCPR General Comment No. 29 (72), para.4; also European Court of Human Rights, Case of *McCann and Others v. the United Kingdom*, Series A, No. 324, p. 46, paras. 148 & 149.

53 UN Resolution 95(1): Affirmation of the Principles of International Law recognized by the Charter of the Nuremberg Tribunal. Resolution 95 (1) of the United Nations General Assembly, 11 December 1946. The UN committee on the codification of international law was directed to establish a general codification of "the principles recognized in the Char-

The original international human rights instruments served as both foundation and inspiration for the Convention on the Rights of the Child. Indeed, the preamble and text of the Convention on the Rights of the Child have pledged and renewed their commitment to all the fundamental human rights principles contained in the original UN declarations and covenants, principles which include the child's right to legal protection before as well as after birth.

This powerful historical context makes nonsense of Lopatka's claim that "decisions as to the form and scope of legal protection of the child before birth have been left to individual States". Moreover, the implication in Lopatka's introduction that Dr. Janusz Korczak's "new concept" of protection for children would have endorsed exclusion of the unborn is an insult to his memory. His central admonition to mothers was to respect and love the child as having equal rights with adults. He would never have conceded that mothers had ownership and disposal rights over their unborn children: "Love the child... Renounce the deceptive longing for perfect children...Know yourself so that you do not take advantage of a defenceless child... We must end despotism... The child, being small, has little market value... Children are not people of tomorrow; they are people today"; and two posters displayed in the Warsaw ghetto and recorded by "the Old Doctor" in his *Diary*, read:

> OUR CHILDREN, OUR CHILDREN MUST LIVE.
> A CHILD IS THE HOLIEST OF ALL BEINGS.[54]

---

ter of the Nuremberg Tribunal and in the judgment of the Tribunal". These were among the foundation stones of modern international human rights law.

54 Korczak, Janusz, *Ghetto Diary*, New York: Holocaust Library, 1978.

Chapter 9 Selective Abortion on Grounds of Disability

Reclaiming the human rights of children with disabilities at risk of abortion

To understand the human rights protection accorded by the *Convention on the Rights of Persons with Disabilities* (2007) to children at risk of abortion because of disabilities, it must be read in conjunction with and as an extension of the object and purpose of the *Universal Declaration of Human Rights* (UDHR), the *Convention on the Rights of the Child* (CRC) and other relevant UN conventions. In spirit and substance, the great human rights instruments of modern international human rights law must be consistent with each other and so manifest a clear and logical coherence. Genuine progress in international human rights law must result in a deepening and widening of human rights protections, and never in a retraction of rights already recognized.

The Preamble to the Convention on the Rights of Persons with Disabilities recognizes this need to mesh new obligations with older obligations of an earlier convention:

> Recognizing that children with disabilities should have full enjoyment of all human rights and fundamental freedoms on an equal basis with other children, and recalling obligations to that end undertaken by States Parties to the Convention on the Rights of the Child...

One of the obligations to that end undertaken by States Parties to the Convention on the Rights of the Child is recognition of the special needs of the child by reason of his physical and mental immaturity, and specific commitment to provide special safeguards and care, including appropriate legal protection before as well as after birth.[1]

This Preambular commitment has immense significance for children who are at risk of abortion because of disabilities in that the State must provide legal protection for these children *on an equal basis with other children*—that is, on an equal basis with children after birth and also on an equal basis with children who do not have disabilities.

---

1 For historical evidence that the Convention on the Rights of the Child recognized the child before birth as entitled to human rights protection, see above Chapter 8: Rights of the child before birth—*Legislative History of the Convention on the Rights of the Child.*

Preambles—negligible or significant?

Some governments have tried to wriggle out of this commitment by advancing the theory that preambular paragraphs do not entail legally binding obligations on States Parties to a Convention. This theory, however, is not credible as it is a direct contradiction of Article 31 General rule of interpretation of the *Vienna Convention on the Law of Treaties*.[2]

The operative provisions within the convention (i.e., in the text) shall be interpreted in good faith in accordance with the ordinary meaning to be given to the terms of the treaty in their context (i.e., in the context of its preamble in addition to the text). Operative provisions must be read consistently with the preambulatory paragraphs, which set out the themes and rationale of the convention.

Ensuring "...appropriate legal protection before as well as after birth"

The second clause of the Preamble to the Convention on the Rights of Persons with Disabilities recognizes that the United Nations, in the Universal Declaration of Human Rights and in the International Covenants on Human Rights, has proclaimed and agreed that everyone is entitled to all the rights and freedoms set forth therein, without distinction of any kind. The Universal Declaration has recognized children before birth as members of the human family, each child entitled to be provided by the State with *special safeguards and care...before as well as after birth.*[3]

The *International Covenant on Civil and Political Rights* (ICCPR) also recognizes the unborn child as a member of the human family. The State, in order to protect the child's inherent right to life, must prohibit and prevent the death penalty for the unborn child's mother.

---

2 "1. A treaty shall be interpreted in good faith in accordance with the ordinary meaning to be given to the terms of the treaty in their context and in the light of its object and purpose. 2. The context for the purpose of the interpretation of a treaty shall comprise, in addition to the text ... its preamble..."

3 A general misconception identifies the "special safeguards...before as well as after birth" language as concepts newly-coined in the Preamble to the *Declaration on the Rights of the Child* (1959). A more careful reading of this Preamble reveals that on November 20th, 1959, the UN General Assembly agreed in this Preamble that the Universal Declaration of Human Rights (1948) *had already* "recognized" the human rights of the child before birth. Significantly, this General Assembly of November 1959, among whom were a considerable number of the original drafters of the Universal Declaration of 1948, provided incontrovertible evidence that the Universal Declaration was understood to have recognized the child before birth as a juridical personality entitled to legal protection. Formal universal recognition of the child before birth as a legitimate subject of inherent and inalienable human rights including entitlement to legal protection is critical for it is the nature of inherent and inalienable human rights that they can never be de-recognized by courts of law or legislatures.

> Sentence of death shall not be imposed for crimes committed by persons below eighteen years of age and shall not be carried out on pregnant women. [ICCPR Article 6(5)]

This article was formulated precisely "in order to save the life of an innocent unborn child" when the child's life is at risk.[4]

Selective abortion: discrimination against children—"a serious violation of rights"

In 2005, the UN Committee on the Rights of the Child (CRC Committee) signalled a reaffirmation of the Universal Declaration's recognition of the need to provide legal protection for all children before as well as after birth. In its General Comment No 7, entitled *Right to Non-discrimination*, the CRC condemns selective abortion as discrimination against children and as a serious violation of their rights, affecting their survival.

The Committee denounces not only selective abortion of girl children on the grounds of sex discrimination, but also goes on in the same paragraph to condemn "multiple discrimination (e.g., related to ethnic origin, social and cultural status, gender and/or disabilities)".[5]

The Convention on the Rights of Persons with Disabilities takes up this "multiple discrimination" against girls, and requires that in this regard States Parties take measures to ensure for them the full and equal enjoyment of all human rights.[6] This means, *inter alia*, that where a prenatal selection process for abortion is based on discriminatory grounds such as sex and/or disabilities, States must ensure legal protection of the human rights of those children at risk.

Recalling that "... protection of the law was denied to the unborn children..." (Nuremberg)

Indeed, the new Convention on the Rights of Persons with Disabilities has clear application to children at risk of abortion on the grounds of disability. The very first clause of the Preamble recognizes the inherent dignity and worth and the equal and inalienable rights of "all members of the human family". Right from the beginning

4 The *travaux préparatoires* (explanatory notes written at the time the Covenant was negotiated) stated this explicitly: "The principal reason for providing in paragraph 4 [now Article 6(5)] of the original text that the death sentence should not be carried out on pregnant women was to save the life of an innocent unborn child." Marc J. Bossuyt, *Guide to the 'Travaux Préparatoires' of the International Convenant on Civil and Political Rights*, Dordrecht: Martinus Nijhoff Publishers, 1987, A/C.3/SR.810 para 2; A/C.3/SR.811 para 9; A/C 3/SR.812 para 7; A/C.3/SR.813 para 36; A/C 3/SR 815 para. 28.

5 UN Committee on the Rights of the Child (CRC) Comment No 7 (2005), Right to Non-discrimination, para. 11.

6 *Convention on the Rights of Persons with Disabilities* (2007) Article 6 (1).

of modern international human rights law, children before birth were recognized as members of the human family.

The Nuremberg judgments recognized the entitlement of unborn children to legal protection. Condemnation of the crime of "compelling and encouraging abortion"[7], in the judgment of the Nuremberg Tribunal, was thus one of the principles incorporated into the International Bill of Rights under *UN Resolution 95*.[8] Abortion, as "a crime against humanity", was not simply limited to the practice of forced abortions but extended to voluntary abortions as well.[9] Prosecutor James McHaney who drew up the indictment and conducted the *RuSHA/Greifelt* trial sought and attained recognition of the unborn as children entitled to legal protection and it is now part of the Nuremberg record of the trial testimony that: "...protection of the law was denied to the unborn children".[10]

Decriminalization of abortion—condemned at Nuremberg

Yet in many countries around the world today, there is a concerted scheme to remove legal protection from children at risk of abortion because they have detectable disabilities. A global campaign for decriminalization of these and all other abortions is being waged by a number of UN and non-government organizations such as the UN CEDAW Committee [which monitors the *Convention for the Elimination of All Forms of Discrimination Against Women* (CEDAW)] and the New York-based Cen-

7 Though the Nazis had decriminalized abortion in Poland and the Eastern Territories, two SS officers, Richard Hildebrandt and Otto Hofmann, were sentenced to 25 years imprisonment for "compelling and encouraging abortion". See *Nuremberg Trials Record*: "The RuSHA Case", Opinion and Judgment, "War Crimes and Crimes Against Humanity", Vol. V, pp. 152 to 154) and pp. 160-2. Available at: http://www.mazal.org/archive/nmt/05/NMT05-T0152.htm.

8 *Affirmation of the Principles of International Law recognized by the Charter of the Nuremberg Tribunal*, Resolution 95 (1) of the United Nations General Assembly, 11 December 1946. The UN committee on the codification of international law was directed to establish a general codification of "the principles recognized in the Charter of the Nuremberg Tribunal and in the judgment of the Tribunal". These became the foundation of modern international human rights law.

9 John Hunt:
- "Out of Respect For Life: Nazi Abortion Policy in the Eastern Occupied Territories", *Journal of Genocide Research* Vol. 1 (3), 1997, pp. 379-385.
- "Abortion and The Nuremberg Prosecutors: A Deeper Analysis", *Life and Learning*, Vol. VII, Proceedings of the Seventh University Faculty for Life Conference, June, 1997.
- "Perfecting Humankind: A Comparison of Progressive and Nazi Views on Eugenics, Sterilization and Abortion", *Life and Learning*, Vol. VIII, Proceedings of the Eighth University Faculty for Life Conference, June, 1998.
- "The Abortion and Eugenics Policies of Nazi Germany", *Association for Interdisciplinary Research in Values and Social Change*, Vol. 16, (1), 2001.

10 *Nuremberg Trials Record:* RuSHA/Greifelt Case, March 1948, Volume IV, p. 1077. Available at: http://www.mazal.org/archive/nmt/04a/NMT04-T1076.htm.

ter for Reproductive Rights. This campaign for decriminalization of abortion contravenes a founding principle of international human rights law—that children are entitled to legal protection before as well as after birth.

At Nuremberg, Nazi directives to decriminalize abortion were furnished as evidence for the count of crimes against humanity:

> Abortion must not be punishable in the remaining territory... Institutes and persons who make a business of performing abortions should not be prosecuted by the police.[11]

In Nazi occupied Poland, decriminalized abortion was the order of the day. Abortion was removed from prosecution in Polish courts:

> Abortions on Polish women in the General Government were also encouraged by the withdrawal of abortion case from the jurisdiction of the Polish courts. The defendants Greifelt, Creutz, Meyer-Hetling, Schwarzenberger, Hofmann, Hildebrandt, Schwalm, Huebner, Lorenz, and Brueckner are charged with special responsibility for and participation in these crimes.[12]

The significant point to be made here is that even though the Nazi authorities had removed abortion from prosecution under Polish domestic law, abortion was still judged and condemned as "a crime against humanity", a category of crime that cannot be excused by altering domestic law to condone it:

> Crimes against humanity: namely, murder, extermination..., and other inhumane acts committed against any civilian population, before or during the war... whether or not in violation of the domestic law of the country where perpetrated.[13]

Professor Hersch Lauterpacht, international law consultant to the Nuremberg judges and member of the International Law Commission entrusted with the first *Draft code of offences against the peace and security of mankind* was very clear about the role of international law to intervene where States either legalized or failed to punish inhuman acts that violated human rights:

> ... crimes in violation of international law could be distinguished from crimes in municipal law by means of the following test: all inhuman acts committed by the organs of the State, or other individuals employed by the State to commit those acts, were international

11 Trial of Ulrich Greifelt and Others Indictment [Tr. pp. 1-18, 7/1/1947], p. 10. Available at: http://www.mazal.org/archive/nmt/05/NMT05-T0111.htm.

12 Ibid., para. 13.

13 Agreement for the Prosecution and Punishment of the Major War Criminals of the European Axis, and Charter of the International Military Tribunal: London, 8 August 1945. Charter - II : Jurisdiction and general principles Article 6(c).

> offences if ...*authorized by the law of the State or if left unpunished by it.* In those cases, the sanctity of human rights prevailed over the sovereignty of the State.[14] [Italics added]

Clearly, the State can have no mandate to authorize by law or to leave unpunished the extermination through medicalized abortion of large groups of children with disabilities such as Down Syndrome and Spina Bifida. Currently, in many parts of the world, about 90% of children detected through prenatal testing to have one of these disabilities are aborted[15] and public concern is now finding expression in mainstream media.[16] The sanctity of the human rights of children at risk of abortion because of their disabilities is meant to prevail over the sovereignty of the State. Therefore, the State must restore legal protection for these children at risk and must prosecute those who perform the ultimate inhuman act, the extermination of these children.

Lauterpacht understood the vital importance of establishing under international law human rights protection against "inhuman acts" (specifically including "extermination") which are "committed by the authorities of a State or by private individuals against groups of the civilian population":

> By proclaiming that certain fundamental human rights transcended internal legislation, the Commission would be continuing the work commenced at Nurnberg and would be taking a great step forward in the progress of international law.[17]

To this day, irrespective of internal legislation, it remains a grave human rights violation to "encourage abortions" i.e., to decriminalize, to fail to punish, and so to endorse lethal discrimination against children on the grounds of ethnic origin, social and cultural status, gender and/or disabilities. Decriminalization of these abortions in domestic law is spurious, for domestic law has no authority to legitimize grave human rights violations against these children.

---

14 Hersch Lauterpacht, *Yearbook of the International Law Commission*, Vol. 12, 69th meeting, 16 July 1954, A/CN.4/SR.269. *Draft code of offences against the peace and security of mankind (Part I)*, paras. 38-40.

15 Mansfield C, Hopfer S, Marteau T.M.:"Termination rates after prenatal diagnosis of Down syndrome, spina bifida, anencephaly, and Turner and Klinefelter syndromes: a systematic literature review. European Concerted Action: DADA (Decision-making After the Diagnosis of a fetal Abnormality)", *Prenatal Diagnosis*, Vol. 19(9), 1999 September, pp. 808-12.

16 See, for example, Amy Harmon: "Prenatal Test Put Down syndrome in Hard Focus", *New York Times*, May 9, 2007; also Brian Skotko: "A Brother's Survey Touches a Nerve In Abortion Fight", *Wall Street Journal*, October 3, 2005.

17 Hersch Lauterpacht: *Yearbook of the International Law Commission*, Vol. 12, *op. cit.*, para. 40.

Systematic abortion—a crime against humanity

Indeed, when the scale (around 90%) of the systematic abortion of children identified as having disabilities such as Down Syndrome and Spina Bifida is examined, irrespective of its purported lawfulness under domestic laws, it may well be condemned as a crime against humanity under customary international law.[18]

In fact, Nehemiah Robinson, prominent international legal scholar, writing in 1960 of the *Convention on the Prevention and Punishment of the Crime of Genocide* (1948), identified the difference between crimes against humanity and "ordinary" violations of the criminal code as existing "primarily in the recognition of the necessity of international protection for power-less minority groups" where such protection is not provided by domestic law.[19]

Indeed, Herbert V. Evatt, Prime Minister of Australia at the time the Genocide Convention was finalized by the General Assembly of the United Nations in December, 1948, hailed the Convention as an "epoch-making event in the development of international law." Through the Convention, he said, "we are establishing individual safeguards for the very existence of such human groups" (i.e., the groups to be protected) and "in this field relating to the sacred right of existence of human groups, we are proclaiming today the supremacy of international law once and for all."[20]

At Nuremberg, Prosecutor McHaney condemned abortion as "an act of extermination".[21] He demonstrated conclusively that the Nazi abortion program involved large-scale systematic extermination of children deemed "inferior" or "undesirable" and was thus a crime against humanity. McHaney's understanding of the criminal nature of this abortion program has been strengthened by more recent international court definitions of what constitutes a crime against humanity:

> Crimes against humanity must be widespread or demonstrate a systematic character. (*Vukover Hospital* decision, April 3, 1996, para. 30); and
> The concept of "widespread" may be defined as massive, frequent, large-scale action carried out collectively with considerable seriousness and directed against a multiplicity of victims. the concept of "systematic" may be defined as thoroughly organized and fol-

18 "It is by now a settled rule of customary international law that the crimes against humanity do not require a connection to international armed conflict. Indeed...customary international law may not require a connection between crimes against humanity and any conflict at all." *Prosecutor v. Tadi*, October 2, 1995 para. 141.

19 Robinson, Nehemiah, *The Genocide Convention: A Commentary*, New York: Institute of Jewish Affairs, 1960, pp. 33-4.

20 Ibid., p. 43.

21 See Hunt, John, "The Abortion and Eugenics Policies of Nazi Germany", *Association for Interdisciplinary Research in Values and Social Change*, Vol. 16, (1), 2001. Hunt cites *Records of the United States Nuremberg War Crimes Trials, United States of America v. Ulrich Greifelt, et al.* (Case VIII), October 10, 1947-March 10, 1948, (Trial Vols. 12 and 13), pp. 13-14.

> lowing a regular pattern on the basis of a common policy involving substantial public or private resources." (*Prosecutor v Akeyesu*, September 2, 1998, pp. 579-80.)

Disturbingly, in some countries such as Australia right now, open advocacy for systematic abortion of children with disabilities is being published in mainstream medical journals such as the *Medical Journal of Australia.*

One recent research paper, in evaluating a screening program for Down Syndrome, manifested very clearly indeed just how abortion programs targeted at a specific group can begin to constitute widespread crimes against humanity and demonstrate a systematic character.[22] The description therein of "a coordinated, population-based screening program" for identifying children with Down Syndrome and having the intended result of aborting the lives of some 90% of these children is scholarly but disturbing. This regional program, replicated in many other regions across Australia, does indeed constitute *massive, frequent, large-scale action carried out collectively with considerable seriousness and directed against a multiplicity of victims.* In addition, such abortion programs are systematic in that they are *thoroughly organized and following a regular pattern on the basis of a common policy involving substantial public or private resources.* In Australia, prenatal testing and most abortions of children with Down Syndrome are paid for by a government subsidized medical insurance scheme that is thoroughly organized and follows a regular pattern on the basis of an approved government policy.

Such a programmed decimation of children with Down Syndrome is prohibited under the Genocide Convention which designates the crime of genocide to include specifically the act of "imposing measures intended to prevent births within the group" with the intent to destroy it, in whole or in part.[23]

Convention reaffirms that "person" means "every human being"

Irrespective, however, of whether abortion is perpetrated on a small or a large scale, it is good that governments are reminded in the Preamble of the new Convention on the Rights of Persons with Disabilities that

> ...discrimination against any person on the basis of disability is a violation of the inherent dignity and worth of the human person...

---

22 Coory, Michael D., Roselli, Timothy, and Carroll, Heidi J.: "Antenatal care implications of population-based trends in Down syndrome birth rates by rurality and antenatal care provider, Queensland, 1990-2004", *Medical Journal of Australia*, Vol. 186 (5), 2007, pp. 230-234.

23 For some original research on the Genocide Convention aspects of targeted abortion programs see: Fleming, John I and Hains, Michael G.: What Rights, If Any, Do the Unborn Have Under International Law? *Australian Bar Review*, December 1997, and Hunt, John: "Abortion and Nazism: Is there really a connection?" *Life and Learning*, Vol. VI, 1996, pp. 323-334.

Routine selection of children for abortion on the basis of their disabilities remains a violation of their inherent dignity and worth.

Yet there are some pro-abortion advocates who demand that the human rights of children at risk of abortion because of disabilities be dismissed on the grounds that they are not "persons".

However, in the Right to life Article 10 of the Convention on the Rights of Persons with Disabilities, States Parties reaffirm that every human being has the inherent right to life and shall take all necessary measures to ensure its effective enjoyment by persons with disabilities on an equal basis with others.

The wording of this article has immense significance for the right to life of children before birth for it reaffirms that the right to life belongs to "every human being". It removes any vestige of an excuse for discrimination based on the spurious grounds that children at risk of abortion are not "persons".

Regrettably, there is quite a large and still growing academic literature that has sought perversely to re-define 'persons' in such a way as to reject the unborn child. The term 'persons' now has a formidable amount of philosophical baggage, much of which is at present unhelpful to genuine human rights advocacy. The *travaux préparatoires* for the Convention on the Rights of the Child records that some opposition to reaffirming the phrase 'before as well as after birth' was on the basis that "an unborn child was not literally a person". This theory, however, was soundly rejected.[24]

Nevertheless, abortion advocacy continues to peddle this line of attack; and 'persons' has become an easily manipulated philosophical concept employed to dehumanize children before birth. The term 'every human being', however, has retained a more objective biological truth that includes the unborn child at both the embryonic and fetal stages as a member of the human family. A smaller human being, it is true, but each unborn child is, nevertheless, a human being already identifiable, irrevocably related genetically and biologically to a human father and a human mother, and to the whole human race.

It is good, then, that the Convention on the Rights of Persons with Disabilities by using the terms 'every human being' and 'persons' in the one *Right to Life* clause reaffirms the consensus definition in the *American Convention on Human Rights* (1969) that 'person' means every human being. (Article 1.2)

Human rights not to be subjected to vexatious tests of "personhood"

This great metaphysical truth that 'person' means every human being was recognized by the framers of the American Convention who were determined to confront the historical injustices in their countries where once a corrupted rule of law denied personhood to certain groups of human beings such as native Indians or African slaves.

The original framers of these human rights instruments, coming out of the terrible human rights denials of the Nazi regime, recognized the great danger that 'persons'

24 *1989 report of the Working Group to the Commission on Human Rights*, E/CN.4/1989/48, paras. 25 to 74.

might be interpreted by future national legislatures as excluding some human beings. And they were right. For today there are people in positions of power and authority who question the human rights of the human being at the embryonic stage, the unborn child at any stage, the anencephalic child, the child in persistent vegetative state, the elderly with dementia, people in a comatose condition—anyone with impaired consciousness or personality.

But human rights belong to every human being simply because they are human, and 'being born' cannot be used as an exclusionary criterion to deny any child with Down Syndrome or some other disability the human right to be born equal in dignity and rights. It is not the act of 'being born' that confers human rights, it is being human.[25]

Indeed, human embryology can now provide incontrovertible evidence of the humanity of the newly conceived child and confirm that the life of a new human being commences at a scientifically well defined "moment of conception".[26]

It is important to recognize the inclusive definition of 'person' adopted in all the major foundational human rights instruments. International law clearly affirms that personhood belongs to every human being: Everyone shall have the right to recognition everywhere as a person before the law. (ICPPR Article 16). This crucial human right was formally recognized by the international community after the horrors of World War II and Hitler's persecution of Jewish and other "non-persons".

"Children" with rights to "prenatal care"—not just "foetuses"

In the Convention on the Rights of the Child, the promise in the Preamble to provide "special safeguards and care" for all children "before as well as after birth" is given a specific application in Article 23(2):

> States Parties recognize the right of the disabled child to special care...

The most authoritative statements on human rights obligations under the Convention on the Rights of the Child are the formal General Comments issued by the CRC Committee. The Committee's recent *General Comment on the Rights of Children with Disabilities* reaffirms that children before birth are "children" not just "foetuses"—they are children with rights, and specifically with a right to prenatal care.

25 See Malik, Charles, "The International Bill of Rights", *United Nations Bulletin*, July, 1948. (Malik was rapporteur for the first Human Rights Commission which drafted the *Universal Declaration*.

26 Condic, Maureen L., "When does life begin? A scientific Perspective", The Winchester Institution for Ethics and the Human Person, White Paper, Volume 1, No. 1, 2008. Available at: http://www.westchesterinstitute.net/index.php?option=com_content&view=article&id=351:white-paper&catid=64:white-papers&Itemid=113.

> The Committee recommends that States parties introduce and strengthen prenatal care for children...[27]

The Convention on the Rights of Persons with Disabilities, taking up this initiative for "early intervention" in prenatal care for children with disabilities, requires State commitment to:

> Provide those health services needed by persons with disabilities specifically because of their disabilities, including early identification and intervention as appropriate, and services designed to minimize and prevent further disabilities, including among children...Article 25(b)

Regarding children with Down Syndrome, for example, when the right to prenatal care for these children is implemented, outcomes are good. Newsweek columnist, George Will, who has a son with Down Syndrome, wrote in January 2007:

> Just 25 years ago, the life expectancy of Down Syndrome people was 25. Today, because of better health care, better mental stimulation in schools and homes, and better community acceptance, their life expectancy is 56.[28]

The CRC Committee provides no authorization for following "early detection of disabilities" with selective abortion. Early interventions enumerated by the CRC Committee are all benign and enabling interventions directed towards "attainment of the highest possible standard of health" for that particular child.[29] Health care programs that target children with disabilities for "termination" are incompatible with the human rights principle that "quality health care is an inherent right for all children".[30]

---

27 CRC General Comment No 9, para. 46.

28 George Will, "Golly, What Did Jon Do? — The Attack on Kids with Down Syndrome", *Newsweek*, Jan. 29, 2007.

29 "Attainment of the highest possible standard of health" as well as access and affordability of quality health care is an inherent right for all children. Children with disabilities are often left out because of several challenges, including discrimination, inaccessibility because of the lack of information and/or financial resources, transportation, geographic distribution and physical access to health care facilities. Another factor is the absence of targeted health care programmes that address the specific needs for children with disabilities. Health policies should be comprehensive and must address early detection of disabilities, early intervention, including psychological as well as physical treatment, rehabilitation including physical aids, for example limb prosthesis, mobility devices, hearing aids, and visual aids." CRC General Comment No 9, para. 44.

30 Ibid.

No abortion rights in Convention on the Rights of Persons with Disabilities

Article 25 of the Convention on the Rights of Persons with Disabilities also affirms "the right to the enjoyment of the highest attainable standard of health without discrimination on the basis of disability". In the *travaux préparatoires* and in numerous subsequent statements of interpretation, it was agreed with a broad consensus that the reference in article 25(a) to provision of sexual and reproductive health programs does not create any abortions rights, and cannot be interpreted to constitute support, endorsement, or promotion of abortion and does not create and would not constitute recognition of any new international human rights law obligations to provide abortion.[31] As the United States delegation pointed out:

> ... the phrase "reproductive health" in Article 25(a) of the draft Convention does not include abortion, and its use in that Article does not create any abortion rights, and cannot be interpreted to constitute support, endorsement, or promotion of abortion. We stated this understanding at the time of adoption of the Convention in the Ad Hoc Committee, *and note that no other delegation suggested a different understanding of this term*."[32] [Italicisation added]

However, even with this understanding, the Holy See opposed the inclusion of such a phrase in this article:

> ...in some countries reproductive health services include abortion, thus denying the inherent right to life of every human being, affirmed by article 10 of the Convention. It is surely tragic that, wherever fetal defect is a precondition for offering or employing abortion, the same Convention created to protect persons with disabilities from all discrimination in the exercise of their rights, may be used to deny the very basic right to life of disabled unborn persons.[33]

Indeed, any interpretation that would throw up such a blatant internal inconsistency between Article 10 and Article 25 of the Convention could not be acceptable. The child with disabilities is entitled to the same right to life and the same right to the enjoyment of the highest attainable standard of health, including prenatal care, as the child without disabilities.

In particular, health professionals are required:

31 The United States, the Marshall Islands, Peru, Honduras, Uganda, Egypt, Iran, Nicaragua, Libya, Costa Rica, the Philippines, Canada, Syria, El Salvador and the Holy See all made interventions to this end.

32 United States Statement of Interpretation, Plenary Session of the UN General Assembly, December 13, 2006.

33 Address delivered by Archbishop Celestino Migliore, the Holy See's permanent observer to the United Nations, to the General Assembly Plenary Session, 13th December, 2006.

> to provide care of the same quality to persons with disabilities as to others, including...inter alia, raising awareness of the human rights, dignity, autonomy and needs of persons with disabilities through training and the promulgation of ethical standards for public and private health care; Article 25(d)

A State Party's human rights obligation to provide prenatal care *of the same quality* for children with disabilities is being breached when the State permits "invasive diagnostic testing" that leads in 90% of "positive diagnostic tests" to selective abortion. These children are denied their *right to life, survival and development to the maximum extent possible.*[34]

As an intended outcome, selective abortion *per se* is seriously incompatible with prenatal care *of the same quality* for children with disabilities as for children without disabilities.

The right to prenatal care is not to be seen as a "favour" to be bestowed or withheld by the State (or by expectant parents) but rather as "fulfilling clear legal obligations to each and every child".[35]

Exposing attitudes of "stigmatization and rejection"

So given that all these human rights principles are in place, why then is it that today the unborn child detected to have a disability is increasingly at risk of abortion?

Three factors need to be considered when assessing the current environment in which these children are selected for abortion:

- Biomedicine has equipped physicians with new technological powers to determine if the child in the womb has disabilities;[36]

34 CRC General Comment No 5 (10): 'Article 6 of the Convention on the Rights of the Child [affirms] the child's inherent right to life and States parties' obligation to *ensure to the maximum extent possible the survival and development of the child.* The Committee expects States to interpret "development" in its broadest sense as a holistic concept, embracing the child's physical, mental, spiritual, moral, psychological and social development. Implementation measures should be aimed at achieving *the optimal development for all children*." [Italicisation not in the original]

35 UN Committee on the Rights of the Child: General Comment No 5 (9): "The Committee emphasizes that, in the context of the Convention, States must see their role as fulfilling clear legal obligations to each and every child. Implementation of the human rights of children must not be seen as a charitable process, bestowing favours on children."

36 Such tests are problematical; see, for example, "Down's syndrome test 'risk to healthy babies'" *Telegraph (UK)*, August 16, 2007. Rebecca Smith, Medical Editor writes: "Ultrasound screening to establish a couple's risk of having a baby with Down's is done at 11 or 12 weeks into the pregnancy, measures the fluid at the back of the foetus's neck and this, together with maternal age, is calculated to give an individual risk of Down's. Parents use this score to decide whether to have a test called an amniocentesis. This involves taking a sample of fluid from the womb. The test determines if the baby does have Down's, but carries a one in 200 risk of causing a miscarriage. Dr Hylton Meire, formerly of King's College Hospital, wrote in *Ultrasound* (August 2007) that if all pregnant women in the

- Economic trends have intensified pressures to rationalise healthcare costs and develop utilitarian strategies which include routinely aborting children with disabilities;
- Some Governments are directly enlisting the medical profession in an agenda of population eugenics aimed at reducing the numbers of human beings born with disabilities by aborting them surgically or administering lethal drugs before birth.

Consequently, many of the States parties to the Convention on the Rights of Persons with Disabilities may be said to demonstrate in their current selective abortion policies objectionable attitudes of rejection and stigmatisation of the unborn child with disabilities. Such attitudes are in direct contravention of the meaning and purpose of this new treaty. Such States parties may be said to be precluded from being genuine signatories to this treaty: the retention of such gross discriminatory attitudes cannot with any logical consistency be reconciled with the treaty's core commitment—acceptance and respect for all human beings with disabilities.

Decriminalization of abortion—contravenes *General Principles* of Convention

Domestic laws that condone selective abortion are in contravention of the Article 3 General Principles of the new *Convention*—selective abortion on the basis of disability violates the principles of
- non-discrimination (3b),
- full and effective inclusion in society (3c),
- respect for difference and acceptance of persons with disabilities as part of human diversity and humanity (3d),
- equality of opportunity (3e), and
- respect for the right of children with disabilities to preserve their identities (3h).

Decriminalization of selective abortion of children with disabilities contravenes these most basic human rights principles. In fact, decriminalization of abortion represents an unconscionable legal permission to discriminate against these children, to exclude them permanently from society, to exercise a dismissive contempt for these children who are different, to reject children with disabilities, allowing them no part in diversity and humanity, to deny them equality of opportunity with those children who do not have a disability, and to disrespect and destroy forever the identities of these children with disabilities.

Laws play an important educative role especially in promoting the human rights principle laid down in the Convention:

UK underwent the amniocentesis test it could lead to the miscarriage of 3,200 healthy babies a year."

> Respect for difference and acceptance of persons with disabilities as part of human diversity and humanity.

Decriminalization of routine aborting of the lives of children with disabilities sends a very wrong message to expectant mothers and their communities—it indicates to them that these unborn children because of their disabilities are not "respected for difference" by the law and are not "accepted by society as part of human diversity and humanity".

"...the hidden message...that they should not been born anymore"

In the darkest, most shameful depths of human reasoning is hidden a profoundly disturbing question that this extreme discrimination has promoted, perhaps sometimes involuntarily, more often in resentful intimation: "Why didn't your mother and her doctor abort you?"

Silently, insidiously, this accusatory question arises in encounters with those with disabilities who have survived the prenatal selection process.[37] And survivors of this selection process are becoming fewer:

> ...almost only Moslems and people with strong religions, who are not allowed to have abortions, are giving life to their babies with Spina Bifida and Hydrocephalus.
> The consequence of these actions is that hospitals are cutting down their budgets and closing interdisciplinary Spina Bifida teams.
> In the near future the small group of young survivors will not have access any more to the services for Hydrocephalus & Spina Bifida where our organisations fought for.
> We, the Spina Bifida and Hydrocephalus population, are like the Incas: a dying population.
> We are eliminated totally, probably because people have been influenced by the hidden message of primary prevention: that they should not been born anymore.[38]

Children with disabilities...a right to respect...a right to be different—not a reason for abortion

Protecting the integrity of the child at risk of abortion is covered by Article 17 of the Convention on the Rights of Persons with Disabilities which says:

37 In October 2007, the House of Commons Committee on Science and Technology examining Britain's 1967 Abortion Act, was warned by Britain's Guild of Catholic Doctors that eugenic abortion is degrading public perception of people with disabilities. "We remain deeply concerned about the use of screening tests to identify children with disabilities before birth when the usual outcome is that the children be killed."

38 Pierre Mertens is President of the International Federation for Spina Bifida and Hydrocephalus (IF). His article "A Future With Purpose, A Future With Choice" is available at: http://www.perso.ch/dupuism/AFutureWithPurpose3.pdf.

> Every person with disabilities has a right to respect for his or her physical and mental integrity on an equal basis with others.

Abortion is a lethal abuse of the physical integrity of the child's tiny body growing *in utero*. Abortion is the antithesis of respect for the child's integrity in the womb—some methods of abortion dismember the child with sharp implements, others poison or scald the child—there is no method of aborting a child with disabilities that is consistent with the child's right to respect for his physical and mental integrity on an equal basis with others i.e., others who are not aborted.

The International Federation for Spina Bifida and Hydrocephalus has issued "Resolution Toulouse 2000" concerning the theme, "The Right to be Different."[39] Endorsed by adults and parents of children with spina bifida, its conclusions are summarized by Ann Neville-Jan:

- People with spina bifida and hydrocephalus live a full life with equal value to that of any other citizen;
- Adults with spina bifida stated very clearly that their quality of life is not a reason for abortion;
- Parents and adults state that the impairment is not the burden. The burden is the constant struggle against inaccessible environments and inadequate systems, which should be allies and should be supportive of them.[40]

Indeed, the quality of life of children with any disability is "not a reason for abortion".

Intentional "deprivation of life" of the unborn child in situations where the child is selected for abortion because of a disability contravenes ICCPR *Right to Life Article 6*[41] and fails the common law tests of absolute "necessity" and strict "proportionality.[42]

Recognition of their right to "prenatal care" follows on from their "right to life, survival and development": it is under this right that the Committee on the Rights of the Child condemns *the systematic killing of children because of their disability*.[43]

---

39 Proceedings of the International Federation's 12th world conference and "Resolution Toulouse 2000—the right to be different". Available at: http://www.ifglobal.org/pregnancy.asp?lang=1&main=8&sub=3.

40 Neville-Jan, Ann, "The Problem With Prevention: The Case of Spina Bifida", *American Journal of Occupational Therapy*, Vol.59, 2005, pp. 527–539 at p. 536.

41 See footnote 3 above.

42 CCPR General Comment No. 29 (72), para. 4; European Court of Human Rights, Case of *McCann and Others v. the United Kingdom*, Series A, No. 324, p. 46, para. 148 & p. 46, para. 149.

43 CRC General Comment No 9, para. 17.

Aborting children with disabilities—abrogating *respect for difference*

It is the irrational nature of human prejudice that we claim to be able to respect the human rights of those who are "permitted" to be born with disabilities while at the same time showing contempt for those selected for abortion. Yet this is nonsense. The two concepts, respect and contempt, are logically incompatible.

Children with disabilities who are at risk of abortion are being condemned as stereotypes, victimized by prejudices and threatened with a lethally harmful practice. The Convention on the Rights of Persons with Disabilities now requires States:

> To combat stereotypes, prejudices and harmful practices relating to persons with disabilities, including those based on sex and age, in all areas of life; Article 8 (1)(b)

But, contrary to this human rights obligation, many States are denying legal protection to children at risk of abortion because of their disabilities and are permitting lethal discrimination against them on the basis of age—specifically on the basis of the child's *physical and mental immaturity.* These children with disabilities are at risk of abortion because of a contempt rather than respect for their particular stage of life—the prenatal *area of life.*

Indeed, today human life *in utero* is a clinically verifiable and easily monitored *area of life.* Children detected in these earliest stages of life to have disabilities are entitled to the same protection from *stereotypes, prejudices and harmful practices relating to persons with disabilities* as in other stages and areas of life.

Selective abortion, "foetal abnormalities" and the non-discrimination principle

The Committee on the Rights of the Child has reaffirmed that selective abortion violates the fundamental human rights principle of non-discrimination.[44]

This non-discrimination principle imposes a legal obligation to eliminate the practice of treating some children with respect because they are 'normal' and other children with contempt because they have 'foetal abnormalities'. This term, 'foetal abnormalities', is often preceded by the adjectives 'serious', 'severe' and 'gross'. But none of these qualifying adjectives can divest the child of his/her inherent humanity nor can they negate the dignity and rights that belong to the child because of that humanity. These children remain human beings with disabilities—they are not as abortion 'providers' like to describe them—serious, severe, or gross 'foetal abnormalities'. Their identity is not to be diminished, falsified or reduced to their disability.

The term 'foetal abnormalities' is being promoted by abortion advocates as a replacement term for 'unborn children with disabilities'. The new term has become exceedingly elastic and is currently being stretched to include treatable conditions

44 UN Committee on the Rights of the Child (CRC) Comment No 7 (2005), *Right to Non-discrimination.*

such as cleft palate and club foot.[45] Routine abortion for manageable conditions is on the increase. In one recent study, genetic screening for Gaucher disease was found to result in termination of pregnancies for generally mild conditions, even in a highly educated population.[46] An editorial in the *Journal of the American Medical Association* "Carrier Screening or Gaucher Disease: More Harm Than Good..." makes a chilling point:

> Had the mother of my patient with Gaucher disease been conceived in Israel in this century, rather than in the early 1900s, she might never have been born...[47]

The question is raised by the authors of this original research as to the true goal of the classic carrier screening paradigm to common, low-penetrance disease. They insist that programs offering such screening should determine "whether the true goal is knowledge and presymptomatic risk assessment or pregnancy termination of fetuses with a specified genetic status".

Quite. This searching question should be applied to all genetic screening of children *in utero*.

Is the true goal of genetic screening knowledge that will be used to help the mother and her child? Or is the true goal of genetic screening a discriminatory one: to eliminate children with disabilities?

Selective abortion—"exclusion on the basis of disability"

Selective abortion constitutes for children before birth an exclusion on the basis of disability as defined by Article 2 of the *Convention on the Rights of Persons with Disabilities* and has the purpose or effect of nullifying the recognition, enjoyment or exercise, on an equal basis with others, of all human rights and fundamental freedoms. The definition includes all forms of discrimination, "including denial of reasonable accommodation".

Both chemical and surgical abortion amount to a denial of reasonable accommodation for children with disabilities. When selection of a child for abortion is authorized on the discriminatory grounds of disability, such an abortion comprises an arbitrary eviction from his/her mother's womb where, as a natural place of safety, the

45 See for example, Clout, Laura, "Babies with disabilities aborted", *Daily Telegraph*. October 21, 2007. "In one area of England in a three year period (2002-5), over 100 babies with minor disabilities were aborted: data from the South West Congenital Anomaly Register records that 54 babies with club feet, 37 babies with cleft palates or lips, and 26 babies with extra or webbed fingers or toes were aborted."

46 Zuckerman, Shachar; Lahad, Amnon; Shmueli, Amir; Zimran, Ari; Peleg, Leah; Orr-Urtreger, Avi; Levy-Lahad, Ephrat; Sagi, Michal, "Carrier Screening for Gaucher Disease: Lessons for Low-Penetrance, Treatable Diseases", *Journal of the American Medical Association*, Vol. 298(11), 19 September, 2007, pp. 1281-1290.

47 Beutler, Ernest, "Carrier Screening for Gaucher Disease: More Harm Than Good...", *Journal of the American Medical Association*, Vol. 298(11), 2007, pp. 1329-1331.

child has by nature a right to development which includes a right to legal protection from arbitrary interference or attack:

> No person with disabilities, regardless of place of residence...shall be subjected to arbitrary or unlawful interference with his or her privacy, family, home... Persons with disabilities have the right to the protection of the law against such interference or attacks. Article 22 (1)

When the Universal Declaration of Human Rights recognized the child before birth (while still *in utero*) as a member of the human family entitled to appropriate legal protection without discrimination, that recognition included the need to protect children at risk of abortion from all forms of discriminatory interference and attacks.

So when the Convention on the Rights of Persons with Disabilities (which acknowledges the foundational principles of the Universal Declaration and the Conventions that comprise the Bill of Rights) instructs governments to:

> Prevent discriminatory denial of health care or health services... on the basis of disability. (25(f)

It is, in effect, urging the prevention of abortion of children on the basis of disability. Abortion *per se* is the ultimate, most extreme form of denial of health care and health services to these children.

Prenatal care on an equal basis with other children

Selective abortion of children detected to be with disabilities before birth has the purpose or effect of nullifying their right to be born free and equal in human rights "on an equal basis with other children" i.e., on an equal basis with other children before a well as after birth, with or without disabilities.

> States Parties shall take all necessary measures to ensure the full enjoyment by children with disabilities of all human rights and fundamental freedoms on an equal basis with other children.[48]

The most vital of all human rights is the right to life expressed in Article 10 of the Convention on the Rights of Persons with Disabilities:

> States Parties reaffirm that every human being has the inherent right to life and shall take all necessary measures to ensure its effective enjoyment by persons with disabilities on an equal basis with others.

The Preamble to the Convention warns against "attitudinal and environmental barriers" that hinder persons with disabilities from full and effective participation in

48 *UN Convention on the Rights of Persons with Disabilities* (2007), Article 7(1).

society on an equal basis with others. Surely one such barrier is the threat of selective abortion for children detected to have a disability. An environment of rejection of children with possible impairments, an attitude that condones, facilitates and even promotes abortion of these children manifests a reprehensible failure to recognize the child's inherent right to life.

Such attitudinal and environmental barriers fail to abide also by the principle: "Respect for difference and acceptance of persons with disabilities as part of human diversity and humanity."[49]

Instead of respect for difference, abortion registers disrespect for difference. Instead of acceptance, the current widespread practice of abortion represents the ultimate rejection of children with disabilities, a rejection of their humanity and of their rightful place as part of human diversity.

Data collection and information should be used to help assess the implementation of obligations under the present Convention and to identify and address the barriers faced by children with disabilities.

Particularly significant for children at risk of abortion because of their disabilities is the States Parties' obligation under the Convention "to identify and address the initial barriers faced by persons with disabilities in exercising their rights".[50] Abortion presents an insurmountable barrier to the right of the child with a disability to be treated on an equal basis with others in regard to human rights entitlement to *special safeguards and care, including appropriate legal protection before as well as after birth*.

Children "in situations of risk..." and pre-natal testing

Far too often now prenatal testing places children with disabilities at grave risk of abortion.

> States Parties shall take, in accordance with their obligations under international law, including international humanitarian law and international human rights law, all necessary measures to ensure the protection and safety of persons with disabilities in situations of risk...[51]

There can be few more seriously threatening "situations of risk" for persons with disabilities than the situation of children at risk of abortion because of disabilities such as Down Syndrome. A recent Victorian study found that "most cases [Down Syndrome] diagnosed prenatally result in a termination of pregnancy":

---

49 *UN Convention on the Rights of Persons with Disabilities* (2007), General principles Article 3.

50 *UN Convention on the Rights of Persons with Disabilities* (2007), Article 31(2).

51 *UN Convention on the Rights of Persons with Disabilities* (2007), Article 11.

> In fact, only 5% of the pregnancies diagnosed prenatally resulted in a live birth. A similar termination rate has been reported for the UK, with slightly lower rates seen in Belgium, Hungary, and Scotland.[52]

That first "attitudinal and environmental" barrier faced by children with such disabilities is the extremely high risk of abortion following the use of testing.

Dr Hylton Meire, in his article "Is Ultrasound as Useful as We Think?" questions the rational and moral bases for this testing.[53] Dr Meire reveals that pre-natal testing for Downs and Edwards syndrome is "not very accurate", throws up "false positives" and on Dr Meire's calculations results in 160 healthy babies "lost" for every 50 cases of Down's or Edward's detected.

Studies such as this affirm the need for education and "Awareness-Raising" as called for in Article 8 of the Convention on the Rights of Persons with Disabilities.[54] Education is not just ensuring that parents understand the medical facts as well as the moral issues raised by the loss of lives resulting from false positives. It is also necessary to educate parents and doctors in order to "change discriminatory attitudes" towards children with disabilities.

Dr Meire's study sheds a disturbing light on the extreme prejudice among some parents and some doctors, discriminatory attitudes so extreme that they would rather sacrifice 160 babies without these disabilities in order to be able to eliminate 50 babies with this disability.

The London-based Lejeune Clinic for Children With Down Syndrome in its submission to the *House of Commons Committee on Science and Technology Enquiry* (October 2007) into time limits on abortion revealed that in 2005 alone, 429 abortions were carried out on babies with Down Syndrome and decried that the law in the UK sets no time limits for abortions on babies that are held to be disabled. The clinic also commented that after Down Syndrome is detected, some women feel pressured to abort their babies, and that very few women are offered information on help available to raise a child with the chromosomal disorder. The submission argued that most children with Down Syndrome are happy, sociable and enjoy friendships. Around 80% attend mainstream primary school, either full or part time, and nearly all integrate in a loving fashion into their families. Behavioral problems can occur and can be addressed successfully; and so:

> Down Syndrome is not a reason for termination. We recognise a valid role for prenatal genetic testing, but the primary goal of prenatal testing should not be to reduce the birth

52 Collins,V.R., Muggli, E.E., Riley, M., Palma, S., Halliday, J.L., "Is Down Syndrome a Disappearing Birth Defect?", *The Journal of Pediatrics*, Vol. 152 (1), January, 2008, pp. 20-4, at p. 23.

53 Meire, Hylton: "Is Ultrasound as Useful as We Think?", *Ultrasound*, Vol.15 (3), August 2007.

54 *UN Convention on the Rights of Persons with Disabilities* (2007), Article 8 (1)(a): "To raise awareness throughout society, including at the family level, regarding persons with disabilities, and to foster respect for the rights and dignity of persons with disabilities".

prevalence of Down Syndrome. Prenatal testing should not be offered or promoted using outdated information, negative stereotypes, prejudicial images or offensive terminology which have the potential to stigmatise people with Down Syndrome and increase the fear of disability.[55]

Routinely, it seems, opinions by doctors assessing the life prospects of children at risk of abortion because of their disabilities are being heavily and purposefully weighted towards the negative.

The International Federation for Spina Bifida and Hydrocephalus, for example, has researched just how much the perception of "Quality of life of persons with spina bifida" influences ethical attitudes towards abortion:

> Perception of spina bifida and hydrocephalus is negative in general and the information given to parents is often too negative...the information on all medical deficits and not on the positive potentials. In Europe more that 90% of the parents follow the advice of doctors to terminate.[56]

The Research Project concluded:

> ...the existence of spina bifida and hydrocephalus in the foetus is not sufficient reason for the termination.[57]

Dr Carla Verpoorten, Belgian spina bifida and hydrocephalus specialist, has challenged the outdated views of Lorber[58] that have for many decades influenced the medical profession towards using abortion and euthanasia to eliminate children with these disabilities.

> The prognosis for children with spina bifida anno 2000 is much better than indicated by Lorber. Professionals should change their pessimistic view on long-term prognosis and need to counsel parents about the full spectrum of impairment in addition to the effects of modern forms of treatment on the outcome of unborn infants with spina bifida. The pessimistic public opinion has to be changed before we can assure prospective parents

---

55 Submission by Lejeune Clinic for Children with Down's Syndrome (SDA03). Available at: http://www.publications.parliament.uk/pa/cm200607/cmselect/cmsctech/1045/1045we04.htm.

56 "Ethical discussion on prenatal selection in EU countries involving spina bifida/hydrocephalus user groups network", Final Report, PS/2004/035.

57 Ibid.

58 Lorber, J.: "Results of treatment of myelomeningocele: An analysis of 524 unselected cases, with special reference to possible selection for treatment", *Developmental Medicine & Child Neurology*, Vol. 13 (3), 1971, pp. 279-303.

> that they and their future child will be welcomed whether or not the child has a disability.[59]

State's obligation "to raise awareness and to foster respect"

In the light of these truths, it is clear that there is still great fear and ignorance in society and among families regarding disabilities. The Convention on the Rights of Persons with Disabilities requires States:

> to raise awareness throughout society, including at the family level, regarding persons with disabilities, and to foster respect for the rights and dignity of persons with disabilities; Article 8(1)(a)

Education programs at the family level should be instituted to help families overcome fear and prejudice regarding children with a disability, including children at risk of abortion.

In initiating and maintaining effective public awareness campaigns, governments are

> to foster at all levels of the education system, including in all children from an early age, an attitude of respect for the rights of persons with disabilities; 8(2)(b)

Children from an early age are very sensitive to adult attitudes at home. Where parents have aborted a sibling with a disability, children will discern the hypocrisy of formal education programs fostering *an attitude of respect for the rights of persons with disabilities.*

"...including those who require more intensive support"

In the Preamble to the Convention on the Rights of Persons with Disabilities, the States Parties

> recognize the need to promote and protect the human rights of all persons with disabilities, including those who require more intensive support (j);

This is significant for the legal protection of the human rights of those children who are at risk of abortion on the grounds of what some abortion "providers" label as "major fetal abnormalities". Australian obstetrician, Professor Lachlan de Crespigny in his advocacy of decriminalization of abortion in the Australian state of Victoria, claims that women are being denied abortion for "fetal abnormality". Professor de Crespigny

59 Verpoorten, C.:"Termination of pregnancy when the unborn child has spina bifida and/or hydrocephalus: An overview on international literature" (2000). Available at: http://www.ifglobal.org/human_rights.asp?lang=1&main=9&sub=.

identifies Down Syndrome as a "major fetal abnormality" and approves abortion on request of children with Down Syndrome:

> Most women will request abortion after the diagnosis of a major fetal abnormality—95% do so after the diagnosis of Down Syndrome in Victoria (J Halliday, Head, Public Health Genetics, Murdoch Children's Research Institute, Melbourne, personal communication).[60]

The term "fetal abnormality" to refer to a child with a disability should be outlawed by the medical profession. These children at risk of abortion are children with disabilities "who require more intensive support".

Provision of abortion services to terminate the life a child with disabilities is not an acceptable substitute for provision of more intensive support for the child. Parents who are identified as having children *who require more intensive support* should be reassured that such support will be available.

Adequate standard of social protection for children and families

Careful reading of the *Convention on the Rights of Persons with Disabilities* discovers no obligation on the State to provide expectant mothers with abortion services that permanently delete children with disabilities from their families and communities. On the contrary, the *Convention* is very clear as to the obligations of the State to provide an adequate standard of social protection and economic assistance for these children and their families.[61]

---

60 See, for example, De Crespigny, Lachlan J., and Savulescu, Julian, "Pregnant women with fetal abnormalities: the forgotten people in the abortion debate", *Medical Journal of Australia*, January 2008; Vol. 188 (2), pp. 100-103: "In 30 years of obstetric ultrasound practice, one of us (L J d C) has seen how the diagnosis of a fetal abnormality affects couples hoping to raise a family—it is their worst nightmare."—the authors go on to speak of "the shocking news of a major fetal abnormality" and "the devastating outcome to their much wanted pregnancy" and to argue from this perception for decriminalization of late abortions.

61 "Convinced that the family is the natural and fundamental group unit of society and is entitled to protection by society and the State, and that persons with disabilities and their *family members should receive the necessary protection and assistance* to enable families to contribute towards the full and equal enjoyment of the rights of persons with disabilities", (Preamble) [italicisation added]

"States Parties shall ensure that children with disabilities have equal rights with respect to family life. With a view to realizing these rights, and to prevent concealment, abandonment, neglect and segregation of children with disabilities, States Parties shall undertake *to provide early and comprehensive information, services and support to children with disabilities and their families.*" Article 23(3) [italicisation added]

States Parties recognize the right of persons with disabilities to social protection and to the enjoyment of that right without discrimination on the basis of disability, and shall take appropriate steps to safeguard and promote the realization of this right, including measures: ...(c) To *ensure access by persons with disabilities and their families living in*

And in the event that the immediate family of a child with disabilities fears that it will be unable to care for that child after birth, there is no question of a State obligation to provide for an abortion of that child. On the contrary:

> States Parties shall, where the immediate family is unable to care for a child with disabilities, undertake every effort to provide alternative care within the wider family, and failing that, within the community in a family setting. [Article 23(5)]

Restoring legal protection for children with disabilities at risk of abortion

Regarding discrimination of any kind on the basis of disability, States Parties to the Convention on the Rights of Persons with Disabilities commit:

> To take all appropriate measures, including legislation, to modify or abolish existing laws, regulations, customs and practices that constitute discrimination against persons with disabilities; 4(1)(b)

This commitment requires States Parties to legislate for the protection of children at risk of abortion because of their disabilities.

It requires also that States abolish "customs and practices that constitute discrimination against persons with disabilities"—routine abortion of some 90% of children with Down Syndrome constitutes just such a custom or practice that must be abolished under this Convention. This abolition must extend to hospitals, health clinics and such public authorities as provide funding or facilities for such abortions, in order to ensure that public authorities and institutions act in conformity with the present Convention.[62]

Governments have promised also to

> take all appropriate measures to eliminate discrimination on the basis of disability by any person, organization or private enterprise; and to promote the training of professionals and staff working with persons with disabilities in the rights recognized in this Convention so as to better provide the assistance and services guaranteed by those rights.[63]

This implies that every person involved in any capacity with the well-being of a child who is at risk of abortion because of disabilities must be trained to recognize the human rights of the child with disabilities and to reject on the child's behalf any

situations of poverty to assistance from the State with disability-related expenses, including adequate training, counselling, financial assistance and respite care; Article 28 (2.) [italicisation added]

62 *Convention on the Rights of Persons with Disabilities*: States Parties undertake to "refrain from engaging in any act or practice that is inconsistent with the present Convention and to ensure that public authorities and institutions act in conformity with the present Convention.", Article 4(1)(d).

63 *Convention on the Rights of Persons with Disabilities*, Articles 4(1)(e) and 4(1)(i).

discrimination against that child. This applies to individuals working in both public hospitals and private clinics where children are at risk of abortion because of their disabilities. The Preamble to the Convention on the Rights of Persons with Disabilities articulates the realization that the individual, having duties to other individuals and to the community to which he or she belongs, is under a responsibility to strive for the promotion and observance of the rights recognized in the International Bill of Human Rights.

Children with disabilities—equal recognition before the law

Other commitments undertaken by States Parties to the Convention include:

> States Parties recognize that all persons are equal before and under the law and are entitled without any discrimination to the equal protection and equal benefit of the law. (Article 5(1))

Children with disabilities who are at risk of abortion are "entitled without any discrimination to the equal protection and equal benefit of the law". Decriminalization of abortion removes the guarantee to these children of "equal and effective legal protection against discrimination on all grounds":

> States Parties shall prohibit all discrimination on the basis of disability and guarantee to persons with disabilities equal and effective legal protection against discrimination on all grounds. Article 5(2)

Discrimination against children at risk of abortion on the basis of disability is to be "prohibited". Discrimination on the grounds that the child is still *in utero* is not to be validated or tolerated.

Under Article 12, persons with disabilities [including children at risk of abortion] have

- the right to *recognition everywhere as persons before the law,* (1)
- the right to *enjoy legal capacity on an equal basis with others in all aspects of life* [including in the child's *physical and mental immaturity* during that initial dependent and developmental state in the womb], (2) and
- a right to *the support they may require in exercising their legal capacity.* (3)

This last duty of the State is often ignored—children at risk of abortion because of their disabilities are given no support, no legal representation of their best interests.

It has become ideologically fashionable to proclaim that the medicalized killing of these children is "a private matter" between the child's mother and her abortionist. Not so.

Privacy cannot be invoked to conceal human rights abuses of children with disabilities, particularly violations of their rights to survival and development. International human rights law has consistently rejected the right to privacy as a defence against human rights violations by adults in positions of power over children in positions of dependency.[64] Major human rights treaties have laid down the principle that "neither privacy nor State sanction can be a defence for human rights violations".[65]

"...appropriate and effective safeguards to prevent abuse"

The need for legislative protection by the State and public support is especially urgent for children at risk of abortion.

To this end, governments must ensure, also under Article 12, that

> all measures that relate to the exercise of legal capacity provide for appropriate and effective safeguards to prevent abuse in accordance with international human rights law.

This relates directly and especially back to the Universal Declaration, which recognizes the child's entitlement to *special safeguards and care, including appropriate legal protection before as well as after birth* and thus includes safeguards for the child at risk of abortion.

Article 12 goes on to stipulate:

> Such safeguards shall ensure that measures relating to the exercise of legal capacity respect the rights...of the person, are free of conflict of interest and undue influence, are proportional and tailored to the person's circumstances...The safeguards shall be proportional to the degree to which such measures affect the person's rights and interests.

Clearly, because the rights and interests of the child at risk of abortion are serious and substantial, indeed of life and death proportions, the legal safeguards must be of the very highest degree possible.

Preventative measures against cruel, inhuman or degrading treatment

Article 15 of the Convention on the Rights of Persons with Disabilities also has direct application to the child at risk of abortion. Building on Article 5 of the Universal Declaration and on Article 37 of the Convention on the Rights of the Child, it states:

> 1. No one shall be subjected to torture or to cruel, inhuman or degrading treatment or punishment. In particular, no one shall be subjected without his or her free consent to medical or scientific experimentation.
> 2. States Parties shall take all effective legislative, administrative, judicial or other measures to prevent persons with disabilities, on an equal basis with others, from

64 HRC General Comment No 31 (2004), para. 8: "It is also implicit in article 7 that States Parties have to take positive measures to ensure that private persons or entities do not inflict... cruel, inhuman or degrading treatment... on others within their power".

65 *UN Declaration on the Elimination of Violence Against Women* (1993), Article 1 & Article 2(c); also the *UN Convention on the Elimination of All Forms of Racial Discrimination* (1969), Article 5(b).

> being subjected to torture or cruel, inhuman or degrading treatment or punishment.

Selective abortion practiced against a child with disabilities is *per se* a lethal form of treatment, a medicalized maltreatment that is cruel, inhuman and degrading to that most extreme point of being exterminatory.

Article 37 of the Convention on the Rights of the Child requires States to ensure that no child shall be subjected to cruel, inhuman or degrading treatment. The Committee on the Rights of the Child addresses this right and points out that it is complemented and extended by Article 19, which requires States

> to take all appropriate legislative, administrative, social and educational measures to protect the child from all forms of physical or mental violence, injury or abuse, neglect or negligent treatment, maltreatment or exploitation...while in the care of parent(s), legal guardian(s) or any other person who has the care of the child.

The Committee concludes:

> There is no ambiguity: "all forms of physical or mental violence" does not leave room for any level of legalized violence against children.[66]

The Committee goes on to condemn any act of violence which directly conflicts with the equal and inalienable rights of children to respect for their human dignity and physical integrity.

Thus, intrinsic use of lethal force (albeit in a clinical or surgical setting) in terminations following identification of children with Down Syndrome or other disabilities cannot be justified. Governments are required under international human rights law to provide appropriate legal protection for all children before as well as after birth.

Abortion—an act of violence, a lethal form of abuse

Article 16 of the Convention on the Rights of Persons with Disabilities relates to protection of those with disabilities from all forms of violence and abuse, *both within and outside the home*. This has particular significance for the child at risk of abortion. There is no private place, not even in the home of the mother's womb, where the tiny person of the child with disabilities can be violated, abused and destroyed with impunity. Professor Lachlan de Crespigny, an abortion advocate, has nonetheless observed truthfully:

> The uterus is indeed the best intensive care unit; fetuses with the most terrible abnormalities usually do not die before birth.[67]

66 CRC General Comment No 8 (2006, para. 18).

67 De Crespigny, Lachlan J., and Savulescu, Julian, (2008), *op. cit.*, pp. 100-103. Unfortunately, de Crespigny uses the effectiveness of the ideal intensive care conditions of the mother's

The Convention on the Rights of Persons with Disabilities Article 16(2) requires that States Parties must ensure that protection services

- are age-sensitive and disability-sensitive,
- take all appropriate measures to prevent all forms of violence and abuse by ensuring, *inter alia*, appropriate forms of age-sensitive assistance and support for persons with disabilities and their families and caregivers, and
- include the provision of information and education on how to avoid, recognize and report instances of violence and abuse.

The tiny immature child in his/her mother's womb is not to be subjected to the violence of abortion because of age or disability. The unborn child with disabilities is not to be abused, his/her small life must not be deliberately ruptured. All the forms of medicalized violence and child abuse that threaten children at risk of abortion because of their disabilities are to be "avoided". Instances of such violence and abuse are to be "recognized and reported".

The immaturity of the child before birth does not call for a lesser form of legal protection against abuse. On the contrary, as recognized by the Universal Declaration, the child *by reason of his physical and mental immaturity* is to be provided by the State with *special safeguards and care, including appropriate legal protection before as well as after birth.* The Committee on the Rights of the Child is right:

> The distinct nature of children, their initial dependent and developmental state, their unique human potential as well as their vulnerability, all demand the need for more, rather than less, legal and other protection from all forms of violence.[68]

Child-focused protective legislation and policies

The Convention on the Rights of Persons with Disabilities Article 16(5) directs States Parties to put in place effective legislation and policies, including child-focused legislation and policies, to ensure that instances of exploitation, violence and abuse against persons with disabilities are *identified, investigated and, where appropriate, prosecuted.* Legislation is to be "women-and child-focused". The child whose disabilities are detected before birth is not to be ignored but is to be included in protective legislation and policy.

This commitment rules out decriminalization of abortion of children with disabilities. Abortion as a particularly lethal instance of violence and abuse against children with disabilities must be *identified, investigated and, where appropriate, prosecuted.*

Insistence on a child-focused approach is supported by the UN Committee on the Rights of the Child which has mandated the State's obligation to ensure that health

womb for the child with the "most terrible" disabilities to argue for the necessity to proactively abort the child: "Denying abortion may only delay the inevitable".

68 CRC General Comment No 8 (2006), para. 21.

professionals working with children with disabilities and engaged in "prenatal care for children" are required to "practice with a child centered approach".[69]

Regrettably, many medical professionals have for some years now ignored this requirement. Typically, in medical journal articles relating to detection of disabilities in unborn children as a prelude to abortion, the children themselves fail to rate a mention. The exclusive focus is on "women". The child is blotted out, referred too only in such abusive dehumanizing language as "fetal abnormality", language that focuses exclusively on the disability and ignores the living presence of the child in his/her mother's womb.[70]

Progressive corruption of human rights language

Even the most cursory reading of mainstream medical journals today will shed a disturbing light on the extreme prejudice that exists against children detected before birth to have disabilities. Discriminatory attitudes are revealed in the discriminatory language. For example:

> Australia does not currently have a coordinated, population-based screening program for Down Syndrome (as it does for breast and cervical cancer)...[71]

This language dehumanizes the child, identifies and equates the disability with the child and treats children with the disability as a disease, like breast or cervical cancer, to be detected and progressively eliminated from the population through selective abortion.

The modern revolution in human rights for the disabled seems to have passed by such authors. One in every 400 pregnancies[72] involves a child with Down Syndrome —they are not "abnormal fetuses"—they are children with a not uncommon disability.

When advocacy of "a coordinated, population-based screening program" puts children with Down Syndrome at risk, authors cannot proffer the feeble excuse that they are merely giving more expectant parents more 'information', more "access to services" and more "choices". Authors, too, are bound by UDHR Article 7 which prohibits "any incitement to discrimination". Discriminatory, demeaning opinions regarding the value of persons with disabilities should be retracted:

> When the costs of screening are offset against the life-time costs of caring for a person with Down Syndrome, screening is less costly...[73]

---

69 CRC General Comment No 9, paras. 45 & 46.

70 See for example Michael D Coory, Timothy Roselli and Heidi J Carroll, *op. cit.*

71 Ibid.

72 Available at: http://www.mcri.edu.au/Downloads/Themes/LCG/PublicHealthGenetics/PrenatalTestingDecisionAid.pdf.

73 Michael D Coory, Timothy Roselli and Heidi J Carroll, *op. cit.*, Concluding Comment.

This contravenes universal human rights values. A person with Down Syndrome is entitled to the same recognition of inherent dignity and worth and of inalienable rights as all other members of the human family. Their violation can never be justified by economic rationalism.[74] Moral credibility cannot be retrieved with a spurious claim to be upholding the principle of equality:

> Some regard such calculations as distasteful because of the impossibility of placing a monetary value on human life. However, few would disagree with the principle that all expectant parents should be provided with the same information and have the same access to services so that they all have the same choices.[75]

Glib words cannot disguise the violation of the rights of the child here. Neither the State's duty nor the health professionals' duty to provide information and services for expectant parents can be performed at the neglect of the more fundamental duty to uphold the rights of children to "special safeguards and care including appropriate legal protection before as well as after birth". The right to life is "the supreme right" and "basic to all human rights".[76]

Nor is it valid under international human rights law to plead a defence that terminations of children with Down Syndrome are legal and/or common practice in a member country of the UN—the *Convention on the Rights of the Child* does not permit violation of children's rights on the grounds that local or customary law or common practice tolerates such violations.[77]

An "excess" of Down Syndrome births?

A human rights approach rejects offensive language such as "the excess of Down Syndrome births" used by these same authors.

History has too many appalling examples of people in positions of power declaring "an excess of births" in vulnerable groups—the Egyptian Pharaohs instituted "a coordinated, population-based screening program" to reduce the "excess" of male Israelite births. Hitler's doctors implemented "a coordinated, population-based screening program" for Jewish children, and children with Down Syndrome and other disabilities.

In researching the history of Nazi eugenics, Professor Hartmut Hanauske-Abel has highlighted the 19 August 1933 edition of *Deutsches Arzteblatt* which asserted that "every doctor must be a genetic doctor," and published the first article on this topic, entitled "The physician and genetic improvement" by Professor F Lommel:

---

74 HRC General Comment No 3, para. 11; also CRC General Comment No 5, para. 6.

75 Michael D Coory et al: *op. cit.*, Concluding Comment.

76 HRC General Comment 6, paras. 1 & 3. See also Inter-American Court of Human Rights in *Jailton Neri Da Fonseca* v. Brazil, (2004), para. 68: "The human right to life is a fundamental human right, the basis for the exercise of the other human rights. ... enjoyment of the right to life is essential for the exercise of all other human rights. If it is not respected, all rights lack meaning."

77 CRC General Comment No 5, para. 19.

> Key phrases are "extermination of life not worth living," "legally enforced sterilisations," "creation of a new, biologically based nobility," and "the goal of breeding in the interest of the race." As part of eugenic considerations "extermination of life not worth living" is thus introduced as a legitimate part of continuing medical education and becomes a standard technical term.[78]

Subsequently, the Nazi eugenics program was promoted by the head of the Nazi organization of physicians, Dr Gerhard Wagner, as

> ...saving the German people from a steady stream of new moral and economic burdens resulting from genetic illnesses...saving children and their children from new and enormous misery...let all that is unworthy of life perish to make room for the strong and healthy to whom the future belongs...We have a good conscience before the world when we eliminate life that is unworthy of life...[79]

These infamous attitudes towards children with disabilities are echoed in today's medical journals in such passages as the one below:

> Because the percentage of births to older mothers is increasing, the number of Down Syndrome births should have increased, all else being equal. More specifically, if the age-specific rates for 1990 to 1999 had continued, there would have been about 70 Down Syndrome births in 2004 (a crude rate of 1.4 per 1000 births, compared with the current crude rate of 1.0 per 1000 births) instead of the 49 reported. Moreover, if the age-specific rates for women who received their antenatal care from private obstetricians could be replicated across the whole of Queensland, the number of Down Syndrome births would have been as low as 27 (a crude rate of 0.5 per 1000 births).[80]

Careful analysis of the text reveals a clear agenda: that the antenatal 'care' provided by private obstetricians should be replicated across the whole of Queensland so that the number of Down Syndrome 'births' can be reduced to as low as 27.

The authors are telling us that of the 70 children with Down Syndrome that would have been born without this particular form of antenatal 'care' (i.e., selective termination), 21 children were terminated but another 22 of these children could have (and by implication should have) been terminated—had they and their mothers been given the recommended antenatal 'care' by private obstetricians.

---

78 Hanauske-Abel, Hartmut, M.: "Not a slippery slope or sudden subversion: German medicine and National Socialism in 1933", *British Medical Journal*, Vol. 313, NUREMBERG DOCTORS' TRIAL Special Edition, December 7, 1996, pp. 1453-1463.

79 Wagner, Gerhard, "Rasse und Bevölkerungspolitik," *Der Parteitag der Ehre*, Vom 8, bis 14. September 1936. Offizieller Bericht über den Verlauf des Reichsparteitages mit sämtlichen Kongreßreden, Munich: Zentralverlag der NSDAP., 1936.

80 Michael D Coory, Timothy Roselli and Heidi J Carroll, *op. cit.*, p. 231.

Principle of indivisibility—human rights protection for mother and unborn child

At the centre of the rationalization of such abortion programs lies the invalid argument that a woman's "right to abortion" trumps the human rights of her child with disabilities who is at risk of abortion. Such rationalization contravenes *the universality, indivisibility, interdependence and interrelatedness of all human rights... and the need for persons with disabilities to be guaranteed their full enjoyment without discrimination.*[81]

Claims that suicide threats by the child's mother justify the child's abortion are invalid—they contravene a fundamental principle of international human rights law, *viz.*, the indivisibility of human rights. This principle demands that the abuse of one person's rights cannot be justified by upholding another person's rights. The indivisibility principle requires that human rights protections for both mother and child be observed—both mother and child are entitled to the best possible health care.

While suicide threats by the mother should be treated with compassion and professional competence, giving in to irrational demands that her child be aborted on the discriminatory grounds of disability can amount only to a grave human rights offence.

In medical journals and the popular press, Professor Lachlan de Crespigny has attempted to justify his infamous abortion at 33 weeks gestation of Jessica, a child with "probable dwarfism"[82] on the grounds that the life of Jessica's mother could be saved only by aborting Jessica's life.[83] Andrew Bolt, in the *Herald Sun*, tells a different story:

> It was de Crespigny, an obstetrician and associate professor, who told a mother from a very different culture that the child she was carrying could be a dwarf. The woman was deeply superstitious and, it seems, not mentally strong. She believed giving birth to a dwarf would bring her terrible luck and was so distraught that she threatened suicide if the girl was not aborted. But the girl, later named Jessica, was already 32 weeks old in the womb, and healthy. She could have been born alive and adopted out. Instead, de Crespigny injected Jessica's heart with potassium chloride, and two minutes later she was dead.[84]

---

81 *Preamble* to the *UN Convention on the Rights of Persons with Disabilities* (2007).

82 Gerber, Paul, "Late-term abortion: what can be learned from Royal Women's Hospital v Medical Practitioners Board of Victoria?", *The Medical Journal of Australia*, Vol. 186 (7), 2007, pp. 359-362, at p. 359.

83 Professor de Crespigny injected potassium chloride into Jessica's heart—"It was lifesaving," he says now of the procedure that he insists he had a moral obligation to perform. "If we didn't do it and the woman died we would have potentially been charged with manslaughter and gone to jail. So in a legal sense, you could argue that we were compelled to offer it." Carol Nader: "Controversial abortion case that brought a doctor years of anguish", *The Age*, December 13, 2007.

84 Andrew Bolt, "Be sad for Jessica's lost life", *Herald Sun*, December 14, 2007.

The human rights principle of indivisibility prohibits the State from abandoning its duty towards such children with disabilities on the grounds that it must protect expectant parents' choices. Parents' right to "choices" is not absolute—it is contingent on ensuring the rights of others.[85]

Violation of the human rights of the child selected for abortion on the grounds of disability cannot be justified by appeals to saving the child's mother from distress. The overwhelming majority of terminations of children with disabilities are elective surgery, and as in all elective surgeries for pregnant women, if it seriously endangers the life of the mother or her child, it should not be attempted.

Inadequate monitoring of the consequences of selective abortions[86] has allowed concealment of many double tragedies resulting in irreparable harm to the mother as well as the preventable loss of her child.

Growing recognition of post-abortion depression and post-abortion suicide further discredits elective abortion as a life-saving, health-giving procedure to be recommended for the mother suffering psychological distress.[87]

The rational response to health-threatening pregnancy these days is to improve delivery of holistic pre-natal and post-natal healthcare including education and social

---

85 UDHR article 29. Also the *Preambles* to both *ICCPR* and *ICESCR*.

86 Ruth Hill: "Abortion researcher confounded by study", *New Zealand Sun-Herald*, January 5,2006. New Zealand's Professor David Fergusson's reading of the literature on abortion suggested that it was "one of the most methodologically flawed and illiterate research areas" he had ever encountered, that the idea behind the law that abortion was a mental health issue was "based on conjecture". No one, he said, had examined the costs and benefits: "If the legislation was based on health grounds, you would naturally think this would lead to monitoring of people who had had abortions' but, he said, "the health aspect is always secondary to personal choice". Despite Professor Fergusson's own admission ("I'm pro-choice but I've produced results which... favour a pro-life viewpoint"), he has concluded: "It verges on scandalous that a surgical procedure that is performed on one in ten women has been so poorly researched and evaluated given the debates about the psychological consequences of abortion."

87 Professor David Fergusson's long-term study, *Journal of Child Psychiatry and Psychology* (January, 2006), linked those having abortions with elevated levels of subsequent mental health problems, including depression, anxiety, suicidal behaviours and substance use disorders. Researchers found that at age 25, 42% of women in the study group who had had an abortion also experienced major depression at some stage during the past four years. This was 35% higher than those who had continued the pregnancy.

See also Sharain Suliman, Todd Ericksen, Peter Labuscgne, Renee de Wit, Dan J. Stein, Soraya Seedat, "Comparison of pain, cortisol levels, and psychological distress in women undergoing surgical termination of pregnancy under local anaesthesia versus intravenous sedation", *BMC Psychiatry* 2007, Vol. 7(24). This more recent study found unexpectedly high levels of Post Traumatic Stress Disorder in a study of 155 women who had abortions. Their psychological health was assessed before the abortion, again at one month after abortion, and then again at three months. Nearly one in five women had symptoms that met the criteria for Post Traumatic Stress Disorder. The researchers observed that "high rates of PTSD characterize women who have undergone voluntary pregnancy termination."

and financial support. A revealing and distressing aspect of de Crespigny's attitude towards Jessica's mother after her abortion is confirmed in his admission in a recent newspaper interview that "He has not seen or spoken to the woman since".[88]

Changing discriminatory attitudes among medical professionals

Education is our most valuable tool for eliminating attitudes of discrimination towards unborn children at risk of abortion, especially towards children like Jessica. Abortion "on request" is the wrong response to current individual and community attitudes of discrimination towards these children. The child with disabilities is not to be blamed. The child is not to be punished, his or her life is not to be forfeited, aborted because of his or her disabilities. Rather, the child's "unwantedness" is *per se* an attitudinal prejudice of the child's mother (and/or sometimes of the child's father and/or other family members and/or the community). Such prejudice needs to be examined out in the open.

In initiating and maintaining effective public awareness campaigns, States Parties to the Convention on the Rights of Persons with Disabilities are

> to nurture receptiveness to the rights of children with disabilities and to promote positive perceptions and greater social awareness towards such children. Article 8(2)(a).

Children with disabilities who are at risk of abortion should be spoken of with respect, especially by medical personnel when speaking to the parents of the child. Regrettably, parents of children with disabilities report consistent failure by their doctors to show such respect:

> Most parents follow the doctor's advice to do therapeutic abortion. This is of course another incorrect word. How can an abortion be therapeutic? If the unborn child is already viable and he can survive termination of pregnancy, there is a major ethical problem. What to do at birth with a viable child that is not wanted by the mother? Therefore physicians prefer to be sure that the child is not a life at birth. They give the unborn baby an injection with Kalium (Potassium) through the womb of the mother in the heart of the child and the baby is stillborn. A therapeutic death. This practice is carried out in many centres and openly discussed in medical conferences and published in their medical magazines, explaining exactly how to do it and how to avoid risks for the mother.[89]

See also the recent admission and warning by the Royal College of Psychiatrists, Position Statement on Women's Mental Health in Relation to Induced Abortion, March 14, 2008.

88 Carol Nader's article, "Controversial abortion case that brought a doctor years of anguish", *The Age*, December 13, 2007.

89 Pierre Mertens, President of the International Federation for Spina Bifida and Hydrocephalus (IF): *A Future With Purpose, A Future With Choice*, p. 9. Available at: www.perso.ch/dupuism/AFutureWithPurpose3.pdf.

The gruesome practice of abortion is indeed routinely sanitized in reporting and discussion. See, for example, Professor de Crespigny's chilling description of his late term abortion (at 33 weeks gestation) of baby Jessica:

> Fetal intracardiac potassium chloride was administered, as recommended by the UK Royal College of Obstetricians and Gynaecologists (RCOG), with rapid cessation of fetal heart movements and labour induced.[90]

This is chilling also in its revelation—that support for such an atrocity is to be found in the Royal College of Obstetricians and Gynaecologists (RCOG) publication: "A consideration of the law and ethics in relation to late termination of pregnancy for fetal abnormality". Clearly, this Report of the RCOG Ethics Committee, published in London in 1998, needs radical revision in the light of the latest instrument of international human rights law, the Convention on the Rights of Persons with Disabilities (2007). The Royal College of Obstetricians and Gynaecologists is not a law unto itself and must comply with universal human rights obligations to protect children with disabilities before as well as after birth and to uphold the 'best interests of the child' principle.

The principle of best interests of the child

The Convention on the Rights of Persons with Disabilities asserts:
- In all actions concerning children with disabilities, the best interests of the child shall be a primary consideration; *Article 7(2)*
- In all cases the best interests of the child shall be paramount. *Article 23(2)*

The Convention on the Rights of the Child (Articles 3, 9, 18, 20, 21, 37 and 40) requires that this principle be applied to each and every proposed or existing law or policy or administrative action or court decision directly or indirectly affecting the well-being of children.[91] The best interests of the child principle, legally binding on expectant parents and prenatal health care providers, prohibits treatment that entails harm or damage to the child's health and development.[92] Aborting the child's life is surely the most lethal of all such treatments.

Intentional killing of a child before birth is never in the best interests of that child. Who decides whether a life is worth living? This is a judgment that the rule of law has always cautioned human beings against making on their own behalf (suicide), and especially on behalf of another human being at one's mercy so to speak ('mercy' killing). What are the rights of the unborn child? Who can judge if a life is worth liv-

90 Lachlan J de Crespigny and Julian Savulescu, "Abortion: time to clarify Australia's confusing laws", Medical Journal of Australia , 2004, Vol. 181 (4), pp. 201-203.

91 CRC General Comment No 5, para. 10.

92 The Inter-American Court of Human Rights concurs with the European Court of Human Rights on this: see Inter-American Court of Human Rights advisory opinion: oc-17/2002 on children's juridical status and human rights. See paras. 74 & 137.9.

ing? These questions were asked at the International Conference of IF (2000) and 270 people with Spina Bifida and Hydrocephalus, considered the best consultants on the quality of life of people with these conditions, answered as follows:

> Most adults with spina bifida underline that their quality of life is not automatically—and should not be given as—a reason for abortion...Doctors are focussing too much on the medical deficit and not on the opportunities of people with disabilities. This is a societal evolution related to the increased availability of diagnostic tools. Information given to future parents is often biased, leading to a termination of the pregnancy.[93]

"When human reason begins to rationalize its own exterminatory projects..."

Termination of the lives of children with disabilities remains an intentionally lethal, pseudo-medical procedure. Genuine medicine does no deliberate harm to an unborn child. The original noble aims and purposes of the medical profession to safeguard the health of mothers and their children *in utero* [94] are being profaned when they are put in the service of a screening program the thinly disguised purpose of which is quite literally decimation of the future population of persons with disabilities such as Down Syndrome and Spina Bifida.

Anyone rationalizing such a programmed decimation should heed Michael Ignatieff's grim warning in the Tanner Lectures (2000) on the prudential necessity of human rights and their ultimate fragility:

> If one end product of Western rationalism is the exterminatory nihilism of the Nazis, then any ethics that takes only reason for its guide is bound to be powerless when human reason begins to rationalize its own exterminatory projects.[95]

93 "Ethical discussion on prenatal selection in EU countries involving spina bifida/hydrocephalus user groups network", Final Report, PS/2004/035 p. 3.

94 The British Medical Association's June 1947 submission *War Crimes and Medicine* reaffirmed "the duty of curing, the greatest crime being co-operation in the destruction of life by murder, suicide and abortion". The *Declaration of Geneva (1948)* vowed: "...the utmost respect for human life from the time of conception". This was reaffirmed by the World Medical Association *ad verbatim* in the *Declaration of Geneva (1968)*. International Code of Medical Ethics (1949) asserted specifically the importance of "...preserving human life from the time of conception".

95 Ignatieff, Michael, *Human Rights as Politics and Idolatry*, (ed.) Amy Gutmann, Princeton, N.J.: Princeton University Press, 2001.

Chapter 10 European Convention (1950) and the Unborn Child

The historical background to the *European Convention for the Protection of Human Rights and Fundamental Freedoms (1950)* reveals that a broad consensus for inclusion of the child before birth in human rights protection was operating universally and without controversy at that time. So compelling is the evidence that it places the intellectual objectivity and competence of the current European Court of Human Rights in serious doubt when that Court continues to insist that in the European Convention there is no definitive right to life protection for the child before birth, that individual states are to be allowed "a margin of appreciation" to decide for themselves when life begins.[1]

The flaw in permitting each State's domestic law to define the term 'everyone' to include or to exclude classes of human beings as they wish is that such an arrangement would allow for a re-enactment of the human rights violations perpetrated by Nazi doctors in the 1930's and 1940's. Such permission for each State to decide for itself who is to have the right to life would be perfectly compatible with any emergence in Europe or elsewhere of a neo-Nazi domestic law that would allow lethal experiments on embryonic children of Jewish parentage. In order that there should never again be a Hitler or a Holocaust, the *Universal Declaration of Human Rights* established right from the beginning the critical obligation to eschew definitions which would 'exclude' some human beings from human rights defence.

The great legal expert on genocide, Raphael Lemkin, writing at the time of the drafting of the Universal Declaration about the "recent Nuremberg proceedings against Nazi doctors who experimented on human beings in concentration camps" verifies the understanding of abortion at that time as a form of killing:

---

1 European Court of Human Rights, *Vo v France*, Judgment of 8 July 2004: "...the issue of when the right to life begins comes within the margin of appreciation which the Court generally considers that States should enjoy in this sphere, notwithstanding an evolutive interpretation of the Convention, a "living instrument which must be interpreted in the light of present-day conditions" (see *Tyrer v. the United Kingdom*, judgment of 25 April 1978, Series A no. 26, pp. 15-16, § 31, and subsequent case-law)." para. 82.

> … the defendants practiced experiments in order to develop techniques for outright killings and abortions.[2]

Given that both the Universal Declaration and the European Convention were written with the object and purpose of preventing any repeat of Nazi contempt for vulnerable, 'defective' or unwanted human beings, this new 'permission' today for European States to de-universalize human rights is absolutely unacceptable. It is incompatible with the original object and purpose of the treaty.

Permission to define the term 'everyone' to exclude some human beings contravenes the universality of the human rights recognized in the Universal Declaration and international human rights law.

European Court's "margin of appreciation" incompatible with non-derogable right to life

Perversely now, the European Court of Human Rights has made a mockery of the Universal Declaration's recognition of the State's duty to provide appropriate legal protection for the child before birth. Claiming that "there is no European consensus on the scientific and legal definition of the beginning of life",[3] the Court has appropriated the weasel term 'a margin of appreciation' in a ludicrous attempt to use purported scientific disagreement as to when life begins as a legal excuse for some European states' liberalized abortion laws. Yet the right to life in international human rights covenant law is a non-derogable right.[4] It is the universal nature of non-derogable human rights that States, including all European Union states who are party to the *International Covenant on Civil and Political Rights* (ICCPR), do not have 'a margin of appreciation'.

In *Vo v. France* (2004), the European Court declares "the unborn child is not regarded as a 'person' directly protected by Article 2 of the Convention".[5]

Yet Article 2 says:

> Everyone's right to life shall be protected by law. No one shall be deprived of his life intentionally save in the execution of a sentence of a court following his conviction of a crime for which this penalty is provided by law.

When the European Court of Human Rights declares in *Vo v. France* (para. 84) that no one knows the meaning of 'everyone', we need to ask whether these judges are being naïve or are they intentionally complicit in a deliberate attempt to manipulate the historical record?

---

2 Lemkin, Raphael, "Genocide as Crime under International Law", *American Journal of International Law*, Vol. 41(1), Jan. 1947, pp. 145-151 at (pp. 147-8).

3 *Vo v. France* (2004), para. 84.

4 *International Covenant on Civil and Political Rights* Articles 4(2) & (6).

5 *Vo v. France* (2004), para. 80.

"...no one knows the meaning of 'everyone'"?

It is not credible to claim that the European Convention on Human Rights could have been either drafted originally or interpreted initially by the European Court of Human Rights to exclude legal protection for the child before birth in direct contradiction to the stated need for special safeguards and care before as well as after birth recognized by the Universal Declaration. This could not be so—not when the great French jurist, René Cassin, one of the most eminent drafters of the Universal Declaration, presided as a judge on the European Court of Human Rights from 1959 to 1970 and was President of the European Court for two periods in this time.[6] It is a gross injustice to imply that René Cassin who received the Nobel Peace Prize in 1968, as a recognition for his work in the drafting of the Universal Declaration, would have gone along with such a radical reinterpretation as to remove legal protection for any group of human beings in vulnerable situations, such as children at risk of abortion. René Cassin himself had lost many members of his family in the Holocaust.

Albert Verdoodt wrote the first detailed legislative history of the drafting of the Universal Declaration, a history that was prefaced by René Cassin himself.[7] The section on the drafting of Article 3—"Everyone has the right to life, liberty and security of person."— begins with Cassin's initial statement before the Secretariat explaining the need to establish something so elementary as "the protection of human life and the right to existence", pointing to 1933 "when Germany commenced to violate these principles".[8]

This, together with a second notable statement before the Secretariat, formed the rationale for the right to life article. This second proposition formulated by and borrowed from the Inter-American Council of Jurists began with: "Everyone has the right to life. This right is understood to be the right to life from the moment of conception..."[9]

Verdoodt records that this right can be understood only in the context of the entire Declaration. From the travaux préparatoires, he says, the right to life is to be interpreted as follows: *Each individual has the right to physical existence.*[10] Though a "precise" mention was not made in the final text of "when this existence begins", Verdoodt makes it clear that it was understood that legislation permitting abortion [even] in certain cases was incompatible with the holistic meaning of the right to life.[11] In the same way, he says, there was no "explicit condemnation" in the text of euthanasia of incurables and the mentally disabled. For these too, Verdoodt quotes the drafters,

6 Cassin was also Chairman of the UN Commission of Human Rights in 1955.

7 Verdoodt, Albert, *Naissance et Signification de la Déclaration Universelle des Droits de l'Homme*, Société d'Etudes Morales, Sociales et Juridiques, Louvain-Paris: Editions Nauwelaerts, 1964.

8 Ibid., p. 95.

9 Ibid., pp. 95-6.

10 "Chaque individu a droit à l'existence physique." ibid., p. 100.

11 "Il n'est pas précisé quand cette existence commence eu égard à des législations permettant l'avortement dans certains cas." ibid., pp. 99-100.

"Each individual has the right to liberty and security of person, as is settled in the articles that follow."[12]

In the original Cassin draft of Article 3 of the Universal Declaration, it was proposed that each man "owes to society fundamental duties which are: obedience to law, exercise of a useful activity, acceptance of the burdens and sacrifices demanded for the common good."[13] It was Cassin who convinced the Drafting Committee that they must start with "the fundamental principle of the unity of the human race" precisely because Hitler had started his pogroms "by asserting the inequality of men".[14] Cassin also put forward a second principle, that every human being has "a right to be treated like every other human being"; and a third principle, "the concept of solidarity or brotherhood among men".[15]

It would be contrary to the clear context of that time to impute to the drafters of the European Convention on Human Rights or the Universal Declaration an intention to exclude the child before birth from human rights. Both documents were truly creatures of post-war revulsion against all human rights abuse—and the focus of those times was firmly, even passionately on 'non-exclusion'. One authority on the drafting history of the Universal Declaration, Johannes Morsink, places great emphasis on this aspect of the drafting of the Declaration. From his study of the copious documents and records of the drafting sessions, he discerns "…an intended literal meaning of the words 'everyone' and 'no one'" and goes on to assert confidently: "They intentionally chose words like 'everyone' and 'no one' and meant them to be taken literally."[16]

It appears that the European Court on Human Rights, in its *Vo v France* majority judgment, did not consult a reputable history of the drafting of the Universal Declaration, when it opined that no one knew the meaning of 'everyone' (para. 84).

In any case, no matter how the Court wriggles here, the Court is in error: it is a matter of historical fact that the European Convention did ensure legal protection for the child before birth and in view of the Court's own admission[17] that a valid al-

---

12 "De meme aucune condamnation explicite n'est portée contre l'euthanasie des incurables et des faibles d'esprit, ni contre la condamnation légale pour crime grave à la peine capitale ou contre le manque de protection de l'Etat contre les tentatives criminelles. Chaque individu a droit à la liberté et à la sureté de sa personne, comme cela est précisé dans les articles suivants." ibid., p. 100.

13 See the June 1947 Draft revised by Cassin (Cassin Draft) in Glendon, Mary Ann: *A World Made New,* Appendix 2.

14 Ibid., p. 39.

15 E/CN.4/AC.1/SR.2, p.2.

16 Morsink, Johannes: "Women's Rights in the Universal Declaration", *Human Rights Quarterly*, Vol. 13, p. 256.

17 "…there is no European consensus on the scientific and legal definition of the beginning of life." *Vo v. France* (2004), para. 82.

ternative consensus has not yet been crafted,[18] the original consensus must remain in effect.

"...and I find it frightening" (Dissenting European Court Judge)

So it is a shameful evasion of the truth when the European Court of Human Rights, in a recent judgment (*Tysiac v Poland* 2007), denies that there is any mandatory protection of the right to life for the unborn child in the European Convention and goes on to rebuke the Polish State for failing to comply "with the positive obligations to safeguard the applicant's [the mother's] right to respect for her private life in the context of a controversy as to whether she was entitled to a therapeutic abortion."[19]

In contrast to the ignorance and confusion of the majority decision in *Tysiac v Poland* (2007), it is immensely encouraging that there are still conscientious and courageously honest judges on the European Court like Justice Borrego Borrego. He deplores the implication that any consideration of the right to life of an unborn Polish child at risk of abortion can be ignored, and he accuses the European Court's majority judgment of having gone too far in urging a more permissive approach to facilitating abortion.[20]

The conclusion to his Dissenting Opinion in the *Tysiac v Poland* case deserves to be publicized far and wide:

> All human beings are born free and equal in dignity and rights. Today the Court has decided that a human being was born as a result of a violation of the *European Convention on Human Rights*. According to this reasoning, there is a Polish child, currently six years old; whose right to be born contradicts the *Convention*.
> I would never have thought that the *Convention* would go so far, and I find it frightening.[21]

---

18 The validity of any consensus that would seek to de-recognize the human rights of any particular group of human beings is dubious. The concept of formal universal recognition of the child before birth as a legitimate subject of inherent and inalienable human rights including entitlement to legal protection is critical for it is the nature of inherent and inalienable human rights that they can never be de-recognized.

19 European Court.of Human Rights, *Tysiac v Poland* Judgment of 24 September 2007, para. 128.

20 European Court.of Human Rights, *Tysiac v Poland* Judgment 2007, Dissenting Opinion by Justice Borrego Borrego.

> The Court appears to be proposing that the High Contracting Party, Poland, join those States that have adopted a more permissive approach with regard to abortion. It must be stressed that "certain State Parties" referred to in paragraph 123 allow "abortion on demand" until eighteen weeks of pregnancy. Is this the law that the Court is laying down to Poland? I consider that the Court contradicts itself in the last sentence of paragraph 104: "It is not the Court's task in the present case to examine whether the Convention guarantees a right to have an abortion." para. 13.

21 Ibid., para. 15.

Lacking a coherent understanding of the historical and metaphysical foundations of the *Convention*, many members of the European Court of Human Rights appear unable at present to form ethically and logically cohesive arguments to defend the truth about the human rights of the unborn child and the inherent dignity and equal worth of each and every human life. Their judgments are skewed by a contemporary bias towards the extreme pro-abortion prejudices being peddled by the dominant ideology of our day.

Denying the right to exist "shocks the conscience of mankind"

By reducing the unborn child at risk of abortion to an inferior kind of being with potentiality and capacity only, the European Court of Human Rights has denied "it" the right to continue to exist:

> The potentiality of that being and its capacity to become a person…require protection in the name of human dignity, without making it a "person" with the "right to life" for the purposes of Article 2.[22]

Regrettably, the European Court of Human Rights appears to have lost sight of its original purpose. The European Convention was drafted with the purpose of ensuring that European law-making would always recognize what the United Nations in 1946 called "the conscience of mankind" which condemns outright the "denial of existence" to entire groups of human beings.[23]

Explaining in August 1949 the need for a European treaty guaranteeing human rights, one of its leading proponents, Pierre-Henri Teitgen, a former French Minister of Justice, put the case for conscientious protection of all human beings to the Consultative Assembly of the Council of Europe as follows:

> Democracies do not become Nazi countries in one day. Evil progresses cunningly…Public opinion and the entire national conscience are asphyxiated…
> It is necessary to intervene before it is too late. A conscience must exist somewhere which will sound the alarm in the minds of a nation menaced by this progressive corruption, to warn them of a peril and to show them that they are progressing down a long road which leads far, sometimes even to Buchenwald or to Dachau.[24]

It was to proof the nations of Europe and of the world against this human susceptibility to "progressive corruption" of universal human rights by new extreme ideolo-

22 *Vo v. France* (2004), para. 84.

23 "…a denial of the right of existence of entire human groups… shocks the conscience of mankind…, and is contrary to moral law and to the spirit and aims of the United Nations…", *UN Resolution on Genocide*, 11 December, 1946.

24 Quoted in Robertson, A.H.: *Human Rights in Europe*, Manchester University Press (2nd ed.), 1977, p. 4.

gies that the modern human rights instruments, including the European Convention, were established.

Historical background to the European Convention

Indeed, it was painfully honest confrontation of the record of Nazi atrocities that led after World War II to a clear condemnation of abortion as "a crime against humanity". This condemnation was made by the international community, *inter alia* through the United Nations, the Nuremberg War Crimes Tribunals and the World Medical Association Organization.

Historian Dr. John Hunt, researching the Nuremberg Trials involving abortion, has established that condemnation of abortion was not simply limited to the practice of forced abortions but included all abortions.[25] James McHaney, Nuremberg prosecutor of the RuSHA or Greifelt Case, in his summation, called abortion an "inhumane act" and an "act of extermination" and stated that even if a woman's request for abortion was voluntary, abortion was still a crime against humanity.

It is part of the Nuremberg record of the trial testimony that the unborn were considered to be human beings entitled to the protection of the law: "...protection of the law was denied to the unborn children..."[26] As one of the Nuremberg judgments, this principle was mandated to be codified in the International Bill of Rights. [UN Resolution 95(1)[27]].

Regarding the term 'compelling abortions', it is important to note that it is the abortion itself that is judged an atrocity against human life, against the lives of unborn children who should have been given "protection of the law". Compulsion is an additional factor of rights violation but it is clear from the Nuremberg Judgments that it does not constitute the whole violation.[28]

25 Hunt, John, "Out of Respect For Life: Nazi Abortion Policy in the Eastern Occupied Territories", *Journal of Genocide Research*, Vol. 1(3), 1997, pp. 379-385; and "Abortion and the Nuremberg Prosecutors: A Deeper Analysis", *Life and Learning*, Vol. VII, Proceedings of the Seventh University Faculty for Life Conference, June, 1997.

26 *Nuremberg Trials Record*: "The RuSHA Case", March 1948, Volume IV, p. 1077. Available at: http://www.mazal.org/archive/nmt/04a/NMT04-T1076.htm.

27 *Affirmation of the Principles of International Law recognized by the Charter of the Nuremberg Tribunal. Resolution 95 (1) of the United Nations General Assembly*, 11 December 1946. The UN committee on the codification of international law was directed to establish a general codification of "the principles recognized in the Charter of the Nuremberg Tribunal and in the judgment of the Tribunal". These became the foundation of modern international human rights law.

28 Historian John Hunt, after extensive research of Nazi abortion programs and the Nuremberg prosecution's evidence, concludes that the Nazis saw abortion as "an act of killing" and that Nuremberg condemned both the violations of liberty and the violations of life as far as abortion was concerned:" Like the kidnapping of children and the seizing of newborns also prosecuted at this trial, abortions were seen as wrong at any time, not just when done for racial-genocidal reasons." Hunt, John: "Abortion and the Nuremberg Prosecutors: A Deeper Analysis", *op. cit.*, p. 205.

Decriminalization of abortion–evidence at Nuremberg for the count of crimes against humanity

The Nazi record of decriminalizing abortion in Poland and the Eastern Territories was still fresh in the public perception when the Universal Declaration (1948) and the European Convention for the Protection of Human Rights (1950) were drafted. Instructions by Nazi authorities issuing directives to decriminalize abortion were furnished as evidence for the count of crimes against humanity:

> Abortion must not be punishable in the remaining territory... Institutes and persons who make a business of performing abortions should not be prosecuted by the police.[29]

Eastern women workers were induced or forced to undergo abortions. In addition to the charge of "compelling" abortions, there was also the charge of "encouraging" abortions among Polish women by removing abortion from prosecution in Polish courts:

> Abortions on Polish women in the General Government were also encouraged by the withdrawal of abortion case from the jurisdiction of the Polish courts. The defendants Greifelt, Creutz, Meyer-Hetling, Schwarzenberger, Hofmann, Hildebrandt, Schwalm, Huebner, Lorenz, and Brueckner are charged with special responsibility for and participation in these crimes.[30]

Decriminalization of abortion was judged and condemned at Nuremberg as encouraging abortions. The fact that the Nazi authorities had removed abortion from Polish domestic law did not nullify the fact that abortion was still judged "a crime against humanity". This was in accord with the working definition:

> Crimes against humanity: namely, murder, extermination...and other inhumane acts committed against any civilian population, before or during the war... whether or not in violation of the domestic law of the country where perpetrated.[31]

Though the Nazis had decriminalized abortion, the Nuremberg Tribunal still judged that "...protection of the law was denied the unborn children" and two SS Officers

---

29 *Nuremberg Trials Record: Trial of Ulrich Greifelt and Others Indictment* [Tr. pp. 1-18, 7/1/1947.] Vol. V. at pp. 95-6. http://www.mazal.org/archive/nmt/05/NMT05-T0095.htm.

30 *Nuremberg Trials Record: Trial of Ulrich Greifelt and Others Indictment* [Tr. pp. 1-18, 7/1/1947.] Vol. IV, para. 12, at pp. 613-4. http://www.mazal.org/archive/nmt/04a/NMT04-T0613.htm.

31 *Agreement for the Prosecution and Punishment of the Major War Criminals of the European Axis, and Charter of the International Military Tribunal,* London, 8 August, 1945. Charter II: Jurisdiction and general principles Article 6(c).

Richard Hildebrandt and Otto Hofmann were convicted for "compelling and encouraging abortion"; they received sentences of 25 years.[32]

It is immensely significant that the Universal Declaration was drafted on the foundation of Nuremberg principles and judgments such as these. In the *Affirmation of the Principles of International Law recognized by the Charter of the Nuremberg Tribunal, Resolution 95 (1) of the United Nations General Assembly*, 11 December 1946, the UN committee on the codification of international law was directed to establish a general codification of "the principles recognized in the Charter of the Nuremberg Tribunal and in the judgment of the Tribunal".

Merging "Hippocratic ethics and human rights into a single code"

The Hippocratic Oath with its age-old condemnation of doctors who perform abortions was still the yardstick of universal medical ethics both at the time of the Nuremberg Trials, and in 1947-9 when the *Geneva Doctors' Oath* and the *International Medical Code of Ethics* were being drafted more or less contemporaneously with the Universal Declaration (1948) and the European Convention (1950). Evelyne Schuster has perceived a critically important truth:

> The key contribution of Nuremberg was to merge both Hippocratic ethics and the protection of human rights into a single code.[33]

Hippocratic medical ethics were referenced many times in the Nuremberg record. Brigadier-General Telford Taylor in his opening statement at the *Doctors' Trial* (December 9, 1946) described the 20 physicians in the dock as ranging from leaders of German scientific medicine, with excellent international reputations, down to the dregs of the German medical profession. He went on to say:

> All of them violated the Hippocratic commandments which they had solemnly sworn to uphold and abide by, including the fundamental principles never to do harm - "primum non nocere."[34]

32 Richard Hildebrandt was Higher SS and Police Leader at Danzig-West Prussia from October 1939 to February 1943, and simultaneously he was leader of the Administration District Danzig-West Prussia of the Allgemeine SS and deputy of the RKFDV. From 20 April 1943 to the end of the war, he was chief of RuSHA. Also Otto Hofmann, as chief of RuSHA from 1940 to 1943. See *Nuremberg Trials Record*: "The RuSHA Case", Opinion and Judgment, "War Crimes and Crimes Against Humanity",Vol.V, pp. 152 to 154 and pp. 160-2. Available at: http://www.mazal.org/archive/nmt/05/NMT05-T0152.htm .

33 Schuster, Evelyne: "The Nuremberg Code: Hippocratic ethics and human rights", *Lancet*, Vol. 351, 1998, pp. 974-978.

34 Opening statement by Brigadier General Telford Taylor, December 9, 1946, p. 67. Available at: http://www.ushmm.org/research/doctors/telfptx.htm (United States Holocaust Memorial Museum)

Although Hippocratic ethics specifically precluded under this principle the practice of abortion, the medical profession cooperated in programmed evil and perpetrated decriminalized deprivation of life against selected unborn children.

For the Nazi leadership, decriminalization of abortion was a significant tool in the genocidal program to prevent births in particular groups that were deemed ideologically or socially unwanted.

States must at all times take positive steps to protect the right to life

We are told by abortion advocates today that 'decriminalization' is not the same as 'legalization' of abortion. Pro-abortion feminist lawyers have commended the *Vo v. France* (2004) decision by the European Court of Human Rights:

> ...the Court declined to treat the fetus as a "person" or require a homicide prosecution even though, as in this case, there was no conflict with the rights of the woman (Paras. 89, 92, 93). This decision protects all of Europe's liberal abortion laws, as well as doctors and providers, from being deterred from providing abortions for fear of such sanction.[35]

But why should there not be fear of sanction for violating the right to life of a child selected for abortion? Notably the judges in this case did not have even the least vestige of the ubiquitous excuse that it was 'necessary' to sacrifice the right to life of the child in order to maintain the right to life of the mother: "...even though, as in this case, there was no conflict with the rights of the woman".

Yet for the child before birth as for the child after birth and as for all adults, the right to life, as proclaimed in the Universal Declaration, is equally valid, and indeed, the Universal Declaration "recognizes" that "the child, by reason of his physical and mental immaturity, needs special safeguards and care, including appropriate legal protection, before as well as after birth".[36]

Codification of legal protection of the right to life principle in the *International Covenant on Civil and Political Rights (ICCPR),* has meant that the right to life is protected by international human rights law which means, *inter alia,* that States must at no time engage in, or condone arbitrary or extrajudicial killings of children before or after birth; and that the States have a strict legal duty to prevent, investigate, prosecute, punish and redress violations of the right to life. "No one may be deprived of their life arbitrarily", says Article 6(1) of the *ICCPR*. This means that the law must strictly control and limit the circumstances in which the State may condone deprivation of life.[37] The legal duty to take positive steps effectively to protect the right to life for everyone is equally valid in times and states of public emergency, in war time, for example, or in national disasters, or in refugee camps.

35 Copelon, R., Zampas, C., Brusie, E., Devore, J., "Human rights begin at birth: international law and the claim of fetal rights", Reproductive Health Matters, November 2005, Vol. 13(26), pp. 120-9.

36 Preamble to the UN Declaration of the Rights of the Child (1959).

37 UN Human Rights Committee General Comment 6, para. 3.

Decriminalization of abortion represents, then, a betrayal of the State's legal duty at all times take positive steps to protect the right to life of every human being "before and after birth", and to prevent, investigate, prosecute, punish and redress violations of the right to life.

Legalization of abortion—regulating abortion as a 'health procedure'

We are told now also that the term 'legalization of abortion', implies that abortion is a health procedure that is under state control and interest. Pro-abortion feminist lawyers have declared: "*Vo* also protects women's access to reproductive health care, including abortion".[38] Such logically absurd ideological redefinition of a fatal assault on the unborn child, however, represents a patently dishonest ploy. Indeed, this is a grotesque reclassification of abortion from a criminal procedure that involves the intentional deprivation of the life of a child in his/her mother's womb to a health procedure which ignores the most pertinent fact: what is classified as a health procedure for the child's mother is in reality an intentionally lethal procedure for her child.

Both the health and the life of the child are destroyed in an abortion 'health procedure'.

Increasingly, more substantial research is uncovering long-term psychological and physiological consequences of abortion that bring into grave doubt the unsubstantiated claims propagated by radical feminists since the 1970s that abortion is a health-giving procedure for women.[39]

In most States where decriminalization of abortion has been replaced with legalization, the State's control and interest under diverse Health Acts has amounted almost entirely to making the procedure 'safe' for the mother by providing regulations on where and how and by whom an abortion may be performed. There is very little regulation in domestic health legislation to protect the child at risk of abortion. The State's focus is on pragmatic issues such as whether the abortion 'provider' complies with the safety regulations attached to the 'procedure'. Such regulations include, for example, getting the signature of two doctors and ensuring that the health facility where the child's life is to be aborted is formally accredited.[40]

38 Ibid.

39 See for example Pedersen, Willy, "Abortion and depression: A population-based longitudinal study of young women", *Scandinavian Journal of Public Health*, Vol. 36 (4), 2008, pp. 424-428.

Also the recent admission and warning by the Royal College of Psychiatrists: "Position Statement on Women's Mental Health in Relation to Induced Abortion", March 14, 2008.

Also New Zealand's Professor David Fergusson's large long-term study reported in the *Journal of Child Psychiatry and Psychology* (January, 2006) linked those having abortions with elevated levels of subsequent mental health problems, including depression, anxiety, suicidal behaviors and substance use disorders.

40 For example, see Hilary White, "Eugenic Abortion for Minor Problems Criticised by Pro-Abortion Doctor", October 22 2007, (LifeSiteNews.com):

Meantime, the terrible human rights abuse at the heart of each abortion is ignored—concern for the child at risk of abortion is blotted out by the facile assumption that every abortion is a 'necessary health procedure' for the child's mother. In a very similar way, Nazi authorities regulated abortion claiming that it was 'necessary' to the health of the German people and issuing quite specific instructions as to the conditions that were to be met in establishing abortion programs.

Making abortion "a simple and pleasant affair"

Just as with today's pro-abortion rhetoric, Nazi propaganda too was deviously persuasive. In Poland, Russia and the Eastern Occupied Territories, Nazi ideologues had set about "encouraging" abortion of the unwanted:

> ...the press, radio, and movies, as well as pamphlets, booklets, and lectures, must be used to instill... the idea that it is harmful to have several children. We must emphasize the expenses that children cause, the good things that people could have had with the money spent on them. We could also hint at the dangerous effect of child-bearing on a woman's health... It will even be necessary to open special institutions for abortion, and to train midwives and nurses for this purpose. The population will practice abortion all the more willingly if these institutions are competently operated. The doctors must be able to help out, there being any question of this being a breach of their professional ethics. [41]

Himmler's March 1943 decree coined the excuse (familiar these days) that "the pregnancy is being interrupted for reasons of social distress".[42] Abortion of "racially substandard offspring of Eastern workers and Poles" was to be sanitized:

Vincent Argent, a gynecologist and former medical director of one of Britain's largest abortionist organisation, British Pregnancy Advisory Service, in his evidence to the House of Commons Committee on Science and Technology enquiry into lowering the age limit for abortions (October, 2007) told of abuses of the current system of abortion with the consent of two-doctors. He told of the signing of batches of consent forms before patients are even seen and forms signed without doctors having met or spoken with patients or reading medical histories. Some, he said, signed consent forms after the abortion had been committed. Others faxed their consent forms to abortion facilities to be used in their absence.

41 Dr. Erich Wetzel, Director of the Nazi Central Advisory Office Memorandum: "Stellungnahme und Gedanken zum Generalplan Ost des Reichsführers SS" (Opinion and ideas Regarding the General Plan for the East of the Reichsführer SS), 27 April, 1942. (Presented as evidence in the RuSHA/Greifelt Case). This excerpt is quoted in Poliakov, Léon: *Harvest of Hate: The Nazi Program for the Destruction of the Jews of Europe*. New York: Holocaust Library [distributed by Schocken Books,], 1979, p. 274.

42 *Nuremberg Military Trials, Vol.* 5, p.109. Available at: http://www.mazal.org/archive/nmt/04a/NMT04-T0687.htm.

> A pregnancy interruption should go off without incidents and the Eastern worker or Pole is to be treated generously during this period in order that this may get to be known among them as a simple and pleasant affair.[43]

On abortion, the European Court of Human Rights in *Tysiac v Poland* (2007) reveals a curious similarity in tone with Himmler's decree—a chilling pragmatism that portrays abortion as a 'simple' harmless procedure:

> The Court notes that the Ordinance provides for a relatively simple procedure for obtaining a lawful abortion based on medical considerations: two concurring opinions of specialists other than the doctor who would perform an abortion are sufficient. Such a procedure allows for taking relevant measures promptly...[44]

Zero concern is shown for the Polish child who loses his/her life in the "pregnancy interruption" being approved in Himmler's decree. Similarly, zero consideration is given to the Polish child who, it was averred, should have been "promptly" and "lawfully" aborted according to the "relatively simple procedure" set out in the Ordinance approved by the European Court of Human Rights in their Tysiac v Poland (2007) judgment.

"...the greatest crime being co-operation in...murder, suicide and abortion" (British Medical Association 1947)

How has the European Court of Human Rights come to this apostasy of the human rights of the unborn child? Why has the Court now in 2007 imposed the provision of "timely abortions"[45] on the State and on doctors as a positive obligation to secure effective respect for the "private life[46] of any pregnant woman who requests abortion?

In 1947, the British Medical Association (BMA) had no qualms about condemning abortion, stating that the trials of medical war criminals have shown that the doctors who were guilty of these crimes against humanity lacked both moral and professional conscience and had "departed from the traditional medical ethic which maintains the value and sanctity of every individual human being". The BMA went on to insist: "Although there have been many changes in Medicine, the spirit of the Hippocratic Oath cannot change." The international medical profession was urged to reaffirm "the duty of curing, the greatest crime being co-operation in the destruction of life by murder, suicide and abortion..."[47]

---

43 "On 18 February 1944, a letter went out from the SD office in Koblenz to the branch offices..." *Nuremberg Military Trials, Vol IV*, p. 687. Available at: http://www.mazal.org/archive/nmt/04a/NMT04-T0687.htm.

44 *Tysiac v Poland* (2007), para. 121.

45 Ibid., para. 18.

46 Ibid., para. 164(3).

47 Statement by the Council of the British Medical Association to the World Medical Association, June 1947 (re-issued by The Medical Education Trust and reproduced at http://www.donoharm.org.uk/leaflets/war.htm).

How has this horror and condemnation of the abortion of unborn children been transformed so radically? How has provision of abortion now become a 'positive' human rights duty imposed by the European Court of Human Rights on the State and, in turn, to be imposed by the State on doctors?

"...utmost respect for human life from the time of conception" *Declaration of Geneva*

Again, in claiming "there is no European consensus on the scientific and legal definition of the beginning of life",[48] the European Court of Human Rights appears to have forgotten that in 1948, the World Medical Association issued the *Declaration of Geneva* which included in the *Physician's Oath* the solemn pledge:

> I will maintain the utmost respect for human life from the time of conception; even under threat, I will not use medical knowledge contrary to the laws of humanity...

This was followed in 1949 with the *International Code of Medical Ethics* which declared:

> A doctor must always bear in mind the importance of preserving human life from the time of conception until death.

For the post-World War II medical profession worldwide, the concept of a duty to protect the child before birth from the time of conception and according to the laws of humanity was recognized as an important and essential principle of medical ethics.

This duty was reaffirmed *verbatim* in the *Declaration of Geneva* (1968). From three months before the Universal Declaration (1948) until two years after the International Covenant on Civil and Political Rights (ICCPR) was completed, this understanding of human rights to include the child before birth ("from the time of conception") was indeed universally established. Not only "a European consensus on the scientific and legal definition of the beginning of life" had been established but also a global consensus.

Historical evidence for consensus on legal protection before birth

There is considerable supplementary historical evidence to invalidate the assumption currently in vogue that the European Convention for the Protection of Human Rights as agreed to in 1950 was somehow diametrically opposed to this consensus at that time and had rejected legal protection for children at risk of abortion. This evidence is summarized under the following headings.

48 *Vo v. France* (2004), para. 84.

1. *No record of exclusion of the unborn child from human rights protection*

In the European Convention for the Protection of Human Rights (1950), the High Contracting Parties undertook to "secure to everyone within their jurisdiction" the right to life.[49] The High Contracting Parties included Belgium, Denmark, France, Ireland, Italy, Luxembourg, the Netherlands, Norway, Sweden and the United Kingdom. These founding member states of the Council of Europe framed and signed the European Convention in 1950. All these governments were represented at and in agreement with the Universal Declaration in 1948. They were also represented at and in agreement with the UN General Assembly in 1959 which, in the *Declaration on the Rights of the Child*, reaffirmed that the right to legal protection for the child before birth was recognized in the Universal Declaration. On the right to life, the European Convention was in complete agreement with the Universal Declaration and the detailed history of the negotiations records no discussion whatsoever about excluding the child before birth from legal human rights protection.[50]

2. *Modelled on the draft Covenant on Civil and Political Rights "as it existed in 1950"*

It should be noted furthermore that John P. Humphrey, a prominent Canadian professor of international law who was appointed by the UN to oversee the drafting of all the foundational human rights instruments, has reminded us of the real source for the drafting of the European Convention:

---

49 In the drafting history, the original reference to "all persons residing within their territories" was changed to all persons "within their jurisdiction". The reasons given related directly to a clear commitment to ensuring that human rights protection was to be inclusive rather than restrictive:

> "The Assembly draft had extended the benefits of the Convention to 'all persons residing within the territories of the signatory States'. It seemed to the Committee that the term 'residing' might be considered too restrictive. It was felt that there were good grounds for extending the benefits of the Convention to all persons in the territories of the signatory States, even those who could not be considered as residing there in the legal sense of the word. The Committee therefore replaced the term 'residing' by the words 'within their jurisdiction' which are also contained in Article 2 of the Draft Covenant of the United Nations Commission." *Collected edition of the 'Travaux Préparatoires'of the European Convention on Human Rights*, Vol. III, The Hague: Martinus Nijhoff Publishers, 1975-85, p. 260.

50 Committee on Legal and Administrative Questions Report, Section 1, Para.6, 5 September 1949, in *Collected edition of the 'Travaux Préparatoires'of the European Convention on Human Rights*, Vol. III, The Hague:Martinus Nijhoff Publishers, 1975-85, p. 194.

> ...the European Convention for the Protection of Human Rights and Fundamental Freedoms was modelled on the draft of the Covenant on Civil and Political Rights as it existed in 1950.[51]

The draft of the Covenant on Civil and Political Rights "as it existed in 1950" affirmed very clearly that the right to life belonged to every human being from the moment of conception.

The UN Commission on Human Rights at the *6th Session* (1950) had agreed on the following text:

> Every human being from the moment of conception has the inherent right to life.[52]

During the *5th Session* (1949), *6th Session* (1950), and *8th Session* (1952) of the *UN Commission on Human Rights*, "consideration for the interests of the unborn child" was a persistent concern which was recorded as having "inspired" the on-going discussions on the draft ICCPR prohibition of the death sentence on pregnant women.[53] The subsequent prohibition of execution of pregnant women, emerging from this consideration, acknowledged that the child, from the State's first knowledge of that child's existence, is to be protected. The unborn child's life is to be protected even though the child's mother is guilty of a most serious crime punishable by death. "That protection", it was affirmed by the Third Committee of the UN General Assembly at its 12th Session (1957), "should be extended to all unborn children".[54] It was argued also at that same session that "it was only logical to guarantee the right to life from the moment life began."[55]

3. UDHR recognition of the rights of the child before birth

The Preamble to the UN Declaration of the Rights of the Child (1959) provides incontrovertible historical proof that the Universal Declaration of Human Rights "recognized" that the child before birth, no less than the child after birth, is an appropriate subject of human rights law and is entitled to appropriate legal protection:

51 John P. Humphrey's Preface to Marc J. Bossuyt: *Guide to the "Travaux Préparatoires" of the International Convenant on Civil and Political Rights*", Dordrecht, Boston, Lancaster: Martinus Nijhoff Publishers, 1987, p. xv.

52 E/CN.4/L.365 p. 24.

53 A/2929 Chapter VI, para. 10.

54 Ibid., p. 121, A/C.3/SR.810, para. 2; A/C.3/SR.811, para. 9; A/C 3/SR.812, para 7; A/C.3/SR.813, para. 36; A/C 3/SR 815, para. 28.

55 Marc J. Bossuyt: *Guide to the "Travaux Préparatoires" of the International Convenant on Civil and Political Rights*, Dordrecht: Martinus Nijhoff Publishers, 1987, p. 121. A/3764, para. 113; A/C.3/SR 813, para. 5; A/C.3/SR 815, para. 5; A/C.3/SR 816, para. 8; A/C.3/SR 819, para. 3; A/C.3/SR 821, para. 9.

> Whereas the child, by reason of his physical and mental immaturity, needs special safeguards and care, including appropriate legal protection, before as well as after birth,
> Whereas the need for such special safeguards has been stated in the Geneva Declaration of the Rights of the Child of 1924, and recognized in the Universal Declaration of Human Rights and in the statutes of specialized agencies and international organizations concerned with the welfare of children…

Insertion of the word 'such' here and repetition of the words 'special safeguards' makes it unmistakably clear that these two clauses are to be read together, and that the Universal Declaration of Human Rights was understood to have committed governments to provide special safeguards, including appropriate legal protection for the child before birth.

The legal force of the 1959 *Declaration* lies in the formal evidence it provides that, as of November 20th 1959, the whole international community understood and agreed that the Universal Declaration (now legally binding) had for that first decade of its jurisdiction *already recognized* the legal status of the child before birth and the child's entitlement to human rights protection. Universal recognition of the child before birth as a juridical personality entitled to legal protection had been established and accepted in the very foundation instrument of modern international human rights law.

4. Common heritage of the rule of law

The Council of Europe, signing in Rome on 4th November 1950 a document that was billed in the international media as the first international legal instrument to guarantee the protection of human rights, could not have dissented so radically from the Universal Declaration on such a fundamental issue as legal protection for the child before birth. This is especially true considering that the Preamble to the European Convention proclaims:

> Being resolved, as the governments of European countries which are like-minded and have a common heritage of political traditions, ideals, freedom and the rule of law, to take the first steps for the collective enforcement of certain of the rights stated in the Universal Declaration…

This "common heritage of…the rule of law" included, we must remember, abortion laws; and "certain of the rights stated in the Universal Declaration" included the right to life. The European Court of Human Rights today would be wrong if it seeks to infer that the right to life in the European Convention is a substantially different right to the right to life in the Universal Declaration. Given it is specifically stated in the Convention that the governments of Europe are "resolved" (i.e., have the stated purpose in this Convention) to take the first steps for the collective enforcement of certain of the rights stated in the Universal Declaration, then the right to life in the European Convention could not be so substantially different as to exclude legal protection for a whole group of human beings, i.e., children before birth, a group recognized by the Universal Declaration to have the same right to "appropriate legal protection" as children after birth.

5. *Same parties to the European Convention and UN Declaration on the Rights of the Child*

For the European High Contracting Parties to have excluded the child before birth from their jurisdiction cannot make sense in the light of the fact that these same Council of Europe member governments subsequently agreed in 1959 that the need for legal protection for the child before as well as after birth was recognized "in the Universal Declaration of Human Rights and in the statutes of specialized agencies and international organizations concerned with the welfare of children." If the Council of Europe had excluded the child before birth from human rights jurisdiction in the 1950 Convention, would it have been sensible for member states to recognize in 1959 the need for legal protection for the child before birth? That would have been nonsensical.

6. *European Court established to ensure observance of codified UDHR obligations*

Just as it is nonsensical to claim now that the right to legal protection for the child before birth was never accepted by the European Court of Human Rights. How could this be when this Court was established in Strasbourg under the European Convention on Human Rights, specifically to ensure observance of the codified UDHR obligations undertaken by contracting states? The Court was brought into existence by the Council of Europe on 18th September 1959. This was just two months before these same Council of Europe member governments agreed publicly and formally at the UN General Assembly that the Universal Declaration of Human Rights "recognized" the right to legal protection for the child "before as well as after birth".

7. *Absence of formal reservations regarding the right to life*

In the absence of any formal reservation or statement of interpretation to the contrary by the Council of Europe, or by any of the individual member states who were signatories both to the Universal Declaration (as member states of the UN) and to the European Convention (as member states of the Council of Europe), it stands to reason that recognition of the child before birth as needing legal human rights protection must have been accorded.

The European Convention's Article 2 Footnote 1—"Right to Life" declares:

1 Everyone's right to life shall be protected by law. No one shall be deprived of his life intentionally save in the execution of a sentence of a court following his conviction of a crime for which this penalty is provided by law.

2 Deprivation of life shall not be regarded as inflicted in contravention of this article when it results from the use of force which is no more than absolutely necessary:

a in defence of any person from unlawful violence

b in order to effect a lawful arrest or to prevent the escape of a person lawfully detained;

c in action lawfully taken for the purpose of quelling a riot or insurrection…

There are clearly no grounds here for intentionally depriving the child before birth of the right to life. For the child before birth, there has been no crime, no conviction and therefore no sentence of a court following a conviction. The child before birth is utterly incapable of offering any person unlawful violence or of participating in a riot or insurrection.

Failure to make any lawful provision here for intentional deprivation of the life of the unborn child is consistent with the general understanding at the time that the child before birth is entitled to human rights and to appropriate legal protection as recognized in the Universal Declaration, upon which the European Convention is based.

The European Convention's Article 17 asserts:

> Nothing in this Convention may be interpreted as implying for any State, group or person any right to engage in any activity or perform any act aimed at the destruction of any of the rights and freedoms set forth herein or at their limitation to a greater extent than is provided for in the Convention.

When read together, Article 2 and Article 17 secure legislative protection of the right to life for the child before birth. Any other interpretation of Article 2 is prohibited by Article 17, for it would require the limitation of the right to life to a greater extent than is specifically provided for in Article 2 of the Convention:

- The child before birth has no criminal conviction (1);
- The child before birth is totally incapable of unlawful violence 2(a);
- The child before birth is neither evading lawful arrest nor escaping lawful detention 2(b); and
- The child before birth is not involved in rioting and insurrection 2(c).

Therefore no European state who is a party to this Convention and no group such as the European Court of Human Rights have any right to introduce a new limitation to the right to life as set out in this Convention. Any limitation aimed at the destruction of the right to life of the child before birth is prohibited by Article 17.

8. *"in the light of its object and purpose"*

To insist on any other interpretation of the Right to Life article would be to infringe the international rules governing treaty interpretation, viz., the *Vienna Convention on the Law of Treaties* (1969). The Vienna Convention provides that:

> A treaty shall be interpreted in good faith in accordance with the ordinary meaning to be given to the terms of the treaty in their context and in the light of its object and purpose" (Article 31, "General Rule of Interpretation 1").

The European Court of Human Rights needs to be reminded that the object and purpose of the European Convention for the Protection of Human Rights (1950) has not changed. It is still as agreed in Article 1 – Obligation to respect human rights:

> The High Contracting Parties shall secure to everyone within their jurisdiction the rights and freedoms defined in Section 1 of this Convention.

The European Convention begins with a clear preambular context for understanding the rights defined in Section 1.[56] It acknowledges that the Universal Declaration "aims at securing the universal and effective recognition and observance of the Rights therein declared". Given that the Universal Declaration "recognized" the right of the child before birth to legislative protection and given that in drafting the European Convention there was no recorded exception taken to that recognition, then the Contracting Parties must be held to be obliged to secure the rights of the child before birth who in the absence of specific exclusion must be "within their jurisdiction". Under Section I Article 2—Right to life, everyone's right to life is entitled to protection by the law with a single exception—save in the execution of a sentence of a court following his conviction of a crime for which this penalty is provided by law. This singular validation of lawful deprivation of life cannot be extended or otherwise distorted to condone the intentional deprivation of the life of an innocent unborn child in an abortion.[57]

A "living documents" approach masks disturbing rupture, not organic growth

Yet the European Court of Human Rights has now reneged on the original universally recognized rights of the child before birth, human rights that were agreed at the time

56 The Governments signatory to The European Convention on Human Rights (1950)
Considering the Universal Declaration of Hums Rights, proclaimed by the General Assembly of the United Nations on 10 December 1948;
Considering that this Declaration aims at securing the universal and effective recognition and observance of the Rights therein declared...
Being resolved, as the Governments of European countries which are like-minded and have a common heritage of political traditions, ideals, freedom and the rule of law to take the first steps for the collective enforcement of certain of the Rights stated in the Universal Declaration;
Have agreed as follows:
Article 1 – Obligation to respect human rights:
The High Contracting Parties shall secure to everyone within their jurisdiction the rights and freedoms defined in Section I of this Convention.

57 For further elaboration on this point, see Rita Joseph, "Abortion and the Death Penalty—Different Subjects, Shared Sentence", *Voices*, Vol. XXIII (1), 2008.

that the European Convention for the Protection of Human Rights (1950) was completed. The Court, in certain comparatively recent majority decisions involving abortion, has practiced intellectual dishonesty with an indefensible return to neo-Nazi values on abortion. In an attempt to rationalize blatant contravention of the original commitment to human rights protection for the child before as well as after birth, a shallow fashionable argument has been developed that all human rights instruments are "living documents" that allow for radical fundamental change that includes even (unconscionable) reversals of the original human rights protections promised and agreed.

Radical feminism has fabricated and promoted this deceptive line under 'gender mainstreaming'—an ingenious tool for ideological indoctrination—which asserts that all human rights are relative, culturally constructed, and need reinterpretation over time. "Old male rights," such as religious freedom and conscientious objection[58], recede as "new women's rights," such as abortion 'rights' emerge. But such a reinterpretation is incompatible with the deontological basis of the original international instruments which are irrefutably based in natural law.

Development, expansion, deepening of original human rights is good, a legitimate form of natural progression; but excising and discarding the human rights of any one group of human beings constitutes a disturbing rupture that violates human rights which remain irrevocably and fundamentally equal and inalienable. Such a withdrawal of human rights protection from a vulnerable group cannot be seen as part of a benign natural organic growth. On the contrary, it is an ignoble abrogation from the understanding and implementation of the human rights that have solemnly been declared and agreed.

Such a rupture has occurred because the European Court of Human Rights has fallen under the influence of radical feminist ideology.[59] The Court has been unduly

58 The UN Committee on the Elimination of Discrimination against Women (CEDAW Committee), for example, has sought to repeal conscience rights for doctors in order to force them to perform abortions. For example:

re Italy: "The Committee expressed particular concern with regard to the limited availability of abortion services for women in southern Italy, as a result of the high incidence of conscientious objection among doctors and hospital personnel." Committee on the Elimination of Discrimination Against Women, Concluding Observations: Italy, U.N. Doc. A/52/38/Rev.1, Part II (1997), para. 353.

re Croatia: "The Committee…is also concerned about information regarding the refusal, by some hospitals, to provide abortions on the basis of conscientious objection of doctors. The Committee considers this to be an infringement of women's reproductive rights." "Report of the Committee on the Elimination of Discrimination against Women," U.N. Doc. A/53/38 (1998), part I, para. 109.

59 See Cornides, Jakob: "Human rights pitted against Man" *International Journal of Human Rights*, Vol.12 (1), February, 2008, pp. 107-134. On the basis of two examples (Opinion 4.2005 of the EU Network of Experts on Fundamental Rights and the ECHR Decision in the case of *Tysiac v. Poland*), this article expresses the author's concern over the increasing estrangement between a new voluntaristic doctrine of human rights and the most basic precepts of ethical reason. This novel doctrine, Cornides says, is not based

influenced by well-organized, well-funded abortion advocacy groups such as the radical feminist lawyers' organization, the New York based Center for Reproductive Rights (CRR). One recent case in which the European Court appears to have been seriously misled by the CRR as *amicus curiae* was the Vo *v France* case. The CRR Submission was logically flawed and used misleading language.

'unborn foetus' or 'child before birth'?

The submission throughout used the term 'unborn foetus' which, apart from being tautologous, is not the language of the foundational international human rights instruments which 'recognize' the right of 'the child' to legal protection 'before as well as after birth.'

Contained within the major human rights instruments is the vocabulary of the human rights of the child before birth. Yet this vocabulary is being ignored—pro-abortion groups such as the CRR are exercising a sleight of hand by replacing the term 'child' with 'foetus' or 'embryo' and then claiming that 'the foetus' or 'the embryo' are not mentioned in human rights instruments.

The definitive language of "expectant mothers" (Geneva Conventions) and their "unborn children" (Nuremberg judgments) has been corrupted. Pro-abortion rhetoric has eschewed the genuine language of human rights and replaced it with mere physiological terms belonging more properly to academic embryology. The medical text book terms 'foetus' and 'embryo' have replaced the human rights terms in an attempt to dehumanize the unborn child and to deny human membership and human rights to the child before birth.

Law makers must recognize the dignity and worth of all human beings and their equality before the law, irrespective of subjective views of how, where and why each human being has been brought into existence, and irrespective of the number of days they have been in existence. Age should never be accepted as an authentic discriminating factor to justify the withholding of basic human rights entitlement. Human rights belong to all human beings by virtue of their being human—size or immaturity do not count as disqualifying factors.

The humanity of each and every human being is the singular and sufficient qualifying factor for equal and inalienable human rights entitlement. The German High Court articulated this seminal truth back in 1975:

> Where human life exists it merits human dignity; it is not decisive whether the holder of this human dignity knows of it and is able to maintain it by himself. The potential ca-

on the concept of an objective and inalienable natural law, but on the radical ideology of certain NGOs and international bureaucracies, which pretend having authority to 'make' new human rights, thereby assuming the role of supreme global law-makers. "This power shift to the unelected, if not halted, could seriously damage or even destroy the credibility the concept of human rights is enjoying worldwide."

pabilities, lying in human existence from its inception on, are sufficient to justify human dignity.[60]

In the light of this truth, the European Court of Human Rights has presented a *totum revolutum* (muddled opinion) when it attempts to "require protection in the name of human dignity" for an embryonic human being while at the same time denying this small human being the very first and most critical of all protections—protection of the "right to life" as promised in Article 2 of the European Convention.[61]

UDHR—the "permanent accession of every human being to the rank of member of human society" (Cassin)

Indeed, there is neither historical foundation nor ethical defence for this newly fabricated notion that a regional court of human rights can de-recognize the human rights of a particular group of human beings (such as children before birth) and exclude them from the entitlements that were originally agreed for their protection. As explained by René Cassin, the distinguished French jurist who was most deeply involved in framing the foundational international human rights instruments, the UN *Charter of Human Rights* has a very definite and practical application to "the whole of juridically organized mankind":

> This will mean two things: first, the permanent accession of every human being to the rank of member of human society - in legal parlance one would say to the rank of subject of international law; second, it will mean that the states consent to exercise their sovereignty under the authority of international law...[62]

It is unthinkable that the permanent accession of the child before birth to the rank of member of human society and subject of international law has become now ephemeral, non-existent even, to be granted or withheld at the whim of a Court of Law under the influence of an extreme ideology.

Deceptive terms such as 'embryo' and 'margin of appreciation' are being used to first undermine and then destroy completely the embryonic human being's "permanent accession to the rank of member of human society" and "subject of international law". For example, in *Evans v. the United Kingdom* (2006), the European Court of Human Rights held unanimously that in destruction of a human embryo there is no violation of Article 2 (right to life) of the European Convention. Recalling that the

60 German High Court, Basic Law for the Federal Republic of Germany (GBL) 2.2: 39 B verf GE 1 (1975).

61 "The potentiality of that being and its capacity to become a person...require protection in the name of human dignity, without making it a "person" with the "right to life" for the purposes of Article 2." *Vo v. France* (2004), para. 84.

62 Cassin, René, "The Charter of Human Rights", Nobel Lecture, December 11 1968. From *Nobel Lectures, Peace 1951-1970*, (Ed.) Frederick W. Haberman, Amsterdam: Elsevier Publishing Company, 1972.

issue of when the right to life began came within the margin of appreciation of the State concerned, the European Court argued that under English law a human embryo did not have independent rights or interests and could not claim—or have claimed on its behalf—a right to life under Article 2 of the European Convention.[63]

Such a decision eerily echoes Nazi attitudes which also were deviously dismissive of the right to life for unborn children as well as for Jewish children, children with disabilities and other groups who were judged of negligible human value because they too were deemed not to have "independent rights or interests".

The Nazi eugenic programs at home and in the Occupied Territories targeted the unwanted and the expendable, and peddled the original seductive notion of 'saving' parents from burdensome children, of "saving the German people from a steady stream of new moral and economic burdens…".[64]

The atrocities and disastrous consequences of errant Nazi morality attest to the extreme danger of conforming morality to prevailing ideologies. Moral relativism untethers human behaviour from the natural law, and purports to be able to justify even the most heinous crimes against humanity, to justify Court-approved and State-approved exterminatory programs against the most vulnerable.

Teitgen, writing back in 1949, was right:

> Evil progresses cunningly…Public opinion and the entire national conscience are asphyxiated…the minds of a nation menaced by this progressive corruption…[65]

It seems that the further we move in time away from the atrocities of the Nazi era, the easier it becomes for our health officials, our legislatures and our judiciaries to slide into a neo-Nazi contempt for the human rights of those we deem expendable—the unwanted, the disabled, the burdensome, the unborn.

The European Court and the limits of authority

In truth, under the European Convention the European Court of Human Rights can authorize neither the abuse of the human rights of children at risk of abortion in some States nor the removal of legal protection from such children in any State.

The *1945 Statute of the International Court of Justice, an International Court*, established by the *Charter of the United Nations* as the principal judicial organ of the United Nations, laid down the rule that international law and judicial bodies must function in accordance with "the general principles of law recognized by civilized nations".[66]

---

63 European Court of Human Rights, Case of Evans v. the United Kingdom, Judgment of 7 March 2006, para. 46.

64 Wagner, Gerhard: "Rasse und Bevölkerungspolitik", *Der Parteitag der Ehre*, Vom 8. bis 14, September 1936. *Offizieller Bericht über den Verlauf des Reichsparteitages mit sämtlichen Kongreßreden* (Munich: Zentralverlag der NSDAP., 1936), pp. 150-160

65 See footnote 24 above.

66 Statute of the International Court of Justice, June 26, 1945, Articles 1 and 38 (c).

In one of the earliest comprehensive studies of the codification of international human rights law in the International Bill of Rights, the distinguished legal scholar R.P. Dhokalia identifies the "general principles of law recognized by civilized nations":

> ...the fundamental and universal principles accepted for many centuries by jurists and philosophers as constituting the natural law, and thus their recognition by Article 38...is recognition of natural law without naming it.[67]

The Universal Declaration (1948) and the European Convention (1950) were grounded firmly and inextricably in the deontological approach. The hard truth is that international human rights law cannot be converted now to a utilitarian or consequentialist approach without a catastrophic unravelling of all the human rights protections that have been painstakingly built on principles such as:

- equal protection before the law of all members of the human family,
- equal safeguards including appropriate legal protection for the child before birth as for the child after birth, and
- an equal right to life, development and survival for all members of the human family.

Dr. Charles Malik, Rapporteur for the Human Rights Commission that drafted the Universal Declaration and the follow-up *Conventions* constituting the *International Bill of Rights*, wrote in 1948 about the Commission's implied agreement on the nature and origin of human rights:

> Where do they come from? What is their metaphysical status? Are they arbitrarily conferred upon me by some external visible agency, such as my state or parliament or the United Nations, so that this visible power can conceivably one day withdraw them from me at will, without thereby violating a higher law? Or do they belong to my essence, so that the function of any external visible power with respect to them is not to create and constitute them but only to recognize and respect them, and so that if in any way it violates them it will thereby trespass against the natural law of my humanity?
>
> This is clearly the problem of natural versus positive law. If these rights are the mere products of positive law, namely of law as it happens to be at a particular stage in evolution, then clearly, since positive law changes, my rights, and therewith my very human nature, will change with it. But if, on the other hand, these rights express my nature as a human being, then there is a certain compulsion about them: they are metaphysically prior to any positive law, and any such law must either conform to them or else be by nature null and void. Either man has an eternal essence which can be grasped and expressed by reason, or he dissolves without any remainder into the general flux.[68]

67 Dhokalia, R.P.: *The Codification of Public International Law*, Manchester: Manchester University Press, 1970, p. 348.

68 Charles Malik: "The International Bill of Rights", *United Nations Bulletin*, July, 1948.

The foundation members of the UN Commission on Human Rights were agreed that human rights do belong to the "*essence*" of being human. Every human being at the embryonic and foetal stages of life is essentially human, so that when the European Court of Human Rights reinterprets the European Convention to deny these smaller human beings their essential human rights, they are trespassing against the natural law of our common humanity upon which the entire modern international human rights law is built.

When conflict develops between universal natural law principles and domestic law

Where such conflict develops, Article 103 of the UN Charter sets out clear obligations:

> In the event of a conflict between the obligations of the Members of the United Nations under the present Charter and their obligations under any other international agreement, their obligations under the present Charter shall prevail.

European members of the United Nations must reject spurious newly coined "obligations" to decriminalize and legalize abortion and now must honour their original obligations under the UN Charter to promote "universal respect for, and observance of human rights".

Stephen Hall, writing in the *European Journal of International Law*, has argued cogently:

> ...states are not free to transform moral wrongs into human rights with complete juridical effect; i.e., with the positive law's usual moral obligation of observance attached. The establishment of a human or fundamental right to abortion under the positive law would be an example of an attempt to transform a moral wrong into a human right. Laws authorizing abortions, and buttressing access to abortions, are radically unjust (and radically immoral) in that they permit choosing directly against a self-evident form of human flourishing; i.e., life. This has certainly occurred at the level of international law partly as a result of such widespread practice. The temptation to turn moral wrongs into human rights arises when, unmindful of the richness of the common good under the natural law, every person's desire or preference is a potential candidate for promotion to the ever-expanding pantheon of positive human rights.[69]

Indeed, no international, regional or domestic human rights court can withdraw legal protection of natural law human rights from the child at risk of abortion. The International Court of Justice has found quite rightly that

69 Hall, Stephen: "The Persistent Spectre: Natural Law, International Order and the Limits of Legal Positivism", *European Journal of International Law*, Oxford: Vol. 12 (2), 2001, p. 269.

> rules concerning the basic rights of the human person in international law are *erga omnes* in nature: they are considered to be 'the concern of all States'. In view of the importance of the rights involved, all States can be held to have a legal interest in their protection.[70]

Tawhida Ahmed and Israel de Jesús Butler observe that the Court of First Instance(CFI) recently appeared to consider all human rights to have attained the status of jus cogens in international law.[71] In its Kadi and Yusuf judgments, the CFI considered that

> ...the obligation to protect human rights (with no more precision) formed a rule of jus cogens in international law and any Security Council Resolution and consequently any EU action taken to implement such a resolution that violated human rights would be void in international law.[72]

In considering which rights fall into this category, the CFI resorted to the Universal Declaration and the ICCPR rather than the European Convention on Human Rights.[73] Regardless of the perspectives of EU bodies, Ahmed and Butler argue, the EU as an International Government Organization is bound to respect rules of Customary International Law. The right to life and the right to equality before the law and non-discrimination were assumed by the Court to have been accepted and recognized by the international community of States as peremptory norms, as jus cogens in nature by virtue of their presence in the Universal Declaration and the ICCPR.

> ...any ıule created through the EU which conflicts with rules that are jus cogens in nature will be void. As well as being accepted in international law, these principles have been accepted by the EU itself through the CFI...[74]

The CFI finding that the Member States of the EU are bound by the terms of the Charter, and are obliged to implement obligations deriving from the Charter above those deriving from the EU, has considerable significance. Almed and Butler say that it can

> logically be extended to the obligation to promote respect for human rights established by the UN Charter, which would oblige Member States to ignore any part of EU law that

70 *Barcelona Traction, Light and Power Company, Ltd.* (*Belgium v Spain*) [1970] Imternational Court of Justice.

71 Ahmed,Tawhida and Butler, Israel de Jesús, "The European Union and Human Rights: An International Law Perspective", *European Journal of International Law*, Vol. 17 (4), 2006, p. 780.

72 Ahmed and Butler cite Kadi (Case T-315/01, *Kadi v Council and Commission*, Judgment, 21/09/2005)and Yusuf (Case T-306/01, *Ahmed Ali Yusuf and Al Barakaat International Foundation v. Council and Commission* 21/09/05).

73 Kadi judgment, paras. 241, 287 and Yusuf judgment, paras. 292, 342.

74 Ibid., pp. 780-1.

> violated human rights as articulated in the UDHR or ICCPR as an expression of 'human rights' in the Charter.[75]

Working from Almed and Butler's conclusion, we can proceed to argue that the European Court of Human Rights is now shaping EU abortion law that violates the human rights of the child before birth as articulated in the Universal Declaration and the ICCPR, i.e., EU abortion law that violates an expression of human rights in the UN Charter. Member States are obliged to ignore any part of EU law that purports to authorize the abuse of the human rights of children at risk of abortion in some States or the removal of legal protection for such children in any State.

Erroneous reasoning by European Court in *Tysiac v Poland*

In this respect, for example, Poland may be said to be obliged to ignore the ruling in March 2007 (*Tysiac v Poland*) by the European Court of Human Rights (6-1) that elevated "the applicant's right to respect for her private life" over and above the right to life of her unborn daughter whom she had wanted her doctors to abort. The European Court ordered the Polish government to award 25,000 euros to a woman who claimed her human right to "a private life" was violated when she was denied an abortion.

The Court ruled that the Polish State had not complied with

> the positive obligations to safeguard the applicant's right to respect for her private life in the context of a controversy as to whether she was entitled to a therapeutic abortion.[76]

Spanish Judge Borrego Borrego, in a sole dissenting opinion, analyzes the feeble reasoning behind the Court's conclusion and asserts boldly that "it is not the task of the Court to make such statements, to advance a decision that favors 'abortion on demand'". He revealed the logical inconsistencies between this decision and a previous decision D. v. Ireland (July 5, 2006):

> ...in the Polish case all the debate is focused on the State's positive obligation of "effective respect" for private life in protecting the individual against arbitrary interference by the public authorities... No reference is made to "the complex and sensitive balancing of equal rights to life ... of the mother and the unborn" mentioned in D. v. Ireland... In D. v. Ireland, everything must be objective. In the present case, everything is subjective...[77]

Indeed, Judge Borrego Borrego is right in his criticism that the judgment goes too far in that it "favors 'abortion on demand'".

75 Ibid.

76 *Tysiac v Poland* (2007), para. 128.

77 *Tysiac v. Poland* Judgment—Dissenting Opinion of Justice Borrego Borrego, paras. 8, 9.

Right to life overrides "respect for private life"

Such a judgment is logically inconsistent with previous decisions of the Court regarding the duty of the State to protect life. With regard to the duty of the State to secure for everyone within its jurisdiction the right to life, the European Court has held that it "involves a primary duty" to put "in place effective criminal-law provisions to deter the commission of offences against the person backed up by law-enforcement machinery for the prevention, suppression and punishment of such provisions".[78] In addition, in both the public sphere and into the field of private life,

> [this duty] also extends in appropriate circumstances to a positive obligation on the authorities to take preventive operational measures to protect an individual or individuals whose life is at risk from the criminal acts of another individual....[79]

Other judgments have discerned that States also have a duty to take 'reasonable' measures to protect individuals [e.g., children in utero] whose lives are in danger because of intentional acts of other individuals [e.g., abortionists]. The State's obligations in this respect extend beyond the duty to establish effective criminal law provisions to deter the commission of offences [e.g., abortion as an intentional act of lethal violence against an unborn child] and may imply the duty to take preventive operational measures to protect an individual [such as an unborn child] whose life is at risk. If a State does not protect the right to life by, for example, failing to penalise dangerous behaviours or, if in well-defined circumstances, it fails to provide security to protect an individual at risk, this gives rise to State responsibility even though the harm may have been committed by private individuals.[80]

> The test that the European Court has established is that the 'authorities knew or ought to have known at the time of the existence of a real risk to the life of an identified individual from the criminal acts of a third party and that they failed to take measures within the scope of their powers which, judged reasonably, might have been expected to avoid that risk' (para 116). In other words, failure of the state to take positive measures to prevent and suppress offences against the person at risk in the above mentioned circumstances would entail a violation of the right to life.[81]

When this is applied with logical consistency to legal protection of the right to life of the child before birth at risk of abortion, the authorities are seen to have a primary

78 European Court of Human Rights, Case of *Mahmut Kaya v. Turkey*, Judgment of 28 March, 2000, paras. 85-6.

79 Ibid.

80 See e.g. HRC: Delgado v. Colombia, Communication No. 195/1985, Views of 12 July 1990 and ECHR: *Osman v. The United Kingdom* (Case No 87/1997/871/1083, Judgment of 28 October, 1998) and Kaya v. Turkey (2000).

81 European Court of Human Rights, Case of *Mahmut Kaya v. Turkey*, Judgment of 28 March 2000.

duty to put in place effective criminal-law provisions to deter the commission of offences against the unborn child backed up by law-enforcement machinery for the prevention, suppression and punishment of such lethal acts. And, further, that this duty "also extends in appropriate circumstances to a positive obligation on the authorities to take preventive operational measures to protect the individual [the child before birth]...whose life is at risk from the criminal acts of another individual [the abortionist]". The grave implication is that the States' international legal obligations extend beyond the public sphere into the field of private life.

Clearly the European Court is in error in its *Tysiac v Poland* judgment. Where the life of a child before birth is at risk, the right to life overrides appeals to respect for privacy.

Given enough rope—European Court now entangled in ideological deceits

And so today we have a group of judges in the European Court of Human Rights, having committed to an imprudent stand on the key moral issue of abortion, now reduced to shallow posturing and compromise in vain attempts to shore up their shifting ground. They have been given enough rope, and now as they try to rationalize their ethically untenable position on abortion this way and that, squirming, wriggling, somersaulting and devising all sorts of ingenious deceits, their arguments in the end are left dangling—mid-air, without foundation, without merit, without truth.

There appears to be no limit to the absurd lengths to which the European Court is now prepared to go in order to shore up the original unprincipled opinion that in destroying "a human embryo" there is no violation of Article 2 (Right to Life) of the European Convention. Once again in order to rationalize the willful destruction of a small embryonic human being, the Court cites an exaggerated right to respect for private life as "a broad term, encompassing, *inter alia*, aspects of an individual's physical and social identity including the right to personal autonomy, personal development and to establish and develop relationships with other human beings and the outside world (*Pretty*, § 61)".[82] This time, the Court opines that the term 'respect for private life' incorporates also "the right to respect for both the decisions to become and not to become a parent".[83] This is an absurdity—this totally irrational denial that the human embryo is already a human being with an irrevocably designated biological father as well as an irrevocably designated biological mother.

The decision to become a parent has already been made and can now be physically, genetically, materially and conceptually verified in the very real existence of an embryonic human being carrying genes of the father and the mother. The Court's ability to rule on this particular case depends precisely on the understanding that the particular 'human embryo' whose life is at stake can be unmistakably distinguished from other 'human embryos' in the same clinic, and that the identity of the mother and the father of this 'human embryo' can be satisfactorily established.

82 *Evans v. the United Kingdom*, Judgment of 7 March, 2006, para. 57.

83 Ibid.

The right *not* to become a parent must be exercised *before* a son or daughter is brought into existence as a human embryo. It is too late *post facto*. The reality of having fathered a particular child, already in existence whether *in utero* or *in vitro*, cannot be reversed simply by destroying that child. Unborn children at whatever stage of the life cycle have the inherent right to life, survival and development "to the maximum extent possible"[84]—the right to life does not depend on their mothers or fathers furnishing them with a gratuitous permission to continue to exist.

What has led the European Court to such specious reasoning? It is becoming clear that the European Court, having been buffeted by the prevailing ideological winds into abandoning the truth that the unborn child at risk of abortion has a right to legal protection, is now trying to maintain, by hook or by crook, an untenable position.

The Court is trying to do the impossible—to reconcile a woman's so-called right to abortion, a belief fundamental to the extreme feminist ideology of today, with the original international and regional human rights legal framework which recognized the child's right to *legal protection before as well as after birth*.

Growing criticism of the European Court's abortion decisions

Jakob Pichon in a recent paper entitled *Does the Unborn Child Have a Right to Life? The Insufficient Answer of the European Court of Human Rights in the Judgment Vo v. France* asserted that the Court "did not give satisfactory reasons for its decision to stay silent on this point" while ignoring there are strong arguments that the fetus, at least a *viable* one,[85] is in fact covered by "everyone" within the meaning of Article 2:

> First, neither the ECtHR nor the former Commission has ever completely excluded the possibility of application of Article 2 to the fetus. Instead, the ECtHR has repeatedly applied the "even assuming" formula which would not have been necessary if Article 2 had been considered to be entirely inapplicable.
>
> Second, there is no crucial difference between a fetus and a child already born, because both are similarly dependent upon their mother...specific laws on voluntary abortion

84 Committee on the Rights of the Child: General Comment No 5 (10): "Article 6 of the Convention on the Rights of the Child [affirms] the child's inherent right to life and States parties' obligation to *ensure to the maximum extent possible the survival and development of the child*. The Committee expects States to interpret "development" in its broadest sense as a holistic concept, embracing the child's physical, mental, spiritual, moral, psychological and social development. Implementation measures should be aimed at achieving *the optimal development for all children*."(italics not in the original)

85 The idea of 'viability', however, as a reliable marker for the beginning of recognition of a right to human rights protection is both philosophically and scientifically flawed. Britain's Cardinal Cormac Murphy-O'Connor discerns the fundamental problem here: "The idea of 'viability'... is a concept dependent on the availability of resources and technology; not one that is able to found a moral distinction between a life that is worth our respect and protection and one that is not." Cardinal Cormac Murphy-O'Connor: "The abortion debate is only just beginning", *Telegraph* (UK), 23 May, 2008.

> existing in all the Contracting States would not have been necessary if the fetus did not have a life to be protected. [Pichon cites here the dissenting opinion of Judge Ress] Third…it is not possible to ignore the major debate that has taken place on the national and international level in recent years on the subject of bioethics and the desirability of introducing or reforming legislation on medically assisted procreation and prenatal diagnosis, in order to prohibit techniques such as the reproductive cloning of human beings and provide a strict framework for techniques with a proven medical interest.[86]

Consequently with these new developments, Pichon says, interpretation of Article 2 now requires "the inclusion of the right to life of the fetus".[87] It should be noted, he concludes, that a number of recent conventions and the prohibition on the reproductive cloning of "human beings" under the *Charter of Fundamental Rights of the European Union* show that the protection of life extends to the initial phase of human life. Consequently, the ECtHR must take such a development into account in order to define in accordance with the *Vienna Convention on the Law of Treaties Article 31*, the "ordinary meaning" of the right to life.

Pichon's arguments are a valuable supplement to the case we make here that European law makers must recognize the historical truth: that the right to life was always applicable to the child before as well as after birth.

In a recent issue of the *International Journal of Human Rights*, Jakob Cornides of the European Commission also criticizes the European Court's interpretation of the human rights Conventions. Proponents of a right to abortion rely on "inventing and distorting reality" and they "manipulate" human rights language precisely because it is so unlikely that a new treaty recognizing abortion as a fundamental human right could ever be adopted.[88] Cornides argues.

> Instead of saying that they want to impose new laws (like abortion on demand) on society, they pretend that international law obliges them to do so, and that the new laws they are making represent the true and original sense of the relevant Conventions.[89]

86 Pichon, Jakob: "Does the Unborn Child Have a Right to Life? The Insufficient Answer of the European Court of Human Rights in the Judgment Vo v. France", *German Law Journal*, Vol. 07 (04), 2006, pp. 439-440. Pichon cites the debate in the European Parliament about the legal protection of biotechnological inventions, available at: http://www.europarl.eu.int/news/expert/background_page/008-1777-300-10-43-901-20051024BKG01776-27-10-2005-2005--false/default_p001c012_en.htm.

Pichon directs us further to *Vo*, para. 32 with a summary of the debates in and Laws of the French National Assembly; to the results of the European Group on Ethics in Science and New Technologies at the European Commission, *Vo* para. 40; and to summaries of the parliamentary debate in the *Deutscher Bundestag* (German Federal Parliament) about Law and Ethics of modern medicine and biotechnology, available at: http://www.berlinews.de/archiv/1997.shtml.

87 Ibid., p. 441.

88 Cornides, Jakob, "Human rights pitted against Man", *International Journal of Human Rights*, Vol. 12, Issue 1, 2008, pp. 107-134.

89 Ibid.

Cornides makes a careful thorough analysis of two recent examples of how European bureaucracies are overstepping their mandates and pushing a pro-abortion ideology using language, supposition and selectivity to usher in a right to abortion by "the backdoor." He concludes that nations have naively "handed over too much power to self-styled 'human rights experts'" which is seriously damaging, perhaps even destroying, the credibility of the concept of human rights.

Court needs more intellectual integrity, more moral fortitude

It is scandalous that the recent evasive, confused and feeble arguments of the European Court on abortion would not meet acceptable academic or legal standards on any other issues in its gambit. It is time for both the intellectual integrity and the moral fortitude of the European Court in abortion cases to be seriously questioned. The Court, for example, in *Vo v France* (2004) presented a wary though somewhat confused set of legal opinions which nevertheless evinced a unanimous agreement that the human embryo could *not* be excluded definitively from the "*Right to Life*" as set forth in Article 2 of the European Convention for the Protection of Human Rights and Fundamental Freedoms (1950). The High Contracting Parties undertook to "secure to everyone within their jurisdiction" the right to life. The Court went on to affirm that this right to life

> requires the State not only to refrain from the "intentional" taking of life, but also to take appropriate steps to safeguard the lives of those within its jurisdiction.[90]

The judgment is notable for its rather grudging recognition of the common ground between States that 'the embryo' i.e., the embryonic human being "belongs to the human race". Yet the Court failed to recognize that under international law as set out in the UN Charter and the foundation instruments, it is precisely this most fundamental of characteristics viz. 'belonging to the human race' that entitles human beings at the embryonic stage (along with all other "members of the human family") to human rights that are equal, inalienable and inherent.

As was agreed in the majority judgment,

> they [human embryos] are beginning to receive some protection in the light of scientific progress and the potential consequences of research into genetic engineering, medically assisted procreation or embryo experimentation.[91]

This admission that 'human embryos' are beginning to receive *some* protection is of immense significance: for in the international language of human rights instruments, the fundamental principles of equality and non-discrimination must apply: *some* protection must be understood as *equal* protection.

90 European Court of Human Rights, *Vo v France*, Judgment of 8 July 2004.

91 Ibid., para. 84.

Regrettably, it seems, fear of upsetting current laws in some European states tolerating abortion on demand appears quite clearly to present the most notable obstacle that prevented this Court from reaching the logical conclusion of their deliberations: *viz.* that the High Contracting Parties must secure to 'human embryos', whom they have all agreed are "within their jurisdiction", that most fundamental of non-derogable rights—the right to life.

From some curiously revealing observations aired in *Vo v France*, it is clear that the justices in Strasbourg are caught on the horns of a political rather than a legal or ethical dilemma. They cannot with intellectual honesty or good conscience exclude the 'human embryo' from the legal protection promised in "*The Right to Life" Article* 2; at the same time they are quite unable, politically speaking, to rock the boat or to disturb the *status quo* in some European states where abortion is liberally available. Nor do they appear to be able to weather the storm of outrage and protest that would eventuate if legislative protection was restored to all children before birth so that abortions "on request" were no longer tolerated.

It is an overly-cautious, faint-hearted, dissembling Court that claims:

> ...it is neither desirable, nor even possible as matters stand, to answer in the abstract the question whether the unborn child is a person for the purposes of Article 2 of the Convention.[92]

No doubt it is the "undesirability" and the "impossibility" of having to confront the political outcry over any requisite tightening up of abortion laws in order to protect the unborn child in European states that has led, among other considerations, to the above prevarication.

The truth remains that the European Convention for the Protection of Human Rights (1950) in conformity with the Universal Declaration (1948) includes a solemn obligation to provide legal protection for the child before as well as after birth. No amount of prevarication can revoke that obligation.

92 Ibid., para. 85.

Chapter 11 American Convention on Human Rights: "...in general, from the moment of conception"

The Inter-American human rights system was adopted by the Organization of American States in 1948, seven months before the United Nations *Universal Declaration of Human Rights* (1948) and two years before the Council of Europe's *European Convention for the Protection of Human Rights* (1950). From the very first draft (1947) of the human rights principles that comprise the *American Declaration on the Rights and Duties of Man* (1948) to their final codification in the *American Convention on Human Rights* (1969), it was consistently recognized that unborn children were included in the human rights protections being drawn up.

The *American Convention on Human Rights* recognizes that every person has the right to have his life respected. Article 1(2) says:

> For the purposes of this Convention, "person" means every human being.

and Article 4(1) declares:

> Every person has the right to have his life respected. This right shall be protected by law and, in general, from the moment of conception...

Together, these provide for protection by the law for every human being "in general, from the moment of conception". This is an invaluable and irrevocable recognition of the inalienable human rights of newly conceived children in international human rights law.

"'person' means every human being..."

Perhaps the greatest contribution made by the drafters of the American Convention on Human Rights to modern international human rights law is the consensus definition that 'person' means every human being. Modern international human rights law owes a great debt to the eminent Latin-American jurists[1] who wrote this defini-

1 For an appreciative evaluation of the Latin American contribution see Glendon, MaryAnn, "The Forgotten Crucible: the Latin American Influence on the Universal Human Rights Idea", *Harvard Human Rights Journal*, Vol. 16, Spring 2003, pp. 27-39.

tion and did so expressly to prohibit the use of the concept of 'personhood' as an exclusionary tool. The original framers of the American human rights instruments purposefully eschewed any definition of 'persons' that might be construed by future national legislatures to exclude some human beings.

It is not by accident or mere chance that it was from the continents of the Americas that this great metaphysical truth that 'person' means every human being emerged and was endorsed. The violent histories of North and South America and the Caribbean served as an invaluable lesson to the framers of the American Convention, as a constant reminder of just how easily the rule of law is corrupted when certain groups of human beings such as native Indians or African slaves are denied personhood.

From bitter experience, they understood that human rights belong to every human being because they are human. They understood that it is not in the gift of governments to confer human rights on some human beings and withdraw them from others. The State has no authority to divide the human race into 'persons' and 'non-persons', while deeming the privileged group only to be 'persons' worthy of human rights protection.

In examining the history of the *Pan-American Declaration of the Rights and Duties of Man* (later known as the *Bogotá Declaration*) and its influence on the Universal Declaration, Mary Ann Glendon, Harvard Learned Hand Professor of Law, traces an important connection between the Latin American concepts of human rights and personhood and the Catholic philosophical tradition with which Latin American jurists were familiar:

> That document in 1948, just before the Universal Declaration itself was adopted, became the first international human rights declaration and that document, that Latin American document, had in turn been influenced by Catholic social thought. That is why certain verbal formulations in the Universal Declaration of Human Rights have a familiar ring to persons who are familiar with say "Rerum Novarum" and " Quadragesimo anno" [Papal Encyclicals: "Rerum Novarum", Leo XIII, 15 May, 1891; "Quadragesimo anno", Pius XI, May 15, 1931]. For example, the consistent use of the word «person» rather than "individual"...By the 1940s, those ideas had found their way into the legal systems, constitutions of many Latin American and continental European countries, via the political programs of Christian Democratic and Christian Social political parties and Christian labour organizations.[2]

Glendon's research on this provides valuable confirmation that many of the delegates doing double duty on drafting both the American Declaration of the Rights and Duties of Man and the Universal Declaration in the late 1940s shared the universal Catholic concept of 'person' as including all human beings by virtue of their humanity.

2 "A world made new—Interview with Mary Ann Glendon", Radio National Encounter Programme: August 11, 2002. Transcript available at: http://www.abc.net.au/rn/encounter/stories/2002/642595.htm.

Human rights, not "person" rights

Under international human rights law, human rights belong to all human beings, "all members of the human family" (these words are present in all three Preambles of the foundation documents of the International Bill of Human Rights). Human beings even in the earliest stages of life, and irrespective of age or size or disabilities, must not be subjected to discriminatory, arbitrarily defined, logically inconsistent and vexatious tests of 'personhood'.[3]

The concept of introducing 'person rights', a separate set of allegedly superior human rights which apply only to human beings who are judged to be persons, is totally incompatible with the original *UN Charter*, the UN Declaration on Human Rights, the *International Covenant on Civil and Political Rights* (ICCPR) and the *International Covenant on Economic, Social and Cultural Rights* (ICESC).

The Preamble to the American Convention on Human Rights recognizes:

> that essential rights of man are not derived from being a national of a certain state, but are based on attributes of the human personality...

The State cannot deny children at risk of abortion the human right to be born equal in dignity and rights—human rights protection was never to be premised on the exclusionary pre-condition that the child must be born first. It is stated clearly that "essential rights...are based on attributes of the human personality..." It is not the act of 'being born' that bestows or confers human rights, it is being human.[4]

Medical science confirms that the newly conceived child is related physically, biologically and genetically to human parents. Each child comes into being already possessing an identifiable place in human genealogy. Science leaves no doubt that each newly conceived child, even at this earliest stage of existence, belongs to the human race. Each new distinctly personal genetic identity belongs uniquely to the one human being from conception to adulthood and old age. This personal genetic identity is not going to change mid-gestation, or mutate at birth or at any later stage of human existence. Each child at risk of abortion is and remains forever a unique member of the human family.

Abortion advocacy was not widely accepted in the 1950s.[5] Reductionist views of the unborn child were advanced by a few academics in a tentative push to justify

3 See, for example, the Constitutional Court of Colombia, DECISION C-355/06, Bogotá, D. C., May 10, 2006, which, declaring that "the right to life is restricted to human persons", decided that the right to life could not be "afforded to those who have not yet reached the human condition" *i.e.*, to children at risk of abortion.

4 See Charles Malik, "The International Bill of Rights", *United Nations Bulletin*, July, 1948. (Malik was rapporteur for the first Human Rights Commission which drafted the *Universal Declaration*.)

5 The International Planned Parenthood Foundation, established in 1953, was rejected in 1955 when it applied for consultative status with the UN's ECOSOC precisely because

"abortion reform" only amidst much controversy.[6] No doubt, the Inter-American Council of Jurists, who drew up the original 1959 draft of the American Convention on Human Rights, were aware of the possibility of problematic abuse of the term 'person' to exclude children before birth from human rights entitlement. Their solution to this problem was to insert the following words that we saw above, officially adopted in 1969:

> For the purpose of this Convention, "person" means every human *being. (American Convention on Human Rights 1969, Article 1(2)*

It is important to recognize that the Inter-American Council of Jurists was simply clarifying here the inclusive definition of 'person' that was already established in all the initial human rights instruments as well as in the drafts of the conventions in progress at that time. All human rights derive from "the dignity and worth of the human person".[7] International law clearly affirms that personhood belongs to every human being:

> Everyone shall have the right to recognition everywhere as a person before the law *(ICCPR Article 16)*

Residual international revulsion towards Hitler's persecution of Jewish and other "non-persons" was sufficient to ensure the unqualified assertion of this right.

Yet in the excess of current speculative and revisionary philosophical baggage that seeks now to redefine children before birth as "non-persons", the American Convention's definition 'person' means every human being should be acknowledged not just as being true for the purpose of this Convention but also as being implicitly true for all human rights instruments that have been built on the foundations of the UN Charter and the Universal Declaration which tied human rights irrevocably to the dignity and worth of the human person in the UDHR Preamble:

---

its aims (which included promotion of abortions) were "not in conformity with the UN Charter" as those aims were understood at that time.

6 See, for example, Williams, Glanville, *The Sanctity of Life and the Criminal Law*, London: Faber & Faber, 1958. Glanville, a high-profile jurist at Cambridge and a prominent member of the Eugenics Society, was proposing in the 1950s an infamous reductionist view of the unborn child and advocated that abortion should be treated like a tonsillectomy, a minor operation to remove unwanted or harmful "tissue growth". Both tissues are alive, he argued, and contain material substances, chemical compounds, DNA and RNA molecules that may vary a little, but they are "mainly matter which is composed of cells which are composed of chemicals". He promoted abortion especially as a tool to eliminate "a horrible evil"—"the breeding of defectives". pp. 31-33 & p. 212.

7 See the Preambles to the *UN Charter*, the *Universal Declaration*, the *ICCPR*, the *ICESCR*, *CEDAW*, the *Convention on the Rights of the Child*, the *Convention on the Elimination of All Forms of Racial Discrimination*, the *Convention against Torture* and the *Convention on the Rights of Persons with Disabilities*.

> Whereas the peoples of the United Nations have in the Charter reaffirmed their faith in fundamental human rights, in the dignity and worth of the human person.

It is both metaphysical nonsense and legalistic prevarication to claim, as many pro-abortion advocates now do, that children become human beings or persons only from birth. This pretentious posture has spawned a growing disjunction between the medical and legal treatment of unborn children.[8] The invisibility of unborn children as persons before the law in many domestic legal systems contrasts dramatically with their increased visibility in prenatal medical care, including during foetal surgery.

The American Convention on Human Rights got it exactly right when it asserted of the right to life:

> This right shall be protected by law and, in general, from the moment of conception. No one shall be arbitrarily deprived of his life.

Liberal abortion laws that allow for arbitrary deprivation of the life of the unborn child are in contravention of the State's duty to ensure that the right to life of the child at risk of abortion is "protected by law and, in general, from the moment of conception."

1981 *Baby Boy* Resolution—ideologically driven misinterpretation

Regrettably, in the 1980 *Baby Boy* case[9], the Inter-American Commission on Human Rights tried to discredit this clear provision for legal protection for the child *in general, from the moment of conception.* This attempt was made by mounting two extremely flawed reconstructions of the arguments that pertained to the right to life of unborn children at two key meetings of earlier Inter-American Commissions, one engaged in drafting the original American Declaration and the other engaged in reviewing the *Draft American Convention on Human Rights*:

- First, the 1981 *Resolution* misconstrues completely the agreement to remove the phrase "including those who are not yet born" from the right to life article in the Draft American Declaration on the Rights and Duties of Man at the Ninth International Conference of American States (Bogotá, 1948);
- Second, the 1981 *Resolution* renders a peculiarly esoteric reading of the *travaux préparatoires* of the San José conference (1969) regarding the alleged meaning of the phrase 'in general' in the right to life article in the American Convention on Human Rights.

Both misrepresentations by the majority Commissioners in the 1981 *Resolution* appear to have been shaped by a pre-existing ideological commitment to the popular

8 Mary Joseph, "Medical and Legal Treatment of the Fetus: a Growing Disjunction?" Available at: http://www.catholicculture.org/library/view.cfm?recnum=710.

9 Inter–American Commission on Human Rights, Resolution No 23/81, Case 2141 (United States), 1980.

belief in 1980 that abortion does not contravene the right to life. Through the distorted lens of the 1980 high-point of the Feminist Revolution with its central tenet of "a woman's right to abortion", these Commissioners have looked back and read into the historical records what is just not there—and indeed what was never there.

Misconstrual of the drafting history of the 1948 *American Declaration*

The majority opinion commissioners in the 1981 *Baby Boy Resolution* completely misconstrued the drafting history of the concept of the right to life that prevailed at the negotiating sessions in Bogotá for the 1948 American Declaration. They dismissed the original 1947 Draft Declaration which established the concept of the right to life as being understood to apply from conception, and failed to trace the demonstrable continuity of this same concept to the Inter-American Council of Jurists' Draft Convention of 1959 and to the final Convention in 1968.

The protection for "those who are not yet born" was a fundamental human rights concern from the very beginning—it is in the very first 1947 Draft. It was retained in the Inter-American Juridical Committee's 1948 draft of Article I of the American Declaration:

> Toda persona tiene derecho a la vida, inclusive los que están por nacer así como también los incurables, dementes y débiles mentales. (Every person has the right to life, including those who are not yet born as well as the incurable, the insane, and the mentally retarded.)[10]

Entirely without foundation and quite wrongly, the 1981 majority opinion writers surmise that a "completely new article 1" was composed back in 1948 when the phrase "including those who are not yet born as well as the incurable, the insane, and the mentally retarded" was removed and the phrase "liberty, security and integrity of this person" was added.[11] They failed to grasp here the really significant factor that the right to life was still the first right and still applied to "every person". As such, it retained its importance as the core of Article 1 and included every person.

Right to life of the unborn—"not discussed or put in doubt by anyone"

Again quite wrongly, removal of the phrase "including those who are not yet born..." was characterized by the 1981 majority opinion "as a compromise" to resolve an alleged conflict existing back in 1948 between the laws of those States permitting abortion in certain cases and the draft of the Juridical Committee.[12]

Dr. Luis Demetrio Tinoco Castro of the Inter-American Commission on Human Rights dissented. He rejected outright this view that the elimination of the concept

10 *Novena Conferencia Internacional Americana*, Actas y Documentos, Vol. V, 1948, p. 449.

11 Inter-American Commission on Human Rights, Resolution No 23/81, para. (d).

12 Ibid.

that explicitly recognizes the right to life of unborn human beings resulted from "a compromise to resolve the problems raised by the Delegations of Argentina, Brazil, Cuba, the United States of America, Mexico, Peru, Uruguay, and Venezuela, mainly as a consequence of the conflict existing between the laws of those states and the draft of the Juridical Committee":

> ...of which compromise or of which problems or objections *I find no mention whatever* in the minutes of the Working Group, of the Sixth Committee, or of the plenary session of the Conference that met in Bogotá. [13] [Italics not in the original]

On the contrary, Dr. Castro says:

> ...the fact that there does not appear in the volumes of Actas y Documentos any specific motion of a written draft by any delegation that expressly requests the elimination of the phrase of the Juridical Committee's draft that was prepared by the eminent jurists Dr. Francisco Campos, Dr. José Joaquin Caicedo Castilla, Dr. E. Arroyo Lameda, and Dr. Charles G. Fenwick, in my opinion indicates that the supplementary phrase was eliminated because it was considered unnecessary, and that the concept—*not discussed or put in doubt by anyone*—that every person has the right to life, including those yet unborn, as well as incurables, imbeciles, and the insane, was implicitly maintained.[14] [Italics not in the original]

Dr. Marco Gerardo Monroy Cabra, also of the Inter-American Commission on Human Rights, could find no evidence to support the majority opinion claim that the phrase "including those who are not yet born" was removed in order to accommodate existing laws permitting abortion in certain cases:

> Indeed, a review of the report and the minutes of the Working Group of the Sixth Committee shows that no conclusion was reached to permit the unequivocal inference that the intention of the drafters of the Declaration was to protect the right to life from the time of birth—much less to allow abortion, since this topic was not approached.[15]

Dr. Castro is forthright, even scathing, in his criticism of the majority report's fabricated history:

> Study of the Minutes and Documents of the Working Group concerned, and of the Sixth Committee, which was responsible for consideration of these articles of the Draft Declaration, leads me to conclusions contrary to those established in the vote of the majority. In fact, I do not find, either in the Report of the Working Group (Document CB-310/CIN-

13 Dr. Luis Demetrion Tinoco Castro, Dissenting opinion, Inter-American Commission on Human Rights, Resolution No 23/81 Case 2141(United States), 1980.

14 Ibid.

15 Dr. Marco Gerardo Monroy Cabra, Dissenting opinion Inter-American Commission on Human Rights, Resolution No 23/81 Case 2141(United States), 1980.

31), signed by its Rapporteur Dr. Guy Pérez Cisneros, or in the Report of the Sixth Committee (Document CB-445/C.VI-36), presented by its Rapporteur Luis Lopez de Mesa, as they appear on pages 472 to 478 and 510 to 516 of Volume V of Actas y Documentos of the Ninth International Conference of American States, published by the Ministry of Foreign Affairs of Colombia, any specific explanation of the reasons that motivated the elimination of the supplementary phrase contained in the Draft Declaration of the International Rights and Duties of Man presented by the Inter-American Juridical Committee (Document CB-7), which recognized "the right to life for all persons, including (a) the unborn, as well as (b) "incurables, imbeciles, and the insane."[16]

Errors of historical fact in majority resolution

Why were these errors of historical fact introduced into the majority resolution in the 1980 *Baby Boy* case? What ideological pressures by pro-abortion advocates were being brought to bear on this case? What skewered source furnished in 1980 the misleading information that a majority of American States were seriously concerned back in 1948 to protect an allegedly extensive list of laws permitting abortion? Such a list was not supplied to the Working Group in 1947-8 and does not appear in the volumes of *Actas y Documentos*. Such a list could be provided only by dint of studying the 1946 volumes of Penal Codes with the pro-abortion mindset of 1980 and thus deliberately misrepresenting legal tolerance of the unavoidable loss of a child in saving the life of the mother as a law permitting abortion. Where did the 1980 Commission come by the misinformation in their resolution?

In connection with the right to life, the definition given in the Juridical Committee's draft was incompatible with the laws governing the death penalty and abortion in the majority of the American States. In effect, the acceptance of this absolute concept—the right to life from the moment of conception—would imply the obligation to derogate the articles of the Penal Codes in force in 1948 in many countries because such articles excluded the penal sanction for the crime of abortion if performed in one or more of the following cases: A—when necessary to save the life of the mother; B—to interrupt the pregnancy of the victim of a rape; C-to protect the honor of an honest woman; D-to prevent the transmission to the fetus of a hereditary on contagious disease; E-for economic reasons (angustia económica).

In 1948, the American States that permitted abortion in one of such cases and, consequently, would be affected by the adoption of article I of the Juridical Committee, were; Argentina—article 86 n.1 , 2 (cases A and B); Brasil—article n.I, II (A and B); Costa Rica—article 199 (A); Cuba—article 443 (A, B and D); Ecuador -article 423 n.l, 2 (A and B); Mexico (Distrito y Territorios Federales)—articles 333e 334 (A and B); Nicaragua—article 399 (frustrated attempt) (C); Paraguay—article 352 (A); Peru—article 163 (A-to save the life or health of the mother); Uruguay—article 328 n. 1-5 (A, B, C. and F—the abortion must be performed in the three first months from conception); Venezuela—article 435

16 Dr. Luis Demetrion Tinoco Castro, Dissenting opinion Inter-American Commission on Human Rights, Resolution No 23/81 Case 2141(United States), 1980.

(A); United States of America—see the State laws and precedents[4]; Puerto Rico S S 266, 267 (A) (*Códigos Penales Iberoamericanos*—Luis Jiménez de Asua—Editorial Andrés Bello—Caracas, 1946—volúmenes I y II).[17]

These paragraphs are misleading given *inter alia* that:

- Many of the Latin American penal codes were based on the abortion provisions of the French Napoleonic Code of 1810 under which any person who by any means procured the abortion of a pregnant woman was punished with imprisonment, as was a pregnant woman who procured her own abortion; and that
- It was commonly understood that there was to be no prosecution where loss of the life of an unborn child occurred during medical treatment necessary to save the life of the mother;[18] and that
- In addition, the reference supplied for *United States of America—see the State laws and precedents[4]* is less than satisfactory—as footnote number 4 furnishes only "a list of the articles of State's Penal Codes and similar statutes on abortion in existence in a majority of states in 1973"—and not in 1948.[19]

One can only suppose that it might have upset their case if the majority commissioners had listed all the states in the United States that had protective laws in place in 1948 to deter abortion. Of abortion laws in the United States contemporary with the drafting of the American Declaration of the Rights and Duties of Man (1948), Dr. John Hunt makes a significant connection that should dispel the impression that legal attitudes towards abortion were quite liberal at that time:

> In 1948, the very year the Nazis were convicted [for compelling and encouraging abortions] in the RuSHA Case and abortionists were being convicted in the United States, the World Medical Association formulated the Declaration of Geneva...'I will maintain the utmost respect for life from the time of its conception'....[20]

---

17 Inter–American Commission on Human Rights, Resolution No 23/81 Case 2141 (United States), 1980, paras. (e) & (f).

18 The 1939 French version of the Napoleonic Code was amended by decree to allow formally for such a defence *i.e.,* if it is the only means to save the mother's life. At the same time, legislation prohibiting abortion was strengthened and penalties were extended to include removal of licences of doctors and pharmacists who facilitated illegal abortion.

19 Footnote [4] reads: "Daniel Callahan—Abortion: Law, Choice and Morality. William A.Nolen—The Baby in the Bottle—Cowarn, McCann & Geoghengan, Inc.—New York, 1978; 410 U.S. 113 provides a list of the articles of State's Penal Codes and similar statutes on abortion in existence in a majority of states in 1973 (pp. 118-119)."

20 John Hunt, "Abortion and The Nuremberg Prosecutors: A Deeper Analysis?", *Life and Learning,* Vol. VII, Proceedings of the Seventh University Faculty for Life Conference, June, 1997, p. 205 Hunt cites specific cases of abortionists convicted in the United States in 1948: *The New York Times,* November 15, 1947, p. 19; July 15, 1948, p. 24; July 16, 1948, p. 40.

Certainly the Latin American countries were not opposed to legal protection for the unborn children—as Mala Htun in her study of abortion history in Latin America has pointed out:

> In the civil law countries of Latin America, laws on abortion...are embedded in civil and criminal codes. They are not short-term policies introduced and withdrawn by each incoming government, but weighty tomes passed from one generation to the next...some date from the nineteenth century. Historically, these codes have provided a continuous framework for the administration of justice amidst coups, constitutional changes and chaotic economic conditions." [21]

Resolving conflict between *Declaration* principles and laws in some American States

While it is conceded that there were laws in some of the American States, which in certain cases permitted abortion, Dr. Marco Gerardo Monroy Cabra says that this incompatibility [with the right to life of the unborn], however, does not lead to the conclusion that the IX International Conference of American States in Bogotá intended to take the position that life should be protected only from birth and not from conception, since this conclusion is not evident from the Minutes of the Sixth Committee. He goes on to observe:

> The Commission's position implies that a conflict between domestic and international law is possible, which in each case would be resolved according to the principles of international doctrine, international jurisprudence, and the constitutional laws of each State. Needless to say, the now-prevalent concept is the monist position held by Kelsen, that in case of conflict international law takes procedence over domestic law, a principle adopted as a general rule in Articles 27 and 46 of the Vienna Convention on the Law of Treaties. This would imply that if the Declaration ran counter to the laws of some American States, international law would prevail.[22]

Indeed, it has been a consistent and clear guiding principle in negotiating all the modern human rights instruments that existing domestic laws are to comply with international human rights laws, and not *vice versa*.

"...including those who are not yet born"

And so it is regrettable that the Inter-American Commission on Human Rights misinterpreted the deletion (from the draft of the American Declaration on the Rights and Duties of Man) of the proposed right to life wording 'including those who are not

21 Htun, Mala, *Sex and the State: Abortion, Divorce, and the Family Under Latin American Dictatorships and Democracies*, Cambridge: Cambridge University Press, 2003, p. 2.

22 Dr. Marco Gerardo Monroy Cabra, Dissenting opinion Inter –American Commission on Human Rights, Resolution No 23/81 Case 2141 (United States), 1980.

yet born" as meaning that the States Parties rejected the right to life for the unborn child. Indeed, they overlooked the fact that the draft of the same right to life clause went on to say "as well as the incurable, the insane, and the mentally retarded" and that this wording was also deleted.

The reason, of course, for both deletions, as pointed out by the two dissenting Commissioners, was that, according to the Rapporteur of the Bogotá conference, the States Parties explicitly intended to express the rights "in their mere essence, without exemplary or restrictive listings" i.e., lest specifying vulnerable groups might exclude other groups not mentioned. But the majority Commissioners, in 1981, to their shame, selectively used this evidence and misinterpreted it to the detriment of the unborn child and to the advantage of liberal abortion laws.

Dr. Marco Gerardo Monroy Cabra, as a dissenting Commissioner, argues that one cannot conclude from the elimination of the sentence "This right extends to the right to life from the moment of conception" that life should not be protected from conception, inasmuch as the phrase "to the right to life of incurables, mentally defectives, and the insane" was also eliminated.[23] No one, he argues, could reasonably say that the life of incurables, mentally defectives, or the insane should not be protected.

The other dissenting Commissioner, Dr. Luis Demetrio Tinoco Castro, goes further—having searched the historical documents in vain for the alleged reasons the majority justices claimed to have found:

> ...I must deduce that the reason for that elimination was none other than that expressed by the Rapporteur, Mr. Lopez de Mesa, in these terms: "likewise, it was decided to draft them (the rights and duties) in their mere essence, without exemplary or restrictive listings, which carry with them the risk of useless diffusion and of the dangerous confusion of their limits." And the reason cannot be other, because there would not be another for explaining the elimination of the phrase that recognizes the right to life for "incurables, mentally defectives, and the insane".[24]

Regarding the 1947 Draft American Declaration, the phrase "and women" was considered briefly for addition to certain articles but was rejected. It is amusing to speculate on the kind of outrage that might have erupted had the Inter-American Commission on Human Rights in 1981 extended their argument to women: "...the conference faced this question but chose not to adopt language which would clearly have stated that principle". Such reasoning may have led to an unwarranted exclusion of women, together with the unborn, the mentally defective and the insane, from the protection of their rights under the Declaration!

Dr. Castro makes the further point:

23 Dr. Marco Gerardo Monroy Cabra, Dissenting opinion Inter –American Commission on Human Rights, Resolution No 23/81 Case 2141(United States), 1980.

24 Dr. Luis Demetrion Tinoco Castro, Dissenting opinion, Inter –American Commission on Human Rights, Resolution No 23/81 Case 2141(United States), 1980.

> That principle [right to life of the unborn child] was not one exclusively of the Internationalists of the Inter-American world, but the predominant one on the matter in the broader circles of the United Nations as is shown by considerandum III of the Declaration of the Rights of the Child on November 20, 1959, by the XIV Session of the General Assembly...[25]

In further support of this reasoning, Dr. Castro points to the *International Code of Medical Morality* and the *Declaration of Geneva* as principles of professional ethics that together with the scientific principles cited from a number of eminent medical texts, establish widespread recognition of the unborn child that pertained at the time.

Given this widespread recognition of the unborn child in 1948, it seems reasonable to conclude that it was the need for conciseness that accounted for dropping the specific inclusion of unborn children, incurables, mentally defectives and the insane in the right to life article.

Baby Boy Resolution—wrong on question faced by drafters of the Declaration

The truth which emerges here is that the 1981 majority *Resolution* on the *Baby Boy* case by the Inter-American Commission on Human Rights was wrong when it denied that "article 1 of the declaration has incorporated the notion that the right of life exists from the moment of conception". It was wrong when it claimed that: "... the conference [in 1948] faced this question but chose not to adopt language which would clearly have stated that principle". Any careful reading of the negotiations will reveal that the conference did not face "this question" for they were in total agreement that the right to life exists from the moment of conception, just as they were in total agreement that the right to life exists for the incurable, the mentally deficient and the insane.

The question that was actually faced was whether there was a need to enumerate exhaustively the more vulnerable classes of human beings. In the context of that post-World War II determination to ensure human rights protection for absolutely everyone, to absolutely every vulnerable group, a common sense decision was made that there was no need to mention by name the unborn, the mentally deficient, the insane and the incurable. All these vulnerable groups were recognized as human beings with equal rights in keeping with the purpose and intention of the whole Declaration of the Rights and Duties of Man, where "Man" was so clearly understood to encompass everyone, all human beings, including women, children, the unborn, the mentally defective and the incurable.

25 Ibid.

Convention's drafting history confirms right to life from the moment of conception

The majority Commissioners in the 1981 *Resolution* brought the same careless disrespect for historical accuracy to their reading of the *travaux préparatoires* of the San José conference (1969) regarding the alleged meaning of the phrase 'in general' in the right to life Article 4 (1) in the *American Convention on Human Rights.*

The drafting history of Article 4(1) records that an argument developed over whether or not it was necessary to include the specific term 'from the moment of conception'. But a more careful reading of the drafting history reveals that the disagreement was about the practicalities of the wording and not about the essential entitlement of the unborn child to have his life respected. The outcome of this argument was a clear and steadfast recognition of the right to life of every human being—in general, from the moment of conception. This is indeed the plain and "ordinary meaning" required by the the Vienna Convention on the Law of Treaties (1969). The Vienna Convention provides that:

> A treaty shall be interpreted in good faith in accordance with the ordinary meaning to be given to the terms of the treaty in their context and in the light of its object and purpose.[26]

The term "in general" was added not as "a compromise" that would allow some States with current laws that allowed abortion in certain cases to evade this commitment but rather as a practical indication that the term "from the moment of conception" was to be read figuratively rather than literally. That is, the phrase "in general, from the moment of conception" is to be understood as roughly from earliest moments of existence, or more practically speaking, from first knowledge of the child's existence by the mother, her doctor and/or the State.

Negotiating the inclusion of the phrase "from the moment of conception"

This history is not reflected in the *Baby Boy* case majority report's summary of the negotiations surrounding the term "from the moment of conception" in the American Convention:

> 25 To accommodate the views that insisted on the concept "from the moment of conception" with the objection raised, since the Bogota Conference, based on the legislation of American States that permitted abortion, *inter alia*, to save the mother's life, and in case of rape, the IACHR, redrafting article 2 (Right to life), decided, by majority vote, to introduce the words «in general.» This compromise was the origin of the new text of article 2 "1. Every person has the right to have his life respected. This right shall be protected by law, *in general*, from the moment of conception" (Yearbook, 1968, page 321).

26 *Vienna Convention on the Law of Treaties* (1969), Article 31, "General Rule of Interpretation 1".

> 26 The rapporteur of the *Opinion* proposed, at this second opportunity for discussion of the definition of the right of life, to delete the entire final phrase "...in general, from the moment of conception". He repeated the reasoning of his dissenting opinion in the Commission; based on the abortion laws in force in the majority of the American States, with an addition: "to avoid any possibility of conflict with article 6, paragraph 1, of the United Nations Covenant on Civil and Political Rights, which states this right in a general way only" (*Yearbook*, 1968, page 97).

In fact, there was no possibility of conflict with Article 6 of the ICCPR which goes on to be quite specific about protecting the unborn child from sentence of death. This article prohibiting execution of pregnant women acknowledges that the child, from the State's first knowledge of that child's existence, is to be protected. This concern for protecting the unborn child is accommodated neatly in the phrase *in general from the moment of conception*. Recall that the *travaux préparatoires* for the ICCPR refers specifically to the intention to save the life of the unborn child:

> The provisions of paragraph 4(5) [now Article 6(5)] of the draft article aimed at the protection of the life of the unborn child whose mother was sentenced to death; that protection should be extended to all unborn children.[27]

and

> The principal reason for providing in paragraph 4 [now Article 6(5)] of the original text that the death sentence should not be carried out on pregnant women was to save the life of an innocent unborn child'[28]

Given this principal reason, it may be seen that the phrase "in general, from the moment of conception" does not represent any conflict or inconsistency with the established purpose and intent of Article 6 of the ICCPR. On the contrary, the right to life was always understood to apply from conception and this understanding pertained with demonstrable continuity from the original Draft Declaration 1947 to the Declaration 1948, through to the Draft Convention 1959 and in the Convention 1968.

Getting the Bogota Declaration right—a reaffirmation, not a modification

The introduction in this 1981 Resolution of an alleged rejection of the concept of a right to life from the moment of conception is not consistent with the historical facts.

27 Marc J. Bossuyt, *Guide to the 'Travaux Préparatoires' of the International Convenant on Civil and Political Rights*, Dordrecht: Martinus Nijhoff Publishers, 1987, A/C.3/SR.810 para. 2; A/C.3/SR.811 para. 9; A/C 3/SR.812 para. 7; A/C.3/SR.813 para. 36; A/C 3/SR 815 para. 28.

28 A/C.3/SR.819, para. 17 & para. 33.

Nonetheless, the majority Resolution in the *Baby Boy* case is right in saying:

> The addition of the phrase "in general, from the moment of conception" does not mean that the drafters of the Convention intended to modify the concept of the right to life that prevailed in Bogota, when they approved the American Declaration.[29]

Indeed, a more careful reading of the drafting history of the concept of the right to life that prevailed at the negotiating sessions in Bogota for the 1948 American Declaration, reveals that the addition of the phrase is simply a reaffirmation, a restatement and not a modification of the concept of the right to life that prevailed in Bogota.

The meaning of "in general"—substantially different or totally different?

Unfortunately, the 1981 Resolution goes on to make a clumsy attempt at ideological modification of the phrase "in general, from the moment of conception". Having complained that:

> ...The legal implications of the clause "in general, from the moment of conception" are substantially different from the shorter clause "from the moment of conception" as appears repeatedly in the petitioners' briefs. (30)

The majority commissioners in their Resolution go on themselves to misrepresent the phrase, not as being substantially different, but as being "totally different". Their mistake here has proved critical since it has been used in subsequent legal disputes to deny the right to life of *every* child from the moment of conception.[30] In effect, the phrase has been so mangled as to appear to encompass now the radically different concept "and *never*, from the moment of conception".

The drafting history of the clause, even as summarized in the *Yearbook, 1968* and sketchily presented in this 1981 resolution, does not indicate any such intention.

> 26. The rapporteur of the *Opinion* proposed, at this second opportunity for discussion of the definition of the right of life, to delete the entire final phrase "...in general, from the moment of conception." He repeated the reasoning of his dissenting opinion in the Commission; based on the abortion laws in force in the majority of the American States, with an addition: "to avoid any possibility of conflict with article 6, paragraph 1, of the United Nations Covenant on Civil and Political Rights, which states this right in a general way only." (*Yearbook*, 1968, page 97).

The reasons put forward here need more searching analysis than was accorded them by the majority justices in the *Baby Boy* case.

29 Inter-American Commission on Human Rights, Resolution No 23/81, para. 30.

30 See for example, CRR's *amica curia* submission to *Vo v. France* paras. 22 & 23.

Keeping the text without change "for reasons of principle"

It is more than a little misleading to claim that Article 6(1) states the right to life "in a general way only"—it is a very definite, clearly-stated principle which, in keeping with its gravity, is not to be easily exempted. It recognizes a profound principle that posits an essential right for all human beings without qualification or limitations. It should be remembered also that conciseness has always been an expressed guideline to the process of drafting common to all the drafting committees of all the human rights instruments to date. In any case, the subsequent Article 6(5) prohibiting execution of pregnant women adds a specificity that cannot be ignored. It acknowledges that the child, from the State's first knowledge of that child's existence (if not *precisely* from the moment of conception), is to be protected. It was indeed "for reasons of principle" that the majority of the drafting Commission decided to retain the right to life in general from the moment of conception:

> 27 However, the majority of the Commission believed that, for reasons of principle, it was fundamental to state the provision on the protection of the right to life in the form recommended to the Council of the OAS in its Opinion (Part One). It was accordingly decided to keep the text of paragraph 1 without change. (*Yearbook*, 1968, page 97).

The Yearbook goes on to record:

> 28 In the Diplomatic Conference that approved the American Convention, the Delegations of Brazil and the Dominican Republic introduced separate amendments to delete the final phrase of paragraph 1 of article 3 (Right to life) "in general, from the moment of conception". The United States delegation supported the Brazilian position. (*Conferencia Especializada Interamericana sobre Derechos Humanos*—ACTAS Y DOCUMENTOS—Washington 1978 (reprinted)—pages 57, 121 and 160.)
>
> 29 Conversely, the Delegation of Ecuador supported the deletion of the words "and in general". Finally, by majority vote, the Conference adopted the text of the draft submitted by the IACHR and approved by the Council of the OAS, which became the present text of article 4, paragraph 1, of the American Convention (ACTAS Y DOCUMENTOS - pages 160 and 481.)

In fact, as seen from the excerpts above, all the indications, including the refusal to delete the phrase "in general, from the moment of conception", confirm the plain "ordinary meaning" of the phrase—an agreement to protect the right to life from the moment of conception in general. In other words, some concession is made to the practical difficulty that the American States may not always be able to protect the right to life of the child, at least not precisely "from the moment of conception".

Clearing up two practical issues

The reasoning for inclusion of the phrase "in general, from the moment of conception" cannot be interpreted as establishing a liberal tolerance for legal abortion up until the moment of birth. Indeed, achievement of the final text appears to have been driven by distinctly different and quite specific concerns. The reasons mirrored those put forward by many of these same delegates in the drafting discussions of Article 6 of the ICCPR, where the grounds for opposing insertion of the words "from the moment of conception" were two practical issues that were perceived as problematic:

- That it was impossible for the State to determine the moment of conception and hence, to undertake to protect life literally from that moment;[31] and
- That the proposed clause would involve the question of the rights and duties of the medical profession in different countries where legislation on the subject was based on different principles and it was, therefore, inappropriate to include such a provision in an international instrument.[32]

The first of these practical points provides the most reasonable and the most likely explanation of the addition of "in general" to the concept of protection of the right to life "from the moment of conception". This practical concern had been raised in the General Assembly debate on the Declaration of the Rights of the Child in 1959 when the impossibility of determining the exact moment of conception led to adoption of the less exacting but nevertheless comprehensive term "before as well as after birth". This is satisfactorily in keeping with the decision made some years earlier by the drafters of the Universal Declaration—that it was simply not necessary to state precisely the moment existence begins. Albert Verdoodt examined closely this point in the drafting history of the Universal Declaration and concludes that the drafters did not intend to allow any legality for provoked abortions.[33] In reaching this conclusion in the early 1960s in his research on the birth and significance of the Universal Declaration, Verdoodt had enjoyed the advantage of personal consultation with many of the original drafters (especially with René Cassin, who wrote the preface to Verdoodt's work).

The Diplomatic Conference reviewing the draft text of the American Convention in 1969 reached a similar conclusion—that it was not necessary to specify the exact moment of conception and that the right to life was to be protected in general from the moment of conception. Indeed, the Diplomatic Conference rejected both the Brazilian and Dominican motions to delete the whole term "in general, from the moment of conception" and thus reaffirmed commitment to protecting the right to life in general from the moment of conception. No confirmation can be found in the entire drafting history to indicate that the Conference, with the addition of the phrase

31 A/C.3/SR.817, para. 37.

32 A/C. 3/SR 815, para. 37; and A/C.3/SR.818, para. 13.

33 Verdoodt, Albert, *Naissance et Signification de la Déclaration Universelle des Droits de l'Homme*, Société d'Etudes Morales, Sociales et Juridiques, Louvain-Paris, Editions Nauwelaerts, 1964. pp. 95-100. (Verdoodt had extensive consultations with many of the drafting committee and the Third Committee that were present at the negotiations, including Cassin, Malik, Santa Cruz, Garcia Bauer and Austregesilo de Atheida. Verdoodt also listened to tape recordings of the critical sessions, so he was able to distinguish the nuances of the debate.)

"in general" was removing protection of the right to life of the unborn for the entire pre-natal period of physical development from conception to birth.

In regards to protecting the right to life from the moment of conception, the second practical concern raised by some of the ICCPR drafting delegates was echoed in the opinion of the Inter-American Commission's dissenting rapporteur at the San José Conference, convened to finalize the text of the American Convention. Vague doubts were raised about the feasibility of establishing a universal standard across national medical associations and different legal jurisdictions.

Yet this reason could not have carried much weight at that date. The World Medical Association had already achieved a well-publicized international consensus from doctors in all parts of the world across many different jurisdictions on the need to protect life from the moment of conception. Three months before the UN General Assembly adopted the Universal Declaration of Human Rights (December 1948), the World Medical Association (an association of national medical bodies) issued the Geneva Declaration (September 1948). This established clearly the concept of a duty to protect the child before birth. The declaration included a solemn duty "to maintain respect for human life from the time of conception" and to protect human life from the time of conception "according to the laws of humanity". This promise *verbatim* was reaffirmed unanimously by the World Medical Association in the amended *Declaration of Geneva* (August 1968).

It is absurd to believe that substantial change on this matter could have occurred by November 1969 when the Organization of American States (OAS) convened the Inter-American Specialized Conference on Human Rights, in San José, Costa Rica.

Inter-American Court yet to pronounce on rights protection for the unborn

And so, on November 21, when this Conference adopted the American Convention on Human Rights, the final text affirmed:

> Every person has the right to have his life respected. This right shall be protected by law and, in general, from the moment of conception...

It is a matter of great shame that the majority resolution on the 1980 *Baby Boy* case emptied this text of a significant part of its original meaning and that this misleading reinterpretation of the text has been used in subsequent cases in other jurisdictions to imply that the addition of "in general" totally nullifies the right to life of the child from the moment of conception to the moment of birth.

As shown above, faulty reasoning and much ingenuity in reinterpretation was exercised to produce the ideologically required result—to disenfranchise children at risk of abortion from the human rights protection promised in the American Convention: the right to have their lives protected by law, in general from the moment of conception.

Sooner or later, the *Baby Boy* Resolution will be challenged and/or the Inter-American Court, which has not yet pronounced on this issue, will be brought to make a more authoritative and consistent assessment regarding the human rights protection afforded by Article 4(1) to children at risk of abortion. The Inter-American Court can be brought to clarify this important issue either by means of an individual petition or through a request for an advisory opinion.

Ten principles from the Inter-American Court ensuring rights are permanently protected

Both the serious scholarship and careful, logical and measured tone of the Inter-American Court's advisory opinions to date auger well for a clarification that will affirm rather than reduce legal protection for children "in general, from the moment of conception". In advisory opinions to date, the Inter-American Court has upheld the following ten principles:

1. *Equality before the law (Article 24)*

The Court has discerned that ultimately, the international system of human rights has been created and functions on the basic premise of equality among all human beings, by virtue of which all discrimination is precluded from that system:

> The notion of equality springs directly from the oneness of the human family and is linked to the essential dignity of the individual. That principle cannot be reconciled with the notion that a given group has the right to privileged treatment because of its perceived superiority. It is equally irreconcilable with the notion to characterize a group as inferior and treat it with hostility or otherwise subject it to discrimination in the enjoyment of rights which are accorded to others not so classified. It is impermissible to subject human beings to differences in treatment that are inconsistent with their unique and congenerous character.[34]

This is a superbly inclusive definition which has clear application to and a profound understanding of the unity of all persons "in general, from the moment of conception" that forms the basis of their equality before the law. The implication to be drawn here is that both children at risk of abortion and their mothers have equality before the law and that the State must strive to respect equally the rights of the mother and her child—rights to have their lives respected and protected—in general from the moment of conception to the natural end of each of their lives. Equality before the law means that the same life-long legal protection must be afforded to both mother and child as equal members of the human family. The Court has affirmed:

34 Inter-American Court of Human Rights, Proposed Amendments to the Naturalization Provisions of the Constitution of Costa Rica, Advisory Opinion OC-4/84 of January 19, 1984, Series A, No. 4, p. 104 & para. 55.

> and ensure the exercise of such rights and freedoms by means of the respective guarantees (Art. 1.1), that is, through suitable measures that will in all circumstances ensure the effectiveness of these rights and freedoms.[43]

So what are the guarantees that *through suitable measures...will in all circumstances ensure the effectiveness* of the right of every person to have his life respected and protected by law and in general, from the moment of conception? Surely the first and most obvious guarantee is for the State to provide and enact laws that protect each person's right at that earliest stage of existence. The child at risk of abortion is entitled to the same level of legal protection of the right to have his/her life respected as the child's mother has been entitled to receive, also in general, from the moment of conception.

5. The need to balance competing interests with the need to preserve the Convention's object and purpose

The Inter-American Court has observed also that when concepts are invoked as a ground for limiting human rights, they must be subjected to an interpretation that is strictly limited to the "just demands" of "a democratic society", which takes account of the need to balance the competing interests involved and the need to preserve the object and purpose of the Convention.[44] Careful consideration of the competing interests of mothers and their children at risk of abortion must take into account the need to preserve the object and purpose of the Convention which, the Court has declared elsewhere, is "the protection of the basic rights of individual human beings..."[45] The right to life has been called "the supreme right".[46] The Inter-American Court has said that it is "basic" to all human rights:

> The human right to life is a fundamental human right, the basis for the exercise of the other human rights. ...the enjoyment of the right to life is essential for the exercise of all other human rights. If it is not respected, all rights lack meaning.[47]

The need to preserve the object and purpose of the Convention is predicated on the need to protect the right to life, the most basic of all "the basic rights of individuals" and "essential for the exercise of all other human rights". This need can be "balanced"

43 Ibid, para. 25.

44 *Compulsory Membership in an Association Prescribed by Law for the Practice of Journalism (Arts. 13 and 29 American Convention on Human Rights)*, Advisory Opinion OC-5/85 of November 13, 1985, (Series A), No. 5, paras. 66 and 67.

45 *The Effect of Reservations on the Entry Into Force of the American Convention on Human Rights (Arts. 74 and 75)*, Advisory Opinion OC-2/82, September 24, 1982, Inter-American Court of Human Rights, (Series A) No. 2 (1982), para. 29.

46 UN Human Rights Committee General Comment 6 (1) & (3).

47 *Jailton Neri Da Fonseca* v. Brazil, Case 11.634, Report No. 33/04, Inter-American Court of Human Rights, OEA/Ser.L/V/II.122 Doc. 5 rev. 1 at 845 (2004), para. 68.

only by "competing interests" that are of equally essential value, i.e., interests of grave life and death proportions.

Contrary to this principle, pro-abortion advocates in some parts of the world are currently employing a ruse that routinely pits the 'health' of the mother against the life of the child to be aborted—the 'health' grounds for this ruse are all too often spurious. They present abortion routinely and falsely as an absolute necessity and are dismissive of all other alternative 'treatments' that may alleviate the mother's health problems.[48] New medical research is revealing just how wrong they are and just how damaging physically, psychologically and emotionally such abortions can be for these poor mothers. Increasingly, such grounds are being recognized as having little medical validity in view of the rapid advances that have been made in holistic pre-natal health care for mothers and children, and the phenomenal progress in obstetrics, in fetal medicine and in pre-natal and post-natal psychological care for mothers. Moreover, growing recognition of post-abortion depression and post-abortion suicide further discredits abortion of the child as a life-saving, health-giving procedure for the mother.[49]

The rational response to life-threatening pregnancy these days is to improve the availability and delivery of best practice programmes that will bring both the mother and her baby safely through pregnancy. The basic human rights principle of indivisibility demands that the right to life of both the mother and the child must be protected with equal vigor by both the health and legal professions. The 'best interests of the child' principle, legally binding on expectant parents and prenatal health care providers, prohibits treatment that entails harm or damage to the child's health and development.[50]

---

48 See for example, the New Zealand Government's 2007 Abortion Supervisory Committee Report: 98.9% of the 17,934 abortions in 2006 were approved on mental health grounds.

49 See, for example, the recent admission and warning by the Royal College of Psychiatrists: Position Statement on Women's Mental Health in Relation to Induced Abortion, 14 March, 2008.

See also Fergusson, David M.' John Horwood, L.; Ridder, Elizabeth M., "Abortion in young women and subsequent mental health", *Journal of Child Psychology and Psychiatry and Allied Disciplines*, Volume 47 (1), January 2006, pp. 16-24. The longterm study of young New Zealand women found: "Those having an abortion had elevated rates of subsequent mental health problems including depression, anxiety, suicidal behaviours and substance use disorders." Available at: http://www.ingentaconnect.com/content/bpl/jcpp;jsessionid =31u5dqihfosum.alexandra.

50 Inter-American Court of Human Rights advisory opinion: OC-17/2002 on children's juridical status and human rights: "That the States Party to the American Convention have the duty, pursuant to Articles 19 and 17, in combination with Article 1(1) of that Convention, to take positive steps to ensure protection of children against mistreatment, whether in their relations with public officials, or in relations among individuals or with non-State entities." para. 137.9. "Recognition of the authority of the family does not mean that the family can arbitrarily control the child, in a manner that would entail damage to the minor's health and development.", para. 74.

6. *The non-derogability of the right to life*

The Inter-American Commission on Human Rights has recognized the *jus cogens* status of the right to life as defined in Article 53[51] of the *Vienna Convention on the Law of Treaties* (1969):

> ... the Inter-American Commission on Human Rights must stress... that the right to life, understood as a basic right of human beings enshrined in the American Declaration and in various international instruments of regional and universal scope, has the status of jus cogens. That is, it is a peremptory rule of international law, and, therefore, cannot be derogable. The concept of jus cogens is derived from a higher order of norms established in ancient times and which cannot be contravened by the laws of man or of nations. The norms of jus cogens have been described by public law specialists as those which encompass public international order. These are the rules that have been accepted, either explicitly in a treaty or tacitly by custom, as necessary to protect the public interest of the society of nations or to maintain levels of public morality recognized by them.[52]

Laws protecting the right of the child at risk of abortion to have his/her life respected and protected by law, in general from the moment of conception, are meant to be non-derogable. Pursuant to Article 27(2) of the American Convention,[53] the right to life is a right that cannot in any circumstances be derogated from, not even in times of public emergency.

> The right to life entails, for States, the obligation to guarantee it. In accordance with Article 1(1) of the American Convention, this implies their obligation to prevent violations of that right, to investigate violations of the right to life, to punish the perpetrators...[54]

51 *Vienna Convention on the Law of Treaties* (1969) Article 53: "...a peremptory norm of general international law is a norm accepted and recognized by the international community of States as a whole as a norm from which no derogation is permitted and which can be modified only by a subsequent norm of general international law having the same character".

52 Inter-American Commission on Human Rights Report Number 47/96 Case 11.436 *Victims of the Tugboat "13 de Marzo" v Cuba*, October 16, 1996, para. 79.

53 Article 27(2): The foregoing provision does not authorize any suspension of the following articles: Article 3 (Right to Juridical Personality), Article 4 (Right to Life), Article 5 (Right to Humane Treatment), Article 6 (Freedom from Slavery), Article 9 (Freedom from Ex Post Facto Laws), Article 12 (Freedom of Conscience and Religion), Article 17 (Rights of the Family), Article 18 (Right to a Name), Article 19 (Rights of the Child), Article 20 (Right to Nationality), and Article 23 (Right to Participate in Government), or of the judicial guarantees essential for the protection of such rights.

54 *Jailton Neri Da Fonseca* v. Brazil, Case 11.634, Report No. 33/04, Inter-American Court of Human Rights., OEA/Ser.L/V/II.122 Doc. 5 rev. 1 at 845 (2004), para. 69.

Moreover, all acts directed towards the suppression of the right to life of children at risk of abortion are illicit under the Convention in Article 29(a).[55] The current campaign mounted by international abortion advocacy lawyers to pressure Latin-American countries into decriminalizing abortion and removing all legal protection for children at risk of abortion is fundamentally in contravention of the object and purpose of the Convention. It seeks to deny children at risk of abortion a right guaranteed them "in general, from the moment of conception" by the Convention or to impair or deprive that right of its true content. (See Article 29 (a))[56]

The Inter-American Court has discerned:

> The meaning of the word "laws" in the context of a system for the protection of human rights cannot be disassociated from the nature and origin of that system.[57]

The nature and origin of the modern system for the protection of human rights is to be found in the very first and singularly important affirmation in all three foundational human rights instruments of the International Bill of Rights:

> ...in accordance with the principles proclaimed in the Charter of the United Nations, recognition of the inherent dignity and of the equal and inalienable rights of all members of the human family is the foundation of freedom, justice and peace in the world...

At the foundation of modern international human rights law is this recognition that "the equal and inalienable rights of all members of the human family" cannot be legitimately restricted through arbitrary exercise of governmental power or even through arbitrary exercise of the majority's democratic will.

7. *Localized majorities may not pass laws in violation of universal human rights*

> In order to guarantee human rights, it is therefore essential that States' actions affecting basic rights not be left to the discretion of localized or domestic governments but, rather, that they be surrounded by a set of guarantees designed to ensure that the inviolable attributes of the individual not be impaired.[58]

---

55 "The Word 'Laws' in Article 30 of the American Convention on Human Rights", Advisory Opinion OC-6/86, May 9, 1986, Inter-American Court of Human Rights (Series A) No. 6 (1986), para. 14.

56 Article 29: "No provision of this Convention shall be interpreted as: (a) permitting any State Party, group, or person to suppress the enjoyment or exercise of the rights and freedoms recognized in this Convention or to restrict them to a greater extent than is provided for herein..."

57 "The Word 'Laws' in Article 30 of the American Convention on Human Rights", Advisory Opinion OC-6/86, May 9, 1986, Inter-American Court of Human Rights, (Series A), No. 6 (1986). para. 21.

58 Ibid., para. 22.

It is true that one of these guarantees is the requirement that restrictions to basic rights only be established by a law passed by the Legislature in accordance with the Constitution. Such a procedure, according to the Inter-American Court of Human Rights, not only clothes these acts with the assent of the people through its representatives, but also allows minority groups to express their disagreement, propose different initiatives, participate in the shaping of the political will, or influence public opinion so as to prevent the majority from acting arbitrarily.[59] The Court, however, goes on to sound a timely warning:

> Although it is true that *this procedure does not always prevent a law passed by the Legislature from being in violation of human rights*—a possibility that underlines the need for some system of subsequent control—there can be no doubt that it is an important obstacle to the arbitrary exercise of power.[60] [Italics added]

Of special relevance to human rights protection for children at risk of abortion is this understanding that the political will of a democratic majority *does not always prevent a law passed by the Legislature from being in violation of human rights—a possibility that underlines the need for some system of subsequent control.* Liberal abortion laws that permit lethal disrespect for the lives of so many children from conception right up until birth demonstrate just such a need for some system of subsequent control, when a localized majority has acted arbitrarily to pass a law that has abrogated the human rights of these children at risk of abortion.

In this respect, the Court has emphasized that the term "peace, order and good government" may under no circumstances be invoked as a means of denying any right guaranteed by the *American Convention on Human Rights* or to impair or deprive it of its true content.[61]

The Court has emphasized that there are some human rights that cannot be legitimately removed by the State:

> The protection of human rights, particularly the civil and political rights set forth in the Convention, is in effect based on the affirmation of the existence of certain inviolable attributes of the individual that cannot be legitimately restricted through the exercise of governmental power.[62]

59 Ibid.

60 Ibid.

61 "Compulsory Membership in an Association Prescribed by Law for the Practice of Journalism" (Arts. 13 and 29 American Convention on Human Rights), Advisory Opinion OC-5/85 of November 13, 1985. Series A No. 5, paras. 66 and 67.

62 The Word "Laws" in Article 30 of the American Convention on Human Rights, Advisory Opinion OC-6/86, May 9, 1986, Inter-American Court of Human Rights, (Series A), No. 6 (1986), para. 21.

The right of every person, in general, from the moment of conception, to have his life respected and protected by law is surely based on those inviolable attributes of the human person as affirmed here by the Court.

8. *No permissible limitation on a right may entail the total denial of that right*

There can be no rational doubt that abortion entails a total denial of the right to life of the child selected for abortion. The selection process itself is a rejection of the concept of universal respect for human life as described by the Inter-American Court of Human Rights:

> In the context of the Charter of the United Nations the concept of universal respect for human rights is inalienably linked to the principle of non-discrimination. That is, inclusion by opposition to exclusion is a distinctive feature of the international system of human rights founded in the framework of the United Nations. Furthermore, the Charter of the United Nations requires states to ensure the effectiveness of rights and freedoms.[63]

When the Court's discernment here is applied to children at risk of abortion, this principle "inclusion by opposition to exclusion" will be seen clearly to require that states "ensure the effectiveness" of the rights of these children to be included in fundamental human rights protection.

This requirement by the Charter of the United Nations to ensure the effectiveness of these rights is to be seen as a real obligation to be exercised in full, an obligation not to be reduced or toyed with in clever and manipulative ways. The Inter-American Court of Human Rights has issued a sharp warning on this:

> Finally, it is essential to mention that no permissible limitation on a right may entail the total denial of that right. In other words, the exercise of a right may be regulated, limited, or conditioned, but in no circumstances may it be converted into a mere illusion on the pretext of its limitation.[64]

This warning has immense significance for all pro-abortion legislation that attempts to regulate, limit or condition the right to life of the child at risk of abortion.

In too many domestic legislatures today, decriminalization and/or legalization of selective abortion has converted the right to life of children at risk of abortion into *a mere illusion on the pretext of its limitation*. The Inter-American Court would be absolutely right if and when it rules that the child at risk of abortion is included in right to life protections guaranteed in international human rights law, and that selective abortion is an impermissible limitation on the child's right to life because it "entails the total denial of that right".

63 Inter-American Court of Human Rights, Annual Report 2002, Section 1V, Chapter 6, para. 74. Available at: http://www.cidh.org/Migrantes/chap.4.2002eng.htm.

64 Ibid., para. 99.

9. *Interpretation must be guided by the primacy of the text*

The Inter-American Court of Human Rights in an advisory opinion on the death penalty examined the meaning and scope of Article 4 of the Convention and applied the rules of interpretation set out in the Vienna Convention Articles 31(1) and 32, which specify that treaties must be interpreted "in good faith in accordance with the ordinary meaning to be given to the terms of the treaty in their context and in the light of its object and purpose" and that supplementary means of interpretation, especially the preparatory work of the treaty, may be used to confirm the meaning.[65]

> This method of interpretation respects the principle of the primacy of the text, that is, the application of objective criteria of interpretation. In the case of human rights treaties, moreover, objective criteria of interpretation that look to the texts themselves are more appropriate than subjective criteria that seek to ascertain only the intent of the Parties. This is so because human rights treaties, as the Court has already noted, "are not multilateral treaties of the traditional type concluded to accomplish the reciprocal exchange of rights for the mutual benefit of the contracting States;" rather "their object and purpose is the protection of the basic rights of individual human beings..." (The Effect of Reservations, supra 42, para. 29.) [66]

Applying this principle of the primacy of the text to interpretation of Article 4 of the *Convention* with regard to the right to life of children at risk of abortion should result in the Court's reaffirmation of their right to life in accordance with the object and purpose of all human rights treaties—*the protection of the basic rights of individual human beings.*

10. *Domestic law may not be invoked to justify nonfulfillment of human rights obligations*

International obligations to protect the right to life guaranteed by Article 4 of the *American Convention* must be fulfilled in good faith; domestic law may not be invoked to justify nonfulfillment.[67] In addition, there is an obligation not to adopt measures that may threaten human rights:

65 Restrictions to the Death Penalty (Arts. 4(2) and 4(4) of the American Convention on Human Rights), Advisory Opinion OC-3/83, September 8, 1983, , Inter-American Court of Human Rights, (Series A) No. 3 (1983) paras. 48-9.

66 Ibid., para. 50.

67 "International Responsibility for the Promulgation and Enforcement of Laws in Violation of the Convention (Arts. 1 and 2 of the American Convention on Human Rights)", Advisory Opinion OC-14/94, December 9, 1994, Inter-American Court of Human Rights, (Series A) No. 14 (1994), para. 35.

> There can be no doubt that...the obligation to adopt all necessary measures to give effect to the rights and freedoms guaranteed by the Convention includes the commitment not to adopt those that would result in the violation of those very rights and freedoms. [68]

Domestic measures that would result in the violation of the right to life of children at risk of abortion would surely include decriminalization and/or legalization of abortion. State-sanctioned legislation that fails to guarantee the very right to life of these children and that results in the violation of those very rights cannot be legitimated. The fact that the action complies with domestic law is no justification from the point of view of international law:

> The Court finds that the promulgation of a law that manifestly violates the obligations assumed by a state upon ratifying or acceding to the Convention constitutes a violation of that treaty and, if such violation affects the guaranteed rights and liberties of specific individuals, gives rise to international responsibility for the state in question.[69]

Canadian Government's ironic endorsement of the inclusive meaning of Article 4(1)

Ironically, one of the most valuable endorsements of the American Convention's recognition of 'the right to life in general from the moment of conception' comes from the Canadian Government's express fear to ratify the American Convention precisely because Article 4(1) raises "concerns related to the preservation of the status quo, in Canadian law, with respect to abortion". [70]

A recent Canadian parliamentary committee enquiry reported a consensus among the witnesses that the American Convention should not be ratified without a reservation or an interpretative declaration regarding article 4(1):

> ...one cannot dismiss the concerns expressed by many witnesses about article 4(1) in the light of the current absence of Canadian legislation on the matter of abortion.

The specific worry is expressed that Article 4 "may impose an obligation to regulate" abortion in Canada where all regulations have been removed.

The excerpt below from the *Proceedings of the Standing Senate Committee on Human Rights* in 2003 is delightfully illuminating in that it affirms a recognition under the American Convention that life does begin from the moment of conception. The text of Article 4(1) of the Convention does indeed cast doubt on the legitimacy of domestic legal systems that do not provide legal protection for those lives at risk of abortion.

---

68 Ibid., para. 36.

69 Ibid., para. 50.

70 "Enhancing Canada's Role in the OAS: Canada's Adherence to the American Convention on Human Rights", Recommendations. Available at: http://www.parl.gc.ca/37/2/parlbus/commbus/ senate/com-e/huma-e/rep-e/rep04may03part1-e.htm.

> **Senator Beaudoin:** What do you do with the sentence "from the moment of conception"?
> **Mr. Fleming [Professor Don Fleming, Faculty of Law, University of New Brunswick]:** There is a recognition under the American convention that life does begin from the moment of conception, but the protection of that life is to protect the life in general. There can be exceptions to the rule. The rule of choice is a legitimate exception because it is not an arbitrary deprivation of life.
> **Senator Beaudoin:** What do you mean there is a choice? There is a choice or no choice.
> **Mr. Fleming:** It is not arbitrary. Law provides it.
> I would desperately hate to see Canadian government get tied up in the intricacies of this, even though it is clear in our minds that we do not need any kind of stipulation on accession to the convention about this article. There is nothing wrong with Canadian accession to the article with a so-called interpretive declaration about article 4.1 indicating what Canada accepts to be the interpretation of that rule. Even if the worst-case scenario of an absolute interpretation of the right to life from the moment of conception is made, Canada could make an interpretive declaration, rather than a reservation to the convention, which I do not think is necessary. We have to say there is one article that we want to indicate is an article that we interpret in a certain way.
> **Senator Beaudoin:** I hope you are right when you say it is enough to have a declaration.
> **Mr. Fleming:** If you read the Baby Boy case, the preparation of that article and the arguments as to why the term "in general" was put only for the section of the right dealing with the moment of conception, you will see the opportunities that can be made for legitimate argument there. We are as convinced as anyone could be.
> **Senator Beaudoin:** I hope that you are right. I will not be surprised if the court disagrees.

Indeed it is very likely that the Court will disagree. Pro-abortion advocates like Professor Fleming may find it hard to maintain that abortion is not arbitrary deprivation of life simply because "Law provides it". In fact, the UN Human Rights Committee has pronounced that "interference authorized by States can only take place on the basis of law, which itself must comply with the provisions, aims and objectives of the Covenant". Regarding the expression "arbitrary interference", the Committee goes on to say:

> The introduction of the concept of arbitrariness is intended to guarantee that even interference provided for by law should be in accordance with the provisions, aims and objectives of the Covenant...[71]

Legal abortion may be seen then to be "interference provided for by law" that nevertheless is not "in accordance with the provisions, aims and objectives of the Covenant".

71 UN Human Rights Committee, General Comment No 16 on *ICCPR* Article 17, para. 3.

The Canadian Government will face a very real dilemma if it accedes to the *American Convention* Article 4(1) while trying to maintain Canada's extremely liberal abortion practices. The difficulty lies in designing a reservation or a statement of interpretation that will satisfy the conditions set down by the Inter-American Court of Human Rights:

> In interpreting reservations, account must be taken of the object and purpose of the relevant treaty which, in the case of the Convention, involves the "protection of the basic rights of individual human beings, irrespective of their nationality, both against the State of their nationality and all other contracting States." (The Effect of Reservations, supra 42, para. 29.) The purpose of the Convention imposes real limits on the effect that reservations attached to it can have. If reservations to the Convention, to be permissible, must be compatible with the object and purpose of the treaty, it follows that these reservations will have to be interpreted in a manner that is most consistent with that object and purpose.[72]

A further excerpt from the *Proceedings of the Standing Senate Committee on Human Rights* in Ottawa 2003 is remarkably revealing in that it shows just how heavily pro-abortion lawyers are relying on the Inter-American Court of Human Rights to interpret the right to life article in accordance with the dominant ideology of the day rather than in accordance with "the primacy of the text" principle:

> **Mr. McEvoy [Professor John McEvoy, Faculty of Law, University of New Brunswick]:** One of the responses to be made is that there is an institutional inertia in every group. For 20 years, the commission has taken the position that abortion is not inconsistent with the right under article 4.1. It is almost like it is common law age of majority—it is 22 years old now. They have believed this. This is how they interpret the convention. That is why there have not been more complaints from the United States or other cases brought to the commission. This is their interpretation.
> Therefore, if it went to the court, it would be a very different situation for a court, within a structure where there has been a long-standing interpretation upon which people have relied, to suddenly have the members of the court take a different interpretation. Those persons are inculcated in the same interpretation of the convention.
> **Senator Beaudoin:** I am ready to take the risk, but you will need a very good lawyer.[73]

It may take a very smart lawyer indeed to manipulate the Inter-American Court of Human Rights into abandoning the Court's principled stands already made on interpreting the *Convention*. (See these principles outlined above.) It would be a great shame if the Court succumbs to the *institutional inertia* that has allowed abortion to

72 "Restrictions to the Death Penalty (Arts. 4(2) and 4(4) of the American Convention on Human Rights)", Advisory Opinion OC-3/83, Inter-American Court of Human Rights, (Series A), September 8, 1983, para. 65.

73 "Proceedings of the Standing Senate Committee on Human Rights", Ottawa Issue 3 - Evidence, March 31, 2003.

flourish for more than 22 years now, that has allowed an interpretation of the right to life from the moment of conception to entail a total denial of that right for so many children. The Court must not be pressured into replacing their pledged commitment to the genuine principles of interpretation with a facile subservience to the current ideologically "inculcated" reinterpretation. The text of Article 4(1) means what it says:

> Every person has the right to have his life respected. This right shall be protected by law and, in general, from the moment of conception...

As long as the Inter-American Court of Human Rights adheres to its well-articulated principles, competent interpretation of this right will protect by law the right of every child at risk of abortion to have his life respected.

Chapter 12 Reclaiming Rights of the African Child at Risk of Abortion

Reasons for revoking new "authorising medical abortion" Protocol language

The "authorising medical abortion"[1] language in Protocol to the *African Charter on Human and People's Rights on the Rights of Women in Africa* (2003) contravenes one of the founding principles of modern international human rights law—that unborn children are entitled to the protection of the law. As one of the Nuremberg judgments, this principle was mandated to be codified in the *International Bill of Rights.*[2]

The original commitment to recognition of the State's duty to protect the rights of the child before as well as after birth was made in the *Universal Declaration of Human Rights* (1948)—this was confirmed and reaffirmed in the *UN Declaration on the Rights of the Child* (1959) as well as in the *International Covenant on Civil and Political Rights* (1966).[3]

These international human rights instruments served as the foundation of the African regional human rights declarations and charters, especially the following:

- *Declaration on the Rights and Welfare of the African Child* (1979)
- *African Charter on Human and Peoples' Rights* (1981)
- *African Charter on the Rights and Welfare of the Child* (1990)

The preambles and texts of these subsequent African human rights instruments have all pledged and renewed African commitment to all the fundamental human rights principles contained in the original UN declarations and covenants.

---

1 *Protocol to the African Charter on Human and People's Rights on the Rights of Women in Africa* (2003), 16(c).

2 UN Resolution 95(1): Affirmation of the Principles of International Law recognized by the Charter of the Nuremberg Tribunal. Resolution 95 (1) of the United Nations General Assembly, 11 December 1946. The UN committee on the codification of international law was directed to establish a general codification of "the principles recognized in the Charter of the Nuremberg Tribunal and in the judgment of the Tribunal". These became the foundation of modern international human rights law.

3 See above Ch.1: UDHR Recognition of Child before Birth: the Historical Context and Ch.2: UDHR Recognition of the Child before Birth: Analysis of the Texts.

Abortion language irreconcilable with human rights

By removing the protection of the law from selected unborn children, the *Protocol to the African Charter on Human and People's Rights on the Rights of Women in Africa* (2003) *(Women's Protocol)* has broken grievously with one of the original human rights principles—to provide legal protection for the child before as well as after birth. This principle was recognized at Nuremberg, enshrined from the earliest years of the United Nations as a fundamental obligation in the International Bill of Rights and reaffirmed in the relevant subsequent international and regional human rights instruments. The African Women's Protocol breaks with this human rights tradition when it instructs States to:

> ...protect the reproductive rights of women by authorising medical abortion in cases of sexual assault, rape, incest, and where the continued pregnancy endangers the mental and physical health of the mother or the life of the mother or the foetus. [16(c)]

This language of "authorising medical abortion" of "the foetus" is incompatible with the language of all previous UN human rights instruments in which it was understood that "legal protection" was to be provided for the child "before as well as after birth". To exclude the child before birth from the protection of human rights law is to return to Nazi concepts condemned by the international community at Nuremberg:

> "...protection of the law was denied to the unborn children..."[4]

Abortion language incompatible with African values

The abortion language of the Women's Protocol is incompatible also with the language of African values, and in particular with the language of the African Charter on Human and Peoples' Rights (1981) which upholds the human rights of the mother and the child. A specific commitment is made to "the rights of the woman and the child":

> The State shall ensure the elimination of every discrimination against women and also ensure the protection of the rights of the woman and the child as stipulated in international declarations and conventions. [Article 18(3)]

In the Preamble to the Women's Protocol, it is legally questionable and morally indefensible to have distorted Article 18 of the African Charter by removing the significant words "and the child" from the original text:

> Further considering that Article 18 of the African Charter of Human and Peoples' Rights calls on all States Parties to eliminate every discrimination against women and to ensure

4 *Nuremberg Trials Record*: "The RuSHA Case", March 1948, Volume IV, p. 1077. Available at: http://www.mazal.org/archive/nmt/04a/NMT04-T1076.htm.

> the protection of the rights of women as stipulated in international declarations and conventions;

Removal of protection of the rights of the child from this Women's Protocol flouts fundamental principles of legal precedent and logical consistency. African values have consistently upheld the rights of both the mother and the child. This is made very clear in the human rights language of the Organization of African Unity's Declaration on the Rights and Welfare of the African Child (1979)

> Bearing in mind that the welfare of the African child is inextricably bound up with that of its parents and other members of its family, especially the mother... (Preamble)

The authors of 16(c) of the Women's Protocol in denying protection to the unborn child and authorizing the medical aborting of that child's life have signalled a return to a barbaric practice. It has never been part of the "virtues of their historical tradition and the values of African civilization"[5] to separate the well-being and rights of the mother from the well-being and rights of her child.[6]

Indeed African values in the African Charter on the Rights and Welfare of the Child (1990) have accorded a special emphasis to recognition of the State's duty to protect and support both the child and those who have the care of the child, especially when the child's life or well-being is threatened:

> Protective measures under this Article shall include effective procedures for the establishment of special monitoring units to provide necessary support for the child and for those who have the care of the child. Article 16(2)

Abortion language contravenes not "supplements" the African Charter

The language of the Women's Protocol 16(c) is unacceptable because it removes the human rights of the child from the original African Charter commitment to "ensure protection of the rights of the woman and the child as stipulated in international declarations and conventions". The abortion language is reprehensible in that it reneges on previous commitments made in international human rights instruments already signed, and ratified or acceded to by African countries.

For the newly coined language in 16(c) of the Women's Protocol is incompatible not only with the language of these three foundational human rights instruments of regional Africa but also with the language of international human rights instruments such as the Universal Declaration of Human Rights, the UN Declaration on the Rights of the Child, and the International Covenant on Civil and Political Rights.

5 Preamble to the African Charter on Human and People's Rights.

6 The African Charter on Human and People's Rights states clearly in Articles 17 and 18 that it is "the duty of the State" to promote and protect the "morals and traditional values recognized by the community" and to "assist the family which is the custodian of these morals and traditional values".

Contained within these human rights instruments is the essential vocabulary of the human rights of the child before birth, the unborn child.

The correct human rights terminology long established in the drafting history of these first international human rights instruments refers to 'the child before birth' or 'the unborn child'. Yet this vocabulary has been ignored in this new Women's Protocol. The replacement term 'the foetus' is not mentioned in the human rights instruments which the Women's Protocol claims in its Preamble to be "supplementing". To advocate medical abortion of "the foetus" is to deny the State's prior duty to provide legal protection for every child before as well as after birth. To authorize medical abortion is to *contravene* the original African Charter, not *to supplement* it.

Medical abortion contravenes Articles 4 and 5 of the African Charter

> Human beings are inviolable. Every human being shall be entitled to respect for his life and the integrity of his person. No one may be arbitrarily deprived of this right. (African Charter Article 4)

> Every individual shall have the right to the respect of the dignity inherent in a human being and to the recognition of his legal status… (African Charter Article 5)

The lethal harm inflicted on an unborn child in a "medical abortion" is at odds with the fundamental human rights protections promised in Articles 4 and 5 of the African Charter to every human being, to every individual.

Firstly, the Protocol's "authorisation of medical abortion" denies that human beings are *inviolable*—it selects certain human beings (unborn children) and abrogates their inviolability. Abortion violates the unborn child's *right to the respect of the dignity inherent in a human being.* Logic and reason dictate that there can be no right to abortion in any international or regional human rights instrument. There is no human right for one human being to abort the life of another human being. There is no human right to attack the integrity of any person, no matter how small or dependent. Dependency of a weaker or younger human being on a stronger or older human being confers neither ownership nor disposal rights i.e., there is no right to terminate the life of the one who is dependent. Interdependence is integral to the human condition. Human rights are universally acknowledged to be interdependent and indivisible.[7]

7 *Vienna Declaration and Programme of Action*, as adopted by the World Conference on Human Rights, 25 June 1993. "All human rights are universal, indivisible and interdependent and interrelated. The international community must treat human rights globally in a fair and equal manner, on the same footing, and with the same emphasis. While the significance of national and regional particularities and various historical, cultural and religious backgrounds must be borne in mind, it is the duty of States, regardless of their political, economic and cultural systems, to promote and protect all human rights and fundamental freedoms." para. 5.

Human rights derive from the inherent dignity of the human person.[8] Every human being from even the very earliest stage of existence in the mother's womb through to natural death retains all the human rights of being human, all the rights that derive from his/her inherent dignity. External circumstances cannot impair inherent human dignity. No conceivable condition or deprivation or mental or physical deficiency can ever render a human being "non-human". The inherent dignity of every human being remains immutable from conception to death.

Secondly, authorization of medical abortion denies the child's right as a human being to *the recognition of his legal status*—it denies the child's entitlement to legal protection. To this end, the abortion language of the Protocol deliberately employs the terms 'medical abortion' and 'the foetus' to undermine the child's legal status. The term 'the foetus' is employed to disguise the humanity of the child before birth; and the term 'medical abortion' is used to infer that the killing of the child under 'medical' supervision has some health-giving medicinal value.

Despite popular euphemisms, 'medical abortion' remains an intentionally lethal, pseudo-medical procedure. Medical ethics since the time of the Hippocratic Oath have recognized that it is wrong to cause deliberate harm to an unborn child or to the unborn child's mother. Even where the State has removed legal protection from the child at risk of abortion, the medical profession should not consent to execute "authorised" abortions.

Abortion language contravenes International Bill of Rights

Under international human rights law, each sovereign state's legislature remains the primary defender of the human rights of unborn children. Africa's politicians must conform to universally recognized rights to which the African States are already committed. States are committed to providing protective laws for the child before as well as after birth. States must provide legal protection against abortion which constitutes arbitrary deprivation of life in breach of international human rights law, as established via the Nuremberg principles and judgments and their codification in the International Bill of Rights.

The drafting history of the International Covenant on Civil and Political Rights also verifies the State's duty to provide protection of the lives of all unborn children.

> ...the protection of the life of the unborn child whose mother was sentenced to death... should be extended to all unborn children.[9]

8 See UDHR and ICCPR Preambles.

9 Bossuyt, Marc J., *Guide to the "Travaux Préparatoires" of the International Convenant on Civil and Political Rights*, Dordrecht: Martinus Nijhoff Publishers, 1987, p. 121. A/3764 para. 113; A/C.3/SR.810 para. 2; A/C.3/SR.811 para. 9; A/C 3/SR.812 para. 7; A/C.3/SR.813 para. 36; A/C 3/SR 815 para. 28.

African states which have ratified the ICCPR must at all times take positive steps to effectively protect the right to life, a legal duty of the State that is equally applicable to the child before birth as to the child after birth.[10]

Proposition 16(c) of the Women's Protocol is invalid because it seeks explicitly to disfranchise the unborn child by virtue of a clause that purports to authorize violation of the unborn child's right to life . Such a limitation of a non-derivable right, the right to life, is inadmissible under the provisions of the ICCPR Article 4(2).

The Protocol's proposed authorization of medical abortion contravenes also Article 6 of the ICCPR which protects the right to life of all members of the human family[11] and includes the unborn child.

Aborting children for sins of their fathers—prohibited punishment

The *Right to Life* Article 4 of the Women's Protocol modelled on ICCPR 6(5) reaffirms this fundamental human rights principle ensuring protection of both the mother and the unborn child:

> ensure that, in those countries where the death penalty still exists, not to carry out death sentences on pregnant or nursing women; 4(2) j)

Thus, in Article16(c) of the Women's Protocol, the arbitrary exceptions—assault, rape and incest—which purport to justify "authorisation" of abortion are not consistent with longstanding human rights obligations towards the pregnant woman and her unborn child and so are not valid. The child before birth, being innocent of any crime, may not be deprived lawfully of his/her life, for "the inherent right to life... shall be protected by law [and] (n) o one shall be arbitrarily deprived of his life."[12] Laws that arbitrarily deprive the child before birth of life are bad laws, impermissible under international human rights law because they are not in accord with at least one of the provisions, aims and objectives of the ICCPR *viz.* "to save the life of an innocent unborn child".

10 The child before birth having been recognized by the Universal Declaration of Human Rights as being included in *"all the members of the human family"* cannot be excluded by any subsequent human rights instrument or committee or judiciary without undermining the very foundation of modern international human rights law. Should international society even once permit the 'de-recognition' of the human rights of even one group of human beings, then the human rights of no group of human beings are secure. (This lesson from the Nazi experience of dehumanization of one group after another was still very vivid at the time of writing the *Universal Declaration*.)

11 "...recognition of the inherent dignity and inalienable rights of all members of the human family is the foundation of freedom, justice and peace in the world..." This is a core value of the International Bill of Rights. It appears in the Preamble of all three instruments and as such is a foundational premise upon which all the rights that follow are based. It is "the foundation of...justice" i.e., it must be the foundation of international human rights law.

12 *ICCPR* Article 6(1).

Furthermore, authorization of medical abortion on the grounds of assault, rape and incest in the Women's Protocol 16(c) is logically and legally inconsistent with Article 7(2) of the African Charter on Human and Peoples' Rights on which the Protocol purports to be based:

> Punishment is personal and can be imposed only on the offender.

This article specifically forbids punishment of the innocent. The State is prohibited from authorizing abortion of the unborn child who is personally innocent of the crimes of assault, rape or incest. The child is not to be treated as an offender—the child is not deserving of capital punishment—the child has committed no crime and there can be no lawful authorization of intentional deprivation of the child's life.

Moreover, if it is agreed that in order "to save the life of an innocent unborn child", the unborn child's mother is not to be executed even though the mother is guilty of a most serious crime punishable by death, then it must be agreed also on those same grounds, that the life of the unborn child must be saved irrespective of the serious crime committed by the father (i.e., by either parent). If the unborn child is not to be executed for the crimes of his/her mother then neither should the child be executed for the crimes of his/her father.

Abortion of her child compounds abused mother's tragedy

Genuine human rights such as the right to special care and protection for abused pregnant women and their unborn children are being distorted by the invention and promotion of a pseudo-right, the so-called right to abortion in cases of sexual assault, rape and incest.[13] How little are abortion advocates prepared to understand that the advent of a child into an abused mother's life is not an extension of the tragedy but the coming of hope, the coming of new purpose and a compelling new reason to live. In no way should we ever seek to underestimate or trivialize the excruciating pain, both psychological and physical, that is endured by the victims of rape and incest. But neither should we ever consent to compound that pain (particularly to compound the psychological trauma[14]) by encouraging these victims to abort their

13 For a more in-depth presentation of the mother's rights and needs see Rita Joseph, "Out of the greatest evils...", *Voices*, Vol. XXI, No 3, 2006.

14 See, for example, Pedersen, Willy, "Abortion and depression: A population-based longitudinal study of young women", *Scandinavian Journal of Public Health*, 2008, Vol. 36, No. 4, pp. 424-428.

Also Fergusson, N., Horwood, L. John, Ridder, Elizabeth M., "Abortion in young women and subsequent mental health", *Journal of Child Psychology and Psychiatry*. 2006, Vol. 47 (1), pp. 16-24.

Also Coleman, Priscilla K., "Resolution of Unwanted Pregnancy During Adolescence Through Abortion Versus Childbirth: Individual and Family Predictors and Psychological Consequences", *Journal of Youth and Adolescence*, 2006.

innocent children—for it is these children who have an inimitable potential to bring true love and healing back into their mothers' lives.

Thus cases of pregnant women who have been abused by sexual assault or rape or incest should not be exploited in Women's Protocol 16(c) to advocate that the State authorize abortion. Since these children have committed no wrong, arbitrary[15] deprivation of their lives by an abortionist should not be tolerated by the State.[16] In terms of the human rights of the unborn child, abortion is lethal punishment of the innocent and cannot be validated by human rights law.

A child in her womb threatens the mental and physical health of the mother?

Nevertheless, in many parts of the world, abortion has been deemed to be lawful on the dubious grounds that the child in the womb threatens the mother's life or her physical or psychological health. Increasingly, such grounds are being recognized to have little or no medical validity in view of the rapid advances that have been made in holistic pre-natal and post-natal health care for mothers and babies, and the phenomenal progress in obstetrics, in foetal medicine and in foetal surgery, as well as the positive burgeoning of pre-natal and post-natal psychological care for mothers.

The rational response to life-threatening pregnancy these days, in Africa as in the rest of the world, is to improve the availability and delivery of optimum pre-natal and post-natal healthcare for mothers and their children.

Also Rue V.M., Coleman P.K., Rue J.J., Reardon D.C., "Induced abortion and traumatic stress: A preliminary comparison of American and Russian women", *Medical Science Monitor*, Vol. 10(10). SR5-16, 2004.

See also the recent admission and warning by the Royal College of Psychiatrists: Position Statement on Women's Mental Health in Relation to Induced Abortion, 14 March, 2008.

Also Suliman, Sharain, Ericksen, Todd, Labuscgne, Peter, de Wit, Renee, Stein, Dan J., Seedat, Soraya, "Comparison of pain, cortisol levels, and psychological distress in women undergoing surgical termination of pregnancy under local anaesthesia versus intravenous sedation," *BMC Psychiatry*, June 2007, Vol. 7 (24). Available at: http://www.biomedcentral.com/1471-244X/7/24.

15 Even 'authorised' deprivation of life can still be 'arbitrary'. See UN Human Rights Committee, General Comment No 16 on *ICCPR* Article 17, para. 3: "The introduction of the concept of arbitrariness is intended to guarantee that even interference provided for by law should be in accordance with the provisions, aims and objectives of the Covenant..."

16 The *European Convention on Human Rights* is the only human rights instrument to spell out the conditions under which intentional deprivation of life may be authorized. (Article 2 footnote 1 – "Right to Life") No grounds can be found therein for intentionally depriving the child before birth of the right to life. For the child before birth, there has been no crime, no sentence of a court and no conviction. The child before birth is utterly incapable of offering any person unlawful violence or of participating in a riot or insurrection.

Evidence supports making pregnancy safer

'Safe abortion' is neither an appropriate nor an adequate response to unsafe pregnancy. The truly moral response to unsafe pregnancy is also the most logical pragmatic response. It is to make pregnancy safer by addressing the major causes identified by the World Health Organisation WHO (2006): hemorrhage, infection, hypertension, obstructed labour and treatable conditions such as malaria, anaemia, and heart disease. As these causes come to be more adequately addressed, maternal deaths resulting from pregnancy will be dramatically reduced.[17]

Those who work in refugee camps and slums with the poorest women of the world, like *Caritas* and *Mater International*, all send us the same message—a crying need to help them to make pregnancy safer.

Ten years ago, Dr. Hiroshi Nakajima as Director-General of the World Health Organization said:

> We know what needs to be done to make motherhood safe and the resources needed are obtainable. Pregnant women need special care that is neither sophisticated nor very expensive. An investment of as little as US $3 per person could prevent most of these maternal and newborn deaths and disabilities.[18]

There can be no denying that UN sponsored population initiatives peddling abortion "services" have siphoned off desperately needed money from programmes that provide basic health facilities, clean water, vaccines, antibiotics and food supplements for expectant mothers and their communities.[19] In Africa between 1990 and 2005, estimates of the annual change in maternal mortality rate was 0%.[20]

"Since Cairo [UN International Conference on Population and Development 1994], over 5 million women have died for lack of basic health care during pregnancy" (WHO). One recent analysis of maternal deaths at a tertiary hospital in Mozambique revealed that at least half of all maternal deaths there were due to infectious diseases

17 For a recent well-researched presentation of this argument see Dr. Susan Yoshihara's "Six Problems with 'Women Deliver': Why the UN Should Not Change MDG 5", C-FAM, 2007. Available at: http://www.c-fam.org/index.php?option=com_docman&task=doc_view&gid=29&Itemid=37.

18 Press Release WHO/336, April 1998.

19 For example, it is estimated that under-nutrition accounts for as many as 20% of maternal deaths and that about half of all women still go though childbirth without access to skilled care or emergency obstetric services in the 68 priority countries covered by Countdown to 2015 Maternal, Newborn and Child Survival, 2008 Report, "Tracking Progress in Maternal, Newborn and Child Survival".

20 *Maternal Mortality in 2005*, (Estimates developed by WHO, UNICEF, UNFPA and the World Bank) Appendix 15. Comparison of 1990 and 2005 maternal mortality by United Nations Population Division regions, p. 38.

such as pneumonia, malaria, and meningitis which could have been effectively treated had resources been available.[21]

Even the United Nations Population Fund (UNFPA) admits that pregnancy in developing regions does not have to be dangerous.

> Every woman, rich or poor, faces a 15 per cent risk of complications around the time of delivery, but maternal death is practically nonexistent in developed regions.[22]

Yet pro-abortion propaganda likes to insist that pregnancy itself is a dangerous condition that can be best treated by "safe abortion". Abortion advocates, if they are sincere about saving women's lives, need to revert to a more truthful perspective.[23] They need to acknowledge, for example, that "...tuberculosis kills more women than all the combined causes of maternal mortality."[24] In the aggressive obsession to expand abortion services for the poorest women, pro-abortion ideologues spurn the fundamentals of pre-natal and post-natal care: the real and disturbing lack of access to basic care, to antibiotics and life-saving vaccines[25], to trained midwives[26] and to centres equipped for obstetric complications; and even where those centres exist, lack of transportation to them remains a huge problem for expectant mothers in emergency situations.

In the light of an expectant mother's most pressing needs, the fanaticism of many abortion advocates borders on the ludicrous—they would rather give a penniless, illiterate girl from Somalia a 'safe abortion' than provide for her genuine human rights—a safe pregnancy along with food security, basic health needs, a decent education, development assistance for her community and a good life for herself and her child.

---

21 Menéndez C, Romagosa C, Ismail MR, Carrilho C, Saute F, et al., "An Autopsy Study of Maternal Mortality in Mozambique: The Contribution of Infectious Diseases", *PLoS Medicine* Vol. 5, No. 2, February 19, 2008. Available at: http://medicine.plosjournals.org/perlserv/?request=getdocument&doi=10.1371/journal.pmed.0050044.

22 *UNFPA State of the World's Population 2005: The Promise of Equality - Gender Equity, Reproductive Health and the Millennium Development Goals*, United Nations Population Fund (UNFPA), September 2007.

23 See, for example, World Health Organisation (WHO), Final Report of the Commission on the Social Determinants of Health Report, *Closing the gap in a generation: Health equity through action on the social determinants of health*, Geneva: 2008, especially pp. 8-9.

24 Connolly M., Nunn P., "Women and tuberculosis", World Health Statistics Quarterly, Vol.49 (2), 1996, pp. 115-119.

25 For example, in the year 2000, neonatal tetanus resulted in 200,000 deaths.(UNICEF, April, 2002).

26 "In Africa, less than 50% of births are attended by a skilled health worker, according to most recent available data." WHO, UNICEF, UNFPA, and The World Bank, *Maternal Mortality in 2005* (Estimates developed by WHO, UNICEF, UNFPA and the World Bank), Geneva: WHO Press, 2007, p. 18.

Authorization of abortion ignores legal principles of necessity and proportionality

In the meantime, authorization of medical abortion remains conceptually incompatible with protecting the rights of the woman and the child as set out in the African Charter Article 18(3):

> The State shall ...ensure the protection of the rights of the woman and the child as stipulated in international declarations and conventions.

The right to life, the well-being, of both the mother and the child must be pursued with equal vigour by the medical profession and by all those in positions of authority in public health and law.

Indeed, there is no authority whereby this Women's Protocol 16 (c) may claim to be able to extrapolate that a State must

> protect the reproductive rights of women by authorising medical abortion in cases... where the continued pregnancy endangers the mental and physical health of the mother or the life of the mother or the foetus...

On the contrary. The original universal right to life takes precedence over the newly-coined "reproductive rights". No less an authority than the ICCPR insists that the State must protect both the mother and the child from arbitrary deprivation of life (Article 6). It is each legislature's responsibility to provide laws that "strictly control and limit the circumstances in which the State may condone deprivation of life".[27] Where the intended outcome of a medical intervention is the deprivation of the life of an unborn child, then it must be considered under international law to be "arbitrary" unless it can be justified by reference to both principles of necessity and proportionality. In the interest of universal justice, the common law method of legal interpretation, now routinely adopted by many jurisdictions around the world, should be applied everywhere and with consistency to laws that protect the unborn child.

The drafting history of the ICCPR "right to life" reveals that the concept of 'lawful defence' was tied from the very beginning to "the use of force which is no more than absolutely necessary", and in the lengthy list of instances of "lawful killing" considered by that first Commission on Human Rights, abortion did not figure.[28] Legally speaking, medical abortion of an unborn child can never be routinely "authorized". Always the loss of the life of an unborn child through a medical intervention must be unintended, unavoidable, 'an absolute necessity' which is conceptually and substantially different to a mere 'choice' or 'option'. Legal grounds of necessity for deprivation of the life of an unborn child may be invoked only after all other measures and remedies have been exhausted—necessity means that there is no other option. State-autho-

27 Human Rights Committee General Comment 6, para. 3.

28 Commission on Human Rights 5th Session, 1949. E/CN.4/188.

rized deprivation of life, whether capital punishment or abortion, is a very, very serious matter—a matter of absolute necessity not just routine.

In addition, the State's solemn duty under the ICCPR to provide laws to protect the unborn child from arbitrary deprivation of life requires that the fundamental legal principle of proportionality also be applied. Anything less than the saving of the mother's life is not proportionate to the irreparable and lethal harm done to the unborn child, and is open to the charge of being arbitrary and unjust. The inadvertent loss of the life of an unborn child in the process of saving the life of his/her mother is an outcome that satisfies the legal requirement of proportionality. If failure to preserve the life of the unborn child occurs for any lesser reason, it is not legally justified and should certainly be investigated by the State. Numerous surveys around the world have confirmed that most medical abortions are performed for "family planning" and for "socio-economic" reasons.[29] In these cases, the unborn child is often routinely misrepresented and eliminated under the accommodatingly vague charge "endangers the mental and physical health of the mother". Authorizing medical abortion of these unborn children flouts a fundamental principle of justice—proportionality.

Women's Protocol 16(c) on abortion lacks logic

Women's Protocol 16 (c) is also problematic in that it is seriously lacking in very basic logic. It claims quite irrationally to:

> protect the reproductive rights of women by authorising medical abortion in cases... where the continued pregnancy endangers... the life of the mother or the foetus...

Where the life of "the foetus" (i.e., the child before birth) is endangered, it makes no sense in the rational practice of life-saving medicine to authorize medical abortion of that child. In just the same way, it would make no sense to abort the life of the mother because the mother's life is endangered.

Where the life of "the foetus" (i.e., the child before birth) is endangered, it is contrary to the State's human rights duties towards the child to authorize medical abortion of that child. Such an authorization is in breach of the prior commitment made by these same African countries in the African Charter on the Rights and Welfare of the Child. In particular it contradicts their prior commitment "to ensure, to the maximum extent possible, the survival, protection and development of the child".[30]

---

29 See, for example, Bankole, Akinrinola, Singh, Susheela. and Haas, Taylor, "Reasons Why Women Have Induced Abortions: Evidence from 27 Countries", *International Family Planning Perspectives*, Vol. 24, No. 3, September, 1998, pp. 117-152. "The most commonly reported reason...is to postpone or stop childbearing. The second most common reason—socio-economic concerns..."

30 African Charter on the Rights and Welfare of the Child Article 5.

Women's Protocol contradicts the Charter to which it purports to be a protocol

This African Charter on the Rights and Welfare of the Child is a very fine human rights instrument but it is as though the authors of this Women's Protocol have never even read it so oblivious are they to the solemn obligation therein to protect the child's right to survival, protection and development. In the Survival and Development section, Article 5, this human rights obligation is enunciated with admirable clarity:

1. Every child has an inherent right to life. This right shall be protected by law.
2. States Parties to the present Charter shall ensure, to the maximum extent possible, the survival, protection and development of the child.

The Women's Protocol authors ignore the fact that African countries reaffirmed in the African Child's Charter adherence to "the principles of human and peoples' rights and freedoms contained in the declarations, conventions and other instruments adopted by the United Nations". They fail to acknowledge that these principles include the rights of the child to *appropriate legal protection before as well as after birth.*[31]

This recommitment to the rights of the child (as well as to the woman's rights) is, *as stipulated in international declarations and conventions*, reiterated in 18(3) of the African Charter on Human and Peoples' Rights. Yet such a recommitment is scorned in the abortion language of the Women's Protocol—indeed, in failing to recommit to the rights of the child, the Protocol contradicts the very Charter to which it purports to be a protocol.

Authorization of abortion violates the African Child's Human Rights Charter

Other commitments already made in the African Charter on the Rights and Welfare of the Child and now being contravened in 16 (c) of the Women's Protocol include:

- To ensure the right of every child to the best attainable health. Medical abortion brings arbitrary death to the child and death should never be promoted as *the best attainable state of physical mental and spiritual health* for any child, before or after birth.[32]
- To protect the child from all forms of inhuman treatment and especially physical injury or maltreatment. Medical abortion inflicts lethal physical injury on the child before birth—it is certainly not a benign treatment to be authorized for the unborn child.[33]

31 *UN Declaration on the Rights of the Child*, Preamble.

32 Article 14: "Every child shall have the right to enjoy the best attainable state of physical mental and spiritual health".

33 Article 16(1): "States Parties to the present Charter shall take specific legislative, administrative, social and educational measures to protect the child from all forms of... inhu-

– To eliminate harmful social and cultural practices affecting the normal growth and development of the child and in particular those practices prejudicial to the life of the child. Medical abortion both as a practice lethally *affecting the normal growth and development* of the unborn child and as a practice extremely and intentionally prejudicial to the life of the child should be *eliminated* not *authorized*.[34]

It was originally in the Declaration on the Rights and Welfare of the African Child that the African states pledged to take legal and educational measures to abolish practices that are "harmful to normal growth and development of the child". Can any practice be more *harmful to normal growth and development of the child* than medical abortion? Authorization of medical abortion is the antithesis of this longstanding obligation of African States to abolish such practices.

Authorization of abortion contrary to Declaration on the Rights of the African Child

Indeed, there is yet another respect in which the authors of the Women's Protocol have ignored Africa's comprehensive previous commitments: in the Declaration on Welfare of the African Child, African member states undertook:

> ...to review the current legal codes and provisions relating to the rights of children, particularly by taking into account the UN Declaration of 1959 on the Rights of the Child... (Article 2)

It is important to recall here that this 1959 UN Declaration on the Rights of the Child specifically reaffirmed the rights of the child before birth: because of the child's physical immaturity, the child before birth is entitled to be provided with appropriate legal protection and special safeguards and care—the same safeguards and care as the child after birth is entitled to receive.

The Women's Protocol in 16 (c) directly contradicts this obligation. It proposes the exact opposite—the removal of all legal protection for the child before birth. It introduces instead "authorisation of medical abortion" i.e., it removes the safeguards and authorizes a lethal treatment for the unborn child.

man or degrading treatment and especially physical or mental injury or abuse, neglect or maltreatment..."

34 Article 21(1): "States Parties to the present Charter shall take all appropriate measures to eliminate harmful social and cultural practices affecting the welfare, dignity, normal growth and development of the child and in particular: (a) those customs and practices prejudicial to the health or life of the child..."

Women's Protocol spurns African values

It is admirably clear from the African Charter on Human and Peoples' Rights that African values include a distinctive emphasis on the duties of the individual towards others and especially towards members of their families.

Careful scrutiny of these commitments will affirm that a woman's rights, even her reproductive rights, are not meant to be pursued at the expense of her child's rights:

- A woman shall have duties towards her family, and a woman's rights *shall be exercised with due regard to the rights of others,* including the rights of her child, before as well as after birth.[35]
- A woman shall *have the duty to respect and consider* her fellow beings including her unborn child *without discrimination*; a woman has the duty to accord the same respect and consideration to her child before birth as to her child after birth.[36]
- A woman shall also *have the duty to preserve the harmonious development of the family,* i.e., she has a duty to preserve life, to preserve the life of the newest member of her family developing in her womb—she may not intentionally destroy that new family member. There is a specific corollary to this: the same respect the mother owes to her unborn child, now dependent on her, is to be reciprocated by the child who has a lifelong duty to respect her (the child's mother) *at all times* and the child has the duty in later life *to maintain* her (the child's mother) in *case of need.*[37]

State's duty to assist mothers

A mother, however, is not expected to carry out her human rights duties towards her child entirely on her own—especially *in case of need* she is entitled to all necessary assistance from the State. It is admirably clear also from the African Charter on Human and Peoples' Rights that African values include a praiseworthy emphasis on the duties of the State towards the family, especially towards women and their children:

> Article 18
> 1. The family shall be the natural unit and basis of society. It shall be protected by the State which shall take care of its physical health and moral.
> 2. The State shall have the duty to assist the family which is the custodian of morals and traditional values recognized by the community.

35 Article 27: 1. "Every individual shall have duties towards his family..." 2. "The rights and freedoms of each individual shall be exercised with due regard to the rights of others..."

36 Article 28: "*Every* individual shall have the duty to respect and consider his fellow beings without discrimination..."

37 Article 29:

"The individual shall also have the duty:

1. To preserve the harmonious development of the family and... to respect his parents at all times, to maintain them in case of need..."

3. The State shall ensure the elimination of every discrimination against women and also ensure the protection of the rights of the woman and the child as stipulated in international declarations and conventions.
4. The aged and the disabled shall also have the right to special measures of protection in keeping with their physical or moral needs.

There is no room here for the State to refuse to protect the human rights of every member of the family. This includes *the duty to assist the family*, to care for the physical health of every family member and to protect the rights of both the mother and her child. The African Child's Charter Article 14 is even more specific: it requires that States undertake to pursue the full implementation of every child's right to *enjoy the best attainable state of physical mental and spiritual health* and in particular shall take measures *to ensure the provision of necessary medical assistance and health care to all children* as well as *to ensure appropriate health care for expectant and nursing mothers.*

State's duty to ensure understanding of corresponding obligations

Again, in Article 25 of the African Charter on Human and Peoples' Rights, special attention is given to the State's duty to ensure not just rights and freedoms but also to see to it that the *corresponding obligations and duties are understood.*[38]

The Preamble to the African Charter on Human and Peoples' Rights includes a specific directive and warning that *the enjoyment of rights and freedoms also implies the performance of duties on the part of everyone.* Preambular paragraphs such as this are well understood in international human rights instruments to be intended to be applied in the interpretation of every article in the Charter.[39] Clearly, operative provisions concerning the rights of women must be read consistently with the preambular paragraphs, which set out the themes and rationale of the Charter. Because the Women's Protocol is put forward as "supplementing" the African Charter, it cannot ignore or contravene the themes and rationale of the Charter. This means that a woman's 'enjoyment' of her reproductive rights also implies the performance of duties on her part to recognize the rights of others, including the rights of her child before as well as after birth.

38 Article 25: "States parties to the present Charter shall have the duty to promote and ensure through teaching, education and publication, the respect of the rights and freedoms contained in the present Charter and to see to it that these freedoms and rights as well as corresponding obligations and duties are understood."

39 Article 31 *General rule of interpretation* as set out in *the Vienna Convention on the Law of Treaties* (1969). The operative provisions of the text of the *African Charter on Human and Peoples' Rights* shall be interpreted in good faith in accordance with the ordinary meaning to be given to the terms of the Charter in their context (i.e., in the context of its preamble in addition to the text).

Authorizing abortion violates human rights principle of indivisibility

Performance of duties towards the child on the part of the State are also implied. The State's duty to protect the reproductive rights of women cannot be performed at the neglect of the State's other and equally important duty to protect the rights of children and to provide special safeguards and care for them before as well as after birth. The fundamental human rights principle of indivisibility comes into play here. Applying the principle of indivisibility means that the State may not abandon its duty to provide legal protection for the child before as well as after birth on the grounds that it must *protect the reproductive rights of women.* The enjoyment of women's reproductive rights is not absolute—it is contingent on ensuring the rights of others, ensuring especially that the rights of children to survival, development and protection are enacted *to the maximum extent possible.*[40]

Protecting child's rights –the duty of individuals and the State

So what are these rights of children the protection of which is the duty of individuals and the State?

The rights of children are spelled out with a fine clarity in the African Charter on the Rights and Welfare of the Child. These African values are particularly commendable in the emphasis placed on both the State's duty and the individual's duty towards every child. This African Child's Human Rights Charter is unequivocal in requiring both parents and the State to put the rights of the child first:

> In all actions concerning the child undertaken by any person or authority the best interests of the child shall be the primary consideration. 4(1)

Parental responsibilities towards their children are taken very seriously:

> Article 20: Parental Responsibilities
> 1. Parents… shall have the duty:
>   (a) to ensure that the best interests of the child are their basic concern at all times-
>   (b) to secure, within their abilities and financial capacities, conditions of living necessary to the child's development…

Clearly parents have a duty to ensure the best interests of their child at *all times,* i.e., before as well as after birth. Medical abortion, the intentional deprivation of the life of the unborn child, is never in the best interests of the child and directly contravenes the parents' duty to *secure conditions of living necessary to the child's development…*

In perverse rejection of the child's human rights, medical abortion intentionally destroys for the child the necessary conditions of living and development—it deprives the child of life. (The addition here of the phrase *within their abilities and*

40 African Charter on the Rights and Welfare of the Child Article 5.

financial capacities to qualify parents' duty to secure *conditions of living necessary to the child's development* does not imply that the child may be aborted where the parents' abilities and financial capacities are inadequate. It should be read rather as pointing to the well-articulated duties of the State as set out in this same document, duties that require the State to assist families, specifically to assist the woman and the child in difficult circumstances.)

African values: the child's right to parental care and protection

African values place particular emphasis on the rights of the child to enjoy parental care and protection.[41]

Reproductive rights of women cannot excuse the denial of a child's human rights entitlement to parental care and protection. In particular, women's reproductive rights cannot justify violation of the unborn child's right to reside with his or her mother without the threat of medical abortion. The intended outcome of medical abortion is the deprivation of the life of the unborn child through the forced separation of the unborn child from his or her mother. There is no truly ethical judicial authority and no morally valid law in the world that can ever determine definitively that a contrived premature death is *in the best interest of the child*. All such arbitrary determinations constitute a violation of the ICCPR legal obligation to protect every human being from *arbitrary deprivation of life*.

This new abortion language in the Women's Protocol 16(c) is unacceptable in that it is incompatible with the right to life language of the ICCPR. Put bluntly, it is not permissible in any creditable protocol to a human rights instrument to protect the reproductive rights of women by authorizing the violation of the right to life of their children.

Authorizing abortion—grave breach of the inalienable rights of the child

It is the essential nature of all human rights that they are inalienable. The opening paragraph of the Universal Declaration of Human Rights proclaims:

> Whereas recognition of the inherent dignity and of the equal and inalienable rights of all members of the human family is the foundation of freedom, justice and peace in the world…

The right of the child before birth to legal protection is one of the equal and inalienable rights of all members of the human family. No one may destroy that right, nor

41 Article 19: "Every child shall be entitled to the enjoyment of parental care and protection and shall, whenever possible, have the right to reside with his or her parents. No child shall be separated from his parents against his will, except when a judicial authority determines in accordance with the appropriate law, that such separation is in the best interest of the child."

deprive the child of that right—that's what inalienable means. And when the Preamble goes on to say:

> ...it is essential...that human rights should be protected by the rule of law

It is clear that no one may remove the human rights of the child before birth from being protected by the rule of law.

The "authorising medical abortion" language in the Women's Protocol removes the protection of the rule of law from the child and must be revoked.

Chapter 13 Selective Abortion: An Act of Violence and Discrimination on Grounds of Sex

Reclaiming the rights of the girl-child at risk of abortion

> We are confronted with the slaughter of Eve, a systematic gendercide of tragic proportions.... It starts in the womb. There are societies where male births are preferred, particularly if the number of births are limited. That's where abortion for gender reasons starts...Abortion is now both a moral issue and a health issue—but in quite the opposite manner that abortion advocates have long argued.[1]

Ambassador Dr. Theodor Winkler of the International Institute of Strategic Studies made this incisive comment in launching a 2005 report entitled *Women in an Insecure World*, an investigation by 60 authors. They show that sex-selection abortions and infanticides are the primary cause of a critical global imbalance of the sexes, with a disparity of more than 200 million more males than females worldwide, a disparity which has resulted in increasing problems with child abuse, sibling violence, spousal exploitation, and sex trafficking.[2]

In view of this situation—*a systematic gendercide of tragic proportions*—abortion advocates can have little credibility in lauding unrestricted abortion as a human rights advance for women and girls.

The UN Committee on the Rights of the Child (CRC Committee) has condemned selective abortion as discrimination against children and as a serious violation of their rights, affecting their survival.[3] The Committee denounces not only selective abortion of girl children on the grounds of sex discrimination, but also goes on in the same paragraph to condemn "multiple discrimination (e.g., related to ethnic origin, social and cultural status, gender and/or disabilities)".

---

1 Logai Foundation, "'Gendercide' responsible for 'missing' women in China, other countries", November 29, 2005. Available at: http://www.laogai.org/news/newsdetail.php?id=2431.

2 Vlachová, Marie and Biason, Lea (eds.), *Women in an Insecure World: Violence Against Women—Facts, Figures and Analysis*, Geneva: Geneva Center for the Democratic Control of Armed Forces (DCAF) 2005.

3 UN Committee on the Rights of the Child (CRC) General Comment No 7 (2005), "Right to Non-discrimination".

The CRC Committee is signalling here a re-emerging recognition of the need to protect children at risk of abortion.

The CRC Committee classifies selective abortion as a human rights violation. As such, States are obliged by the international human rights standard established in the UN *Convention on the Rights of the Child* (CRC) (1990) to hold perpetrators accountable.

Selective abortion—prenatal sex selection as "an act of violence"—*Beijing Platform for Action*

The act of "prenatal sex-selection", resulting in selective abortion on the grounds of sex, is included in the official definition of violence agreed at the Fourth UN Conference on Women at Beijing (1995): "acts of violence against women also include...prenatal sex selection..." [4] Governments at Beijing promised to:

- prevent and eliminate all forms of violence against women and girls. [5]
- enact and enforce legislation protecting girls from all forms of violence, including...prenatal sex selection ... [6]
- enact and enforce legislation against the perpetrators of practices and acts of violence against women, such as...prenatal sex selection...and give vigorous support to the efforts of non-governmental and community organizations to eliminate such practices.[7]
- eliminate all forms of discrimination against the girl child...which result in harmful and unethical practices such as prenatal sex-selection and female infanticide; this is often compounded by the increasing use of technologies to determine fetal sex, resulting in abortion of female fetuses. [8]

This last paragraph ties prenatal sex selection to abortion—although there was an immense effort by pro-abortion advocates at the time to try to keep condemnation of abortion out of the text.

Their aim was to restrict condemnation to "prenatal sex selection". This had proved, however, logically impossible, as they had realized by the time the UN Conference known as Beijing+5 came round five years later. There in New York, they resisted all our efforts to review how governments were performing on their Beijing promise to enact and enforce legislation to eliminate the violent act of pre-natal sex selection resulting in abortions. The UN Secretariat and the Chair just pulled a blanket of silence down over the Beijing commitment—in the final report of that conference pre-natal sex selection did not rate even one mention.

4 Fourth UN Conference on Women at Beijing (1995) *Platform for Action*, para. 115.

5 Ibid., Principle 29.

6 Ibid., para. 283 (d).

7 Ibid., para. 124 (i).

8 Ibid., para. 277(c).

This silence was maintained right through the UN General Assembly Special Session on Children in May 2002 (Child Summit) where again the whole terrible injustice of millions of sex-selective abortions was deemed "too sensitive" to raise, and was deliberately stifled by certain delegations (principally, we were told by one European Union delegate, out of deference to the large scale perpetrators India and China).

Grave discrepancies emerging on selective abortion

This dishonest silence has been maintained deftly and diligently at each of the subsequent annual meetings at New York headquarters of the UN Commission on the Status of Women (CSW). Yet at the 2007 meeting[9], the issue finally broke through, largely due to the efforts of the United States delegation. A small number of delegations introduced a resolution condemning sex-selective abortion but pro-abortion ideologues rejected it, even though the specific focus of the Session was the Elimination of all Forms of Discrimination and Violence against the Girl-child.

This irrational rejection of what was formally agreed in the Beijing *Platform for Action* represents a growing chasm between the ideologically driven attitudes of the UN Commission on the Status of Women (CSW) and the more moderate UN Committee on the Rights of the Child.

Such a rejection of a resolution condemning selective abortion of girl-children was in direct contradiction to the necessary protections affirmed by the UN Committee on the Rights of the Child:

> Discrimination against girl children is a serious violation of rights, affecting their survival...They may be victims of selective abortion...and infanticide...[10]

This is powerful language because this gives formal recognition that the victims of selective abortion are not "just foetuses"—the pronoun 'they' refers back to the word 'children'. It is a timely reaffirmation that children before birth have human rights, specifically the rights enumerated below this directive. The "Right to non-discrimination" includes the right to laws that offer "equal protection against violence".[11]

It is common understanding that a General Comment issued by a treaty monitoring body such as the UN Committee on the Rights of the Child is the most formal and authoritative statement that can be issued by these UN bodies.[12] General Comments outrank any statements or resolutions issued by the CSW and also outrank any Concluding Observations and Recommendations on country reports issued by the treaty monitoring committees.

9 51st Session meeting of the CSW, 26 February-9 March, 2007.

10 UN Committee on the Rights of the Child, General Comment No 7 (2005).

11 Ibid., para. 11.

12 McGoldrick, Dominic, *The Human Rights Committee*, Oxford: Clarendon Press, 1994.

These CRC General Comments are binding on every UN member country in the world except the United States (the only UN member not to have ratified as yet the Convention on the Rights of the Child).

Significantly, under the section entitled "*Right to life, survival and development*", General Comment No 7, the CRC affirms perinatal care for mothers and babies:

> Article 6 refers to the child's inherent right to life and States parties' obligation to ensure, to the maximum extent possible, the survival and development of the child. States parties are urged to take all possible measures to improve perinatal care for mothers and babies, reduce infant and child mortality...[13]

In medical textbooks, the term 'perinatal' is generally defined as relating to the period around childbirth, specifically from around week 28 of the pregnancy to around one month after birth.

This concept of perinatal care for 'babies' (i.e. in their own right) from around week 28 gestation also represents a reappraisal—a return to reaffirmation of the 1959 General Assembly consensus that the UDHR recognized the rights of the child to legal protection and to special safeguards and care *before as well as after birth*. The concept that both mother and baby (before as well as after birth) are entitled to health care appears again where States Parties are required to adopt an integrated approach in assisting parents to provide for and protect their children, an approach that includes "perinatal health services for mother and baby".[14]

Serious logical inconsistencies as long as ideology prevails over truth

From various General Comments issued by the different treaty monitoring bodies, there are emerging some very serious logical inconsistencies that cannot be resolved as long as ideology prevails over truth. One of the most serious discrepancies has emerged between the CEDAW[15] Committee's General Comment No 24 advocating the removal of laws restricting reproductive services (abortion) and the Committee on the Rights of the Child's General Comment No 7 which calls for States parties to provide equal protection against violence for all children and asserts that selective abortion is *discrimination against girl children* and is *a serious violation of rights affecting their survival.*

In any conflict between the directives of the CRC Committee (condemning selective abortion and infanticide as violence against children) and the directives of the CEDAW Committee (advocating the removal of all laws against abortion), the CRC Committee must prevail. The 'best interests of the child principle' is universally recognized in international human rights law, and is articulated in both the *Convention*

13 UN Committee on the Rights of the Child. General Comment No 7 (2005). para. 10.

14 Ibid., para. 20(a).

15 The CEDAW Committee monitors the UN *Convention on the Elimination of all Discrimination against Women* (CEDAW) (1979).

on the Rights of the Child and the *Convention on the Elimination of all Discrimination against Women*.[16]

The Commission on the Status of Women is bound to uphold the best interests of the child principle and therefore cannot legitimately reject any resolution on selective abortion that reaffirms exactly what the CRC Committee has already formally expounded and endorsed in General Comment No 7 (2005). Even as state-sanctioned procedures, abortion is never in the best interest of the child being aborted. It flatly contradicts the very nature of human rights for anyone to judge that a violation of the right to life of a child is in the best interests of that child. To make such a judgment, even at the very earliest stage of existence, on the discriminatory grounds of disability, age, 'wantedness' and/or birth status is indefensible.

At the heart of the best interests of the child principle is the truth that children's rights are adults' duties. Consigning a child to the abortionist is a dereliction of the duty of care owed to all children by their parents and the State.

The UN Committee on the Rights of the Child in General Comment No 9 (2006) again provides formal recognition of the human rights of children before birth—specifically that children with disabilities are entitled to "prenatal care", and this right follows on from the "right to life, survival and development". It is under this right that the Committee condemns 'the systematic killing of children because of their disability".[17] The Committee also raises the important issue of prenatal care for children:

> The Committee recommends that States parties introduce and strengthen prenatal care for children...[18]

Again, it is clear that prenatal care is not just for mothers but also for their unborn children who are recognized as 'children' in their own right (not just 'foetuses'). It is a vitally important recognition that children before birth are already rights-holders.

Prenatal sex selection threatens to expose weakness of abortion arguments

So why then has the Commission on the Status of Women (CSW) refused to recognize this? Why then at the 51st Session of the CSW (2007), did the Commission's leadership refuse to allow a resolution (proposed by a group of delegations led by the United States) condemning sex-selective abortion? Why was such a condemnation of a clearly discriminatory practice resisted even though the Session was specifically entitled the Elimination of all Forms of Discrimination and Violence against the Girl-child? And why then at the 52nd Session of the CSW (2008) did the Commission fail to respond with any concrete support for the UN Secretary-General Ban Ki-moon's

16 *Convention on the Rights of the Child* Articles 3, 9, 18, 20, 21, 37 and 40; *Convention on the Elimination of all Discrimination against Women* Article 6 (2b) & (2c); Also *UN Declaration of the Rights of the Child*, Principle 2.

17 UN Committee for the Convention on the Rights of the Child, General Comment No 9 (2006), para. 17.

18 Ibid., para. 46.

condemnation of prenatal sex selection in his opening address? Pointing to the statistics on violence against women, he asserted:

> Through the practice of prenatal sex selection, countless others are denied the right even to exist.[19]

Why this strange silence by the CSW on the practice of prenatal sex selection which denies countless girl-children "the right even to exist"?

The CSW was established 21st June 1946. Like all other UN commissions and agencies it was understood to be obliged to uphold the principles laid down in the United Nations Charter in San Francisco in 1945. The Preamble to the Charter declared a faith "in fundamental human rights, in the dignity and worth of the human person, in the equal rights of men and women and of nations large and small". It is scandalous that this Commission which was set up to advance the human rights of women could end up by rejecting the human rights of the unborn girl-child at risk of abortion.

There is just one clear reason for this apostasy of what was agreed in the *Beijing Platform* (1996)—it is the fear, the growing realization that any condemnation of any abortion whatsoever will expose the paucity of logic and morality in their extreme ideological commitment to abortion as a woman's 'choice', as an absolute right that may not be restricted for any reason or in any way. This extreme ideological position is fundamentally incompatible with the human rights obligations towards children at risk of abortion.

According to Kirsten Moore, president of the pro-choice Reproductive Health Technologies Project, when members of her staff recently discussed whether to recommend that any prenatal tests be banned, they found it impossible to draw a line — even at sex selection, which almost all found morally repugnant:

> We all had our own zones of discomfort but still couldn't quite bring ourselves to say, 'Here's the line, firm and clear' because that is the core of the pro-choice philosophy...You can never make that decision for someone else.[20]

Proponents of this extreme kind of pro-choice ideology are on a collision course with fundamental human rights principles protecting the rights of the child.

All selective abortions—in contravention of Rights of the Child Convention

Certainly such radical feminist rhetoric contravenes the authority of the CRC Committee which recognizes in General Comment No 7(2005) and General Comment No 9(2006), that the *Convention on the Rights of the Child* is to apply to girl children

19 UN Secretary-General Ban Ki-moon, Opening Address to fifty-second Session of the Commission on the Status of Women, New York, 25 February 2008.

20 Quoted by Amy Harmon in her article, "Genetic testing + Abortion", *New York Times*, May 13, 2007.

before birth, to unborn children with disabilities, and also, by logical application of the fundamental human rights principle of equality, to all children before birth.

- In General Comment No 7, under the section *Right to non-discrimination,* the CRC Committee examines Article 2 "which ensures rights to every child, without discrimination of any kind". States parties are "to identify the implications of this principle for realizing rights in early childhood".[21]
- The Committee gives an example of discrimination: "... for example where laws fail to offer equal protection against violence for all children..." Applying the 'appropriate legal protection before as well as after birth' principle as articulated in the Preamble to the Convention, it is clear that laws must not "fail to offer equal protection against violence for all children" including before as well as after birth.
- The Committee goes on to point out in the same paragraph that

  > Young children are especially at risk of discrimination because they are relatively powerless and depend on others for the realization of their rights

  This is, of course, especially the case where children are at risk of abortion: they are absolutely powerless and entirely dependent on their mothers and others for the realization of their rights.
- The Committee says "Article 2 also means that "particular groups of young children [such as children at risk of abortion] must not be discriminated against..." As examples of discrimination expressed through harsh treatment which may be abusive, the Committee begins with:

  > Discrimination against girl children is a serious violation of rights, affecting their survival...They may be victims of selective abortion, genital mutilation, neglect and infanticide...[22]

  and ends with condemning also "multiple discrimination (e.g. related to ethnic origin, social and cultural status, gender and/or disabilities)".[23]

"...girls are more likely to be killed in the womb"

The UNICEF report, *State of the World's Children 2007*, also affirms that selective abortion is a human rights offence against the child "in the earliest phase" of his/her life:

> Gender discrimination begins early. Modern diagnostic tools for pregnancy have made it possible to determine a child's sex in the earliest phase.

21 Committee on the Rights of the Child, General Comment No 7, para. 11.

22 Ibid.

23 Ibid.

The authors of another comprehensive report, *Because I am a Girl: The State of the World's Girls 2007*, issued by UK branch of Plan, an international child-focused community development organization, also acknowledge upfront that discrimination against girls begins "even before they are born".[24] They too jettison the coy language and careful euphemisms of the CSW meetings that refuse to recognize the human rights of the unborn child. They address frankly

> the facts that girls are more likely to be killed in the womb and young mothers are more at risk of developing serious complications both for the mother and her unborn child.[25]

This more truthful language, "killed in the womb" is re-emerging in mainstream newspaper articles. For example, in an article on India "Land without brides", Amrit Dhillon writes of "twenty million female babies—killed before birth by a society that prefers male children".[26]

The UNICEF 2007 report summarizes the appalling human rights offences routinely perpetrated against unborn girl children in India, where nationwide, 7000 fewer girls than expected are born each day, largely due to sex determination.[27] Although the Indian government has made it illegal to perform ultrasounds and abortions for the purpose of sex-selection, the practice is widespread and shows no signs of slowing. UNICEF says that wealthier populations are the worst offenders, since they can afford the cost of testing for sex identification. But in a recent front page article in the *Wall Street Journal*, Peter Wonacott reveals that big business such as General Electric Co. and other companies have sold so many ultrasound machines in India that tests are now available for as little as *US* $8 in small towns where there is no drinking water, electricity is infrequent and roads turn to mud after a March rain shower.[28]

In China, the UNICEF report says, the one-child policy has exacerbated the cultural preference for male children and has led to selective abortion of girl children as routine practice and to further neglect of girls who do survive to birth.[29] The Chinese Government is at last being forced to acknowledge the growing threat to the safety

---

24 Plan, *Because I am a Girl: The State of the World's Girls 2007*, London: Plan, UK Branch, 2007, p. 29.

25 Ibid.

26 Dhillon, Amrit, "Land without Brides", *Sunday Morning Post* (Hong Kong), November 4, 2007.

27 Immense declines, recorded since 1991, have occurred in the number of girl children in the most prosperous states and districts—as much as 50-100 fewer girls per 1,000 fewer than elsewhere. In the northern districts of the country, including the Punjab and Haryana states, fewer than 800 girls are born to every 1000 boys. UNICEF Report, *State of the World's Children 2007: Women and Children: the Double Dividend of Gender Equality*, New York: UNICEF, 2007.

28 Wonacott, Peter, "India's Skewed Sex Ratio Puts GE Sales in Spotlight", *Wall Street Journal* April 18, 2007.

29 UNICEF Report, *State of the World's Children 2007: Women and Children: the Double Dividend of Gender Equality*, New York, UNICEF, 2007.

and social security of women and girls who have survived the gendercide only to be confronted with a growth in human rights abuse in the forms of kidnapping, rape and illegal marriage (wife sharing) exacerbated by the existence of a large group of males who remain unmarried because there are so many fewer women.

Parents tampering with biological laws—"a tragedy of the commons"

In the meantime, a UNFPA report on the sex-ratio imbalance in Asia by Christophe Z Guilmoto examines the deep change in the overall age patterns of sex discrimination now affecting the new generations at the bottom of the age pyramid "including the unborn":

> We recognise here the emergence of a new demographic regime of gender discrimination, in which male dominance is much more pronounced among the young (including the unborn) than it was in the past.[30]

The origin of this rise in the sex ratio at birth (SRB) is linked to the introduction of sex-selective abortions in many Asian countries, where abortion is by far the most common practice accounting for today's skewed SRB values.[31] Guilmoto reminds us that the natural biological distribution which ensures a balanced sex ratio is a public good. Parents are tampering with biological laws when they fail to contribute their due share of girls to the common demographic pool—"a contribution necessary to the stability of the entire marriage and family system".[32]

Guilmoto's understanding of "Asia's masculization process" is astute:

> Given such a situation, environmental economists will recognise a tragedy of the commons: the archetypical social trap, in which free access to a public resource by individual interests leads rapidly to the complete depletion of the shared resource. Skewed sex ratio is therefore a typical "externality"—i.e., the unintended and negative consequence of private decisions that ends up affecting everyone.[33]

Guillmoto's concern is reflected by Joseph Chamie, former director of the United Nations Population Division, who recently warned of the likely consequences of sex-selective abortion in the two largest countries in the world, China and India:

> ...sex imbalances will push many men to look for brides in younger age groups, allowing the re-emergence of customs like child brides or marriage promises. Men unable to marry locally may need to import brides from distant regions. Also, some suggest that

30 Guilmoto, Christophe Z., UNFPA Report: "Sex-ratio imbalance in Asia:Trends, consequences and policy responses ", LPED/IRD, Paris: UNFPA, October 2007, p. 2. Available at: http://www.unfpa.org/gender/docs/studies/india.pdf.

31 Ibid., p. 3.

32 Ibid., p. 9.

33 Ibid.

> large numbers of surplus bachelors are likely to generate crime and civil disorder, such as the growth of urban gangs, increased trafficking of women, prostitution and bride kidnapping. The trends could even lead to the build-up of large militias to provide a safety valve for the frustrations of numerous bachelors.[34]

These demographic concerns are now reaching the popular press.

China's one child policy exacerbates sex-selective abortion

A recent *China Daily* article reported that currently, there are about 18 million more males of marrying age than females.

> An increasing crime rate, growing demand for pornography and illegal marriage are some of the consequences that could result from the widening gender gap in China...[35]

Zhang Weiqing, head of the National Population and Family Planning Commission, acknowledged that China has now "the world's most serious gender discrepancy that will affect social stability and harmony."[36] Zhai Zhenwu, Dean of School of Sociology and Population Studies at China's Renmin University, told *China Daily*: "If a gender imbalance occurs in one or two age groups, it can be adjusted. But when it stays and gets worse, the issue could become irreversible." Zhai called for a more positive attitude toward women while saying that the government was addressing the problem with education, subsidies and a strict regulation of ultrasounds and abortions.[37]

Of course what the Chinese Government fails to acknowledge here is that in introducing and rigidly enforcing for many decades now their infamous one-child policy they have encouraged and endorsed very negative attitudes of indifference or even contempt for unborn children. Knowing that they are permitted to have only one child, and inured to fact that any additional children must by law be aborted, many Chinese parents have opted to use abortion to eliminate a girl child and to ensure that the one child to whom they are permitted to give birth is a son. Having become used to routine and sometimes forced abortion of second or subsequent children, these Chinese parents may no longer be inclined to acknowledge any moral difference between aborting a child for demographic reasons at the behest of the government and aborting a child for their own private reasons such as preference for one sex over another.

34 Chamie, Joseph, "The Global Abortion Bind: A woman's right to choose gives way to sex-selection abortions and dangerous gender imbalances", *YaleGlobal*, May 29, 2008.

35 "Gender imbalance linked to serious social ills", *China Daily*, August 23, 2007.

36 Ibid.

37 Ibid.

India's sex-selective abortion debacle: "...they don't want to abort their babies"

Extreme liberal attitudes towards sex-selective abortion are identified in another 2007 UNFPA report on the sex-ratio imbalance: Guilmoto, the author, traces the history of sex-selective abortion in India. In the 1970s, India had established

> a new and rather liberal law on abortion, which in many cases rendered the termination of a pregnancy considerably easier, for reasons ranging from foetal physical defect to contraception failure.[38]

But in the 1980s, the combination of new technologies for pre-natal sex determination and abortion proved to be "a dramatic cocktail, which would quickly become an efficient sex-selection device".[39] He comments also on the fact that while in the initial trial period of prenatal testing, women expressed great interest in knowing the sex of their child, "other family members, such as the father or his parents, also understood its potential for sex selection, and encouraged women to overcome their physical or psychological reservations on abortion if they wanted to avoid the birth of a girl."[40]

The harmful effects on women in India of being pressured by their families and their society to abort their girl children are revealed by Gita Aravamudhan in her recently published book "Disappearing Daughters: the Tragedy of Female Foeticide".[41] In an interview with *The Hindu*, Aravamudhan reveals:

> What bothered me the most was that women were forced to undergo abortion after abortion. In their heart of hearts, they didn't want to abort their babies but social and filial pressures, the fear that they would be thrown out of home otherwise, made them do it. It had affected the health of so many women. Women were inflicting such injuries on themselves; they were ruining themselves—and nothing was in their hands.[42]

Aravamudhan identifies the adverse link that research has established between education and the skew between sexes in India. The more educated a women is, the more likely she is to actively choose a boy if she decides to have one child:

---

38 Guilmoto, Christophe Z., UNFPA Report, "Characteristics of sex-ratio imbalance in India and future scenarios", Report presented at the 4th Asia Pacific Conference on Reproductive Health and Rights, Hyderabad, India, October 29-31, 2007. Published by the United Nations Population Fund, 2.2. p.3. Available at: http://www.unfpa.org/gender/case_studies.htm.

39 Ibid.

40 Ibid., p. 4.

41 Aravamudhan. Ghita: *Disappearing Daughters: the Tragedy of Female Foeticide*, New Delhi: Penguin, 2007.

42 Quoted in an interview in *The Hindu*, May 27, 2007.

> I started looking at census figures...I realised that infanticide happened not in pockets, among the poor and disempowered but foeticide happened among the rich, the powerful, the educated; those who were aware of family planning... There was a deep link between female foeticide and factors like wealth, education, success of family planning, and medical progress.[43]

Identifying sex-selective abortion as "big business", she places significant blame on the doctors:

> There should be a lecture series on the subject in medical colleges. Doctors should be made aware that aborting female babies is a crime. We need to shock them into understanding what is happening.[44]

Doctors, who don't understand the gravity of the situation, are playing with lives: "Instead of helping to stabilise society, they are creating the skew."[45]

Aravamudhan says that the ultrasound machine has mutated into an instrument of murder and likens female foeticide to "a holocaust" in which "a whole gender is getting exterminated"; she calls sex-selective abortions "an organized crime" and "a silent and smoothly executed crime which leaves no waves in its wake."[46]

Visibility and abortion violence

It is this silent smooth invisibility of the violence against the girl child in sex-selective abortion crimes that must be made visible. Regarding acts of violence against children, the Committee on the Rights of the Child says:

> Once visible, it is clear that the practice directly conflicts with the equal and inalienable rights of children to respect for their human dignity and physical integrity.[47]

This quote from the CRC Committee's General Comment No 8 (2006) deals with "the practice" of corporal punishment and other forms of cruel or degrading treatment and cannot be inappropriate in the context of abortion violence perpetrated against girl children who also are surely entitled to protection of the law against lethal physical abuse. The Committee defines "corporal" or "physical" punishment as "any punishment in which physical force is used and intended to cause some degree of pain or discomfort, however light."[48] While abortion is not strictly speaking "punishment" (well, perhaps in the sense that the girl child is being punished for being a girl),

43 Ibid.

44 Ibid.

45 Ibid.

46 Aravamudhan: *Disappearing Daughters, op. cit.*, p. xv.

47 Committee on the Rights of the Child, General comment No 8 (2006), para. 21.

48 Ibid., para. 11.

it is certainly not a benign health-giving treatment intended to comfort or to heal the girl child *in utero*. Abortion is certainly "corporal" (Latin: *corpus*—the body): there is a tiny body to be scalded by saline solution, her head, torso and limbs sometimes to be dismembered, sometimes to be expelled whole and in tact, her tiny *corpus* forced prematurely from her mother's womb.

The CRC Committee condemns as "invariably degrading" all treatment that involves kicking, shaking or throwing children, burning, scalding or forced ingestion (for example, washing children's mouths out with soap or forcing them to swallow hot spices). Under this definition, forced ingestion of abortifacients by the child in the womb would certainly qualify for prohibition as cruel, inhuman and degrading treatment. Article 37 of the Convention on the Rights of the Child requires States to ensure that "no child shall be subjected to torture or other cruel, inhuman or degrading treatment or punishment".

The CRC Committee goes on to explain the basis and scope of this rights entitlement:

> Before the adoption of the Convention on the Rights of the Child, the International Bill of Human Rights - the Universal Declaration and the two International Covenants, on Civil and Political Rights and on Economic, Social and Cultural Rights—upheld "everyone's" right to respect for his/her human dignity and physical integrity and to equal protection under the law. In asserting States' obligation to prohibit and eliminate all corporal punishment and all other cruel or degrading forms of punishment, the Committee notes that the Convention on the Rights of the Child builds on this foundation. The dignity of each and every individual is the fundamental guiding principle of international human rights law.[49]

No room for any level of legalized violence against children

With further reference to the Convention on the Rights of the Child Article 37, the CRC says that it is complemented and extended by Article 19, which requires States to

> take all appropriate legislative, administrative, social and educational measures to protect the child from all forms of physical or mental violence, injury or abuse, neglect or negligent treatment, maltreatment or exploitation...

The Committee condemns all forms of violence, rejects all excuses:

> There is no ambiguity: "all forms of physical or mental violence" does not leave room for any level of legalized violence against children. Corporal punishment and other cruel or degrading forms of punishment are forms of violence and States must take all appropriate legislative, administrative, social and educational measures to eliminate them.[50]

49 Ibid., para. 16.

50 Committee on the Rights of the Child, General Comment No 8 (2006), para. 18.

Indeed, at the UN Women's Conference in Beijing, all the governments of the world made a public commitment to the *Platform for Action* which included "Strategic objective L.7. Eradicate violence against the girl child". Although not fully appreciated at the time, it is becoming increasingly clear that to eradicate violence against the girl child, it is necessary to eradicate all prenatal selection of girl children for abortion, not just those prenatal selections made on the grounds of the sex of the unborn child.

Selective abortion—not just sex discrimination but also "an act of violence"

Ironically, the New York based pro-abortion Women's Caucus (major authors of the 1995 Beijing *Draft Platform for Action*), in their official strategy document distributed to all heads of delegations present at Beijing, attempted to frame abortion exclusively as a sex discrimination problem. They attempted to discount the real violence enacted in every abortion and argued that their preferred term 'pre-natal sex selection' emphasizes that the wrong involved is not abortion *per se*, but abortion for the purposes of limiting the birth of girls. The indifference of the Women's Caucus to the violence involved in the killing of these girl children *in utero* is revealed in their terse rejection of the term 'female foeticide'.

> Foeticide should be deleted because it does not address the gender discrimination problem but rather introduces anti-abortion language through the back door.[51]

But to the girl child selected for abortion, there can be no meaningful distinction between the violence of the act for which she is selected on the grounds of her sex and the violence of the same act for which she is selected on other grounds *e.g.* that the girl child represents an unwanted education or career interruption, or a potentially cumbersome economic burden to her mother or family or community.

The violence is not in the selection *per se* but rather in selection for abortion, for destruction, for elimination. The discrimination is not only a discrimination of the mind, it is a mental attitude that crosses into physical action, that finds expression in the physically destructive act of abortion. It is not just a conceptual selection—it is a physical selection, selection for physical violence, selection for an elective surgical or medical procedure in which an instrument or a chemical poison is used to procure the miscarriage of a girl child.

To decriminalize sex-selective abortion or to enforce protective legislation?

There are very confusing and conflicting goals being advanced on sex-selective abortion.

---

51 Women's Environment and Development Organization (WEDO), *Take the Brackets Off Women's Lives! Women's Linkage Caucus Advocacy Chart*, New York: Women's Environment and Development Organization (WEDO), August 30, 1995, "Reproductive & Sexual Health Rights", p. 7.

At Beijing, the international community made a formal commitment to "enact and enforce legislation protecting girls from all forms of violence, including...prenatal sex selection";[52] at the same Conference it was proposed that States consider reviewing laws containing punitive measures against women who have undergone illegal abortions.[53] The UN CEDAW Committee is pressing countries to remove all restrictive and punitive laws on abortion[54] while others in the UN are calling for new effective legislation against selective abortion.[55] On 25 February 2008, the UN Secretary-General urged all States to review and, when necessary, revise or create applicable laws to ensure that violence against women, in which he specifically included prenatal sex selection, was "always criminalized". He said "Far too often the crimes go unpunished, the perpetrators walk free."[56]

The introduction to UN discourse on human rights of this concept of protection of the unborn girl child from the violent act of prenatal sex selection, namely the act of aborting the girl child, confirms that the girl child's period of gestation is indeed part of the life cycle throughout which the human rights of women are an inalienable, integral and indivisible part of universal human rights:

> The *UN World Conference on Human Rights* in Vienna in 1993, reaffirmed clearly that the human rights of women throughout the life cycle are an inalienable, integral and indivisible part of universal human rights.[57]

Selective abortion as "an act of violence"—conceptual violence only?

If prenatal sex selection represents "acts of violence" based on sex discrimination, then every abortion is an act of violence against women or against men as the violence cannot lie in merely selecting the sex, but rather in aborting the girl child (or the boy child) selected. For it should not be forgotten that pre-natal sex selection may be perpetrated against the boy child as well. In Japan, for example, there is high preference expressed for pre-natal sex-selection of male children for abortion; it has been suggested that female babies are preferred partly because they are considered 'more cute' or more reliable carers for elderly parents.[58]

---

52 *Beijing Platform for Action*, para. 283(d).

53 *Beijing Platform for Action*, para. 106(k).

54 CEDAW Committee, General Recommendation 24, on article 12 of the Convention on the Elimination of All Forms of Discrimination against Women, Women and Health, UN Doc. A/54/38 Rev. 1, 20th Session, 1999, paras. 14 & 31(c).

55 See Committee on the Rights of the Child, General Comments Nos 7, 8 & 9 re the necessity for legislation to protect children from all forms of discrimination and violence.

56 UN Secretary-General Ban Ki-moon, Opening Address to fifty-second Session of the Commission on the Status of Women, New York, February 25, 2008.

57 Beijing Platform for Action, para. 216.

58 National Institute of Population and Social Security Research Survey Series, No. 14, January 10, 1999.

The violence of the act of performing an abortion cannot lie in the criteria for selection of the victim to be targeted by that act of violence, for it is the same act (abortion) that follows the selection. The degree of violence in the act (abortion) is always the same in that it is intentionally lethal—a young human entity is physically assaulted, surgically dismembered, chemically poisoned, or suctioned powerfully and fatally from the safety of the mother's womb.

It is a fact that prenatal sex selection (resulting in abortion) and female infanticide are coupled throughout the Beijing *Platform of Action* as "acts of violence" and as "harmful and unethical practices" with a clear implication that they are deprivation of life offences of equal gravity. Only fanatical ideologues could have really believed they could establish and maintain the fiction that 'pre-natal sex selection' (a mental act) against the girl child is an act of violence whereas the subsequent physical act (often gruesomely bloody) of 'abortion' is not.

Emerging necessity to monitor reasons for all abortions

Given the case that abortions on the discriminatory grounds of sex selection are not to be tolerated by UN members, it may be argued that all governments have both the authority and the duty to override privacy concerns in order to monitor the motives for all abortions. They must exercise their authority to "enact and enforce legislation" to protect all children (both the girl child and the boy child) from the violence of prenatal sex selection resulting in abortion.

In the light of these Beijing *Platform for Action* promises to enact and enforce protective laws for the unborn girl child, there is logical inconsistency in the current push by some UN treaty monitoring bodies to pressure Latin American countries and others into removing all laws against abortion.[59]

See also Fuse, Kana: "Daughter preference in Japan: a Shift in Gender Role Attitudes? A Working Paper", Available at: http://paa2006.princeton.edu/download.aspx?submissionId=60747.

See also the Fertility Survey conducted July 1992 by the Institute of Population Problems of the Ministry of Health and Welfare (MOHW), cited in JOICFP News, November, 1993, (233) 7, "A Preference for Girls".

See also Macer, Darryl R. J., "Bioethics in Japan and East Asia", Turkish Journal of Medical Ethics, Vol. 9, 2001, pp. 70-77.

59 Human Rights Watch, "International Human Rights Law and Abortion in Latin America":

> U.N. treaty bodies, which take a measured approach to interpreting international human rights law, have consistently and extensively opined on abortion access and restrictions. By our count, as of early 2005, at least 122 concluding observations on ninety-three countries spanning more than a decade by U.N. treaty bodies have substantively addressed how abortion relates to fundamental human rights. These bodies reason that firmly established human rights are jeopardized by restrictive or punitive abortion laws and practices.

Available at: http://www.hrw.org/backgrounder/wrd/wrd0106/.

Of course, the Beijing Conference document has no concrete authority to change international human rights law. But since, ironically, abortion advocates like the Center for Reproductive Rights have been claiming for years that the Cairo and Beijing UN Conferences established the 'reproductive rights of women' including 'a woman's right to abortion', it may be time to remind them of what the Beijing Platform actually enjoined governments to do in order to protect the girl-child from the violent act of abortion.

An immovable barrier of logic and reason proscribes "abortion rights"

Guilmoto has identified the immovable barrier of logic and reason that prevents pro-abortion advocates from proclaiming 'a woman's right to abortion' while condemning prenatal sex selection. He relates social acceptability and perception of the legitimacy of sex selection to the acceptability of using "rational reasoning" (such as the cost-benefit analysis) to make a decision about one's offspring:

> To a large extent, rapid fertility decline itself has shown that people have accepted the principle of controlled fertility, and it may therefore logically follow that manipulating the "contents" of one's fertility is part of this fundamental behavioural change.[60]

The true human rights reform needed here is a return to universal respect for children *in utero*. They are unborn children with a right to legal protection—male or female, they are not to be manipulated and aborted as mere "contents" of one's fertility.

With the authority of the CRC Committee on the Convention on the Rights of the Child,[61] we can claim that the right to prenatal care and protection against discrimination and violence is to apply to girl children before birth, to unborn children with disabilities, and also, by logical application of the fundamental human rights principle of equality, to all children before birth.

This, of course is consistent with the Universal Declaration's recognition that every child "by reason of his physical and mental immaturity, needs special safeguards and care, including appropriate legal protection, before as well as after birth".

60 Guilmoto, Christophe Z., UNFPA Report: "Characteristics of sex-ratio imbalance in India and future scenarios", October 2007, *op. cit.*, para. 4.2.1.

61 Committee on the Rights of the Child (CRC), General Comment No 7(2005); also CRC, General Comment No 9 (2006).

Chapter 14 Children's Rights "...without any exceptions whatsoever"

Reclaiming the right to life for children of rape or incest

In recent years, the UN Committee on the Rights of the Child (CRC Committee) has condemned selective abortion as discrimination against children and as a serious violation of their rights, affecting their survival.[1]

The Committee denounces selective abortion of girl children on the grounds of gender discrimination, and condemnation also extends to abortion on the grounds of "multiple discrimination (e.g., related to ethnic origin, social and cultural status, gender and/or disabilities)".[2]

The Committee on the Rights of the Child is signalling here a re-emerging recognition of the need to protect children at risk of abortion. Selective abortion includes those abortions based on discrimination related to the social and cultural status of the children of rape and incest and to the social and cultural status of their mothers.

These children together with their mothers are entitled to adequate programs of practical assistance including pre-natal and postnatal health care as well as personal and social security such as emergency safe housing and financial support.

There are two sets of reasons that militate against aborting children who are conceived through rape or incest. One set is based on fundamental principles of international human rights law. The other set of reasons is pragmatically humanitarian, based on the child's potential to be loved and to love, and so to bring healing and love to an abused mother.

Protective laws against arbitrary deprivation of life for unborn children

In every premeditated abortion, deprivation of life is the intended outcome. Despite the current massive ideologically-driven campaign to decriminalize abortion around the world, arbitrary deprivation of life, under modern international human rights law, is still strictly prohibited. "No one may be deprived of their life arbitrarily", says Article 6(1) of the *International Covenant on Civil and Political Rights* (ICCPR). This

1 UN Committee on the Rights of the Child (CRC), *General Comment No 7* (2005) under *Right to Non-discrimination.*

2 Ibid.

means that the law must strictly control and limit the circumstances in which the State may condone deprivation of life.

Under international human rights law, the sovereign state's legislature remains the primary defender of the human rights of unborn children. Politicians must conform to universal human rights obligations to provide protective laws against abortion which constitutes arbitrary deprivation of life in breach of international human rights law, as established via the Nuremberg principles and judgments[3] and their codification in the International Bill of Rights.

It is part of the Nuremberg record of the trial testimony (*RuSHA/Greifelt Case* 1947-8) that from this very foundation of modern international human rights law, unborn children are considered to be human beings entitled to the protection of the law: "...protection of the law was denied to the unborn children..."[4] Nuremberg prosecutor, James McHaney, called abortion an "inhumane act" and an "act of extermination" and established that even if a woman's request for abortion was "voluntary", abortion is still "a crime against humanity".[5]

The 1948 *Universal Declaration of Human Rights* (*UDHR*) recognizes that the child "by reason of his physical and mental immaturity" is entitled to "special safeguards and care including appropriate legal protection before as well as after birth."[6] This immaturity is not to be allowed to diminish in any way the child's inherent humanity. The right to life, as protected under Article 3 of the Universal Declaration, is equally valid for the child before birth as for the child after birth, "without any discrimination whatsoever".[7]

3 UN Resolution 95(1): Affirmation of the Principles of International Law recognized by the Charter of the Nuremberg Tribunal. Resolution 95 (1) of the United Nations General Assembly, 11 December 1946. The UN committee on the codification of international law was directed to establish a general codification of "the principles recognized in the Charter of the Nuremberg Tribunal and in the judgment of the Tribunal".

4 Nuremberg Trials Record: "The RuSHA Case", March 1948, Volume IV, p. 1077. Available at: http://www.mazal.org/archive/nmt/04a/NMT04-T1076.htm.

5 See the series of research papers by John Hunt which include:
- "Out of Respect For Life: Nazi Abortion Policy in the Eastern Occupied Territories", Journal of Genocide Research, Vol. 1 (3), 1997, pp. 379-385.
- "Abortion and the Nuremberg Prosecutors: A Deeper Analysis", Life and Learning Vol.VII, Proceedings of the Seventh University Faculty for Life Conference, June, 1997.

6 The UN General Assembly, November 20, 1959, reaffirmed explicitly the UDHR's "recognition" of the rights of the child before birth. The concept of formal universal recognition of the child before birth as a legitimate subject of inherent and inalienable human rights including entitlement to legal protection is critical for it is the nature of inherent and inalienable human rights that they can never be de-recognized by courts of law or legislatures.

7 UN Declaration on the Rights of the Child, Principle 1: "Every child without any exception whatsoever is entitled to these rights ..."

States which have ratified the ICCPR[8] must at all times take positive steps to effectively protect the right to life, a legal duty that is equally applicable to the child before birth as to the child after birth. Protected by international human rights law, the right to life means, *inter alia*, that States have a strict legal duty that is non-derogable, a duty at all times to prevent, investigate, prosecute, punish and redress violations of the right to life wherever such violations occur, both in private and in public, and even in public emergencies threatening the life of the nation.[9] That the right to life is non-derogable means, *inter alia*, that at no time are States permitted to engage in or condone the arbitrary taking of a human life, including the life of a child conceived through rape or incest.

The unborn child's right to life is also protected under Article 6(5) of the ICCPR. The *travaux préparatoires* (explanatory notes written at the time the Covenant was negotiated) stated this explicitly:

> The provisions of paragraph 4(5) [now Article 6(5)] of the draft article aimed at the protection of the life of the unborn child whose mother was sentenced to death; that protection should be extended to all unborn children.[10]

Indeed, special emphasis was placed on the innocence of the unborn child:

> The principal reason for providing in paragraph 4 [now Article 6] of the original text that the death sentence should not be carried out on pregnant women was to save the life of an innocent unborn child.[11]

The State, in order to protect the child's inherent right to life, must prohibit and prevent the death penalty for the unborn child's mother. Just so, the logical imperative of the corollary of this directive requires that the State, also in order "to save the life of an innocent unborn child", must prohibit and prevent imposition of abortion or any other form of death penalty on an unborn child.

8 The US, for example, ratified the ICCPR 8 June 1992. Reservation No. 2 (with the notable exception of pregnant women) reads: "The United States reserves the right, subject to its constitutional constraints, to impose capital punishment on any person (other than a pregnant woman) duly convicted under existing or future laws permitting the imposition of capital punishment, including such punishment for crimes committed by persons below eighteen years of age." US Reservations, Declarations, and Understandings, International Covenant on Civil and Political Rights, 102nd Congress, 2nd Session in 138 Congressional Records S 4781, April 2, 1992.

9 ICCPR Article 4(2).

10 Bossuyt, Marc J., *Guide to the "Travaux Préparatoires" of the International Convenant on Civil and Political Rights*, Dordrecht, Martinus Nijhoff Publishers, 1987, A/C.3/SR.810 para. 2; A/C.3/SR.811 para. 9; A/C 3/SR.812 para. 7; A/C.3/SR.813 para. 36; A/C 3/SR 815 para. 28.

11 Ibid., p. 121. A/3764 para. 113.

Recognition of the existence of another human being *in utero*

The ICCPR recognizes in Article 6(5) that the pregnant woman does indeed carry within her womb another human being who is entitled, by virtue of the child's immaturity to special protection from the death sentence. This article, prohibiting execution of pregnant women, acknowledges that the child, from the State's first knowledge of that child's existence, is to be protected.

Additional recognition of the State's responsibility for legal protection for the child before birth as well as after birth is found in the *Protocol Additional to the Geneva Conventions of 12 August 1949, and Relating to the Protection of Victims of Non-International Armed Conflicts (Protocol II).*[12] The Geneva Conventions are explicit in the kind of special protection and assistance that must be provided to expectant mothers in all situations. The modern concept being pushed by the current UN Secretariat that expectant mothers in war and refugee situations should be provided with abortion 'services' is not consistent with the protection in the Geneva Conventions for expectant mothers and their children. In Articles 14, 38(5) and 50 of the 1949 *Geneva Conventions relative to the Protection of Civilian Persons in Time of War*, special protection measures are enumerated specifically for "children under fifteen, expectant mothers and mothers of children under seven". The mother of a child before birth is to be given equal and the same protection for herself and her child as the mothers of children under seven; and children of expectant mothers are to be given the same protections as children under 15.

Rape and incest—arbitrary exceptions purporting to justify 'lawful abortion'

Even in emergency and post-conflict situations, it is now generally acknowledged:

> The legal bases upon which human rights are applicable to all UN activities can be derived first of all from the inherent nature of human rights. Human rights are part of being a human being and therefore such rights are automatically part of the legal framework applicable to those with power to affect the enjoyment of those rights.[13]

Those with the power to affect the enjoyment of the right to life of those children who have been conceived through rape cannot use that power arbitrarily to deny the right to life to these children. Even "in those countries where abortion is not against the law", abortion of these children remains arbitrary deprivation of life. The domestic

12 *Protocol Additional to the Geneva Conventions of 12 August 1949, and Relating to the Protection of Victims of Non-International Armed Conflicts (Protocol II)*Article 6 (4): "The death penalty shall not be pronounced on persons who were under the age of eighteen years at the time of the offence and shall not be carried out on pregnant women or mothers of young children."

13 White, N., "Towards a Strategy for Human Rights Protection in Post-Conflict Situations" in White, N. and Klasson , D. (eds.), *The UN, Human Rights and Post-Conflict Situations*, New York: Juris Publishing, 2005, p. 463.

law of a country cannot derogate from the universal and non-derogable right to life, not even in public emergencies. The child before birth, being innocent of any crime, may not be deprived lawfully of his or her life, for "the inherent right to life... shall be protected by law [and] (n)o one shall be arbitrarily deprived of his life." Use of the term "arbitrarily" in the framing of the ICCPR right to life Article 6 was directed specifically towards protecting vulnerable human beings in those countries where legal protection is not provided, or where the laws in place are inadequate in their framing or in their interpretation.

In such circumstances, 'legal abortion' can still constitute arbitrary deprivation of life:

> The introduction of the concept of arbitrariness is intended to guarantee that even interference provided for by law should be in accordance with the provisions, aims and objectives of the Covenant...[14]

Legal abortion may be seen then to be an instance of "interference provided for by law" that nonetheless is not "in accordance with the provisions, aims and objectives of the Covenant".[15] This application of the term 'arbitrary' to what may be 'legal' but is nevertheless 'unjust' was reaffirmed very clearly in the *travaux préparatoires* for the International Covenant on Civil and Political Rights.[16]

It is precisely in those countries where abortion is not against the law, where domestic law has failed to provide authentic protection of the inherent right to life of children at risk of abortion, that international human rights law under Article 6 of the ICCPR must be proactively applied. Where there is a gap in the domestic law, international human rights law must be able to fill that gap. The international human rights instruments were put in place to supply any deficiency in the body of domestic law that protects the right to life of all equally, impartially, everywhere and in all circumstances. This was the *raison d'être*, the whole point of formulating and ratifying the codification of fundamental human rights principles such as the right to life in the international human rights instruments.

Throughout numerous drafting sessions, it was clearly understood that deprivation of the life of an unborn child can be arbitrary even when it may be 'legal' under domestic law. It should be remembered that in Poland during Nazi occupation, abortion was not against the law:

> Abortions on Polish women in the General Government were also encouraged by the withdrawal of abortion case from the jurisdiction of the Polish courts. The defendants Greifelt, Creutz, Meyer-Hetling, Schwarzenberger, Hofmann, Hildebrandt, Schwalm,

14 UN Human Rights Committee, General Comment No 16 on *ICCPR* Article 17, para. 3.

15 Ibid.

16 E/CN.4/SR.310 p.9; 5th (1949), 6th (1950) and 8th (1952) Sessions of the Commission on Human Rights.

> Huebner, Lorenz, and Brueckner are charged with special responsibility for and participation in these crimes.[17]

The fact that the Nazi authorities had removed abortion from Polish domestic law did not nullify the fact that at Nuremberg abortion was still judged "a crime against humanity". This was in accord with the original working definition of a crime against humanity:

> "...*whether or not in violation of the domestic law of the country where perpetrated.*"[18]

Liberal abortion laws that purport to legalize the deprivation of the lives of children conceived through rape or incest are bad laws—they are impermissible under international human rights law because they are not in accord with at least one of the founding provisions, aims and objectives of the *ICCPR viz.* "to save the life of an innocent unborn child". If it is agreed that, in order "to save the life of an innocent unborn child", the child's mother is not to be executed even though the mother is guilty of a most serious crime punishable by death, then it must be agreed also on these same grounds, that the life of the child must be saved irrespective of the serious crime committed by the father (i.e., by either parent). Logic dictates that if the unborn child is not to be executed for the crimes of his/her mother, then neither should he or she be executed for the crimes of his/her father.

In response to this compelling logic, radical feminist ideologues have propounded a devious new argument based on fabrication of a new meaning for the legal concept of 'forced pregnancy'.[19] The term 'forced pregnancy' has been hijacked to "describe the violation of women's integrity by forcing her to become and remain pregnant".[20] This ideological re-definition imposes a false construct on a natural biological process—it is deliberately misleading and vexatious, without merit or truth. Their purpose is to misrepresent pregnancy as an unjust imposition that can be alleviated only

17 Trial of Ulrich Greifelt and Others Indictment [Tr. pp. 1-18, 7/1/1947], para.13. Available at: http://www.mazal.org/archive/nmt/05/NMT05-T0111.htm

18 Agreement for the Prosecution and Punishment of the Major War Criminals of the European Axis, and Charter of the International Military Tribunal: London, 8 August 1945. Charter - II : Jurisdiction and general principles Article 6(c).

19 The genuine legal term "forced pregnancy" is defined in *the Rome Statute of the International Criminal Court* (2002) under Article 8 entitled Crimes Against Humanity:

> 2 (f) "Forced pregnancy" means the unlawful confinement of a woman forcibly made pregnant, with the intent of affecting the ethnic composition of any population or carrying out other grave violations of international law. This definition shall not in any way be interpreted as affecting national laws relating to pregnancy.

The term 'forced pregnancy' first entered accepted UN language at the Vienna World Conference on Human Rights (1993) in the specific context of a particular contemporary armed conflict where Serbian soldiers used rape as a tool for ethnic cleansing.

20 Take the Brackets Off Women's Lives! Women's Linkage Caucus Advocacy Chart, New York: Women's Environment and Development Organization (WEDO), August 30, 1995, "Reproductive & Sexual Health Rights", p. 7.

by "legal abortion services" that offer each mother the 'choice' to have her unborn child exterminated. They have advanced a perverted new concept of pregnancy—it is now deprecated as an ordeal of such physical and psychological severity that no woman should ever be "forced" to carry her child to a natural full term. The absence of abortion on demand is identified wrongly with being "forced to bear children".[21] Their underlying premise is that pregnancy *per se* is inhumane treatment forced on women wherever abortion is not accessible and legal.[22]

Extreme negativity of the radical feminist view of pregnancy

Radical feminism rejects "...the male view of reproduction as a natural process."[23] Quite erroneously, the morally repugnant force used in rape and incest is equated with and transferred conceptually to allowing the mother's pregnancy to run its natural (unforced) course. Although this redefinition of the legal term 'forced pregnancy' was rejected in all the preparatory UN meetings for establishing the International Criminal Court, this counterfeit concept continues to be popularized and used to deadly purpose in the *curia amici* briefs written by abortion advocacy groups such as the New York-based Center for Reproductive Rights and submitted to various Latin American Courts in cases where the so-called right to abortion in case of rape and incest is being advanced.[24]

An 'unwanted' pregnancy, the Courts are told, endangers women and girls' health and lives. Regrettably, many health education programs for girls around the world peddle misinformation designed to inculcate irrational fear of pregnancy. Such misinformation when deliberately imparted to women and girls who have been victims of rape and incest, is especially poignant and cruel. Denial of access to 'safe' abortion services, they are told, entails that the victim must undergo the 'terrible' health risks of pregnancy:

21 EGM/GBP/1997/Report, "Gender-based persecution", Report of the Expert Group Meeting, Toronto, Canada, 9-12 November 1997, published by United Nations Division for the Advancement of Women, Department of Economic and Social Affairs, para. 60.

22 In September 1997, the Report of the UN Human Rights Committee (A/52/40), regarding the Third Periodic Report on Peru, recorded that provisions criminalizing abortion even for pregnancies resulting from rape were found by the Committee "to subject women to inhumane treatment" and to be "possibly incompatible with articles 3, 6 and 7 of the Covenant [ICCPR]".

23 Olsen F.: "Do (Only) Women Have Bodies?" in Cheah, P., Fraser, D., and Grbich J. (eds), *Thinking Through the Body of the Law*, St Leonards: Allen and Unwin, 1996.

24 Radical feminist concepts were adopted recently, for example, in Colombia to legalize abortion on these grounds. The Constitutional Court of Colombia opined, "The legislature must not impose the role of procreator on a woman against her will." and portrayed any mother who is denied the opportunity to abort her child as "being treated as a reproductive instrument for the human race". (DECISION C-355/06, Bogotá, D. C., May 10, 2006, 8.1) Similar arguments were also used in Argentina, to authorize tha abortion of two children conceived through the rape of their mentally handicapped mothers. Further details available at: http://www.reproductiverights.org/courts.html.

> According to the World Health Organization (WHO) estimates, more than 585,000 women die each year as a result of pregnancy. At least 7 million women suffer serious health problems, and as many as 50 million suffer some health consequences after childbirth.[25]

The UN's *Reproductive Health in Refugee Situations: An Inter-Agency Field Manual* runs the same line under "Some General Facts About Reproductive Health":

> 585,000 women die each year—one every minute—from pregnancy-related causes...Girls aged 15-19 are twice as likely to die from childbirth as women in their twenties.[26]

The deceitful implication of these claims is that women and girls are unavoidably at risk of dying in childbirth.

Provide "adequate pre-natal and post-natal care" —not more abortions

Not so, says the UNFPA: "Every woman, rich or poor, faces a 15 per cent risk of complications around the time of delivery, but maternal death is practically nonexistent in developed regions."[27] The truth is that these poor mothers are not being provided with First World standards of obstetric and medical care, adequate clean water, sanitation and good nutrition. In some cases too, while abortion is readily provided as a 'quick-fix', a mother's desperate need for social support and real protection from further violence is ignored, or placed in the "too hard" basket.

Especially in these most traumatic situations, both mother and child have a right to comprehensive prenatal care. The unborn child's right to pre-natal care is an enduring concept that has been reaffirmed many times over the years. This principle had appeared in the 1950 *Draft Declaration on the Rights of the Child* and was universally acknowledged in Principle 4 of the *UN Declaration on the Rights of the Child* (1959):

> ...He shall be entitled to grow and develop in health; to this end, special care and protection shall be *provided both to him and to his mother, including adequate pre-natal and post-natal care...*" [Italics added]

In Principle 1 of this UN Declaration on the Rights of the Child, it is made very clear that there are to be no exceptions to the human rights entitlement of children:

---

25 Sadik, Nafis, (at time of publication Executive Director, UNFPA) "Progress in Protecting Reproductive Rights and Promoting Reproductive Health: Five Years Since Cairo", *Health and Human Rights*. Vol.4, 2000, p.15.

26 UNFPA, UNHCR, WHO, *Reproductive Health in Refugee Situations: An Inter-Agency Field Manual*, 1999, p.2.

27 UNFPA Report, State of the World's Population 2005:The Promise of Equality - Gender Equity, Reproductive Health and the Millennium Development Goals, United Nations Population Fund (UNFPA), September 2007..

> The child shall enjoy all the rights set forth in this Declaration. Every child, *without any exception whatsoever*, shall be entitled to these rights, without distinction or discrimination on account of race, colour, sex, language, religion, political or other opinion, national or social origin, property, birth or other status, whether of himself or of his family. [Italics added]

There is no room here for accommodating the lethal discrimination of selective abortion against children who have been conceived through no fault of their own in a criminal act of rape or incest.

UN Committee on the Rights of the Child—"prenatal care for children"

The UN Committee on the Rights of the Child (CRC) recently issued *General Comment on the Rights of Children with Disabilities* which reaffirms that children before birth are "children" not just "foetuses"—they are children with rights, and specifically with a right to prenatal care.

> The Committee recommends that States parties introduce and strengthen prenatal care for children.[28]

Moreover, the Committee insists that each and every child's right is not a "favour" to be bestowed or withheld by the State but rather "a clear legal obligation".[29]

In addition, the CRC Committee has condemned selective abortion as discrimination against children and as "a serious violation of their rights, affecting their survival."[30] Logical consistency must include in the Committee's condemnation of "multiple discrimination (e.g., related to ethnic origin, social and cultural status, gender and/or disabilities)" any specific discrimination against children conceived through rape or incest. It surely includes such discrimination on social or cultural grounds where the child is accorded an inferior social status, denied the right to live, and aborted because of the father's crime.

Inconsistency between "the child's' right to adequate prenatal care" and "legal abortion"

These General Comments (which are the most authoritative statements that can be issued by the UN Committee on the Rights of the Child) affirm that the operative

28 UN Committee on the Rights of the Child, General Comment No 9 (2006) para. 46.

29 UN Committee on the Rights of the Child, General Comment No 5 (2003) para. 9: "The Committee emphasizes that, in the context of the Convention, States must see their role as fulfilling clear legal obligations to each and every child. Implementation of the human rights of children must not be seen as a charitable process, bestowing favours on children."

30 UN Committee on the Rights of the Child (CRC) *General Comment No 7* (2005), Right to Non-discrimination.

provisions of the *Convention on the Rights of the Child* include all children before birth without discrimination.

The *Draft Convention on the Rights of the Child* (1978) in Article IV reaffirmed the rights of the child as well as the mother to adequate prenatal care

> He shall be entitled to grow and develop in health; to this end, special care and protection shall be provided both to him and to his mother, including adequate prenatal and post-natal care.

The problem, initially flagged by Austria, of "inconsistency between 'the child's' right to adequate prenatal care and the possibilities for legal abortion provided in some countries"[31], remains a dilemma of both moral and logical incompatibility. It remains so especially in those States where legal protection for unborn children at risk of abortion is being denied because of exceptions that endorse lethal discrimination against children conceived through rape or incest.

Discrimination on grounds of "social origin" prohibited

Discrimination in prenatal care against a child on social grounds is prohibited: the discrimination clause common to all human rights instruments guarantees all members of the human family equal entitlement to human rights "without distinction of any kind such as...social origin...birth or other status".[32]

Furthermore, the *UN Declaration on the Rights of the Child* (1959) affirms the rights of the child ("before as well as after birth") who is "socially handicapped": Principle 5 asserts that the child who is socially handicapped shall be given the special treatment and care "required by his particular condition".

It is indefensible to respond with a lethal act of violence to the socially handicapped child whose social origin lies in the paternal crime of rape or incest. The selective abortion of such a child is based on prejudice not justice.

Abortion an inappropriate response to rape or incest—another act of violence, another victim

The UN Secretariat appears to be ignorant of the history of international human rights commitments to protecting the child before birth conceived through rape or incest—every child without exception is to be protected from arbitrary deprivation of his or her life as a punishment for the circumstances of his or her social origins. Perversely it would seem, in the Secretary-General's *Report on Violence against Women 2006*, abortion is included in the range of services to be provided for women victims/survivors of violence:

31 From document E/CN.4/1324, *Legislative History of the Convention on the Rights of the Child*, p. 581.

32 *Universal Declaration* Article 2, *ICCPR* Article 2, *Convention on the Rights of the Child* Article 2, *et al.*

> The range of services required to assist victims/survivors of violence against women include: comprehensive medical services, including access to safe abortion.[33]

Since abortion is an act of violence against the child, it is a totally inappropriate response to offer victims/survivors of violence a service that comprises *per se* another act of violence, this time an act of violence in which there are two victims, the hurting mother and her own aborted child. "Safe abortion" belies its benign connotations—it compounds the violence with yet another act of violence against yet another victim. It is logically incompatible with human rights protection owed both mother and child and such an act of violence against the child contravenes the principle of indivisibility. We cannot uphold the human rights of one vulnerable person by violating the human rights of another vulnerable person.

Abortion—lethal punishment of the innocent

It is unconscionable that we have a world where genuine human rights such as the right to special care and protection for abused pregnant women and their unborn children are being largely replaced by the invention and promotion of a pseudo-right, the so-called right to abortion in cases of rape and incest.[34]

Thus do abortion advocates around the world continue to exploit the situations of pregnant women who have been abused by rape or incest to argue their case for lifting all restrictions on abortion. But since these children have committed no wrong, legal deprivation of their lives by an abortion 'provider' should not be tolerated by the State. In terms of the human rights of the unborn child, abortion is lethal punishment of the innocent.

Indeed, one of the most fundamental and consistently proclaimed rights of the child (before as well as after birth) is the right to protection from punishment on the basis of the activities or crimes of someone else (such as the child's father). The *Fourth Geneva Convention* (1949) states) in Article 33:

> No protected person may be punished for an offence he or she has not personally committed.

Also Article 5 (3) of the *American Convention on Human Rights*[35] states:

33 UN Secretary-General's *Report on Violence against Women*, 2006, p. 95, para. (h).

34 See, for example, Committee on Economic, Social and Cultural Rights, Concluding Observations on the Report of Mexico 2006: "The Committee is concerned...about reports on obstruction of access to legal abortion after rape, e.g., by misinformation, lack of clear guidelines, abusive behaviour directed at pregnant rape victims by public prosecutors and health personnel, and legal impediments in cases of incest..." para. 236.

35 US President Jimmy Carter signed this *Convention* in 1977, and although it has not yet been ratified by the US Congress, the US is still understood to be in honor bound to abide by these fundamental human rights principles. Under international law, a country is expected to abide by a treaty it has signed, even as it awaits final ratification. See Inter-

> Punishment shall not be extended to any person other than the criminal.

And for those abortion advocates who argue that the unborn child is not a person, the American Convention on Human Rights Article 1(2) says:

> For the purposes of this Convention, "person" means every human being.

And Article 4(1) of the American Convention declares:

> Every person has the right to have his life respected. This right shall be protected by law and, in general, from the moment of conception...

State-condoned execution of any child for the crimes of the child's parents is prohibited—the child's right to life is to be protected by law in general from the moment of conception.[36]

This principle of protection for children against punishment for the crimes of their parents is reaffirmed in other regional human rights instruments. Article 7(2) of the *African Charter on Human and Peoples' Rights* asserts:

> Punishment is personal and can be imposed only on the offender.

This article specifically forbids punishment of the innocent: the State is prohibited from authorising abortion of the unborn child who is personally innocent of the crimes of rape or incest. The child is not to be treated as an offender—the child is not deserving of capital punishment—the child has committed no crime and there can be no lawful authorization for the intentional deprivation of the child's life.

Similarly, in the *European Convention for the Protection of Human Rights and Fundamental Freedoms* (1950), the High Contracting Parties undertook to "secure to everyone within their jurisdiction" the right to life. The European Convention's Article 2 Footnote 1—"Right to Life" declares:

---

national Commission of Jurists, *Administration of the Death Penalty in the United States*, para. 33, June, 1996.

36 In the 1980 *Baby Boy* case, the Inter-American Commission on Human Rights (resolution 23/81) tried to discredit this clear provision for legal protection for the child "*in general from the moment of conception*" by a very shoddy reading of the *travaux préparatoires* regarding the alleged meaning of the phrase "*in general*". The majority opinion justices completely misread the drafting history of the concept of the right to life that prevailed at the negotiating sessions in Bogota for the 1948 *American Declaration*. They ignored the original 1947 draft Declaration which established the concept of the right to life as being understood to apply from conception, and failed to trace the demonstrable continuity of this same concept to the Inter-American Council of Jurists' Draft Convention of 1959 and to the final Convention in 1968. The introduction in this 1980-1 Resolution of an alleged rejection of the concept of a right to life from the moment of conception is fanciful fabrication and bears no relation to the historical facts. As the dissenting justices pointed out, the drafting history of the clause does not indicate any such rejection.

1 Everyone's right to life shall be protected by law. No one shall be deprived of his life intentionally save in the execution of a sentence of a court following his conviction of a crime for which this penalty is provided by law.

2 Deprivation of life shall not be regarded as inflicted in contravention of this article when it results from the use of force which is no more than absolutely necessary:

a in defense of any person from unlawful violence b in order to effect a lawful arrest or to prevent the escape of a person lawfully detained; c in action lawfully taken for the purpose of quelling a riot or insurrection...

There are clearly no grounds here for intentionally depriving the child before birth of the right to life because of the father's crime of rape or incest. For the child before birth, there has been no crime, and no sentence of a court following any conviction, no grounds here for authorization of a death penalty.[37] The child before birth is utterly incapable of offering any person unlawful violence or of participating in a riot or insurrection.

Aborting her child does not restore a mother's health

Yet jurisdictions around the world are caving in to irrational demands that abortion be legalized on the grounds that the child in the womb threatens the mother's life or her physical or psychological health. Increasingly, such grounds are being recognized to have little or no medical validity in view of the rapid advances that have been made in holistic pre-natal health care for mothers and babies, and the phenomenal progress in obstetrics, in fetal medicine and in pre-natal and post-natal psychological care for mothers. The rational response to life-threatening pregnancy these days is to improve the availability and delivery of optimum pre-natal and post-natal healthcare.

Moreover, growing recognition of post-abortion depression and post-abortion suicide further discredits abortion of the child as a life-saving, health-giving procedure for the mother.[38] The right to life, the well-being, of both the mother and the

37 See Rita Joseph, "Abortion and the Death Penalty—Different Subjects, Shared Sentence", *Voices*, Vol. XXIII (1), 2008.

38 Fergusson, N., Horwood, L. John, Ridder, Elizabeth M., "Abortion in young women and subsequent mental health", *Journal of Child Psychology and Psychiatry*. 2006, Vol. 47 (1), pp. 16-24. This large long-term study linked those having abortions with elevated levels of subsequent mental health problems, including depression, anxiety, suicidal behaviours and substance use disorders. Researchers found that at age 25, 42% of women in the study group who had had an abortion also experienced major depression at some stage during the past four years. This was 35% higher than those who had continued the pregnancy. Despite Professor Fergusson's own admission ("I'm pro-choice but I've produced results which... favor a pro-life viewpoint"), he has concluded: "It verges on scandalous that a surgical procedure that is performed on one in ten women has been so poorly researched and evaluated given the debates about the psychological consequences of abortion." In a letter to the Abortion Supervisory Committee, he wrote that his reading of the literature on abortion suggested that it was "one of the most methodologically flawed and illiterate research areas" he had ever encountered. Professor Fergusson went on to say that the

child must be pursued with equal vigor by the medical profession and by all those in positions of authority in public health and law. Abortion remains an intentionally lethal, pseudo-medical procedure. Genuine medicine, as agreed by all civilized human societies since the time of the Hippocratic Oath, does no deliberate harm to an unborn child. The original noble aims and purposes of the medical fraternity to protect the health of all mothers, and all children, including children *in utero*,[39] are being profaned when they are put in the service of promoting abortion of innocent children.

Abortion flouts legal principles of proportionality and necessity

The common law method of legal interpretation, now routinely adopted by many jurisdictions around the world, should everywhere be applied to laws that protect the unborn. Under this method, all public officials and public and private abortion providers, when the intended outcome of their intervention is deprivation of the life of an unborn child, must justify their actions by reference to both principles of necessity and proportionality.

---

idea behind the law that abortion was a mental health issue was "based on conjecture". No one, he said, had examined the costs and benefits: "If the legislation was based on health grounds, you would naturally think this would lead to monitoring of people who had had abortions' but, he said, "the health aspect is always secondary to personal choice." Ruth Hill: "Abortion researcher confounded by study", New *Zealand Sun-Herald,* January 5, 2006.

See also, for example, Pedersen, Willy, "Abortion and depression: A population-based longitudinal study of young women", *Scandinavian Journal of Public Health*, 2008, Vol. 36, No. 4, pp. 424-428.

Also Coleman, Priscilla K., "Resolution of Unwanted Pregnancy During Adolescence Through Abortion Versus Childbirth: Individual and Family Predictors and Psychological Consequences," Journal of Youth and Adolescence, 2006.

Also Rue V.M., Coleman P.K., Rue J.J., Reardon D.C.., "Induced abortion and traumatic stress: A preliminary comparison of American and Russian women", Medical Science Monitor, Vol.10(10). SR5-16, 2004.

See also the recent admission and warning by the Royal College of Psychiatrists, Position Statement on Women's Mental Health in Relation to Induced Abortion, March 14, 2008.

Also Also Suliman, Sharain, Ericksen, Todd, Labuscgne, Peter, de Wit, Renee, Stein, Dan J., Seedat, Soraya., "Comparison of pain, cortisol levels, and psychological distress in women undergoing surgical termination of pregnancy under local anaesthesia versus intravenous sedation", *BMC Psychiatry*, June 2007, Vol. 7 (24). Available at: http://www.biomedcentral.com/1471-244X/7/24.

39 The *Declaration of Geneva (1948)* vowed: "...the utmost respect for human life from the time of conception". This was reaffirmed by the World Medical Association *verbatim* in the *Declaration of Geneva* (1968). International Code of Medical Ethics (1949) asserted specifically the importance of "...preserving human life from the time of conception".

Abortion should never be misrepresented as an 'option' that must always be 'offered' to the mothers of children conceived through rape or incest. Legally speaking, any act, any use of force that results in deprivation of the life of an unborn child is never a 'choice': always it must be *only* what is 'absolutely necessary' which is conceptually and substantially different to a mere 'choice'.[40] Deprivation of life on legal grounds of necessity is invoked only after all other measures and remedies have been genuinely explored, tried and exhausted—it means that there is no other option. With regards to every mother and unborn child at risk, the objective "necessity" test that every doctor should apply is this: "If this baby were a desperately wanted baby, what could I do 'to save the life of the unborn child' as well as the life of the mother?" If the answer is absolutely nothing, then the involuntary loss of the baby's life while trying to save the mother's life may indeed be considered 'necessary'. Necessity is what remains when all 'choices' have been eliminated. State-condoned deprivation of life, whether capital punishment or abortion, is a very, very serious matter—it should never be trivialized as 'a choice'.

The fundamental legal principle of proportionality should also be applied. Anything less than the saving of the mother's life is not strictly proportional to the irreparable and lethal harm done to the unborn child, and is open to the charge of being arbitrary and unjust. If the life of the unborn child is lost in the process of saving the life of the mother—that is justified. If the unborn child is deprived of the whole of his or her life for any lesser reason, it should certainly be investigated.

Pressuring mothers to abort their children

Many media reports lamented the "failure" of some recent South Dakota anti-abortion legislation to provide for "exceptions for rape and incest".[41] It is a measure of the intellectual and moral confusion that surrounds this issue that so many people seem to exhibit some ambivalence on this politically sensitive matter. Clear logical and ethical imperatives to protect the unborn child tend to be overwhelmed by emotionally-driven public sympathy and heightened public sensitivities relating exclusively to the grief, hurt and shame being experienced by a woman, especially a very young woman, who finds herself pregnant through rape or incest.

It only compounds the tragedy when at the same time, public sympathy towards her tiny innocent child is suppressed—all the concern is focused on the child's mother and provision of a 'choice' to abort the child becomes in itself an insidious pressure. This pressure on mothers to consider abortion takes on the imperative of an obligation. She is told (quite wrongly) that by aborting her child she is exercising her obligation to protect her own mental and physical health. More subtly and insidiously,

40 The drafting history of the *ICCPR* "right to life" reveals that the concepts of "lawful killing" and "the use of force which is no more than absolutely necessary", were never considered by that first Commission on Human Rights to legitimize abortion. Commission on Human Rights 5th Session, 1949. E/CN.4/188.

41 A referendum on the *Women's Health and Human Life Protection Act* was conducted in North Dakota, November 7, 2006.

she may be made aware of an 'obligation' to save her family and friends the anguish of public exposure of her searing experience and to spare them a life-time and living reminder of that experience.

Radical feminists insist that the correct response to the announcement of a pregnancy is a firm affirmation that it is "your choice" and "We will go along with whatever you decide" i.e., to have the baby or to abort the baby. All too often, the problem with this response is that it carries with it an inbuilt bias that tips women, struggling with the normal ambivalence and emotional vulnerability of newly pregnant women, into having an abortion. When a woman tells the news that she is going to have a baby, what she really wants and needs (and is entitled to receive) is an immediate and whole-hearted welcome for her baby. She needs a firm promise that help will be there for her and her child, a comforting and genuine reassurance that all will be fine in the long run. The last thing any woman wants to hear, especially in a situation fraught with hurt and anxiety, is that "it's your choice"—that she alone is to have the responsibility of choosing life or death for her baby. Such a choice implicitly reinforces her deepest fear that she *is* alone, that the formidable responsibility is hers alone, and so inclines her inexorably towards abortion.

Thus to offer abortions to pregnant victims of rape and incest is not a fair, honest or genuine "choice". The very offer of an abortion carries with it a subliminal message that the baby is *not* positively wanted, is *not* going to be warmly welcomed by family, friends and the wider community. Implicit is the concept of mere toleration: the baby's death will be tolerated just as easily as the baby's birth. This is profoundly cruel and unjust. Even an accompanying offer of assistance "should she decide to keep the baby" cannot suffice to undo the damage done by the offer of an abortion at a time when she needs an unqualified affirmation, a straightforward loving acceptance of her child. As the most vulnerable of all pregnant women, the victims of rape or incest need non-ambivalent reassurance, more so than other women.

Irrational prejudice transfers public censure of rape and incest to innocent children

We need to deal with this appalling social climate in which vestiges of public censure of acts of rape or incest spill over quite irrationally to the pregnancies that result from these acts. It is a cruel folly that the injustice and evil of acts of rape and incest are so often transferred to the pregnancies so that the unborn babies themselves begin to be treated as unjust and evil. The pregnancies are portrayed as a continuation of the same terrible imposition, of the same terrible injustice. For this is the tone of much of the recent national and international pro-abortion advocacy that seeks to pressure governments into providing abortion for these mothers as a public duty.[42]

42 Consider, for example, the attitude reported in Maja Kirilova Eriksson's *Reproductive Freedom in the Context of International Human Rights and Humanitarian Law*, The Hague: Martinus Nijhoff, 1999: "…children born as a product of violence were despised…" (pp. 389-90). It is reported that of 3000 rapes during the ethnic cleansing in Croatia, there were 119 pregnancies, of which 88 were aborted (p. 505).

The flawed reasons for condoning the abortion of the lives of these children need to be examined publicly. There seems to be a regrettable reluctance to uncover and condemn the largely hidden prejudice held by the general public towards these children and their mothers. It is precisely this prejudice that subtly pressures these mothers to abort their children. The core of the prejudice, as far as can be judged from anecdotal evidence, is a facile erroneous judgment that rape and incest victims should not carry their children to full term because it will be "too painful"—that the children will be "an unbearable reminder" of the crime perpetrated against these women in the conception of their children.

Often, it seems however, society is just not prepared to experience the discomfort of responding responsibly and generously to the needs of these mothers and their children. Recall how in many euthanasia debates, the caregivers' argument that to continue living is too painful for their patient often masks a deeper and less than honorable concern for the caregivers' own comfort. Just so, there may be something deeper and less honorable lurking behind society's insistence that it is too painful for mothers to bring these children to birth. An honest examination may reveal that public attitudes (with an underlay of censure) towards these children (and their mothers who have "chosen" to bring them to birth) are unjust and must change. It is one of the few remaining vestiges of an earlier barbarism that society will not recognize the vulnerability of both the mother and her child before and after birth and the State and community obligation to protect and provide for them in these difficult circumstances.

It is absolutely critical that these victim mothers be protected from further abuse. This has long been one of the hidden tragedies behind the facile practice of quietly aborting the children of rape and incest: women and girls are sent back into the same situation where further abuse leads to further abortions.

The healing power of a little child

It is good that more and more countries are putting serious effort into the pursuit of justice in the courts for women victims of rape and incest. Of course, it is right and proper to convict and sentence the men who have committed these crimes. But while courts of law appear to be making significant progress in bringing to justice the perpetrators of the crimes of rape and incest, and in exercising a pragmatic justice in awarding compensation in some cases, there are very few judiciaries around the world who are ready to protect from abortion the unborn victims of rape and incest. How little they are prepared to understand that the advent of a child into an abused mother's life is not an extension of the tragedy but the coming of hope, the coming of new purpose, of a compelling new reason to live.

And so for each of these mothers, forgiveness may be more important than justice. The healing necessary for her return to joy in life is contingent ultimately on her being able to forgive the child's father and all those who have hurt, humiliated and abused her. For all human beings, forgiveness is problematical—but not impossible.[43]

In no way should we ever seek to underestimate or trivialize the excruciating pain, both psychological and physical, that is endured by the victims of rape and incest. But neither should we ever consent to compound that pain by encouraging these victims to abort their innocent children who have an inimitable potential to bring true love and healing back into their mothers' lives. These children are the priceless gifts of providence, not retribution. They are sent to show their mothers a way forward out of the valley of darkness, away from despair and hate. Led by a little child, each of these ineffably sad mothers may be drawn on to love and to be loved, to reclaim the heart of life. For here, providentially, is someone to love her, to bring to her life new and deep ties of kinship and meaning, a new someone who will come to know this mother and come to love her forever.

This tiny, fragile new life within each womb calls forth from each mother an heroic love that recognizes that she has here within her a new life, a new hope, a new good, a new beginning. It is the most natural thing in the world to welcome new life—the heart knows that all new life is good. Every mother knows instinctively the first principle of natural law: that life is good, and to be supported and favoured, and all that threatens it is to be avoided. She knows that irrespective of the circumstances of her child's conception, her child has a right to life. From the first knowledge of her child's existence, no one has the authority to thwart and abort that tiny new life. If it is not the case that all human life is sacred, then no human life is sacred. If there is not an inviolable right to life for everyone, then there is an inviolable right to life for no one. Every child, without any exception whatsoever, whenever, wherever and however the child is conceived, has a right to be here.

43 For more on these aspects see Rita Joseph, "Out of the greatest evils..." in *Voices*, Vol. XXI, No. 3, 2006.

Conclusion Ideologies Must Conform to Human Rights—Not Human Rights to Ideologies

Decriminalization of abortion—an ideological aberration

The right to life is a non-derogable right—one of the rights that governments may not derogate from, not even in times of "public emergency".[1] Public emergencies such as internal conflicts and terrorism are not the only exigencies that can threaten the integrity of a nation's legal system. The winds of ideological aberration can sweep across the globe, and States, legislatures, judiciaries and academia cave in to these prevailing winds. One such aberration is the growing insistence that the child before birth is no longer entitled to "special safeguards and care, including legal protection before as well as after birth".[2]

There is a global push towards decriminalization of abortion by some United Nations agencies and international non-government organizations (NGOs). Even some regional bodies such as the Council of Europe have recently mounted the bandwagon.[3] The aberrant goal of this global campaign is to pressure all governments to repeal laws that protect the child before birth from abortion, from violation of the child's right to life. This is, in effect, to promote a corruption of the strict legal duty of the States under Article 6 of the *International Covenant on Civil and Political Rights* (ICCPR) to prevent, investigate, prosecute, punish and redress violations of the right to life.

In the December 1959 *Declaration on the Rights of the Child*, the UN General Assembly formally declared that the *Universal Declaration of Human Rights* (UDHR) "recognized" the human rights of the child before birth. This reaffirmation took place while members of that same UN General Assembly, sitting in that same December session (Session XVI), were drafting the *International Covenant on Civil and Political Rights* (ICCPR) and the *International Covenant on Economic, Social and Cultural Rights* (ICESC).

---

1 *ICCPR* Article 4.

2 Preamble to *UN Declaration on the Rights of the Child* (1959) and Preamble to *UN Convention on the Rights of the Child* (1990).

3 Council of Europe: "Access to safe and legal abortion in Europe", Resolution 1607, April 16, 2008.

Recognition of the child before birth was understood also to apply to the UN Covenants on which committees appointed by the UN General Assembly were working at that very time (December 1959). Furthermore, both Covenants acknowledged in their Preamble their commitment to the principles of the Universal Declaration with the phrase "in accordance with the Universal Declaration of Human Rights".

Since the Universal Declaration recognizes the rights of the child before birth *"including appropriate legal protection"*, nothing in the subsequent Conventions may be interpreted to mean that this legal protection may be repealed, and that the child may be aborted with impunity.

When an ideology hijacks human rights

Yet we know from the Round Table of Human Rights Treaty Bodies on Human Rights Approaches to Women's health, with a Focus on Sexual and Reproductive Health and Rights (held December, 1996)) that a blueprint was developed to reinterpret the human rights treaties to accommodate abortion and to remove legal protection from the child at risk of abortion. The plan was to endorse procured abortion by reinterpreting "recognized rights, to which the States are already committed"[4]. The UN treaty monitoring bodies are now being transformed into treaty-re-interpreting bodies, which effectively re-work the treaties. This reworking was never part of their mandate.[5]

Universal human rights are no longer universal if they are hijacked to serve a single transient ideology. The UN Human Rights Committee, reinterpreting (more than forty years later) the International Covenant on Civil and Political Rights with the stated intention of 'gender mainstreaming' those universal rights, is contravening the universality of those rights. Right from the beginning, it was established that it is the nature of human rights that they are to apply equally to all human beings everywhere at all times. The fundamental principles of universal and inalienable human rights and the inherent dignity and equality of all members of the human family were never to be tampered with. The human rights of any one vulnerable group of human beings were never to be de-recognized by transient ideologies, not even for the purpose of advancing the rights of another group more favoured by those ideologies.[6]

4 Round Table of Human Rights Treaty Bodies on Human Rights Approaches to Women's health, with a Focus on Sexual and Reproductive Health and Rights: Summary of Proceedings and Recommendations, published by United Nations Population Fund, United Nations High Commissioner for Human Rights and United Nations Division for the Advancement of Women, 1998, p. 13.

5 See Rita Joseph: "Compliance with Human Rights or Compliance with an Ideology?" *Voices*, Vol XXII No 1, 2007.

6 See, for example, the influence of radical feminist ideology on the language of the Constitutional Court of Colombia in its DECISION C-355/06, Bogotá, D. C., May 10, 2006. The Court declares that a woman is " being treated as a reproductive instrument for the human race" (8.1) (that is, wherever legislation is in place to protect her child from abortion). The Court goes on to even higher flights of ideological zeal to insist, "The legislature must not impose the role of procreator on a woman against her will." But the

The devious initiative taken by the UN Secretariat in 1996 to reshape human rights law to remove protection from children at risk of abortion was very cleverly masked by the new language of "norm-interpretation" and "gender dimensions":

> The understanding of international human rights law is shaped by the treaty bodies both through norm-interpretation and assessment of compliance of States parties with convention obligations. The challenge is thus to develop approaches to norm-interpretation and monitoring consistent with the objectives of each of the human rights treaties and which increase attention to the gender dimensions of these objectives.[7]

The Feminist Revolution and "abortion rights"—the oppressed have become the oppressors

Unfortunately, however, as "sensitivity to the gender implications"[8] of a woman's putative right to abortion has grown to gross proportions, it has swamped all residual sensitivity to the lethal implications of abortion for the unborn child victims. Under the guise of "reform", the Feminist Revolution has taken the path of excess that so many revolutions before have taken—the oppressed have become the oppressors. Radical feminists, no sooner freed from what they saw as the shackles of subordination of their own interests to those of men, have usurped the power to subordinate to their own arbitrary will the best interests of their own children *in utero*, even to the extent of claiming the right to consign their children to the oblivion of abortion.

In terms of vulnerability, children at risk of abortion are in a far more invidious position than their mothers. Indeed, the mother's new "right to abortion" destroys her child's right to life. Psychologist Dr. Sydney Callahan has challenged the core inconsistency here: she points out that the anti-abortion argument rests on two propositions:

- Accepting the basic democratic claim that all members of the human community are equal in intrinsic worth, and
- Then discerning that the human community must include all members of the human species – both born and unborn.[9]

Court goes too far. The 'role of procreator', i.e., having a baby, is a natural event—it is not "imposed" by the legislature—pregnancy is the natural result of existential biological forces independent of the legislature.

7 Report by the Secretary-General to the tenth meeting of persons chairing human rights treaty bodies, "*Integrating the gender perspective into the work of United Nations human rights treaty bodies*", United Nations HRI/MC/1998/6, Reform of the human rights treaty system, para. 15.

8 Ibid.

9 Callahan, Sydney, "Context of the Abortion Debate" in Merskey, Roy M. and Hartman, Gary R., *A Documentary History of the Legal Aspects of Abortion in the United States.: Webster vs. Reproductive Health Services*, Littleton, CO: Fred B. Rothman & Co., 1990, p. 2 & p. 19.

Callahan's inclusion of the unborn in the human community is based on liberal arguments about moral equivalency that, in other contexts such as racial and gender equality, she believes 'pro-choice advocates' probably would accept:

> ...the less powerful members of the human community must not be denied their equal intrinsic moral worth nor be sacrificed to the interests of stronger and more powerful parties. The abortion debate is one more domain in which persons must challenge those in the society who defend expediency, inequality, and violently destructive solutions to human problems.[10]

UN Human Rights Committee compromised

Given this, it is shameful that the UN Human Rights Committee has not only failed to lead this challenge on behalf of the less powerful members of the human community but continues to make recommendations to remove whatever legal protections remain for unborn children at risk. The Committee's Recommendations now routinely urge States Parties to liberalize abortion laws. In the years since its first ideologically-driven apostasy[11] of the rights of the child before birth, "including appropriate legal protection", this same Committee has, in effect, been compromised. In advancing a woman's "right" to abortion, it has jeopardized the right to legal protection for the child before birth who is at risk of being aborted. In doing so, the Committee has compromised the initial premise, upon which all three instruments of the *International Bill of Rights* are founded:

> Whereas recognition of the inherent dignity and of the equal and inalienable rights of all members of the human family is the foundation of freedom, justice and peace in the world.

Right to life of the child at risk of abortion—not "a private matter"

For the UN Human Rights Committee advocating removal of legal protection for unborn children at risk of abortion, the rights of all members of the human family are not equal. Some members are deemed to be more equal than others. So-called abortion rights for women are quite suddenly deemed "more equal" than the human rights of their children before birth. Quite suddenly, for the Human Rights Committee, the rights of all members of the human family are not inalienable—the right to life of the child at risk of abortion is now deemed transferable to the child's mother who is permitted 'lawfully' to usurp the power at will to quash her child's right to life. Quite suddenly, the universal right to life is privatized—the right to life of the child at risk of abortion is no longer protected by law or by the State—it has become "a private matter between the woman and her abortion provider". Quite suddenly, the

10 Ibid., p. 19.

11 UN Human Rights Committee: *Concluding Observations and Recommendations on Peru's Periodic Report 1995.*

UN Human Rights Committee has caved in to ideological pressure to promote and commend the repeal of laws which protect the child before birth at risk of abortion.

No State may resile from the human rights in the International Bill of Rights

Let us be quite blunt about what the Human Rights Committee is recommending these days: that the rights of the child before birth to legal protection be rescinded. Yet what does the term 'inalienable rights' mean, if it does not mean that no one, not even the Human Rights Committee, can deprive any member of the human family of these rights?

Destruction of human rights recognized by the Universal Declaration is not permissible—not under any circumstances; this is made amply clear in Article 30:

> Nothing in this Declaration may be interpreted as implying for any Sate, group or person any right to engage in any activity or to perform any act aimed at the destruction of any of the rights and freedoms set forth herein.

Not even the UN Human Rights Committee itself, has *any right to engage in any activity* (such as abortion advocacy) *aimed at the destruction of any of the rights and freedoms set forth herein* (such as the right to life of the child at risk of abortion).

There is no treaty-based right for pro-abortion advocates to engage in activity aimed at the destruction of the rights of the child before birth to legal protection. There is no right for any State, group or person to any action aimed at the destruction of laws which protect the child before birth from being aborted

It appears that logical consistency is not a strong point for the UN Committee on Human Rights: the Committee in General Comment No 26 declared that "international law does not permit a State which has ratified or acceded or succeeded to these Covenants to denounce them or withdraw from them". These rights, the Committee says, "belong to the people". Logically, then, the rights of the child before birth *belong* to the child before birth, and no State may resile from them, or denounce or withdraw from any of the human rights protections guaranteed therein—not even when instructed to do so by the UN Human Rights Committee.

Abortion "rights"—a shameful tale of re-interpretation

It was in the 1995 *Concluding Observations and Recommendations to Peru* that the Human Rights Committee made the first of its many recommendations that particular States Parties resile from these human rights obligations and legalize abortion. The government of Peru "...must take the necessary measures to ensure that women do not risk their life because of the existence of restrictive legal provisions on abortion". Such a recommendation conveniently ignores the fact that the restrictive legal provisions on abortion exist to protect the lives of children at risk of abortion as well as the lives of their mothers.

Discriminatory reinterpretation of the international human rights instruments to exclude the rights of the unborn child is legally indefensible.

A masterly stratagem to insinuate "abortion rights" into human rights law

Yet this was the first move in a masterly stratagem that was devised to insinuate a woman's 'right' to abortion into international human rights 'customary' law. This plan was drawn up and agreed to at the 1996 Round Table of Human Rights Treaty Bodies. In agreeing to this plan of reinterpretation, the Human Rights Treaty Monitoring Bodies went not only beyond their mandate but against it.[12]

Nevertheless, the stratagem continues to be enacted as follows: the major objective delineating the "new" direction of the abortion rights agenda is to make access to abortion a human right; and the corollary, to decriminalize abortion in every country in the world.

- The treaty bodies are to examine each article in the transforming light of the new "gender perspective." These reinterpretations are to be translated into binding international human rights law which, in turn, are intended to override not only national sovereignty but individual rights and freedoms relating to conscience and religion as well. Religion and conscience will not be allowed to "excuse" restrictions on the access to abortion.[13]
- Non-governmental organizations are to be funded to assist the treaty bodies by monitoring the new human rights in their countries, and by submitting accusatory shadow reports[14] on alleged violations, and by gathering pertinent statistics (such as suicide rates for pregnant adolescents) to "justify" the need for "effective remedies" such as revoking legislative restrictions on abortion.
- By reinterpreting "recognized rights, to which the States are already committed", the UN Secretariat, together with the UN treaty monitoring bodies, are proceeding to make findings on each country's Periodic Report[15] with a view to using the international "shaming process" to force States to comply with this new pseudo-right to abortion.[16]

12 See Rita Joseph, "Feminist rights agenda storms UN", *Population Research Institute Review*, June / July, 1999. See also Rita Joseph, "Treaty monitors act more like dictators", *The Australian*, Monday 11 September, 2000.

13 Religious belief and the right to conscientious objection are seen as obstacles to providing universal abortion rights. See, for example, "IPPF Charter on Sexual and Reproductive Rights" (1995) Right #5. This IPPF Charter received official UN endorsement in the UNFPA *State of the World Report, 1997*, Chapter 1, Box 8. It condemns "the restrictive interpretation of religious texts, beliefs, philosophies and customs as tools to curtail freedom of thought on sexual and reproductive health care and other issues".

14 For a frank account of this manipulative process, see Brennan, Susan, "Having our say: Australian women's organisations and the treaty reporting process", *Australian Journal of Human Rights*, Vol. 25, 1999.

15 Periodically, each country has to submit a report to each treaty body setting out its successes and failures in complying with the treaty. The treaty monitoring body interrogates a delegation from that country and publicizes its criticisms.

16 See for example: (i)The Human Rights Committee's re-interpretation of Articles 3, 6 and 7 of the *ICCPR* to require repeal of abortion laws, in the Committee's Concluding Observations on the Periodic Reports (1997/8) of Bolivia, Colombia, Zambia, the Sudan and

- Besides these Concluding Observations and Recommendations on each country's Periodic Report, the treaty monitoring bodies issue General Comments about how treaty provisions are to be interpreted. Increasingly, these Observations, Recommendations and General Comments are being used to develop a pro-abortion jurisprudence of international legal standards crafted by radical feminism. For example, all limiting laws on "access to the full enjoyment by adolescents of their sexual and reproductive rights, including access to safe abortion", all protective laws such as parental notification requirements on reproductive services are being "reimagined"[*sic*] as discrimination against adolescents, as exacerbating the dangers of adolescent suicides and of "adolescent vulnerability to reproductive ill-health".[17]
- Once a country has been found in violation of these "rights", it is argued, there can be no immunity from a legally binding obligation to provide effective remedies. The effective remedies recommended by the UN Committees, however, have all too often concentrated exclusively on legalizing abortion to make it 'safe'.

The Committee's ideological blinkers will not let them see that 'safe legal abortions' are no safe remedy for the children at risk of these abortions. Committees should be promoting access to the positive remedy of comprehensive pregnancy support with safe outcomes for mother and child rather than to 'legal' abortion.

When true emphasis is placed on making pregnancy as safe for mothers and babies in the developing world as it is in the developed world,[18] the illegitimacy of abortion advocates' current tactics becomes clear. At present, it suits the pro-abortion lobby to downplay or even to ignore the need for safe pregnancy while they continue to exploit the situation by estimating[19] the number of women and girls who die from "lack

Senegal; (ii) the Human Rights Committee's re-interpretation of Article 24 of the *ICCPR* to intimate that denying suicidal pregnant minors legal abortion is a serious abuse of their rights, in the Concluding Observations on Ecuador's Report (August 1998), and (iii) the CEDAW Committee's reinterpretation of Article 12 of *Convention on the Elimination of All Forms of Discrimination Against Women* (CEDAW) to require that governments legalize abortion services, in the Concluding Observations on Colombia's Report (February, 1999). Also see the more recent recommendations to Honduras, Belize, Brazil, Kenya and Liechtenstein to further liberalize abortion laws. (July 2007).

17 For a research-based assessment of this objective, see Rita Joseph: "Wrong Way—Go Back", *Voices*, Vol.XVII, No 2, 2002.

18 UNFPA Report State of the World's Population 2005: "Every woman, rich or poor, faces a 15 per cent risk of complications around the time of delivery, but maternal death is practically nonexistent in developed regions."

19 The UN Population Division: The World's Women 2005: Progress in Statistics stated "more than a third of the 204 countries or areas examined did not report deaths by cause, sex and age even once…even where the deaths are derived from a civil registration with complete coverage, maternal deaths may be missed or not correctly identified, thus compromising the reliability of such statistics." The report also concluded that the progress in reporting deaths by cause and sex has been very limited since 1975.

of access to safe abortion" and then using those estimates to call for legalization and expansion of abortion services. The higher the numbers[20] of maternal deaths from abortion the more pressure is brought to bear in support of what appears to be their highest priority—to decriminalize and legalize abortion.

However, pregnancies should be made safe, not 'safely terminated'. Social conditions that pressure women towards abortion need to be addressed by 'remedies' other than 'legal' abortion, remedies other than those which destroy their children.

Abortion—like FGM—always a harmful practice

Ideological mendacity lurks behind the perennial claim that abortion should be 'legalized' in order to make all abortions 'safe'. Indeed, it is a curious irony that the same proponents of this argument have rejected strenuously and quite rightly the argument that Female Genital Mutilation (FGM) should be legalized so that the procedure can be performed 'safely' by trained medical personnel. There is logical inconsistency here, for both procedures Female Genital Mutilation (FGM) and abortion, a form of Foetal Mutilation (FM) one might say, are pseudo-medical practices. Both of these mutilating elective surgeries are barbaric, inherently harmful and best avoided altogether. Education and legislative programmes are needed urgently to eliminate both these harmful practices.[21]

At the Cairo and Beijing international conferences, UN member countries having committed to "reducing recourse to abortion" and "eliminating the need for abortion",[22] also committed to eliminating Female Genital Mutilation (FGM).[23]

See also AbouZahr, Carla, "Global burden of maternal death and disability", *British Medical Bulletin*, Vol. 67, 2003, pp. 1-11.

20 These numbers are exceedingly hard to gather with any degree of accuracy. See *Maternal Mortality in 2000: Estimates Developed by* WHO, UNICEF, UNFPA: "The 2000 estimates cannot be used to analyse trends because of the wide margins of uncertainty associated with the estimates."

See also Susan Yoshihara: "Six Problems with 'Women Deliver': Why the UN Should Not Change MDG 5", C-Fam(2007). Available at: http://www.cfam.org/index.php?option=com_docman&task=doc_view&gid=29&Itemid=37.

21 The Beijing Platform underscores the importance of education, particularly of parents, to aid understanding of the harmful health consequences of FGM. [Beijing *Platform for Action* para. 277(d)].

Also, the UN CEDAW Committee General Recommendation No. 14 urges States Parties to "take appropriate and effective measures with a view to eradicating the practice of female circumcision".

22 Cairo International Convention on Population and Development *Programme of Action* (1994)and Beijing Fourth World Conference on Women *Platform for Action*: Consensus was achieved at Cairo ICPD para. 8.25 and Beijing PFA para. 106 (k): "to reduce the recourse to abortion" and "to eliminate the need for abortion".

23 Cairo *Programme of Action* paras. 4.22, 5.5, 7.40; Beijing *Platform for Action* paras. 124(i), 283(d).

As has been argued by certain delegations at the UN for many years now, we cannot reduce FGM by training doctors to perform it safely on women and young girls. Neither, it is argued, should we pretend to be able to reduce abortions that hurt both mothers and their children by training doctors to perform abortions 'safely'.

It should be observed that those arguing for the "medicalization" of abortion because "there are always going to be abortions" do not take such a defeatist attitude towards eliminating FGM: "...female genital mutilation can vanish within a generation."[24] In fact, the World Health Organization Policy Guidelines for Nurses and Midwives asserts:

> In some countries, more affluent families seek the services of medical personnel, in an attempt to avoid the dangers of unskilled operations performed in unsanitary conditions. However, the "medicalization" of FGM—which is willful damage to healthy organs for non-therapeutic reasons—is unethical... A major effort is needed to prevent the "medicalization" of the practice. The World Health Organization, the International Council of Nurses (ICN), the International Confederation of Midwives (ICM) and the Federation of Gynecology and Obstetrics (FIGO) have all declared their opposition to the "medicalization" of FGM, and have advised that it should not be performed by health professionals or in health establishments under any circumstances. FGM violates the basic human rights of girls and women...the performance of FGM by a health professional is a violation of the ethical code governing health practice, which specifically requires that nurses and midwives "do no harm".[25]

One day soon, perhaps, we shall see Guidelines such as this issued by the health professions in condemnation of the "medicalization" of abortion.

An ideological approach—all reasons for abortion to be respected?

The current bias of the UN CEDAW Committee[26] is revealed clearly in the records of their meetings where the country periodic reports are under criticism. For example, at the CEDAW July 2007 session, Committee member Silvia Pimentel asserted dogmatically: "Women have their reasons to seek an abortion, which should be

24 "The consequences of genital mutilation are unacceptable anywhere, anytime and by any moral and ethical standard....If we can come together for a sustained push, female genital mutilation can vanish within a generation." UN Deputy Secretary-General Asha-Rose Migiro, Commission on the Status of Women, Fifty-second Session, 27 February 2008.

25 "The prevention and the management of the health complications of FGM: Policy guidelines for nurses and midwives", World Health Organisation, 2001. See also "Eliminating female genital mutilation: an interagency statement, UNAIDS, UNDP, UNECA, UNESCO, UNFPA, UNHCHR, UNHCR, UNICEF, UNIFEM, WHO", 2008.

26 For a frank account of the machinations that seek to ensure the composition of the CEDAW Committee will deliver "a feminist vision" by "feminist experts", see Obando, Ana Elena, "The CEDAW Committee: A Space for Our Rights", December 2004, WHRnet. Available at: http://lyris.spc.int/read/messages?id=32449.

respected". Unfortunately, there are a myriad purported "reasons" which cannot be respected because they cannot rationally be reconciled with a genuine respect for the human rights of the unborn child singled out for abortion. Despite conceding that reasons for abortion do not always include a threat to the mother's life, Pimentel went on to condemn protective laws for children at risk of abortion, interpreting them as allowing "the interests of the fetus [to] outweigh those of the mother."[27]

Indeed, threading insidiously through so much of the pro-abortion advocacy of the UN Human Rights Committee and the CEDAW Committee is an unsubstantiated assumption that 'safe' abortion is always a health-giving 'service' to be promoted and expanded. Reproductive health is now become so broadly defined that it would encompass as reasons for procuring abortions practically everything and anything across the whole range of physical, mental, emotional, social and economic factors from the most grave circumstances to the most irrational prejudice.

At the 1994 International Conference on Population and Development (ICPD) in Cairo, reproductive health was defined as 'a state of complete physical, mental, and social well-being, and not merely the absence of diseases or infirmity, in all matters relating to the reproductive system and to its functions and processes.' A year later, the Beijing Platform defined 'women's reproductive health' to include "a satisfying and safe sex life",[28] capacity to reproduce, and the freedom to decide if, when, and how to do so. Therefore, abortion advocates conclude:

> at the heart of the reproductive rights movement are the convictions that the right to reproductive health, reproductive choice, and reproductive freedom are essential to the control of one's life…[29]

Not so. Control of one's life is not to be built on abortion. There is truth in feminist dogma proclaiming that a woman cannot exercise the "right to control her own

27 Singson, Samantha, "CEDAW tells Hondurans that Abortion Ban is 'A Crime'", Friday Fax Archives, August 2, 2007, Volume 10, Number 33. Available at: http://www.c-fam.org/publications/id.525/pub_detail.asp.

Singson reports also that Silvia Pimentel criticized the content of Hungary's planning materials—she expressed particular concern over brochures entitled "Life is a Miracle," saying that conservatives often construed such material as reason for not having an abortion.

28 Beijing *Platform for Action* para. 94. It is unreasonable to demand that this "satisfying and safe sex life" should be absolutely guaranteed by provision of 'back-up' abortion. A 'satisfying and safe sex life' is now being re-interpreted to include the right to be made 'safe' from the 'intolerable threat' of having a child that is unplanned. Facilitating routine abortion of any unplanned children seems a disproportionate price to pay for this second-tier 'right'.

29 Bogecho, D, "Putting it to Good Use: The International Covenant on Civil and Political Rights and Women's Right to Reproductive Health", *Law, Social Justice & Global Development Journal (LGD)*, Vol. (1), 2004.

fertility" without unfettered access to abortion.[30] To predicate women's right to reproductive health on abortion "rights" is to pervert the language of human rights. It is to disguise the injustice perpetrated each year against some tens of millions of children who are aborted, in most cases not because of health reasons.[31] Promotion of abortion as a routine solution for dealing with the 'consequences' of on-going dysfunctional behaviours such as sexual violence or sexual incontinence is not valid—it merely compounds dysfunction with injustice.

Genuine reproductive rights of women include adequate access to family and community support and, where necessary, to financial assistance from governments and local communities for each mother and her baby both before birth and after birth. Authentic human rights for expectant mothers also cover access to obstetric care at well-equipped birth centres, good nutrition, clean water, adequate sanitation, safe housing. These are genuinely women's rights and do not require the tragic abrogation of legal protection of the right to life of their unborn children.

Proclamation of Teheran—not an endorsement of abortion

Yet another line of propaganda presents abortion as an essential part of a right to 'family planning'. While it is true that the First International Conference on Human Rights, held in Tehran in 1968, identified the basic right of parents to "determine freely and responsibly the number and spacing of their children", such a right was never meant to include abortion as a *method* for determining the number and spacing of children.[32]

Yet the Center for Reproductive Rights claims that this right of women to choose the spacing of their children includes the right to abort the unwanted ones, that this

30 For a refutation of this dogma, see my entry "Fécondité et continence" in *Lexique des termes ambigus et controversés sur la vie, la famille et les questions ethiques*, Pierre Téqui éditeur, Paris: Conseil pontifical pour la famille, 2005, pp. 525-533.

31 See, for example, Bankole, Akinrinola, Singh, Susheela and Haa, Taylor: "Reasons Why Women Have Induced Abortions: Evidence from 27 Countries", *International Family Planning Perspectives*, Vol. 24, No. 3, Sep., 1998, pp. 117-152. "The most commonly reported reason…is to postpone or stop childbearing. The second most common reason—socio-economic concerns…"

See also Johnston, Wm. Robert, "*Reasons given for having abortions in the United States*", December 4, 2006. Available at: http://www.johnstonsarchive.net/policy/abortion/abreasons.html.

From a compilation of several statistical studies, Johnston has placed the percentage of abortions carried out for reasons of the physical life of the mother at 0.2% (0.1-0.3%). The physical health of the mother is placed at 1% (0.1-3.0%). Quantifying cases involving the "mental health" of the mother is difficult due to the highly subjective use of this term (as demonstrated by the wide range in percentage of abortions reported for this reason). Abortions carried out for reasons of "personal choice" account for 98% (78-99%).

32 ICPD *Programme of Action* (1994) specifically excluded abortion from the term "family planning": "In no case should abortion be promoted as a method of family planning." para. 8.25.

was confirmed in other international conferences during the 1970s and 1980s and, over time, was developed and expanded upon to include a broader understanding of reproductive rights as consisting of a basic right to 'reproductive self-determination and autonomy'.[33]

These claims have no basis in truth. The *Proclamation of Teheran*, 13 May 1968, came out of the First International Conference on Human Rights which met explicitly "to review the progress made in the twenty years since the adoption of the *Universal Declaration of Human Rights* and to formulate a programme for the future". It solemnly proclaims:

- It is imperative that the members of the international community fulfill their solemn obligations to promote and encourage respect for human rights and fundamental freedoms for all without distinctions of any kind such as race, colour, sex, language, religion, political or other opinions; (para. 1)
- The *Universal Declaration of Human Rights* states a common understanding of the peoples of the world concerning the inalienable and inviolable rights of all members of the human family and constitutes an obligation for the members of the international community;(para. 2)
- The protection of the family and of the child remains the concern of the international community. Parents have a basic human right to determine freely and responsibly the number and the spacing of their children. (para. 16)

Pro-abortion advocates have misread into this Tehran Proclamation a right to abort any child that they don't want. This is a gross misinterpretation of "Parents have a basic human right to determine freely and responsibly the number and the spacing of their children". Such an interpretation ignores the word "responsibly" and in effect requires arbitrary removal of the context of protection of the family and of the child called for in the preceding sentence. To interpret the second sentence of Article 16 as a right to abort one's child is in blatant contradiction to the commitment made (in the preceding sentence) to the protection of the child: "The protection of the family and of the child remains the concern of the international community".

The Tehran Proclamation affirming "its faith in the principles of the Universal Declaration of Human Rights and other international instruments in this field" urged

> all peoples and governments to dedicate themselves to the principles enshrined in the *Universal Declaration of Human Rights* and to redouble their efforts to provide for all human beings a life consonant with freedom and dignity and conducive to physical, mental, social and spiritual welfare.

33 The Center for Reproductive Rights and Policy and University of Toronto International Programme on Reproductive and Sexual Health Law, *Bringing Rights to Bear: An Analysis of the Work of UN Treaty Monitoring Bodies on Reproductive and Sexual Rights*, November, 2001, p. 17.

Recalling here that the Universal Declaration of Human Rights recognizes the need for legal protection for the child before as well as after birth, there can be no legitimate reading of a right to abortion into this Tehran Proclamation.

Ideological attack on conscience rights

Indeed, this radical pro-abortion revisionist agenda constitutes a disturbing move away from the truly universal human rights of the *original Universal Declaration.* Promotion of abortion as a human right constitutes a move towards non-universal pseudo-human rights being defined by a particular ideology. Gender mainstreaming—an ingenious but ethically dubious feminist tool for ideological indoctrination—asserts that all human rights are relative, culturally constructed, and need re-interpretation over time.[34]

Naively imprudent adoption of the gender mainstreaming concept by the UN General Assembly[35] has been exploited by ideologues who now use it quite invalidly as a *carte blanche* authority to revamp the values and goals of the UN system, and the entire world. "Old male rights," such as religious and conscientious objection, they say must recede, as "new women's rights," such as the right to abortion, emerge.

The UN CEDAW Committee, for example, has sought to repeal conscience rights for doctors in order to force them to perform abortions on children whose mothers request that they be aborted:

> The Committee expressed particular concern with regard to the limited availability of abortion services for women in southern Italy, as a result of the high incidence of conscientious objection among doctors and hospital personnel.[36]

Issues of religious freedom and conscience rights are also being raised:

> The Committee expresses concern that there is evidence that church-related organizations adversely influence the Government's policies concerning women and thereby impede full implementation of the Convention ... It is also concerned about information regarding the refusal, by some hospitals, to provide abortions on the basis of conscientious objection of doctors. The Committee considers this to be an infringement of women's reproductive rights.[37]

34 "Report of the Expert Group Meeting on the development of guidelines for the integration of gender perspectives into United Nations human rights activities and programmes", E/ CN.4/1996/105, paras. 13, 58.

35 Resolution 52/100 December 12, 1997.

36 CEDAW Committee, Concluding Comments and Recommendations on Italy's Periodic Report, para. 353.

37 CEDAW Committee, Concluding Comments and Recommendations on Croatia's Periodic Report, paras. 108-9.

Other ideologically-driven organizations too have called for overriding conscience rights in order to facilitate access to abortion. On December 14, 2005, the European Union Network of Independent Experts on Fundamental Rights, which monitors and advises the European Union on the status of fundamental rights in the European Union, issued an opinion on health providers' right to conscientious objection.[38] The Network was especially critical of 'concordants' or treaties, on the subject of conscientious objection that EU member states have entered into with the Holy See. Such concordants, they asserted, give providers broad discretion to refuse to perform abortions. Their assertions relied heavily on the 'documentation' by the Center for Reproductive Rights of the alleged effect such concordants have on women's access to legal abortion.

The Network's opinion simply replicated the Center's faulty analysis of the human rights dimensions of conscientious objection. It concluded that EU member states have an obligation under international human rights law to regulate providers' invocation of conscientious objection so as to ensure that no woman is deprived of an abortion in circumstances where the procedure is legal.

How quickly do these ideologues progress from permitting doctors to perform abortions to enforcing them! How radically have they departed from the original purpose and principles of the United Nations Human Rights Charter and Covenants which were enacted precisely because ideologically driven mass killing (including the programmed abortion of countless children) "has outraged the conscience of mankind".[39]

In the same way as human rights recognition has led to the abolition of slavery, human rights recognition of unborn children must lead to abolition of abortion. That is the nature of human knowledge—once a truth is recognized, there can be no going back, no return to 'un-knowing', no retreat into denial. There can be no de-recognition of the human rights of a particular group of human beings.

Extreme feminist ideology has led to a betrayal of universal principles

The UN General Assembly understood this very well in the 1960s. The *Declaration on Social Progress and Development* (1969) was proclaimed. It specifically reaffirms the principles of the Universal Declaration and the Declaration of the Rights of the Child, and goes on to state that social progress and development, founded on respect for the dignity and value of the human person, requires:

38 The EU Network of Independent Experts on Fundamental Rights (2005): "The Right to Conscientious Objection and the Conclusion by the EU Member States of Concordates with the Holy See", Opinion N° 4-2005, December 14, 2005. Available at: http://www.europa.eu.int/comm/justice_home/cfr_cdf/doc/ avis/2005_4_en.pdf).

39 *Preamble* to the *Universal Declaration of Human Rights*: "...disregard and contempt for human rights has resulted in barbarous acts which have outraged the conscience of mankind..."

> The immediate and final elimination of all forms of inequality... including Nazism and apartheid and all other policies and ideologies opposed to the purposes and principles of the United Nations...[40]

It is time for the extreme feminist ideology promoting abortion worldwide to be denounced as one of the "ideologies opposed to the purposes and principles of the United Nations". We must call for the "immediate and final elimination" of abortion as one of the "forms of inequality" that impedes "(s)ocial progress and development... founded on respect for the dignity and value of the human person..."

The ideological conditioning of the last four decades has been insidiously destructive of human rights protection for the child at risk of abortion. Even the World Medical Association which solemnly pledged in 1948 "I will maintain *the utmost respect for human life from the time of conception, even under threat, I will not use my medical knowledge contrary to the laws of humanity*", and reaffirmed that pledge in 1968, succumbed in 1983 to pro-abortion feminist ideology. The term "from the time of conception" was altered in 1983 to "from its beginning", and these words were deleted altogether at the May 2005 meeting of the World Medical Association.

How is this complete betrayal over time of a solemn pledge to be explained? Perhaps it is this: the further in time we move away from the human rights violations of the Holocaust and other atrocities of World War II, the easier it seems to have become to establish a new worldview, not unlike the Nazi worldview. Not only for doctors but also for UN personnel, national legislatures, judiciaries and academics, it seems to have become absurdly easy to set in place laws, judgments and legal theories that comprise an ideologically-based world view which seriously posits perennial extermination before birth of a select group of human beings (unwanted children) and a de-recognition of their human rights as being necessary to the maintenance of the good of another group (women). Only the UN Committee on the Rights of the Child has sounded a return to sanity in recent years in its principled indictment of selective abortion,[41] corporal punishments and other cruel, inhuman and degrading treatment:

> The distinct nature of children, their initial dependent and developmental state, their unique human potential as well as their vulnerability, all demand the need for more, rather than less, legal and other protection from all forms of violence.[42]

Echoes of Nazi compliance by doctors in abortion programs

Yet sadly for many doctors, there remains an acquiescent ambivalence towards the violent act of abortion, a feint-hearted reluctance to speak out for human rights protection for the child at risk of abortion. Dr. Tessa Chelouche, in a recent article "Doc-

40 *UN Declaration on Social Progress and Development* (1969) Article 2(a).

41 UN Committee on the Rights of the Child, General Comment No 7 (2005) and UN Committee on the Rights of the Child, General Comment No 9 (2006).

42 UN Committee on the Rights of the Child, General Comment No 8 (2006) para. 21.

tors, Pregnancy, Childbirth and Abortion during the Third Reich", expresses such an ambivalence about the morality of abortion today:

> Abortion may or may not be a morally defensible act, but it is a different act from that of doctors purposely killing fetuses and newborn babies in order to preserve Nazi racial purity. I will show how pregnancy, childbirth and abortion were used as weapons of mass destruction by physicians, who had been supposedly trained to heal, in their zeal to unquestionably comply with the political paradigm of the time.[43]

However, we have argued in the foregoing chapters that abortion today is not "a different act from that of doctors purposely killing fetuses and newborn babies in order to preserve Nazi racial purity". The act is the same act. And even the purpose of the act as committed by abortionists today—to preserve radical feminist ideological gibberish such as 'reproductive health autonomy' is not dissimilar to that of "preserving" Nazi ideological nonsense such as 'racial purity'. Today's physicians, like their Nazi counterparts, were "supposedly trained to heal", yet they use abortion to effect mass destruction of unborn children (an estimated 40 million annually). Today's political paradigm is differently based—on radical feminism, rather than Nazism—but among many physicians today there is that very same "zeal to unquestionably comply with the political paradigm of the day".

For radical feminists: pregnancy has become "a metaphor for disease"

There are other similarities. A false conflict is set up between the right to health of an expectant mother and the alleged threat to her health posed by allowing her child to be born. Just so was a false dilemma contrived between the health of the Aryan population and allowing Jewish babies to be born. Always the plea is that abortion of the child is 'necessary' for the health of others who are of superior worth. Always the claim is that abortion is 'lawful' and may be performed in good faith because it serves the greater good of others.[44]

In the Nazi era, according to Dr. Chelouche, criteria of what constituted inferiority were elaborated by physicians in collusion with political ideologists:

---

43 Chelouche, Tessa: "Doctors, Pregnancy, Childbirth and Abortion during the Third Reich", *Israel Medical Association Journal,* Vol. 9, March 2007, p. 202.

44 Defendant Otto Hoffmann: "...If today I look back on my work in the Race and Settlement Main Office and on my activity as Higher SS and Police Leader... I think that I may say that at all times I acted in good faith that all the decrees were based on law and that there was no reason for me not to comply with them". *Nuremberg Trials Record,* Vol V, p. 81. Available at: http://www.mazal.org/archive/nmt/05/NMT05-T0081.htm.

Also Defendant Richard Hildebrandt: "... I never did anything, or gave orders for anything to be done which would have brought me into conflict with my conscience... my orders were necessary and lawful" *Nuremberg Trials Record,* Vol. V, p. 82. Available at: http://www.mazal.org/archive/nmt/05/NMT05-T0082.htm.

> The programs of mass murder began when physicians decided that human life was of differential value...[45]

In much the same way as it is said that in Nazi medical programmes, race became a metaphor for disease,[46] so in the modern radical feminist paradigm, pregnancy has become a metaphor for disease. Even the World Health Organization, not immune to ideological indoctrination, now routinely couples pregnancy with AIDS as conditions to be "protected against", marketing condoms as "dual protection". WHO has wasted millions on research in a vain hope of developing what they have chosen to call an "immuno-contraceptive"—a vaccine against pregnancy.

Just as the Nazi "biomedical paradigm provided the theoretical basis for allowing those sworn to the Hippocratic principle of nonmaleficence to kill in the name of the state",[47] today's radical feminist biomedical paradigm provides the theoretical basis for allowing doctors (many of whom are no longer "sworn to the Hippocratic principle of nonmaleficence")[48] to kill in the name of "women's reproductive health".

Regrettably, some health education programs for girls and women today peddle misinformation designed to inculcate irrational fear of pregnancy.[49] The implication is that women and girls are *inherently* at risk of dying in childbirth, rather than the truth that they are not provided with First World standards of good nutrition and medical care, as well as adequate clean water, sanitation and effective protection against infectious diseases.[50]

---

45 Chelouche (*op. cit.*, p. 202) cites here Bock, G.: "Nazi sterilization and reproductive policies", in: *Deadly Medicine: Creating the Master Race*, Washington DC: United States Holocaust Memorial Museum, 2004, pp. 61-2.

46 Ibid. Chelouche cites here Seidelman W.E., " 'Medspeak' for murder: the Nazi experience and the culture of medicine" in: Caplan, AL, (ed.), *When Medicine Went Mad: Bioethics and the Holocaust*, Totowa, NJ: Humana Press, 1992, pp. 271-2.

47 Chelouche ibid cited in Caplan, AL., "How did medicine go so wrong?" in: Caplan AL, ed., *When Medicine Went Mad: Bioethics and the Holocaust,* Totowa, NJ: Humana Press, 1992:71-7.

48 See Orr, R.D., Pang N., Pellegrino E.D., Siegler M., "The Use of the Hippocratic Oath: A Review of Twentieth Century Practice and a Content Analysis of Oaths Administered in Medical Schools in he U.S. and Canada in 1993", *Journal of Clinical Ethics*, Vol. 8 (4), 1997, pp. 377-388, p. 285.

49 "According to WHO and UNICEF's estimates, more than 585,000 women die each year as a result of pregnancy. At least 7 million women suffer serious health problems, and as many as 50 million suffer some health consequences after childbirth." in Sadik, Nafis, (at time of publication Executive Director, UNFPA) "Progress in Protecting Reproductive Rights and Promoting Reproductive Health: Five Years Since Cairo", *Health and Human Rights*, Vol. 4, 2000, p. 15.

50 See for example *UNFPA State of the World Population Report 2006*:

> Maternal mortality remains astoundingly high, at about 529,000 a year, more than 99 per cent in developing countries, and much of it readily preventable. Four out of five deaths are the direct result of obstetric complications, most of which could be averted through delivery with a skilled birth attendant and access to emergency obstetric services. For

The "ideologically unwanted"—at risk of abortion

Among the dogmas of radical feminism underpinning 'abortion rights' is the particularly noxious dictum that pregnancy is a parasitical growth and an unfair imposition on women. Women are told that they must reject "…the male view of reproduction as a natural process."[51]. Women are encouraged to claim their right to abort their children who are ideologically portrayed as threatening their mothers' psychological and physical health. From much the same exclusive mindset, ideologically-driven termination programmes were promoted as being necessary for the German people to regain "the path to health":

> In National Socialism, the German people has once again found its original way of life. It is again on the path to health, and therefore offers the Jewish parasite no further nourishment…[52]

In our radically feminized world today, abortion is once again a matter of destroying the parasitic, unwanted life of a particular child to ensure the "healthy life" of others.

> …the expulsion of the Jews was bound to the health of the national body…National Socialism is the wellspring of health for our people… We can only choose between being devoured by the parasite or destroying it. The Jew must be destroyed wherever we meet him! In so doing, we commit no crime against life, but rather serve life's laws of battle, which always oppose that which is an enemy to healthy life. Our battle serves to maintain life.[53]

Dr. Gerhard Wagner, head of the Nazi physicians in the 1930s, used the health of the adults to justify medical termination of the lives of their children who were deemed burdensome or ideologically unwanted. He asserted that it is the duty of the state to protect the people's health through legal measures:

> Allow us to form our German state according to our laws and needs… it is irresponsible that the state must provide the money for some genetically ill families who may have several family members in institutions costing thousands of marks annually. The National Socialist state cannot repair the failings of the past, but through the "Law for the Prevention of Genetically Ill Offspring," it has seen to it that in the future the inferior will not be able to produce more inferior children, saving the German people from a steady

example, only 10-20 per cent of women deliver with skilled health personnel in the slums of Kenya, Mali, Rwanda and Uganda, compared to between 68 and 86 per cent in non-slum urban areas.

51 Olsen F.: "Do (Only) Women Have Bodies?", Cheah P., Fraser D. and Grbich J. (eds.), *Thinking Through the Body of the Law*, St Leonards: Allen and Unwin, 1996.

52 Parole 21: "Den Juden kennen heißt den Sinn des Krieges verstehen!", *Sprechabenddienst*, Sept./Oct. 1944. Available at: http://www.calvin.edu/academic/cas/gpa/sprech44a.htm.

53 Ibid.

> stream of new moral and economic burdens resulting from genetic illnesses...we prevent unhealthy life from being propagated, saving children and their children from new and enormous misery.[54]

In authorizing the medicalized destruction of selected children (before as well as after birth), Nazi ideologues insisted there could be no guilt.

> This is necessary for the preservation and development of all that lives on this earth...I believe that we have a good conscience before the world when we eliminate life that is unworthy of life...[55]

Aborting children's lives "only to help" their mothers?

The *Nuremberg Trials Record* shows that even when confronted with the enormity of the crimes against humanity, there was stubborn denial of any crime:

> The activity of Lebensborn, however one may understand it, consisted of care for other people. Mistakes may have occurred, errors which one may only be able to judge today in retrospect. The basic motives, however, the basic motive for helping and assisting other people was predominant in every case. I personally at no time had any other motive, nor did I at any other time follow any other intentions.[56]

Similarly, defendants insisted that their 'work' of terminating lives was only to 'help' women and children:

> I did not help women and children in order to be praised for it. I helped them because I wanted to help them, and because I had to help them. I never expected any thanks for that; but that I would be placed before a court because of my helping activities — that is something I never comprehended and I still cannot understand it — at the end of this trial. In the future it will never be comprehensible to me because I cannot believe that my work was ever a crime. [57]

These attitudes towards terminating children's lives in order to "help" their mothers find chilling echoes in respectable medical journals of our own times:

---

54 Wagner, Gerhard: "Rasse und Bevölkerungspolitik," *Der Parteitag der Ehre*, vom 8, bis 14, September 1936. *Offizieller Bericht über den Verlauf des Reichsparteitages mit sämtlichen Kongreßreden*, Munich: Zentralverlag der NSDAP., 1936, pp. 150-60. Available at: http://www.calvin.edu/academic/cas/gpa/pt36rasse.htm.

55 Ibid.

56 Defendant Guenther Tesch, *Nuremberg Trials Record, Vol.V.* p. 87. Available at: http://www.mazal.org/archive/nmt/05/NMT05-T0087.htm.

57 Defendant Inge Viermetz, *Nuremberg Trials Record, Vol.V*, p. 87. Available at: http://www.mazal.org/archive/nmt/05/NMT05-T0087.htm.

> Doctors who perform abortions consider that the lives of women are saved by their performing abortions legally rather than leaving women to kill themselves in the attempt.[58]

There is here the same arrogant insistence as among Nazi doctors that there is no solution possible for these mothers other than "the final solution"—there is no other way "to help them" than to kill their children "safely" and "legally".

In the trial of Adolf Eichmann, "artificial abortion in every case and in all stages of pregnancy" at Theresienstadt and at Kovno Ghetto was identified in Count 4 of the indictment as one of the measures intended to advance the "Final Solution of the Jewish Question."[59] In a dramatic attempt to shift responsibility to the society at the time, Dr. Servatius (Defencè for Eichmannn) insisted that Eichmann could "not be made to pay as a surrogate for the guilt of the human associations, for the guilt of the epoch", and then Dr. Servatius waxed quite prophetic:

> From the interweaving of the various connections must be drawn the lesson that what happened to the Accused can in the future happen to anyone, no one is immune. Concepts are remodelled, the capable ones are needed, they are lured and won over and they are the very ones who become guilty. What happened to the German people can come to pass in every people. The entire civilized world is confronted by this problem. Recognizing this truth should heal and teach us how to prevent new disasters.[60]

The re-emergence of programs of mass abortion today and their spread with the collusion of the medical profession across the entire civilized world is a testimony to the astonishing accuracy of Dr. Servatius's warning.

Progressive corruption of medical ethics

A similar warning was issued by Dr. Leo Alexander, a consultant to the Secretary of war and the Chief Counsel on War Crimes at the Nuremberg Trials, writing in the *New England Journal of Medicine* in 1948. He points out that the Holocaust began with a small modification of traditional medical ethics:

> Whatever proportions these crimes finally assumed, it became evident to all who investigated them that they had started from small beginnings. The beginnings at first were merely a subtle shift in emphasis in the basic attitude of the physicians. It started with the acceptance of the attitude... that there is such a thing as life not worthy to be lived. This attitude in its early stages concerned itself merely with the severely and chronically sick. Gradually the sphere of those to be included in this category was enlarged to encompass

58 Wendy Savage, Doctors for a Woman's Choice on Abortion, Letter to the editor, "Legal abortions save women's lives", *British Medical Journal*, 31 May, 1997, Vol. 314, p. 1623.

59 Shofar FTP Archive File: people/e/eichmann.adolf/transcripts/Sessions/Session-001-01, 11 April, 1961.

60 Shofar FTP Archive File: people/e/eichmann.adolf/transcripts/Sessions/Session-120-03, 13 December, 1961.

the socially unproductive, the ideologically unwanted, the racially unwanted, and finally all non-Germans.[61]

Dr. Alexander speaks of "ideologically conditioned crimes against humanity" being motivated by fear and cowardice, especially fear of "ostracism by the group". He identifies systems in which there is a prevalence of thinking in destructive rather than in ameliorative terms in dealing with social problems. He observes the ease with which destruction of life was advocated for those considered either socially useless or socially disturbing:

> All destructiveness ultimately leads to self-destruction; the fate of the SS and of Nazi Germany is an eloquent example. The destructive principle, once unleashed, is bound to engulf the whole personality and to occupy all its relationships. Destructive urges and destructive concepts arising therefrom cannot remain limited or focused upon one subject or several subjects alone, but must inevitably spread and be directed against one's entire surrounding world, including one's own group and ultimately the self. The ameliorative point of view maintained in relation to all others is the only real means of self-preservation.[62]

Many medical and social researchers today are beginning to uncover the creeping proliferation of the destructive urges and the destructive concepts associated with mass abortion—the tragic escalation of dysfunctional relationships, family breakdown, disintegration of stable communities, increased child abuse, prevalence of alcohol and drug addictions, serious physical and mental health impairment, rising suicide rates. Indeed, Dr. Alexander's observations have a bitter truth for today's suicide ideation statistics for bereaved mothers who have been caught up in the destructiveness of abortion.[63]

Mass abortion—re-emergence of an ideology of stigmatization and rejection

How have we come to this toleration of mass abortion? It would be hard to overestimate the revulsion experienced by the international community immediately after World War II against the Nazi contempt for human lives deemed expendable, a contempt that included programmatic encouragement of abortion and deliberate

---

61 Alexander, Leo, "Medical Science Under Dictatorship," *New England Journal of Medicine*, 14 July, 1949, pp. 39-47.

62 Ibid.

63 See for example, Gissler, Berg, C., Bouvier-Colle, M.-H., Buekens, P "Injury deaths, suicides and homicides associated with pregnancy, Finland 1987-2000", *European Journal of Public Health*, Vol. 15(5), 2005, pp. 459-63.

Also see Reardon D.C., Ney P.G., Scheuren F., Cougle J., Coleman P.K., Strahan T.W.: "Deaths associated with pregnancy outcome: a record linkage study of low income women", *Southern Medical Journal*, Vol. 95(8), 2002, pp. 834-41.

removal of laws that protected unborn children from abortion in Poland and the other occupied territories.

In the context of a determined moral integrity and fierce intellectual honesty, framers of the human rights instruments saw with extraordinary clarity the fundamental principles of natural law that had been violated by the Nazi regime. The international human rights and humanitarian agreements of 1947, 1948, 1949 and 1951 were all forged in this spirit of determination that 'never again' would these moral universals be violated with impunity.

In recent years, legal academics removed sufficiently from the searing catastrophe of Nazi experience have lost that clarity of moral vision. At a safe and comfortable distance from the immense tragedy of those years, they now dabble like dilettantes with notions of changeable human rights and shifting moral norms, an exceedingly elastic positive law, 'law without morality' and other anomalies. The philosopher, Dietrich Von Hildebrand, one of the few academics of the thirties who pierced Nazi propaganda and protested their mass atrocities, once sounded a warning still relevant to academics today:

> Moral good and evil are such elemental realities that even when a philosopher or psychologist tries to deny them, he is faced with them as soon as he quits his desk and comes again into existential contact with reality.[64]

We have not dealt well with the biomedical advances that have invested doctors too suddenly with new technological powers to determine if the child in the womb is imperfect or the wrong sex or even, in the case of 'saviour siblings' the wrong genes or the wrong blood type. Economic trends worldwide have intensified pressures to rationalise healthcare costs and develop utilitarian strategies for promoting abortion as the best cost-saving option where children would need expensive special care or where mothers are in financial or social distress.

National and international political forces, adopting the extreme ideology of a vociferous minority of feminist ideologues, have directly enlisted the medical profession in an agenda of social and economic transformation that provides abortion on demand as a routine procedure. The dominant ideology of our times is an ideology of rejection and stigmatisation that favours and permits the dehumanisation of one of the most vulnerable sectors of the human family, children at risk of abortion.

To delete non-derogable rights—an invalid action in human rights law

Indeed, pro-abortion advocates now use this ideology to 'expand' human rights norms in such a way as to rupture with the original norms set down in the *International Bill of Rights*. They are engaged not simply in expansion of recognized rights but in *deletion* of recognized rights, replacing the right to life of the unborn child with a woman's right to abortion.

64 Von Hildebrand, Dietrich: *Man and Woman: Love & the Meaning of Intimacy*, Manchester, NH: Sophia Institute Press, 1992, p. 78.

This cannot be done without compromising the essential non-derogability of the right to life itself. It cannot be done without rejecting the deontological foundations of human rights law and without contravening the principles of non-discrimination, inalienability, inherence and equality of human rights for all members of the human family. To delete non-derogable rights is an invalid action in human rights law.

Treaty monitoring bodies—turning breaches of the rule of law into attempted recognition of a new law

Deleting fundamental non-derogable human rights for a victimized group of human beings from a natural law-based human rights system cannot be accommodated legitimately. De-recognizing the human rights of a victim group such as unborn children at risk of abortion can be legitimized only by switching to a different system based on a different philosophy of law such as consequentialism or utilitarianism.

And that is what radical feminist ideologues have done—surreptitiously and invalidly. They claim that human rights are constantly evolving over time. Through ideological indoctrination, they are gender mainstreaming human rights to "culturally construct" a right to abortion for women and to "culturally deconstruct" the right to life for the child at risk of abortion.

Proof that their major approach is utilitarian/consequentialist may be found very readily in the way in which they are using the treaty monitoring bodies to reinterpret the right to life to include abortion.

At an International Law Conference on "Implementing Human Rights" at the Australian National University (December 1997), Elizabeth Evatt, then on the UN Human Rights Committee, advised that the best way to establish the right to abortion is for NGOs in each country to gather and send to the treaty committees the pertinent statistics on women dying from illegal abortions and on suicide rates among pregnant adolescents. She said these statistics could be used to "justify" the need for "effective remedies" such as legalizing abortion. She claimed that if the Human Rights Committee finds a violation, the State has a legal obligation under the Covenant to provide effective remedy. Remedies, she insisted, may include repeal of national laws restricting abortion.

So it was no surprise subsequently, in August 1998, that the Human Rights Committee reinterpreted Article 24 of the ICCPR to declare that denying suicidal pregnant minors legal abortion is a serious abuse of their rights[65]—as if abortion is a harmless and reliable remedy against suicide.

It was no surprise either when the CEDAW Committee, in February 1999, reinterpreted Article 12 of CEDAW to require the State to legalize abortion services.[66]

65 Human Rights Committee Concluding Observations and Recommendations on Ecuador's Report, August, 1998.

66 CEDAW Committee: Concluding Observations and Recommendations on Colombia's Report, February, 1999.

Abortion 'rights'—based on cultural pragmatism, not international human rights law

This whole manipulative process is contemptuous of the natural-law based norms of international human rights instruments: it relies rather on pragmatic utilitarian approaches, on constructing consequentialist arguments for legalizing abortion:

A specific number of women die from illegal abortion, therefore abortion must be legalized. Then they broaden the argument—585,000 women die each year from complications related to pregnancy and childbirth, therefore women must not be "forced to remain pregnant"—such a dangerous health risk must be undergone by choice only—safe legal abortion must be accessible. This is abortion advocates' core strategy.

Yet they are careful to conceal the flaw in their argument, that abortion does not make pregnancy safe.[67] While "unsafe" abortion causes the death of the mother and her child, it is illogical. perhaps even obscenely so, to claim that abortion is "safe" where it causes only the death of her child. The fundamental human rights principle of indivisibility is violated when States attempt to expand women's rights and use that expansion as an excuse to obliterate the rights of children at risk of abortion.

Non-derogable rights were never meant to be amenable to change and destruction through manipulation of the processes of customary law. The push to decriminalize abortion is based on a kind of cultural pragmatism, not on international law; and since even widespread cultural practices are frequently contrary to law, we must argue that it is not a sound basis to rely on cultural practice to restrict or narrow the law on human rights.

Alarm bells should ring urgently and loudly when any attempt is made to pressure any government into removing legal protection of non-derogable rights from any select category of human beings.

Abortion 'rights'—"contrary to the purposes and principles of the United Nations"

It was precisely to prevent a large-scale human tragedy like the Holocaust ever happening again that the modern international human rights instruments were drawn up after World War II. It is in direct contravention of these instruments that the current campaign to abolish abortion laws is being waged. The "concluding observations on ninety-three countries spanning more than a decade by U.N. treaty bod-

67 Both maternal mortality and pre-natal mortality can best be addressed by eliminating abortion and transferring scarce health resources to the provision of good pre-natal and postnatal care for mothers and children, including adequate provision of nutritional supplementation, safe water and sanitation, basic supplements (such as iodide and foliate), all necessary vaccinations, tetanus injections as well as emergency obstetrics and skilled birth attendants, and transport to well-equipped birth centres.

ies"[68] pressuring governments to remove protective laws against abortion constitute a premeditated agenda to remove from international law the non-derogable right to life of a particular group of human beings. Truly it is contrary to the purposes and principles of the UN and is thus in violation of UDHR Article 29(iii):

> These rights and freedoms may in no case be exercised contrary to the purposes and principles of the United Nations.

Regrettably some UN delegations remain quite ignorant of this great intellectual and moral battle going on right now between two competing philosophies of human rights law—between the inherent and inalienable natural law values upon which the foundational modern human rights instruments were based and the new flexible human rights based on ever-changing positivist values that yield readily to even the grossest demands of a new ideology.

New Human Rights Council—already misconceptions on abortion creeping in

While the recent dissolution of an ineffective and sometimes corrupt Human Rights Commission was welcomed by many, there is a new challenge to be faced. It is now vitally important for the international community to ensure that the creation of the new Human Rights Council is not being used to attempt to establish a new philosophical foundation (utilitarianism or consequentialism) to human rights law. Meting out legal protection according to means, ends and consequences is both logically and morally incompatible with the original human rights law under which no amount of toting up of ends and consequences is to be allowed to prevail over inherent and inalienable human rights and the equal respect which is due to all members of the human family "without any discrimination whatsoever".

Already some misconceptions are creeping in. Paul Hunt's Special Rapporteur Report to the 7th session of the UN Human Rights Council, January 2008 presents his personal ideological view that few human rights are absolute which allows for his history of abortion advocacy to be accommodated.[69] The Holy See identified the problem this presents:

---

68 Human Rights Watch: *International Human Rights Law and Abortion in Latin America*: "U.N. treaty bodies, which take a measured approach to interpreting international human rights law, have consistently and extensively opined on abortion access and restrictions. By our count, as of early 2005, at least 122 concluding observations on ninety-three countries spanning more than a decade by U.N. treaty bodies have substantively addressed how abortion relates to fundamental human rights. These bodies reason that firmly established human rights are jeopardized by restrictive or punitive abortion laws and practices." Available at: http://www.hrw.org/backgrounder/wrd/wrd0106/.

69 "Report of the Special Rapporteur on the Right of Everyone to the Enjoyment of the Highest Attainable Standard of Physical and Mental Health Document" A/HRC/7/11, 31 January, 2008. Paul Hunt's reputation as an independent expert is dubious as he is currently listed as a member of the International Litigation Advisory Committee to the Cen-

> While the report claims that "few human rights are absolute," it is the firm belief of my delegation, Mr. President, that no compromise can be made with a person's right to life itself, from conception to natural death, nor with that person's ability to enjoy the dignity which flows from that right.[70]

The Holy See sounded a warning to the Human Rights Council that for those who require special protection, for those whose conditions are most vulnerable and may entirely depend on being safeguarded by others, the right to life must never be ignored or denied:

> Particular cases in point are children in the womb and those suffering from grave and life-threatening illnesses. My Delegation urgently hopes that references to "emergency obstetric care" will never be misconstrued to justify the forced ending of human life before birth and that the reference to a state's obligation to "identify a minimum 'basket' of health services" and to "striking balances" will not be interpreted in a manner that denies essential services to the seriously ill. [71]

Human Rights Council must reaffirm the deontological basis of human rights law

The new Human Rights Council must not break with the original deontological system of duties and natural law principles that is woven into the very foundations of modern international human rights law.

The Universal Declaration of Human Rights (1948) and the International Conventions on Civil and Political Rights and on Social, Economic and Cultural Rights (1966) were grounded firmly and inextricably in the deontological approach. The hard truth is that international human rights law cannot be converted now to the utilitarian or consequentialist approach without a catastrophic unravelling of all the human rights protections that have been painstakingly built on principles such as equal protection before the law of every human being, equal safeguards including appropriate legal protection for the child before birth as for the child after birth, and an equal right to development and survival for all members of the human family.

The new Human Rights Council needs to recommit to the spirit and letter of the original foundation documents of modern international human rights law.

Need for reform of the treaty monitoring bodies

In the meantime, maintaining philosophical continuity with the original Human Rights Commission is imperative, as is reforming the treaty monitoring bodies.

---

ter for Reproductive Rights. Available at: http://www.reproductiverights.org/ww_litigation.html.

70 Address by Holy See delegation to the 7th session of the U.N. Human Rights Council, 14 March, 2008.

71 Ibid.

Heribert Golsong issued a stern caution to treaty monitoring bodies that too broad an interpretation of human rights treaties may not always be in line with their "noble purpose"; and that an expansive reading of the treaties may resemble an act "of usurpation of overreaching power or at least an act of *detournement de pouvoir*" beyond the confines of the *Vienna Convention on the Law of Treaties*.[72] The treaty monitoring bodies are now infringing the international rules governing treaty interpretation, viz., the Vienna Convention on the Law of Treaties (1969). The Vienna Convention provides that: "A treaty shall be interpreted in good faith in accordance with the ordinary meaning to be given to the terms of the treaty in their context and in the light of its object and purpose" (Article 31, "General Rule of Interpretation 1"). At least some of the novel human rights now being read into human rights treaties signed more than 40 years ago are not in the "ordinary meaning." They are quite extraordinary, and should therefore be rejected.

Scrutiny of the official transcripts of the treaty committee meetings reveals some appalling standards of logical consistency and rational debate. Across the broad spectrum of General Comments from the different treaty monitoring bodies, there are emerging some very serious logical inconsistencies that cannot be resolved as long as ideology prevails over truth. One of the most serious discrepancies is between the CEDAW's General Comment No 24 insisting on the removal of laws restricting reproductive services (abortion) and the Committee on the Rights of the Child's General Comment No 7 which calls for States parties to provide equal protection against violence for all children and asserts that selective abortion is *discrimination against girl children* and is *a serious violation of rights affecting their survival*.[73]

When interpretation of a treaty provision is not "in good faith"

Interpretations of human rights treaty provisions are not "in good faith" when "contrary to the purposes and principles of the United Nations", which includes the commitment that "all human beings... should act towards one another in a spirit of brotherhood", they are "aimed at the destruction of any of the rights and freedoms set forth herein".

To break with the spirit of brotherhood is to break with human solidarity; it is to set brother against brother, mother against her own child.

It is not "in good faith" when an interpretation breaks with the "faith in fundamental human rights, in the dignity and worth of the human person, in the equal rights of men and women" affirmed on page one of the Charter of the United Nations. It is not "in good faith" when equal rights of men and women are interpreted to mean that because abortion is a medical "service" applying only to women, and because laws

72 Golsong, Heribert, "Interpreting the European Convention on Human Rights beyond the confines of the Vienna Convention on the Law of Treaties" in *The European System for the Protection of Human Rights*, (eds.) R.St.J. MacDonald, F. Matcher & H. Petzold, Dordrecht: Martinus Nijhoff, 1993, p. 162.

73 See Chapter 13 above.

against abortion only affect women, that these abortion laws protecting the child before birth must be abolished.[74]

It is not "in good faith" when Articles 3, 6 and 7 of the International Covenant on Civil and Political Rights are ideologically re-interpreted to mean that legal protection for the child before birth is to be repealed.[75]

It is not "in good faith" when the UN Human Rights Committee and other treaty monitoring bodies have colluded (see the record of their infamous meeting in 1996[76]) to reinterpret human rights instruments to exclude appropriate legal protection for the child before birth.

They are in breach of Article 31 General rule of interpretation of the Vienna Convention on the Law of Treaties which requires that a treaty shall be interpreted in good faith in accordance with the ordinary meaning to be given to the terms of the treaty in their context and in the light of its object and purpose, and then goes on to stipulate:

> A special meaning shall be given to a term if it is established that the parties so intended.
> *Article 31 (4)*

The Human Rights Committee has not established that the parties to the International Bill of Rights "so intended" at the time that a special meaning was given to the term "child" that meant the child after birth only. On the contrary. The child before as well as after birth was recognized at the time to be entitled to special safeguards and care including legal protection.[77]

It is not "in good faith" when the interpretations issued by the Committee are based not on the universal principles agreed at the time that the human rights instruments were drawn up, but rather on a new ideology, radical feminism, which has aimed at

74 CEDAW Committee's General Recommendation No. 24 (20th session, 1999) (Article 12 Women and Health)*:* It is discriminatory for a State party to refuse to legally provide for the performance of certain reproductive health services for women. (para.11) The obligation to respect rights requires States parties to refrain from obstructing action taken by women in pursuit of their health goals…States parties should not restrict women's access to health services or to the clinics…because they are women. Other barriers to women's access to appropriate health care include laws that criminalize medical procedures only needed by women and that punish women who undergo those procedures.(para.14)… When possible, legislation criminalizing abortion could be amended to remove punitive provisions imposed on women who undergo abortion. [para.31 (c)].

75 See for example: the Human Rights Committee's Concluding Observations on the Periodic Reports (1997/8) of Bolivia, Colombia, Zambia, the Sudan and Senegal.

76 *Round Table of Human Rights Treaty Bodies on Human Rights Approaches to Women's health, with a Focus on Sexual and Reproductive Health and Rights*: *Summary of Proceedings and Recommendations*, published by United Nations Population Fund, United Nations High Commissioner for Human Rights and United Nations Division for the Advancement of Women, 1998.

77 See Chapters 1 and 2 above.

the destruction of the fundamental rights of the child before birth in order to promote in their place the grossly esoteric "abortion rights" of women.

These interpretations form the basis of what pro-abortion feminist ideologues see as their ingenious stratagem to move "a woman's right to abortion" into international human rights law. But it can't be allowed to succeed. It awaits merely intellectually honest academic, legislative or judicial critique. Once divested of its ideological trappings, this master plan must collapse, for like other infamous master plans, it has been built on the withdrawal of the protection of the law from a class of the most vulnerable human beings.

A perverse and persuasively articulate ideology may have succeeded, for the time being, in silencing the law and suppressing the truth. But international human rights law is not "silent" on our obligation to protect children at risk of abortion. Sooner or later, the blinding brilliance and insistent din of any ideological madness burns itself out and the agony of remorse and shame begins. Once again, decriminalized mass abortion will be condemned as a crime against humanity—"protection of the law was denied the unborn children". Once again a hurt and shaken humankind will declare in good faith that the universal protection of the human rights of all members of the human family should 'never again' be violated. And once again, for the sake of future generations, we will try to ensure in international law the timeless truth that ideologies must conform to human rights—and not human rights to ideology.

Bibliography

AbouZahr, Carla, "Global burden of maternal death and disability", *British Medical Bulletin*, Vol. 67, 2003.

Ahmed,Tawhida and Butler, Israel de Jesús, "The European Union and Human Rights: An International Law Perspective", *European Journal of International Law*, , Vol.17 (4), 2006.

The Alan Guttmacher Institute, Into a New World: Young Women's Sexual and Reproductive Lives, New York: 1997.

Alexander, Leo, "Medical Science Under Dictatorship", *New England Journal of Medicine*, July 14, 1949.

Alston, Philip, "The Unborn Child and Abortion under the draft Convention on the Rights of the Child", *Human Rights Quarterly*, Vol.12(1), 1990.

Aravamudhan. Ghita: "*Disappearing Daughters:the Tragedy of Female Foeticide*", New Delhi: Penguin , 2007.

Bankole, Akinrinola, Singh, Susheela and Haa, Taylor: "Reasons Why Women Have Induced Abortions: Evidence from 27 Countries", *International Family Planning Perspectives*, Vol. 24, No. 3, Sep., 1998.

Bard-Anders Andreaason, "Article 22" in Godnundur Alfredson and Asbjorn Eide, (eds.), *The Universal Declaration of Human Rights: A Common Standard of Achievement*, The Hague: Martinus Nijhoff, 1999.

Bellieni, Carlo, Buonocore, Giuseppe, "Assisted Procreation: Too Little Consideration for the Babies?", *Ethics & Medicine*, Summer, 2006.

Beutler, Ernest, "Carrier Screening for Gaucher Disease: More Harm Than Good...", *Journal of the American Medical Association*, Vol. 298(11), 2007.

Bogdon, Michael and Olsen, Birgitte Kofod, "Article 6" in Godnundur Alfredson and Asbjorn Eide, (eds.), *The Universal Declaration of Human Rights: A Common Standard of Achievement*, The Hague, Martinus Nijhoff Publishers, 1999.

Bogecho, D, "Putting it to Good Use: The International Covenant on Civil and Political Rights and Women's Right to Reproductive Health", *Law, Social Justice & Global Development Journal (LGD)*, Vol. 1, 2004.

Brennan, Susan, "Having our say: Australian women's organisations and the treaty reporting process", *Australian Journal of Human Rights*, Vol. 25, 1999.

Bossuyt, Marc J.: *Guide to the "Travaux Préparatoires" of the International Convenant on Civil and Political Rights*, Dordrecht: Martinus Nijhoff Publishers, 1987.

Buonocore, Giuseppe & Bellieni, Carlo (eds.): *Neonatal Pain: Suffering, Pain and the Risk of Brain Damage in the Fetus and Unborn*, Milan: Springer, 2008.

Callahan, Sydney, "Context of the Abortion Debate" in Merskey, Roy M. and Hartman, Gary R., *A Documentary History of the Legal Aspects of Abortion in the United States.: Webster vs. Reproductive Health Services*, Littleton, CO: Fred B. Rothman & Co., 1990.

Cassin, René, "The Charter of Human Rights", Nobel Lecture, December 11, 1968, in *Nobel Lectures, Peace 1951-1970*, (Ed.) Frederick W. Haberman, Amsterdam: Elsevier Publishing Company, 1972.

The Center for Reproductive Rights and Policy and University of Toronto International Programme on Reproductive and Sexual Health Law, *Bringing Rights to Bear: An Analysis of the Work of UN Treaty Monitoring Bodies on Reproductive and Sexual Rights*, November, 2001.

Chamie, Joseph, "The Global Abortion Bind: A woman's right to choose gives way to sex-selection abortions and dangerous gender imbalances", *YaleGlobal*, May 29, 2008.

Chelouche, Tessa, "Doctors, Pregnancy, Childbirth and Abortion during the Third Reich", *Israel Medical Association Journal*, Vol. 9, March 2007.

Cohen, Cynthia Price, " Review", The American Journal of International Law, Vol. 89 (4), October, 1995.

Coleman, Priscilla K., "Resolution of Unwanted Pregnancy During Adolescence Through Abortion Versus Childbirth: Individual and Family Predictors and Psychological Consequences", *Journal of Youth and Adolescence*, 2006.

Collins, Vincent J., *Principles of Anesthesiology*, Third Edition, Baltimore:Williams and Wilkins, 1992.

Collins,V.R., Muggli, E.E., Riley, M., Palma, S., Halliday, J.L., "Is Down Syndrome a Disappearing Birth Defect?", *The Journal of Pediatrics*, Vol. 152 (1), January, 2008.

Connolly M., Nunn P., "Women and tuberculosis", World Health Statistics Quarterly, Vol.49 (2), 1996.

Cook, Rebecca and Dickens, Bernard M., "Human Rights dynamics of Abortion Law Reform" *Human Rights Quarterly*, Vol.25, No. 1, February 2003.

Coory ,Michael D., Roselli, Timothy, and Carroll, Heidi J.: "Antenatal care implications of population-based trends in Down syndrome birth rates by rurality and antenatal care provider, Queensland, 1990–2004", *Medical Journal of Australia*, Vol.186 (5), 2007.

Copelon, R., Zampas, C., Brusie, E., Devore, J., "Human rights begin at birth: international law and the claim of fetal rights", *Reproductive Health Matters*, Vol.13 (26), November, 2005.

Cornides, Jakob: "Human rights pitted against Man", *International Journal of Human Rights*, Vol.12 (1), Febuary, 2008.

Collected edition of the 'Travaux Préparatoires'of the European Convention on Human Rights, The Hague:Martinus Nijhoff Publishers, 1975-85.

De Crespigny, Lachlan J., and Savulescu, Julian, "Pregnant women with fetal abnormalities: the forgotten people in the abortion debate", *Medical Journal of Australia*, Vol. 188 (2), January. 2008.

Dhokalia, R.P.: *The Codification of Public International Law* , Manchester: Manchester University Press, 1970.

Eriksson, Maja Kirilova, *Reproductive Freedom in the Context of International Human Rights and Humanitarian Law*, The Hague: Martinus Nijhoff, 1999.

Fergusson, David M.· John Horwood, L.; Ridder, Elizabeth M., "Abortion in young women and subsequent mental health", *Journal of Child Psychology and Psychiatry and Allied Disciplines*, Volume 47 (1), January 2006.

Finnis, John, *Aquinas: Moral, Legal and Political Theory*, Oxford University Press, 1998.

Finnis, John, *Natural Law and Natural Rights*, Oxford; Clarendon Press, 1980.

Fleming, John I and Hains, Michael G., "What Rights, If Any, Do the Unborn Have Under International Law?", *Australian Bar Review*, Vol.16 (2), December, 1997.

Gissler, M., Berg, C., Bouvier-Colle, M.-H., Buekens, P., "Injury deaths, suicides and homicides associated with pregnancy, Finland 1987-2000", *European Journal of Public Health*, Vol. 15(5), 2005.

Glendon, Mary Ann, *A World Made New: A History of the U.N. Charter of Human Rights*, New York: Random House, 2001.

Glendon, MaryAnn, "The Forgotten Crucible: the Latin American Influence on the Universal Human Rights Idea", *Harvard Human Rights* Journal, Vol. 16, Spring 2003.

Godnundur Alfredson and Asbjorn Eide, (eds.), *The Universal Declaration of Human Rights: A Common Standard of Achievement*, The Hague, Martinus Nijhoff Publishers, 1999.

Golsong, Heribert, "Interpreting the European Convention on Human Rights beyond the confines of the Vienna Convention on the Law of Treaties" in *The European System for the Protection of Human Rights*, (eds.) R.St.J. MacDonald, F. Matcher & H. Petzold, Dordrecht: Martinus Nijhoff, 1993.

Guilmoto, Christophe Z., UNFPA Report: "Sex-ratio imbalance in Asia:Trends, consequences and policy responses ", LPED/IRD, Paris: UNFPA, October 2007.

Guilmoto, Christophe Z., UNFPA Report, "Characteristics of sex-ratio imbalance in India and future scenarios", Report presented at the 4th Asia Pacific Conference on Reproductive Health and Rights, Hyderabad, India, October 29-31, 2007. Published by the United Nations Population Fund, 2007.

Hall, Stephen: "The Persistent Spectre: Natural Law, International Order and the Limits of Legal Positivism", *European Journal of International Law*, Vol. 12 (2), Oxford: 2001.

Hanauske-Abel, Hartmut, M., "Not a slippery slope or sudden subversion: German medicine and National Socialism in 1933", *British Medical Journal*, Vol.313, Nuremberg Doctors' Trial Special Edition, December 7, 1996.

Hardy K., Martin K.L., Leese H.J., Winston R.M., Handyside A.H., "Human preimplantation development in vitro is not adversely affected by biopsy at the 8-cell stage", *Human Reproduction*, Vol. 5, No. 6, 1990.

Hernán Santa Cruz„ « *Cooperar o Perecer El Dilema de la Comunidad Mundial* » Buenos Aires: Grupo Editor Latinoamericano, 1984.

Hilgers, Thomas W. and Horan, Denis J., *Abortion and Social Justice*, New York, Sheed and Ward, 1972.

Hoveyda, Fereydoun, "The Universal Declaration and 50 Years of Human Rights", *Transnational Law and Contemporary Problems*, Vol. 8, 1998.

Htun, Mala, *Sex and the State: Abortion, Divorce, and the Family Under Latin American Dictatorships and Democracies*, Cambridge: Cambridge University Press, 2003

Hunt, John, "Abortion and the Nuremberg Prosecutors: A Deeper Analysis", *Life and Learning* Vol.VII, Proceedings of the Seventh University Faculty for Life Conference, June, 1997.

Hunt, John, "Abortion and Nazism: Is There Really a Connection?" *Linacre Quarterly*, November, 1996.

Hunt, John, "Perfecting Humankind: A Comparison of Progressive and Nazi Views on Eugenics, Sterilization and Abortion", *Life and Learning*, Vol.VIII, Proceedings of the Eighth University Faculty for Life Conference, June, 1998.

Hunt, John, "The Abortion and Eugenics Policies of Nazi Germany", Association for Interdisciplinary Research in Values and Social Change, Volume 16 (1), 2001.

Hunt, John, "Out of Respect For Life: Nazi Abortion Policy in the Eastern Occupied Territories", *Journal of Genocide Research*, Vol. 1 (3), 1997.

Ignatieff, Michael, *Human Rights as Politics and Idolatry*, (ed.) Amy Gutmann, Princeton, N.J.: Princeton University Press, 2001.

Joseph, Rita , "Abortion and the Death Penalty—Different Subjects, Shared Sentence", *Voices*, Vol. XXIII (1), 2008

Joseph, Rita, "Compliance with Human Rights or Compliance with an Ideology?" *Voices*, Vol XXII No 1, 2007.

Joseph, Rita, "Feminist rights agenda storms UN", *Population Research Institute Review*, June / July, 1999.

Joseph, Rita, "Wrong Way—Go Back", *Voices*, Vol.XVII, No 2, 2002.

Kamenetsky, Ihor, *Secret Nazi Plans for Eastern Europe: A Study of Lebensraum Policies*, New York: Bookman Associates, 1961.

Korczak, Janusz, *Ghetto Diary*, New York: Holocaust Library, 1978.

Koskenniemi, Martii, "The Preamble of the Declaration of Human Rights" in Godnundur Alfredson and Asbjorn Eide, (eds.), *The Universal Declaration of Human Rights: A Common Standard of Achievement*, The Hague: Martinus Nijhoff Publishers, 1999.

Krug, E.G., Dahlberg, L.L., Mercy, J. A., Zwi, A. B., and Lozano, R., (Eds.), *World Report on Violence and Health*, Geneva: World Health Organization, 2002

Lassen, Nina, "Article 4 ", in Godnundur Alfredson and Asbjorn Eide, (eds.), *The Universal Declaration of Human Rights: A Common Standard of Achievement*, The Hague: Martinus Nijhoff Publishers, 1999.

Lauterpacht, Hersch: *International Law and Human Rights*, London: Stevens and Sons, 1950.

Lemkin, Raphael. "Genocide as Crime under International Law", *The American Journal of International Law*, Vol. 41(1), January, 1947, pp. 145-151, at pp.147-8.

Levy, Daniel and Sznaide, Natan, "The institutionalization of cosmopolitan morality:

the Holocaust and human rights", *Journal of Human Rights*, Vol. 3 (2), June 2004,

Lindholm, Tore, "Article 1" in (eds.) Godnundur Alfredson and Asbjorn Eide, *The Universal Declaration of Human Rights: A Common Standard of Achievement*, The Hague, Martinus Nijhoff Publishers, 1999.

Lorber, J.: "Results of treatment of myelomeningocele: An analysis of 524 unselected cases, with special reference to possible selection for treatment", *Developmental Medicine & Child Neurology*, Vol. 13 (3), 1971.

Macer, Darryl R. J., "Bioethics in Japan and East Asia", *Turkish Journal of Medical Ethics*, Vol. 9, 2001.

Malik, Charles, "International Bill of Human Rights", *United Nations Bulletin*, July, 1948.

Mansfield C., Hopfer S., Marteau T.M., "Termination rates after prenatal diagnosis of Down syndrome, spina bifida, anencephaly, and Turner and Klinefelter syndromes: a systematic literature review. European Concerted Action: DADA (Decision-making After the Diagnosis of a fetal Abnormality)", *Prenatal Diagnosis*, Vol.19(9), September, 1999, pp.808-12.

Maritain, Jacques: *Natural Law: Reflections on Theory & Practice*, (ed.) William Sweet, South Bend: St. Augustine's Press, 2001.

McGoldrick, Dominic, *The Human Rights Committee*, Oxford: Clarendon Press, 1994.

Meire, Hylton: "Is Ultrasound as Useful as We Think?", *Ultrasound*, Vol.15 (3), August 2007.

Menéndez C, Romagosa C, Ismail MR, Carrilho C, Saute F, et al., "An Autopsy Study of Maternal Mortality in Mozambique: The Contribution of Infectious Diseases", *PLoS Medicine*, Vol. 5, No. 2, February 19, 2008.

Mitscherlich A, Mielke F., *Doctors of infamy: the story of the Nazi Medical Crimes*, New York: Schuman, 1949.

Mollmann, M., "Decisions Denied", *Human Rights Watch*, Vol 17, No 1 (B), June 2005.

Morsink, Johannes, "Book Review on the Universal Declaration of Human Rights—a Commentary", *Human Rights Quarterly*, Vol.17 (2), 1995.

Morsink, Johannes, "The Philosophy of the Universal Declaration", *Human Rights Quarterly*, Vol.6(3), 1984.

Morsink, Johannes, *Universal Declaration of Human Right: Origins, Drafting and Intent*, Philadelphia: University of Pennsylvania Press, 1999.

Morsink, Johannes, "Women's rights in the Universal Declaration", *Human Rights Quarterly*, Vol. 13, 1991.

Morsink, Johannes, "World War Two and the Universal Declaration", *Human Rights Quarterly*, Vol. 15, 1993.

Neville-Jan, Ann, "The Problem With Prevention: The Case of Spina Bifida", *American Journal of Occupational Therapy*, Vol.59, 2005.

Office of the High Commissioner for Human Rights (OHCHR), *Legislative History on the Convention on the Rights of the Child*, Geneva: OHCHR, 2007.

Office of the UN High Commissioner for Refugees (UNHCR), *Reproductive Health in Refugee Situations: An Inter-Agency Field Manual*, Geneva, UNHCR, 1999.

Olsen F.: "Do (Only) Women Have Bodies?" in Cheah, P., Fraser, D., and Grbich J. (eds), *Thinking Through the Body of the Law*, St Leonards: Allen and Unwin, 1996.

Organization of American States (OAS), *Inter-American Year-book, 1968*, Washington: 1973

Orr, R.D., Pang N., Pellegrino E.D., Siegler M., "The Use of the Hippocratic Oath: A Review of Twentieth Century Practice and a Content Analysis of Oaths Administered in Medical Schools in he U.S. and Canada in 1993", *Journal of Clinical Ethics*, Vol.8 (4), 1997.

Patten, Bradley, "Human Embryology", Philadelphia: The Blakiston Company, 1947.

Pedersen, Willy, "Abortion and depression: A population-based longitudinal study of young women", *Scandinavian Journal of Public Health*, Vol. 36 (4), 2008.

Pellegrino, Edmund D., "The Nazi Doctors and Nuremberg; Some Moral Lessons Revisited", *Annals of Internal Medicine*, 1997.

Pichon, Jakob: "Does the Unborn Child Have a Right to Life? The Insufficient Answer of the European Court of Human Rights in the Judgment Vo v. France", *German Law Journal*, Vol. 07 (04), 2006.

Plan, *Because I am a Girl: The State of the World's Girls 2007*, London: Plan, UK Branch, 2007.

Poliakov, Léon, *Harvest of Hate: The Nazi Program for the Destruction of the Jews of Europe*, New York: Holocaust Library [distributed by Schocken Books,], 1979.

Pontifical Council for the Family, *The Family and Human Rights*, Vatican City: 1999.

Reardon D.C., Ney P.G., Scheuren F., Cougle J., Coleman P.K., Strahan T.W.: "Deaths associated with pregnancy outcome: a record linkage study of low income women", *Southern Medical Journal*, Vol. 95(8), 2002.

Robertson, A.H.: *Human Rights in Europe*, Manchester University Press (2nd ed.), 1977.

Robinson, Nehemiah, *The Genocide Convention: A Commentary*, New York: Institute of Jewish Affairs, 1960.

Round Table of Human Rights Treaty Bodies on Human Rights Approaches to Women's health, with a Focus on Sexual and Reproductive Health and Rights: Summary of Proceedings and Recommendations, published by United Nations Population Fund, United Nations High Commissioner for Human Rights and United Nations Division for the Advancement of Women, 1998.

Rue V.M., Coleman P.K., Rue J.J., Reardon D.C., "Induced abortion and traumatic stress: A preliminary comparison of American and Russian women", Medical Science Monitor, *Vol.*10(10). SR5-16, 2004.

Sadik, Nafis, "Progress in Protecting Reproductive Rights and Promoting Reproductive Health: Five Years Since Cairo", *Health and Human Rights*. Vol.4, 2000.

Schuster, Evelyne: "The Nuremberg Code: Hippocratic ethics and human rights", *Lancet*, Vol. 351, 1998.

Shue, Henry, *Basic Rights: Subsistence, Affluence, and U.S. Foreign Policy*, Princeton: Princeton University Press, 1980.

Suliman, Sharain, Ericksen, Todd, Labuscgne, Peter, de Wit, Renee, Stein, Dan J., Seedat, Soraya., "Comparison of pain, cortisol levels, and psychological distress in women undergoing surgical termination of pregnancy under local anaesthesia versus intravenous sedation," *BMC Psychiatry*, June 2007, Vol. 7 (24).

UNESCO, (ed.), *Human Rights: Comments and Interpretations*, with an Introduction by Jacques Maritain, London & New York: Wingate, 1949

UNFPA State of the World's Population 2005:The Promise of Equality - Gender Equity, Reproductive Health and the Millennium Development Goals, United Nations Population Fund (UNFPA), September 2007.

UNICEF Report, *State of the World's Children 2007: Women and Children: the Double Dividend of Gender Equality*, New York: UNICEF, 2007.

Van Aggelen, Johannes: "The Preamble of the United Nations Declaration of Human Rights", *Denver Journal of International Law and Policy*, Vol.28 (2), 2000.

Verdoodt, Albert, *Naissance et Signification de la Déclaration Universelle des Droits de l'Homme*, Société d'Etudes Morales, Sociales et Juridiques, Louvain-Paris: Editions Nauwelaerts, 1964.

Von Hildebrand, Dietrich: *Man and Woman: Love & the Meaning of Intimacy*, Manchester, NH: Sophia Institute Press, 1992.

Von Pufendorf, Samuel, *On The Duty of Man and Citizen According to the Natural Law (1673)* [1682 Edition] translated by Frank Gardner Moore, New York: Oxford University Press, 1927.

Vlachová, Marie and Biason, Lea (eds.), *Women in an Insecure World: Violence Against Women - Facts, Figures and Analysis*, Geneva: Geneva Center for the Democratic Control of Armed Forces (DCAF), 2005.

White, N. and Klasson , D. (eds.), *The UN, Human Rights and Post-Conflict Situations*, New York: Juris Publishing, 2005.

WHO, UNICEF, UNFPA, and The World Bank, *Maternal Mortality in 2005* (Estimates developed byWHO, UNICEF, UNFPA and the World Bank), Geneva: WHO Press, 2007.

Williams, Glanville, *The Sanctity of Life and the Criminal Law*, London: Faber & Faber, 1958.

Wilson, Ronald, "Why human rights matter for everyone", *Human Rights*, Volume 3 (3), September 1996.

Women's Environment and Development Organization (WEDO), *Take the Brackets Off Women's Lives! Women's Linkage Caucus Advocacy Chart*, New York: Women's Environment and Development Organization (WEDO), August 30, 1995

World Health Organisation (WHO), Final Report of the Commission on the Social Determinants of Health Report, *Closing the gap in a generation: Health equity through action on the social determinants of health*, Geneva: 2008.

World Health Organization (WHO), *Safe abortion : technical and policy guidance for health systems*, Geneva: WHO, 2003.

Wright-Carozza, Paolo, "From Conquest to Constitutions: Retrieving a Latin American Tradition of the Idea of Human Rights", *Human Rights Quarterly*, Volume 25, Number 2, May 2003.

Yourow, Howard Charles, *The Margin of Appreciation Doctrine in the Dynamics of the European Court of Human Rights Jurisprudence*, London: Martinus Nijhoff Publishers, 1996.

Zuckerman, Shachar; Lahad, Amnon; Shmueli, Amir ; Zimran, Ari ; Peleg, Leah ; Orr-Urtreger, Avi; Levy-Lahad, Ephrat; Sagi, Michal, "Carrier Screening for Gaucher Disease: Lessons for Low-Penetrance, Treatable Diseases", *Journal of the American Medical Association*, Vol. 298 (11), 19 September, 2007.

Index

D